"You desire truth in the inward being; teach me wisdom in my secret heart." This cry of the psalmist [Psalm 51:6] echoes throughout this "unconventional" biography, *Clayton's Chronicles*.

Clayton's life has held profound joys, and profound griefs—recounted here with courage and vulnerability. Again and again, we hear the invitation not to flee from our fears and our deepest wounds, but to share them, to consider what they might teach, and to bring them into the light.

It's been said that our final decades bring us "face to face with our last chance to experience our lives more fully and more freely, to experience it so much more able to love and give and forgive." [Kathleen Dowling Singh] The Steiners have shared a glimpse of one such life. I hope that many readers will be coaxed along a similar path of self-discovery, coming to see their lives "more fully and more freely".

A Mennonite Spiritual Director
Indiana

This is a great story and product and I'm excited to see it go to print. Jere (Clayton's nephew) provides a unique telling of Clayton's story by including a heavenly being to chronicle Clayton's life. The story is written with integrity and vulnerability, not shying away from the struggles and toxicity experienced throughout his life.

An important story about how a negative childhood environment can greatly affect us AND how overcoming those difficulties is possible.

This is a must-read book, especially for those who have hidden their thoughts and emotions within themselves for far too long ... you won't be able to put this book down!

Ben Bouwman
Pastor of Walnut Hill Mennonite Church

Clayton's Chronicles by Jere Steiner and Clayton Steiner is a heartwarming memoir in story form that is hopeful and engaging. There is a grace to this story that holds and never shies away from the hard things that life brings. It is a story of an evolution of faith that I think many readers will identify with. Clayton's story will stay with me for a long time to come.

Lynn Diener
Writer and Mennonite by Choice

Clayton's CHRONICLES

A heavenly perspective of
the down-to-earth life
of Clayton H. Steiner

JERE STEINER
IN PARTNERSHIP WITH CLAYTON STEINER

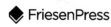 FriesenPress

One Printers Way
Altona, MB R0G 0B0
Canada

www.friesenpress.com

Written by Jere Steiner, partnered with Clayton Steiner

The biography of Clayton's life herein is a true story. Please note that some names have been changed where necessary.

ISBN
978-1-03-916074-3 (Hardcover)
978-1-03-916073-6 (Paperback)
978-1-03-916075-0 (eBook)

1. *Biography & Autobiography, Personal Memoirs*
2. *Religion, Christian Life, Personal Growth*
3. *Religion, Christianity, Literature & the Arts*

Distributed to the trade by The Ingram Book Company

To all our readers—may you find healing within these pages

TABLE OF CONTENTS

PART 2   GROWING

PART 3   OVERCOMING

PREFACE

Life is too short to read boring biographies. At least, that's what I've always thought. So, when my Uncle Clayton asked if I would help him write his biography, primarily for his family, I frankly wasn't very excited. But I knew Clayton had lived an interesting life and wondered if we could make his request into much more.

After pondering the quandary for a few days, I approached him with the idea of having someone not of this world narrating his story. Sounds strange, I know, but this unconventional perspective, I believed, would add layers of depth to his story as well as to all of us wrestling with life.

Now, my uncle knows me. He knows sometimes my ideas can be a little too … shall we say, *out there!*

Fortunately, after contemplating my proposal, he decided to trust me. At times, I won't lie, we both had our doubts about that trustful, albeit dicey, decision.

But after much time and effort, I can confidently say we are more than pleased with this unique narration of riveting stories taken from one man's humble life, and we think you will be too. Stories of family, adventure, romance, disappointment, grief, and overcoming, all with profound and encouraging insight, are sure to capture your curiosity, if not your heart.

Clayton's Chronicles is achingly vulnerable, delving into the deep crevices of his heart to find his paths to healing. This book lends a vivid perspective that will not only present one man's history but also illuminate a rich view of how to navigate the joys and hardships of life. For sometimes we must confront our hurts, those who hurt us, and our need to change—even when we feel broken inside.

But don't worry about sinking too deep into the heaviness of it all. I think you'll find this an enthralling page-turner, as well as a source of hope and direction. Enjoy the story of a farm boy born in Amish country just after the Depression and what he learned throughout a life fully lived.

PART 1
EXPLORING

1
HEAVEN'S CHRONICLE

"Congratulations on your promotion," said the grizzled editor in chief, who was sitting back on his reclining office chair, elbows on armrests, fingertips touching one another like a spider on a mirror. "What did you do at *Heaven's Chronicle* before you made it to this department?"

Beemer, the young lad on the other side of the editor's desk, straightened his tie and sat up straight. "I was a binder." Before his new boss could ruffle his thick brows or make an intimidating comment, Beemer added, "Not the most glamorous of jobs, but I had to start somewhere."

"Indeed." The older, balding man, now thick around the middle from too much on-the-job sitting and not enough in-the-field observation, eyed the young man over his ever-present reading glasses. "And you thought binding our precious memoirs was beneath you?"

Beemer squirmed and cleared his throat. "Oh no, Chief. It's just that, well … as important as binding is, I want to be a part of the really important aspects of the business. You know, like writing about famous people, like the one you wrote about Aristotle."

"Famous people?" The editor closed his eyes mid-eye roll, then he furrowed his bushy eyebrows. He stood. "Come with me." He walked out of the office.

Confused, Beemer jumped up and obediently followed.

The suspended editor led the new employee down a labyrinth of dimly lit hallways to a massive, ornate, wooden door. He pivoted to the taller, thinner pupil before him. "Whenever you're feeling too high on yourself or unmotivated or insignificant, I want you to come here." He turned and pushed the door of all doors with all his might, feet fighting for traction, face reddening. Slowly, the door swiveled open like the earth revolving into a breathtaking sunrise, warm and inviting.

Beemer did not question the light or its source. His eyes took in the immediate wonder of the obvious significance of the sanctuary. Everywhere before him, as far as his eye could see, straight ahead, to his right, to his left, high above him—books!

"Whoa! I've never even imagined so many books in my whole life. What is this, the Big Guy's written fantasies or something?"

The publishing guru stifled his immediate irritation, opting to utilize a teaching moment for the young intern instead. "Look, if you want to stay in my department, you need to get some things straight."

Beemer's eyes froze wide-open.

"First, THE BOSS is in charge of all of this." Chief swept his arm across the unending room. "We don't call our creator and employer, The Big Guy, Old Man, Daddio, Big Mamma, the Ole Storyteller, or any other colorful term that may roll off your profuse tongue. THE BOSS goes by, THE BOSS. Nothing fancy. Nothing mistaken to mean something else. Nothing to show anyone's nuanced opinions. THE BOSS is the fulfillment of male and female, but categorically beyond either. Just, THE BOSS. Got it?"

Beemer, mouth agape, nodded.

"Second," the old journeyman continued, "this sacred room is The Great Hall of Annals, the largest library imaginable. These books are THE BOSS's most prized possessions. These," he looked from side to side, "are THE BOSS's sole purpose. They require skillful depiction on every page. Scrupulous accuracy is our duty here. We hold them in the utmost, highest regard."

The student let go of the book he had just tilted from a bookshelf, dropping it to the floor. He frantically scrambled to place it back on the shelf, only to fumble it to the floor again. He jerked his head back to his mentor, breathing erratically. "Sorry, sorry!"

The stone-faced, red-cheeked editor continued. "And third, THE BOSS doesn't write fantasy … or fiction of any kind. These books are all creatively true. Never forget that!"

Beemer nodded, then he gulped as he placed the rascally book back on the shelf. "So, they're theology or something?"

"No, they're true-life stories. Biographies of every person who ever lived."

"Whoa!" The new hire gawked anew at the billions of books before him.

The editor nodded. "This is the recording sanctuary of humankind's history. Every person's life story ends up here."

"Too cool! So, where are the really famous people books kept?" Beemer stretched his neck to look high above. "I know you wrote tons of them. Are they at the top?"

"We don't use that word up here."

"What word?"

"Famous."

"Why not? Afraid of insulting the schmucks?"

"Because it means nothing," the editor fired back. "Everyone's life is of equal value to THE BOSS ... as are the books."

"Oh, come on! Surely, Abraham Lincoln was more important than John Wilkes Booth. Beethoven more important than a tone-deaf janitor, Thomas Edison more important than a college dropout, and Shakespeare was surely greater than some two-bit reporter ..."

"No!" the chronicling expert cut off his subordinate. "That's not how THE BOSS sees all these prized gems. Surely you accepted this position in my department knowing this?"

"Yeah, well, I guess I did hear that, now that you mention it." The young employee cleared his throat and swallowed again. "But I guess I didn't really believe it. I mean, if I was THE BOSS, I'd be more interested in Socrates than a backslapping minion. I'd delight in one of the great Caesars more than some drab politician. Or ..."

"If you don't stop, I can see to it that you never leave the binding department again."

"Okay, okay." Beemer held his hands up. "I was just trying to think like THE BOSS, sir."

"I go by Chief. You can cut the sir nonsense."

"Yes, sir ... ah, Chief! I mean, Chief."

"And stop trying to 'think like THE BOSS.' Learning is what this phase of your employment is about, not taking charge."

Beemer swayed from side to side. "So … when do I start writing?"

"Oh, you won't be writing for some time."

The young man's jaw hung open. "Ah … I thought I was hired to write."

"You were. You are. But you can't start writing until you know how to write."

Beemer blew a jilted snicker out his nose. "I know how to write. I proved that in all the testing modules."

"Oh, we know you can write. But you need to learn to write from the soul."

"But my writings have shown a lot of soul. My teachers have even said so."

"I'm well aware of that. You wouldn't be here if you hadn't displayed this gift."

"Sooo … what's the problem then? I don't understand."

The sad-faced manager with drooping eyebrows nodded. "I know you don't. You will. You've got to learn to connect with the soul so your writing flows like honey from a ladle."

"But I've shown I can write the hell out of my soul."

The chief editor took two large strides toward his subordinate, his bulbous nose a whisker from Beemer's chin. "If you're serious about this job, that's the last time you ever use that word up here. Understand me?"

Beemer looked down into the steely eyes of his angry editor. "Oh yeah. Sorry, Chief. It will never happen again. I don't know what I was thinking. I just meant that, like you, I'm good at writing from my soul."

"It's not *your* soul we're concerned with here."

Beemer went slack-jawed again. "Huh?"

The exasperated chief gestured to all the books around them and then nodded as if stating the obvious.

Beemer's head jutted back. "Whoa! You mean I'm going to be authoring books like these?"

"Don't get ahead of yourself, tiger. You're not authoring anything."

Beemer squinted his boggled eyes and tilted his head. "But …"

Chief held up his hand. "Authoring suggests you write *your* views or ideas, *your* soul. That's not what we do here. We write the souls of others. You'll be what we refer to as a chronicler. You write only facts. No embellishing."

"But won't that make these books kind of boring? All facts, no imagination?"

"THE BOSS is not boring! Read any book here, and you'll see that THE BOSS and the people THE BOSS authored are wholly imaginative. You'll not find a boring book here. They're all good reads."

"But I've only written from my perspective. I'm not sure I know how to place all the facts of someone's life into a book interestingly."

"Precisely! That's why the first part of the job is to read how others accomplished this."

Beemer's lips bunched to the side. "I'm not real good at those how-to manuals. I'm more of a hands-on kind of guy."

"Good, then you'll learn *real good* when you get your hands on some of these books and see how the pros do it," said the editor, sure to include the novice's grammar faux pas. "Your job is to read, read, read. That's how I learned when I became a chronicler."

The editor headed for the door. "I'll see you in a few."

"But ... whose story will I be writing?"

"That depends on who's ready at your christening."

"You mean, I won't know who I'll be writing about until they're born?"

"That's how it works."

"How will I get all the information on their life if they're just born?"

"You won't get it sitting in a cushy office. This is an in-the-field job. You follow them around and report their experiences, reactions, and choices, and when you get exceptionally adept, their thoughts and feelings."

"For their whole life?"

"That's the only way to be an accurate chronicler."

Beemer looked like he had seen a ghost.

"Relax," Chief said, "you're young. You'll do thousands of these before you're my age."

"How many lives do I cover at one time?"

"Oh, never more than one at a time. We want the full story. It will require your complete concentration. This is not a job for the faint of heart."

"But won't I bother them if I follow them around all their lives?"

"No, that's the brilliance of THE BOSS's plan. No earthly person can see her or his chronicler. You fly under the human's radar wherever they go. In fact, you heavenly chroniclers won't see each other either."

"Hmh. That's rad." Beemer felt the chief's eyes locked onto him. "Where do I start?"

"Just pick one and start reading."

"Can I start with a famous one?"

The chief editor's eyes drooped in coordination with his eyebrows.

"Just kidding!" Beemer retracted. "I'll just pick this one right here." He snagged a book. "Penrose Martha McCarty." He smiled a bit too wide, covering his false optimism.

"Ah, huh. Well, we'll talk when you're ready." The editor walked out the door.

Beemer watched the door close. He looked at the nondescript book in his hands, then around him at the vast millions—no, there had to be billions—of similar books all around him. He sighed. *This could take forever!*

Perusing the interminable library for a *special* book he could sink his teeth into, he longed to find a famous book—one THE BOSS would be especially proud of. After looking up and around, he sighed. He resigned himself to the (likely ordinary) life story of Penrose McCarty in his hand. *What was the harm in reading it like he promised Chief he would? Boredom had never killed anyone, had it?* He looked around the overwhelming book menagerie again. The breath went out of him. The book in his hand opened, and he began reading.

Somehow, Beemer read that first book from The Great Hall of Annals. The interest it fostered in him surprised him. Penrose was not famous by any stretch of the imagination. But Beemer could see how her valuable presence touched others and THE BOSS. Though she made plenty of mistakes and lacked a strong, pronounced character (qualities Beemer assumed famous people possessed), her meager existence made a profound influence on the world.

He soon swallowed hundreds of books a day, curious how each person's life wound through unique twists and turns, joys and trials, failures and successes. He marveled at the provocative purpose each story held. Each life meant something. No one's life was insignificant.

Still, the famous, those noticed most by their peers, intrigued Beemer the most. If these first stories of Joe Blow and Suzi Q Smith could enthrall him, imagine what reaction the high-profile stories of those idolized could generate. Such inspiring stories of hope and promise would surely bless THE BOSS beyond the status quo. He dreamed of one day awing THE BOSS so.

And so, he read. He read and read and read some more. He learned how chroniclers made insignificant characters come alive. The servant boy, Jaffa, of the 1500s in early France came away as a hero, though he was beaten to death at age nine. The angry spinster, Abigail Weebler, raised goats and pigeons and never said no to the weary traveler in need of a bed for the night. One of the lavish-living, but neglected, concubines of King Solomon became known as the old lady who "bestowed wisdom with a ladle" as her outward beauty faded after the king passed away.

Beemer especially noted how so many of the books Chief biographized were of famous people, such as, King David, Alexander the Great, and Michelangelo. Beemer read for months, years. Then, one day, he read the story of one William Clark and was transfixed. His readiness to be a chronicler came from that book.

William, having no formal education in his youth, eventually began writing of his experiences and expertise, and he went on to lead various influential campaigns. Not afraid of hostile enemies, he soon rose to the rank of lieutenant in the US Army, successfully defeating its foes. He was forced to retire at the early age of twenty-six because of health issues, and many assumed his military and outdoorsman careers were over. Not so! When William was thirty-three years old, his friend Meriwether recruited him for the adventure of a lifetime. He accepted. Together, they led a world-renowned expedition of uncharted land that few imagined ever experiencing. The Corps of Discovery mission was to explore the greater region of the *Louisiana Purchase* in 1804 and establish trade with Native Americans. Along with fulfilling their mission, they also discovered a waterway from the United States to the Pacific Ocean and claimed the Oregon territory. William Clark and Meriwether Lewis will forever be known for their heroic exploration known as the *Lewis and Clark Expedition*.

Beemer had never encountered such resolute courage. Discovering the unknown hooked his imagination. Like William Clark, how grand it would be to write about not just a new land, but a new life—a new life with the potential to discover the most valuable and profound insights.

Beemer called the editor for a meeting.

"So, you're ready to write your first biography?"

Beemer glowed. "I am. It was just as you said. I read thousands … more like millions of biographies. I learned a lot from each story. And, suddenly, one day, I knew I was ready."

The bushy-browed, bald editor nodded skeptically. "Okay. Why?"

Beemer's eager grin flattened. "Why?"

"What inspired you to be ready?"

"Well, I read the William Clark story. And now, I want to discover how one life can impact so many."

"But you realize that you may not get a high-profile person to write about, right? You may draw someone few will ever hear of."

Beemer's smile flattened. "But I'm sure I can make their story interesting. From what I've read, like in all of your biographies, everyone has potential, right?"

The chief's leery eyes squinted. "Well, just so you tell their story and not your own." He looked at his eager apprentice and sighed. "You'll start on the next available client."

Beemer shoved his back against his chair and pumped his fists.

"But …" the editor continued, "since this is your first book, you will be under notable scrutiny. I will be your editor, and I will go over your material with a fine-tooth comb. Be prepared to write and rewrite. Then to rewrite and rewrite some more. This is to be a true depiction of a real life. Embellishment is not your job. Accuracy and insight are now the air you breathe. Are you aware and ready to hold to these stringent parameters?"

"Absolutely!" Beemer squinted and chewed the side of his lip as his eyes trailed off to nowhere in particular. "Um … about that insight … how will I know for sure if it's true insight or my personal insight?"

"You'll know because I'll know … and I'll tell you! Such nonsense will not be tolerated. THE BOSS won't allow it, so I can't either. Stick to the truth and learn the soul of your client, and you'll do just fine. Make it *your* story, and you'll be out on your ear before you can say, 'Once upon a time.' Got it?"

Beemer nodded clumsily. "Yes, Chief."

"Okay, your christening begins at 8:00 tomorrow morning in Kidron, Ohio, USA. Your bundle of joy comes out of the hopper one hour after that, when your field operation officially begins. Be prepared for a lifetime of observation and chronicling."

Beemer swallowed and nodded. His big job was really happening!

The following blurb was found in a news clipping put out by *Heaven's Chronicle*:

Beemer, the newest chronicler on record, made it to Kidron, Ohio, on June 7, 1941, an hour before the birth. The editor in chief of Heaven's Chronicle officiated at his small christening ceremony.

The chief directed Beemer to place his writing hand on *The Great Hall of Annals'* greatest book of all, the biography of THE BOSS's Son. "Having read the constitution of *The Heaven's Chronicler's Oath*, do you thoroughly understand your commencing duties to observe and report honestly?"

"I do."

"And do you promise to uphold your duties as a chronicler and to record the soul of your client throughout the client's lifetime so THE BOSS can treasure it for eternity?"

"I do."

The editor then whapped Beemer over the head with the Book of Books.

Dazed, Beemer said, as was the custom of the ceremony, "Thank you, Chief. I'm ready to observe, study, and understand my subject to the fullest of my ability."

"You are hereby christened and are ready to report the life of Homer and Bertha Zuercher Steiner's next forthcoming baby."

The two chroniclers smiled for the camera. Chief leaned over to Beemer and whispered, "Stay with the script. THE BOSS is counting on you."

The editor in chief of *Heaven's Chronicle*, upon christening his newly appointed chronicler, Beemer, left to supervise dispatch duties at headquarters. He was a busy manager.

2

FINDING CLAYTON

Beemer found himself alone on the cusp of his first big-time job in downtown Kidron—if one could call it a town. He saw no metropolitan buildings, smelled no factory or automobile fumes, heard no hustle-bustle of any kind, though he had read of all such goings-on for typical 1941 United States communities. Inexperienced with the human senses he had been given for the job, he wondered if the metaphysical techs had messed up the adaptive process in him, causing his other senses to contradict his thoughts.

He saw rolling hill farmland in every direction, smelled robust earth and animal by-products, and heard the unfamiliar sound of heavy hooves on a blacktop (not asphalt paved, but tarred and oiled) road. His expectations of the modern twentieth century were something else.

He knew Kidron had just gone through the Great Depression, as had all of the United States and most of the world. But, *had this town been somehow demolished by the economic crisis?*

Beemer took in the surroundings. Instead of the industrial city setting he had expected, he saw the *L. E. Sommer Feed Mill*, the *E. P. Gerber Hardware Store*, a slaughterhouse, and a blacksmith shop. Coming out of the blacksmith shop was a long-bearded man who wore vintage pilgrim attire and a straw-brimmed hat. He got into a black buggy that was pulled by an enormous horse. Beemer squinted and scratched his head. *Rural must be way behind urban communities*, he concluded.

Just my luck to get stuck in an insignificant town that no one except its own inhabitants would ever know of. He sighed. *This could be a long assignment!*

Breathing in the proverbial breath of fresh air (laden with animal odors), Beemer set out for the hospital to find his subject. An hour did not allow him the luxury of gawking or pondering his lot, though he couldn't help but wonder if his new little bundle would someday be the headline news—a person everyone revered.

As chroniclers can, Beemer transported himself twenty-five miles away to the nearest hospital, Aultman Hospital in Canton, only to discover the Steiners were not there. He looked at his watch. *They must be at a different hospital.*

In a flash, he whisked away to the next nearest hospital in Akron. He found no trace of a pregnant Bertha Steiner there either. The cockiness Beemer had exuded the day before gave way to panic, knowing the poor impression he would give by missing the birth of his first assignment.

He arrived at Lakeside, the large hospital in Cleveland sixty miles away, at the designated time of birth. Baby Steiner was born right on time, he knew—as there are never untimely births in THE BOSS's birth log. This made Beemer weak-kneed, not with joy, but with fear, because the birth time had come and gone. He plopped into a chair and hung his throbbing head. There was no sign of the Steiners at this hospital either!

Beemer skedaddled back to Kidron to search for the missing child or any clue as to where Bertha Zuercher Steiner had borne her child. As humbling as it was, he had no alternative but to investigate the nearly one hundred households in the unincorporated 449-person village of Kidron.

By midmorning, Beemer found that most country households busied themselves with barnyard chores or outdoor tasks or errands. Those he discovered in their home were women and young children. When he located the mother of the home and realized she was not tending a newborn, he slipped away to the next house, hoping to find a woman named Bertha holding her new baby.

Some seventy households later, Beemer came to a house on Zuercher Rd., addressed as Route 1, Apple Creek, OH (though still considered Kidron). Curiously, a man exited the side door. Beemer watched the man fling an odd-looking, small suitcase into the back seat of his car as a prepubescent girl ducked out the front door and yelled, "Mom says to tell you thank you, Dr. Mayor."

"Glad to oblige. A healthy baby boy is always worth the trouble."

"Are you off to deliver another one?"

The man chuckled. "Not that I know of. I'll head home to Apple Creek, just about six miles from here, to see if anyone's called for me though."

For the first time since his christening, Beemer felt a pang of hope. *A healthy BABY boy!* No wonder Beemer couldn't find the Steiner baby in a hospital. This doctor made house calls.

Beemer inspected the farmhouse and found a teenage girl holding and patting a tiny baby boy. *This had to be Bertha,* though she looked exceptionally young.

Fearing the worst—that his assessment was somehow amiss, and the editor would null and void his christening and reassign him back to binding for incompetence—Beemer searched the house to confirm his assumption. As near as he could tell, all four bedrooms were empty. A middle-aged woman, busying herself in the kitchen, seemed injured or much older than she appeared. Two toddlers, a boy and a girl, played at her feet.

Outside, Beemer found the girl he had seen thanking the doctor with another girl about her age, hanging up laundry on a clothesline.

Two adolescent boys were rough-housing in the nearby barn. "Roy, Dad's gonna kill us if he sees we're not pitching that manure," the taller one shouted.

The smaller one tackled him into a loose straw bale and said, "I don't care. If I hold you down for ten seconds, you have to do my half."

The older boy rolled his opponent over, pushed off him, and stood up. "Now, don't be so dumb and do your chores."

Though Beemer could understand their language (as all chroniclers can), he noticed that they did not speak English, as one would expect Midwestern Americans to speak, but a Swiss-German dialect called *Schwyzerdütsch*.

A slightly older boy, who didn't enter the battle, pitched manure from the pens on the other side of the barn, unphased.

Beemer roamed nearby farmland and spotted a young teenage boy pulling a manure spreader with a pair of horses.

"Watch what you're doing," the older boy walking next to the outfit yelled, "you're trampling the cornrows. Dad'll have a fit if we ruin our corn harvest."

So, where was Dad? And why wouldn't he be home on a Saturday?

Out of clues, Beemer returned to the house. The youthful woman holding the now crying baby jostled him on her hip enroute to the kitchen. "Mom, I think he needs feeding."

The older woman stopped grinding grape nuts and placed her palms on the counter. She sighed deeply. Then, she smiled and turned to take the infant from her daughter's arms. "Come here, my Clayton Harley Steiner." And she breastfed her hungry farmer-to-be.

Beemer got a lot wrong his first day. Now, however, convinced he had found the subject of his oncoming biography, he would never again leave his side for as long as Clayton lived. To make up for all his embarrassing blunders, Beemer began to write.

Because chroniclers never sleep, Beemer wrote and formed his annals when Clayton slept, which during the first weeks of the newborn's life, was more than it was not. Though he had missed Clayton's birth, he used this excess time to formulate his words just right, determined to make his subject's story shine and to cover up all his missteps.

Watching the little guy sleep in such humble surroundings, Beemer wondered just what innovative skill it would take to make his biography pop. Imagining THE BOSS's glowing approval if he succeeded and disappointment if he failed spurred him on. *If only I could be as good a writer as Chief was.*

3

INFANT YEARS
BEGINNING OF GREATNESS?

Meanwhile, back at *Heaven's Chronicle* headquarters, the editor sat in his office chair, reading glasses midway down his bulbous nose, reading the current Master Log that he had retrieved from Beemer. The Master Log at *Heaven's Chronicle* instantaneously recorded whatever Beemer wrote in his biographic book, which allowed the editor to access the writing at any time.

Chronicling editors were busy administrators, proofreading all their chronicler's work, consulting with the newer ones, and hiring and firing whenever the need arose, which was often. A chronicler did not stay a chronicler unless they maintained the highest standard of reporting. Chroniclers often neglected to gauge the subject's *emotional* makeup, *environment*, and *experiences*—the three Es of chronicling—or, as they referred to it in the biz, the *Threeseez*. Once the chronicler understood the subject, they could better understand the subject's thoughts and reactions.

The chief despised firing an incapable chronicler; his favorite part of the job was seeing THE BOSS's joy through the growth and expression of a coming-of-age chronicler. A good chronicler sees THE BOSS's undeniable handiwork in their subject, making all the editor in chief's maddening corrective actions worth the trouble. And novice chroniclers were always that—trouble—sometimes causing the editor to totally cut out or reword whole sections of the chronicler's manuscript.

Chief read the following highlights from the Master Log for Clayton Steiner:

Bertha nurses her child every couple of hours. When she is busy cleaning, preparing a meal, washing clothes through the wringer, or working the garden, Clayton sometimes cries a little longer, usually in his oldest sister Arlene's arms.

These first few days Clayton continues to sleep, cry, poop, repeat.

Today marks the first bath for Clayton. The three oldest girls, Arlene, Viola, and Dorothy help their mother, though she could manage this chore on her own. But this rite of passage is a bonding experience for the girls, if not for the crying Clayton, as they bathe him in a portable washbasin.

Bertha tells her girls, "The doctor told me, 'The cleaner the baby, the healthier he'll be.' He said cleanliness prevents diseases."

"Like the scarlet fever we had this winter and had to be quarterleaned for fifty days?" Viola asks.

"Yes, I suppose staying clean can help keep us from being *quarantined*."

"And like the flu and the mumps we got before that?" adds Arlene.

"And the chickenpox," pipes in the younger Dorothy.

"Yes, this was a hard winter," Bertha says. "Which makes you a miracle baby." She lifts the wet and crying baby and swaddles him with the towel on her shoulder.

Later, in early fall, the chief read:

Clayton cries while Bertha is busy grinding grape nuts for breakfast. Arlene hears the cries and checks his diaper, finding a healthy discharge. It's the morning of their first day of school, and Arlene changes his diaper as Viola observes.

"You're sure good at taking care of Clayton."

The fifteen-year-old Arlene smiles. "I've had a lot of practice."

"Yeah. I don't want to go to school today," says Viola.

17

"I'm not too excited about it either."

"The other kids are going to say our house is a zoo."

"I know," Arlene admits. "I've heard it all before. But they don't know our little Clayton here. If they did, they'd wish they had as big a family as ours."

Viola crinkles her nose. "Even with his messy diapers?"

Arlene snickers. "Yeah, even with his messy diapers."

Initially content with what he read, the chief's wiry eyebrows unified in grave concern the further he read. Though he wanted to trust his novice chronicler, the chief's inward sensor was on high alert. Something did not feel right about this. *Already time for our first chat.* He loathed this part of the job though it was a crucial element.

When Beemer next wrote in his biographic book, the editor transported down to see him, as is an editor's function. Beemer did not expect the visit, so cocky of his writing excellence was he.

"Beemer."

Beemer jumped as if a ghost had called his name in the middle of the night. "Chief! You scared the hel ..." He caught the editor's challenge in his stern expression. Beemer started again, "You scared the ... health out of me. What are you doing here?"

"We've got to talk."

Beemer glanced at the baby in his bassinet. "Okay. But can you make it quick? Hard telling how long our little prince will be out. I've got to record three messy diapers, a major spit-up on his sister Arlene, and a humorous burp during his dad's mumbled prayer that I want to describe hilariously."

Nonplussed, the editor squared his gaze upon his underling. "This will take as long as it takes."

Beemer's darting eyes were eventually held by his formidable mentor's glare. "Of course. But shouldn't we talk in the next room? You might wake him." He gestured to the baby.

The editor smirked and harrumphed. "Beemer, they can't hear us, remember?"

"Oh yeah. I forgot."

"I read your first chapter."

A smile spread over Beemer's face. "Great! What d'you think?"

"I think you're still intent on being an author instead of a chronicler."

Beemer's smile flattened. "What do you mean?"

"Remember the *Chronicler's Oath* you swore to uphold?"

Beemer swallowed, eyes searching for a worthy answer. He nodded.

"Do you remember something in there about, 'Not adding a jot or tittle to the events of the subject?'"

Beemer's nods weakened.

"Then why do you report that Master Clayton was born at *Aultman Hospital* in Canton?"

"Well, how would it look to have our hero born in this puny farmhouse?"

The plump, balding editor stared over his glasses, waiting for a punchline that never followed. "A hero? A hero of what?"

"That's the beauty of it. We've yet to find out. He's an adventure waiting to unfold. An unknown land waiting to be discovered."

Chief held up his hand. "This isn't the *Lewis and Clark Expedition*. You are not the child's author. THE BOSS is. Are you privy to the plans THE BOSS has for Clayton?"

"Well, no, not exactly."

"You're a chronicler. You chronicle. That means you record his life in words. You aren't writing a novel. You're not making a movie thriller. You're in THE BOSS's employ. Do you wish to keep this job or go back to binding?"

Beemer's shoulders slumped. "Keep it. I was born to write."

"So, write the truth. THE BOSS is nothing if not Truth."

"Yes, sir."

The editor's bushy eyebrows furrowed to become one.

Beemer corrected, "I mean … Chief."

"Are we done here?"

Beemer blinked twice, nodded frantically, then halted as if his brain froze.

Chief stayed put. "What is it?"

"It's just that … " Beemer looked down at his shuffling feet. "Well, I'm not really into writing a boring biography."

The editor squinted. "You lied about the subject because you are afraid his life will be too boring?"

"Yeah, sort of."

"Listen, kid, I've been doing this for more days than the total books you've ever read. I have never read of a boring subject. THE BOSS is incapable of making any person boring or without purpose. It can't happen."

"But …"

"But what?"

"Wouldn't it be better if I made his drab situation look more exciting somehow?"

"No."

"You don't think he has too many things going against him?"

"First, even if every conceivable possibility went against him, THE BOSS would see value in him. And you will too if you stick with him his entire life and observe the amazing person THE BOSS has planted in him.

"Second, he's not got it all that bad. He's being fed, clothed, and sheltered extravagantly compared to many on this earth. And he has a mother and father and family that love him."

Chief noticed Beemer's apprehensive glance. "What?"

"Nothing." Beemer refused to make eye contact.

"Have you fabricated more than the birthplace?"

Beemer's eyes darted around the room for refuge.

"What else did you lie about?"

No response.

"Come on. We'd better straighten this out now, rather than later. You keep adding to this faulty foundation and you won't be around to see what's built on this life."

After wincing and a brief shutting of his eyes, Beemer confessed. "Well, Homer, his dad, doesn't actually hold the little guy and play peek-a-boo with him whenever he gets the chance like I wrote he did."

Silence. "I wondered about that. Fathers of this generation aren't inclined to display affection. Provider and protector are their main roles. Personal intimacy for them, with anyone, is rare."

"And he's not always smiling and telling the other kids jokes."

Chief stared at the old wooden floor and narrowed his eyes.

Beemer continued before he lost his nerve. "And he may not actually be thinking of running for mayor."

The editor took a moment to grind his teeth. "Anything else you need to confess?"

Beemer squirmed and took in an uneasy deep breath. "Well, there's been a couple of times when Homer yelled at Bertha when she was breastfeeding the child, to, 'Hurry up and come to bed!'"

The editor looked confused. "Why is that noteworthy? He was probably worn-out from working his full-time job at *Orrville Tile Company* on top of farming and raising eleven children."

"It's just that … the tone in which Homer spoke those words was more of a … I don't know, more of a demand or an ultimatum than a tired man's frustrated request. It came off as kind of mean."

"Hey, you're a chronicler, not a judge. You report what happens, not why it happened or who's to blame. Quit trying to control the story. Tell the story."

"Okay, I will from now on. Sorry."

"Apology accepted. Now stop trying to create a masterpiece. The child is the masterpiece. And he's THE BOSS's masterpiece, not yours. Yours is the joyous privilege to report how this masterpiece unfolds, through all the wonderful—and horrific—events of his life."

The chief clutched his student's shoulders and looked unwaveringly into his eyes. "You can do this. I'm entrusting THE BOSS's joy with you." With a hint of a smile, the weathered editor released his grip. "Now, if there's anything else before I get to my other editing obligations, please ask now, so I'm not forced to confront you down here again. I'm getting too old for this transporting business."

"Well … " Beemer bit the tip of his thumb. "I don't really know just yet, but what if, just for curiosity's sake, the dad does turn out to be mean?"

The editor assumed his dignified editor's stalwart pose—arms folded over his ample belly, thick, black glasses at the end of his bulbous nose, torso at a right angle from his jutting chin, and facing his employee. "Report it. Why is this a question?"

"But, I mean, what would become of young Clayton? Surely, his life will be greatly affected. Surely, his chance for greatness will take a hit."

The bushy eyebrows came together. "Trust me, THE BOSS has *great things* for this Clayton, no matter how rough a start he gets. Sometimes, the rougher the start, the greater the life. THE BOSS has extraordinary means to evoke greatness. You'll see. Report and observe."

Beemer looked over to the wondrous sleeping baby at the foot of his parents' bed. How profound to think this little child, born right after the *Great Depression*, the youngest of eleven hungry children, raised on a measly farm in a less-than-progressive community would someday be ... significant. Maybe, *the rougher the start, the greater the life*, would be Clayton's destiny. Someday, like the famous explorer William Clark, maybe he would discover great things. *Oh, but what will those great things be?*

When Beemer looked back to share his wonder with his esteemed mentor, he found only humans sleeping in the grim room.

4

TODDLER YEARS

LEARNING WHAT TO EXPECT

Several years had passed since Chief's last transport visit with Beemer. That was fine with Beemer. He still wanted to be Heaven's best writer ever (even better than Chief had been) and figured the more job-in-jeopardy conversations he missed, the better. As much as he itched to show his editor and THE BOSS his tantalizing writing skills, following the boring house guidelines seemed a safer bet at the moment.

As he recorded each event in Clayton's life, Beemer reminded himself of the editor in chief's nonnegotiable instructions: *You're a chronicler—chronicle. Tell the story.* As far as Beemer was concerned, he had no wiggle room to add insights, humor, or objective gleanings to his technically sound reporting ... even if he thought he could improve on the format.

Beemer's biographic book of Clayton included these anecdotes through his toddler years:

Clayton, now old enough to sit without assistance, sits next to his mother for breakfast while listening to his father, Homer, as he gives his ritual, twenty-minute lecture on the Bible ... otherwise known as devotions.

Little Clayton eats his grape nuts like the rest of his nine siblings who are still at home, while Homer drones on with the family devotions. Totally oblivious to its meaning, Clayton, only three years old, plays catapult with his spoon, eliciting a few chuckles from his brothers and sisters.

His father stops his serious discourse. "Arlene and Viola," he says, "take Clayton in the other room and spank him, so he remembers to respect the Good Lord's Word."

Arlene and Viola, seventeen and fifteen respectively, dutifully do as they are told. Arlene lifts the toddler from the table, and they march into the living room and place him on the sofa.

"Now what?" Viola asks.

"I guess we bare his bottom," says Arlene.

The girls disrobe him as Clayton looks on, unsure of the unusual game they are playing.

"You first. I'll hold him down," Arlene says.

The little man is face down on the sofa as Viola whacks him on his bum. Clayton looks back to see his adoring sisters, not laughing. He wriggles.

"Here, you hold him." Arlene gets in two quick swats with her open palm.

Now, Clayton sits next to his dad during morning devotions. When Clayton's eyes wander, he gets a kick to his shins from Homer. Over time, Clayton's shins become black and blue, but they are still kicked repeatedly under the table whenever his eyes stray from the ruler of the roost's laborious devotions.

Clayton acts as if he is fully engaged in whatever it is his father is selling during breakfast. He is learning to be silent and appear interested like all his siblings.

After devotions, the girls leave, and the boys stay put to hear their father's instructions for the rest of the day. Clayton finds only one brother, Marion, who is seven years older, that avails his lap to him. Fortunately, only one lap is needed.

Clayton is nearly five years old, and his mother tells him that his father wants him to dress himself. Clayton looks back wide-eyed as if he'd just been given one of his older brother's chores that he couldn't possibly do. Bertha, his mother, graciously shows him the ropes and assists him one last time in this clothes-changing business. The next morning, Clayton changes into his daily clothes without his mother's help.

After the daily evening devotions, where each family member who is capable of reading reads a verse from a Bible chapter, personal prayer time ensues. Clayton and his nearest-in-age siblings, Norma Jean and Kenny, kneel at their mother's feet while she leads them in their nightly prayer, "Now I lay me down to sleep; I pray the Lord my soul to keep; if I should die before I wake, I pray my soul the Lord to take." So convincing is her recital of this comforting prayer that she sounds and looks like she includes herself in its plea.

In the middle of the night, five-year-old Clayton gets sick and throws up all over himself and the bed he shares with his brother, eight-year-old Kenny, at the foot of his parents' bed. His mother tenderly and efficiently cleans up the mess.

Writing in his biographic book one night, Beemer heard his name called. His body tightened as he looked up. Chief was in the room.

Beemer slowly turned to face his editor. "Chief." He thought of a thousand different things to add: "Are you lost? Did you come down to congratulate me on my awesome work? Am I being transferred to the president's son?" His least favorite option was, "What did I screw up this time?" But he said nothing more.

The chief replied in kind. After a staring match, he said, "Beemer, how are you feeling about your recent entries?"

Beemer's frightened mind was blank. "Um, I think I've written everything by the book, just like you asked."

"Beemer, I'm not here to chew you out."

"You told me to write technically sound," said Beemer. "Haven't I written technically sound?"

"Yes."

"Then what? I've not added any of myself in the thing."

"That's what I'm here about."

"I haven't; I swear. None of this," he points at his biographic book, "is my commentary. It's all unadulterated fact. Just like it happened."

"I know."

Beemer tilted his head. "You're complimenting me?"

"In a way, yes. But don't let that get to your head. I'm here for my routine checkup and to encourage you moving forward."

Still wary, Beemer waited for the other shoe to drop … the one that would surely step on his hopefulness.

"You have kept your reporting on the straight and narrow. Thank you for chronicling Clayton's story. You have shown yourself faithful to our mission."

Beemer wanted to pinch himself to see if he was dreaming … though he never slept. *Thank you for chronicling Clayton's story,* the chief had said. Unbelievable! He had been dreaming of hearing those words for the past five years. "Thank you … I mean, you're welcome … I mean, I have?"

"Yes, but it's time to grow up a little and add a splash of life to your writing. Stay technical, just write less like a textbook and more like a true-life adventure."

Beemer's eyes widened. "You mean like the *Lewis and Clark Expedition* with William Clark?"

"Yes, I suppose I do." The staunch editor looked above his glasses, perched on his nose. "But the adventure you need to explore is an emotional one. You remember the first element of the *Threeseez*?"

"Emotional makeup?"

"Right. It's time for you to learn Clayton's emotional makeup so you can write his *felt* story, not just the facts of his life."

"But Clayton's just a little kid. How many emotions can a kid have?"

The squatty man with the too-big eyebrows sighed to tame his own emotions. "Beemer, these humans are a bundle of mixed-up emotions. THE BOSS wired them to feel everything. Little children feel these natural emotions as pure as the driven snow. I guarantee you that Clayton is feeling everything. You need to *learn* what he's feeling, so you can *feel* what he's feeling. That's what makes a profound writer."

Seeing Beemer's blank stare, the editor in chief explained, "Pay attention to his reactions to new and traumatic events. Record these reactions. Make a log and cross-check your findings. This will help you understand his temperament, which will, in turn, help you understand his emotions. These natural inner reactions—emotions—are raw; behavior is manufactured. You learn his true emotions and you can judge his behavior accurately ... but only then. That's why learning his emotions is so critical."

"So, do all kids basically react the same way to new events?"

"Oh no. Not at all. Every kid is different. Some fight it, some laugh it off, some refuse to acknowledge it, and some tackle it head-on."

Beemer smiled. "I wonder if Clayton will learn to come out ahead on his."

"I can't answer that. Most people find their strategy relatively early. You'll just have to log his every reaction and see how he turns out. That's your adventure—to feel your subject's emotions."

Beemer nodded. "So, I'll really be able to feel what Clayton is feeling?"

"Sure, in a dozen years or so ... if you critically observe and log his reactions as I said."

Beemer's shoulders drooped. "A dozen years?"

"Hey, a chronicler doesn't just sign up to be a good chronicler. It takes hard work and dedication. Are you up for the challenge?"

"Of course! It's just ... "

"Good. Is there anything else?" asked the busy manager.

"I ... don't think so."

"Okay, then, carry on." The bald, round editor in chief turned to leave, then turned back. "Oh, you'll likely have some questions as you're plotting his reactions. Just write any such questions or possible insights in the margins. I'll note them and then answer the pertinent ones when I return."

Beemer nodded. "And when will that be, exactly?"

The tired editor smiled. "When I need to."

With that, he was gone.

Beemer smiled ... and frowned. *This is going to take some studying. How do I write technically sound AND write with emotion?* Beemer wondered how

Chief learned to do it. However, unless he was mistaken, as confusing as the editor's instruction had just been, it looked like he'd been given the green light to add a little pizzazz to the storyline. Maybe even encouragement to add a little color. He didn't know how it would look, but Beemer was ready to paint the town read (he sniggered at his own pun). Was he possibly sitting on a biographical masterpiece?

5
CHILDHOOD
STEERING THROUGH FEAR

The *Heaven's Chronicle's* editor in chief rifled through Beemer's lengthy biographic document in his Master Log, deciphering if Beemer was learning to judge his subject's emotions. He masterfully ignored the extraneous parts of the abundant, thorough, daily details and read only the following highlights:

Clayton walks north a mile and a half with his four elementary-aged brothers and sister to the Sonnenberg Public One-Room School for his first day of school. The teacher, Mr. Amstutz, speaks in English. Clayton has heard numerous words spoken in English from his siblings and people from church, but never has he been hit with nonstop sentences of only English. His world just got a little bigger ... or he, smaller.

It rains all day today. Clayton walks to school and drips all over his chair the whole morning.

Today Clayton walks to school through a foot of snow like all the other students.

In class, Clayton is asked what bread is called before it is baked. He says, "teig," the Swiss name for dough. The other children laugh. Many new English words are difficult for Clayton to remember or pronounce. Overall, in the classroom, Clayton avoids expressing out loud what he has learned because of the language hurdle. It appears safer to learn as little as possible rather than learning so much that one will be expected to share one's knowledge more frequently.

> Beemer made a note in the margin to his editor: *Is it safe to say that Clayton felt embarrassed? Maybe even humiliated? I wonder how he processes such feelings.*

Throw the kerosene lamps away (one per room). The Steiner household now has electricity! New electric lights go in every room. Clayton must still adhere to his strict bedtime, but the family no longer needs to trim the wicks and fill the lamps with kerosene every week.

Clayton rips a page out of the Sears catalog while in the smelly outhouse (used by the entire family) and uses it as toilet paper.

Saturday night is bath night. Clayton's older brothers fetch the big metal tub from the basement ceiling shelf and place it in the kitchen. Large pots of hot water that are heated on the stove are poured into the tub. After the girls each take their turn bathing, the boys take their turns, oldest to youngest. Clayton ends up with the dirtiest bath water every week.

> Margin notes to the editor: *Does Clayton feel cheated, being last all the time? Does he feel like the least valuable?*

Sunday. Everybody goes to church this day. Clayton piles into one car driven by his dad, and Lee drives a few of their siblings in the other. Tonight (Sunday), the family goes through the same routine to get to evening church.

Wednesday night, all go to church, except Homer and Bertha. Clayton knows that every time the church doors are open, he must attend. His dad enforces this policy for everyone except himself and his wife.

In a surprise and unprecedented gesture, Homer gives his youngest son a child-sized bicycle. Clayton enjoys riding his bike to school.

Today, it snows so hard after school that Clayton is forced to get off his bike. Since it is difficult to push his bike through the snow, he opts to leave it in the ditch until the storm subsides.

Clayton returns to retrieve his bicycle this morning. It is gone. Homer is not happy! He tells Clayton, "If you are like that, you will not amount to anything," and he informs Clayton that he will never give him a bike again. Clayton must ponder the loss of his pride and the first thing that belonged to only him. He now has one less reason to feel in control of anything.

> Margin notes to the editor: *Does Clayton feel shame or injustice more? He's just a kid, after all. Why is he being told his future has been corrupted by his innocent mistake?*

Clayton smiles and laughs during recess. Not so much in the classroom.

Clayton reads a verse at the evening devotions (like the rest of the family) for the first time. He stumbles a little over the word "chastise," but he performs well other than that. Not bad for a seven-year-old.

Homer mumbles the prayer before the meal. Clayton once witnessed his dad writing out this pre-meal prayer. It spoke of thankfulness for God's provision and protection. Had Clayton not read his notes, he would not have known what his dad is praying. The other hearers no longer question this unintelligible ritual at *every* meal.

During the typical meal of mush (cooked cornmeal from their cornfield), the children all sit in their same seats. Clayton sits on the bench against the wall. No one talks while they eat. Homer likely considers conversation unnecessary for a disciplined family.

Indoor plumbing has arrived. The Steiners now have running water in the kitchen and in the bathrooms. Theoretically, the outhouse and the boys *watering the trees* will be a thing of the past, though the eleven people still at home will need to share the one indoor toilet. And the new shower has hot water! Clayton, however, takes a mostly cold shower tonight because the hot water ran out by the time his turn rolled around. The benefits of being the youngest have not set in just yet.

Clayton sits next to his mother on the piano bench tonight and joins her in singing, "What a Friend We Have in Jesus."

> Notes in the margin: *Does Clayton feel loved and safe next to his mother? Will these feelings be enough to prepare him for hard times?*

Clayton is playing in the barn with Kenny and tells his dad that he will, "Do it later," when asked to sweep around the wood box in the living room. Homer, twisting Clayton's ear between his thumb and forefinger, says, "Why don't you listen to me? You're being like the Zuerchers, that lazy family your mother came from." Afterward, Clayton holds his ear as if worried it will stick out more than it already does.

Dorothy, Clayton's eighteen-year-old sister, finds out from the doctor today that she has tuberculosis. She had been coughing badly for weeks. The doctor says it is highly contagious, so she must go to a sanatorium in Amherst, near Cleveland (two hours away) to be by herself until she recovers.

Because today is Saturday, devotions go over an hour instead of the regular twenty minutes. Clayton keeps his eyes on his father the whole time even though the lesson contradicts Clayton's experience. Homer goes on and on about how sinful their mother is. The message admonishes his children *not* to be like their mother. Clayton, like all his brothers and sisters, says nothing. Bertha, the focus of his accusations, sits still like everyone else.

Margin notes from Beemer: *It seems like Clayton should feel angry, yet he doesn't act like it. But then, neither do any of his other role models who sit around the table. How am I going to figure out Clayton's emotions if he doesn't express his true feelings?*

Clayton awakes to his mother singing "Blessed Assurance" in the kitchen. Clayton wakes before the other children (which is rarely the case) and strolls to the kitchen. He pulls up a chair and watches his mother grind the grape nuts for the family as she sings more hymns from church.

Like his brothers and sisters, Clayton eats as much of the ground grape nuts as he wants for breakfast. He adds milk and sugar to his taste. Where variety lacks, abundance suffices when it comes to breakfast.

It snows so much today that Clayton doesn't go to school. He shares three sleds with his brothers and sisters down the barn bank runway into an open field. They take running starts, hopping onto the sled to see how far they can go. Sometimes, they pile two or more onto one sled at a time. Each time they break a distance record, they mark the ending spot with a stick in the ground. Then, they pull the sled back to test their Olympic skills again.

Margin notes: *Is it safe to say that Clayton feels genuinely happy here?*

As weather permits, Clayton and his three brothers, Kenny, Roy, and Marion ride their one bike to school … at the same time. This morning, Clayton gets his foot caught in the spokes, causing the gang to halt and fall. Clayton cries in pain. They rub off their wounds and ride the rest of the way to school.

Interrupting his play out in the barn with his brothers, Clayton finds a large rock between the old Model A Ford junk heap and the toolshed and takes a dump on it, an all-too-common occurrence that he and his brothers practice when the house is inconvenient. They no doubt learned such behavior from their dad who every morning takes his dump in the same corner of the barn and covers it with straw.

Clayton opts to challenge his mother's directive to carry a bowl of mush to the table and continues disassembling and assembling the batteries into the flashlight instead. Before he knows it, his ear is twisted in his mother's fingers. Clayton carries the bowl to the table, then he holds his sore ear, shocked by either the severity of the pain or the maker of his pain—his mother, who rarely raises a hand against him. He's learning that even authority figures he trusts can hurt him.

Tonight, Clayton cautiously sits by his mother at the piano. She draws him in with a hug. They sing "Jesus Loves Me, This I Know" together. Clayton smiles and sings boldly. After reciting the "Now I lay me down to sleep…" prayer with his mother, Clayton kneels at his bed extra intently.

In the morning, after breakfast and the boring devotions where he learned not to be like Bertha's mother (Clayton's Grandma Zuercher), he finds a dollar bill out in the driveway. Looking at it, front side and back, he tugs it taut. He confides to his mother, "I prayed for money last night, and look." He holds the miracle dollar bill up as proof. She smiles and nods.

> In the margin, Beemer wrote to the editor: *Is Clayton feeling seen and valued by THE BOSS here? Do you think I should corroborate that THE BOSS likely answered his prayers? Is this an occasion that may bolster his faith in THE BOSS from here on out?*

Clayton and Kenny now sleep upstairs in the room next to Marion and Roy. Clayton wets his bed tonight. In the morning, Clayton complains to his mother about his bedsheets being wet. She changes the sheet with the one extra sheet they own. Again, Clayton wets his bed and tells his mother. The weekly washing isn't for another two days, so she is unable to change his sheets. Clayton will have to go to bed with a damp sheet.

Homer discovers that Clayton is chronically wetting his bed. "We can't afford to buy new sheets," he says. "You'll sleep in your wet sheets until you stop this nonsense."

Clayton notices little bedsores on his bottom that worsen every time he lies in the wet sheets on the straw mattress.

> Notes to the editor: *Does Clayton feel like he deserves the bedsores? Does he realize wetting the bed is not his fault?*

Out in the barn, eight-year-old Clayton is learning to pitch manure with a pitchfork. He's frustrated and tells his dad he can't do it because the manure keeps falling through the cracks of the pitchfork.

Homer is not in the mood. He says, "You can do better than that! Don't be like your mother." Homer turns and leaves his teary-eyed eight-year-old son holding a grungy pitchfork that is taller than himself.

This morning, Clayton displays extra interest in devotions, no doubt to show his father his devotion to him. Homer makes no sign of acknowledging Clayton's rapt attention. Instead, he conveys the terribleness of being weak like their mother and like the neighbors who won't farm when it rains.

> In the margin, Beemer writes: *Is Clayton feeling insignificant and defeated? Should I write something about how he must be questioning his dad's love for him? Or is that not necessarily an intuitive thing a kid would wonder?*

Clayton finally gets to participate in a pest hunt. His school will give the class that brings in the most pests a nice prize. Since pests (like mice, rats, starlings, sparrows, and foxes) wreak havoc on farms, placing a bounty on them benefits the farmers and motivates the children. It is a win/win that the community applauds.

Tonight, Clayton follows his brothers to the barn. Marion shines a flashlight on an unsuspecting sparrow in the hay, blinding it momentarily. The other boys run at it. Roy grabs the helpless winged pest and slams it against the wall. Then, he snaps its head off and stuffs the head in a paper bag to be counted by the teacher in the morning. They catch a few more like this, though Clayton's bag remains empty.

At the devotions this morning, Homer tells the kids that Elno (their oldest brother who was the first to move out on his own) is considering the ministry.

As Clayton struggles to milk a cow this morning, Homer tells him, "Marion wouldn't do it like that."

Homer takes Clayton to the doctor today to see if something can be done about his bedwetting. Dr. Iten examines him and asks him how much he drinks before he goes to bed, if he pees regularly, and if it ever hurts to pee. Dr. Iten then turns to Homer and says, "It looks like you have a pretty healthy boy here." Homer and the doctor then go to a separate room for a while, leaving Clayton to play with a stethoscope.

At home, before supper, Homer sits Clayton behind the woodstove in the living room and tells him Dr. Iten told him that Clayton is now old enough to stop wetting the bed.

Clayton awakes this morning to a dry bed.

Clayton has not wet the bed for a week.

Clayton has not wet the bed for a month. That must be a smart doctor!

Since Dorothy may be in isolation for a long time, Homer and Bertha travel two hours once a week to visit her. Clayton asks to go with them but is denied.

After their parents leave, Roy (age fourteen) finds the keys to their second car. With a devilish grin, he convinces Marion, Kenny, and Clayton to ride in the car with him. He drives them all over town, then stops at a neighbor's, gets out, knocks on their door, and asks if the two boys want to come with them. They do.

Before their parents get home, Roy parks the car exactly where he found it and tells everyone to keep the secret so they can do it again the next time.

Clayton sits in the egg room in the house basement with his mother as she grades the eggs. He asks her questions about her family, Homer's family, and the church congregation as she weighs each egg and puts each in the appropriate small, medium, large, or extra-large boxes.

Homer finds Clayton and Kenny wrestling around in the straw stack, trying to put straw down each other's back. He grabs an ear of each. "We don't play around when there's work to be done. Don't be lazy."

Margin notes: *Does Clayton feel bad for being a child?*

Clayton plays softball every recess in the spring. Today, after school, the teacher piles twelve kids into his car (including a few in the open trunk) and drives them to another one-room school to play a softball game against them. Clayton catches a ball in the outfield and gets a hit. He gives it his all like the game depends on him.

In the margin: *Does Clayton finally feel confident at something?*

Popcorn night is every Saturday night after supper and chores. Lee pops the several batches of corn tonight in the usual black kettle with a stirring handle on the top. Clayton eats his fill of popcorn by the handful. Lee pops so much that they store the remainder in old four-quart canning jars and use it for snacks during the week.

A rarity—Clayton, Kenny, and Normie get to go along with their parents to visit Dorothy. But about halfway there, the '38 Dodge breaks down in the middle of the road. Homer goes to the nearest house for assistance. They are nice people, though they are not Mennonite. They invite the family in for a scrumptious meal and to spend the night until they can get help getting the car home the next day.

The head of the house laughs when he sees Clayton's eyes water and when he acts as if his mouth is about to explode after taking a swig of a beverage. "Is that your first taste of soda pop?"

Clayton nods. "It burns your mouth."

"Yeah, it's carbonated. They call it *pop* because the fizz pops in your mouth."

Clayton and his brothers sneak up to the chicken coop tonight, flashlights in hand, and open the door to critters nestling in the warm chicken manure. Then, they make their raid. The varmints scatter to the nearest exits. Clayton stomps on a mouse and a rat tonight on their pest hunt. He gets his pocketknife out and cuts off their tails and stuffs them in his bag.

Clayton's class receives one point for his mouse tail and two points for the rat tail.

Today, when the parents go to visit Dorothy, the boys participate in their favorite pastime—sliding down the barn roof. Clayton slides down on his bottom and catches himself on the silo right next to the barn just before going over the edge. This time, he snags his pants on a nail.

> Beemer's note to the editor: *What is Clayton feeling when he does such daring and impulsive things? Does it make him feel alive? Worthy of attention? A part of his brothers' world?*

Clayton learns to use wrenches, screwdrivers, and other tools to disassemble the '38 Dodge that is now parked in the back of the toolshed next to the last old junker (a Model A Ford). His brothers explain what each part is called and its function as they take it out for possible resale later. They spend hours tenaciously dismantling the junk heap.

Mending day. Bertha asks Clayton how he ripped his pants. Clayton tells her, "Must've got it caught on a nail somewhere."

It rains like Noah's dreams tonight. Kenny and Clayton open their bedroom window, take off their clothes, and step out onto the roof to fully enjoy the weather, evidently. A new pastime called skinny dripping has been born.

Homer shuts down the family softball game after church today. Though it looked like all the kids enjoyed the entertainment, Homer serves notice that Sunday is a day of rest, not for running around like chickens with their heads cut off. Clayton and his siblings walk off the field with frowns on their faces.

Clayton helps his mother with the weekly clothes washing today (Monday) because Normie is under the weather. He keeps the fire going under the hot water kettle and helps pull the clothes out of the hand-cranked wringer after they come out of the single-engine-powered washing machine (that Homer cranks by hand to start).

Clayton changes into his newly laundered clothes. As is the procedure every week, he wears one set of clothes to school, one to do chores, and one set waits in the pile to be washed. Along with these three sets, he has one set of Sunday clothes. His clothes are all hand-me-downs. His mother sews most of the shirts and dresses from the material in feed bags.

> Beemer notes: *Does Clayton realize how materially poor his family is?*

At devotions, Homer relates the passage in scripture about the ten plagues in Egypt to how the Zuerchers do everything wrong.

Clayton laughs when he pulls the one-legged milking stool out from under Kenny while Kenny is milking a cow. Kenny takes off after him. As they turn the corner around the barn, they run into Homer. Homer grabs their ears and says, "If you are like that, you will not amount to anything," and to Clayton when Kenny is back milking his cow, he says, "Elno or Marion would not do that."

Clayton, now in the fourth grade, stutters when answering the teacher's questions.

It is June 20, 1952, on a Friday night. The entire family (except for Elno, Arlene, and Lee) is finishing up supper. The phone rings. Bertha answers. "Just a minute," she says and quickly hands the phone to Homer.

Homer answers and appears to answer some questions. "Yes. It is. Yes." Then he asked some questions. "Where did it happen? Is he okay? Was anyone else hurt? What's that? Where? How much?" Each question sounded more concerning. "Okay. I'll be there." He hangs up. Clayton, like all his siblings, silently stares.

Homer looks at his audience, in no hurry to share. "Lee had an accident."

Clayton tightens his body and looks at his brothers and sisters. They don't seem to know how to react either. No one makes a peep. Lee, twenty-four-years-old, had gone to a Mennonite youth convention with his girlfriend, best friend, and best friend's date.

Homer continues, "In Maumee. It's up by Toledo. About two and a half hours from here, the police said. Lee's in jail. I've got to pay to get him out. They say it's a homicide. He overran a curve and his '49 Ford rolled. The other boy with him died. Everyone else is not too bad."

Clayton sits, not moving a coiled muscle. *Lee's best friend died! And he's in jail.*

Homer and Irvin, Arlene's husband who lives on the other side of Kidron, drive to pick up Lee that night. Clayton asks his mom for details about the accident the day after the horrific accident, but she doesn't know any more than her eleven-year-old son. The rest of the family handles the unknown in silence.

Clayton attends the packed church for Lee's friend's funeral and finds a seat in the balcony. Lee walks in with his date and sits near the middle of the church. Clayton hears many of Lee's friends talking about him and how awful the accident was. Clayton's breathing is uneasy. He avoids eye contact with anyone.

Beemer asks the editor in the margin: *I know I don't know Clayton's emotions yet, but it sure looks like he's doing all he can to avoid feeling his emotions. How will he ever learn to feel the emotions given him if those he looks up to don't show emotions either?*

It's dinnertime (the noon meal). Clayton enjoys the potatoes, corn, and green beans his mother cooks from their summer garden!

Kenny and Clayton step out onto the roof from their bedroom in the hot night. They dare each other to jump off the summerhouse roof—a good eight-foot drop or more. They both take the dare. Clayton lands a little funny and hobbles back inside with a twisted ankle.

Margin comments: *Is this what Clayton must go through to feel like a man? Risk life and limb?*

Clayton is chasing Kenny around the sheets that are hung out to dry. To get an edge, he barrels through a sheet, knocking it to the ground. Bertha is not happy. She takes him by the ear and makes him wash it by hand in a tub until it is completely clean.

His mother lovingly teaches Clayton how to play, "Little Drops of Water" on the piano tonight.

Margin notes: *Is Clayton feeling forgiven?*

When Clayton finishes his chores after school, he asks his mother if his dad is home yet. When she tells him he is not, Clayton turns on the radio to Wooster's WWST's *Request Time* to listen to *worldly music* (according to Homer). On this rare occasion, Bertha joins him in listening though such an action has been declared a sin.

Because Homer is the treasurer for his Sunday school class, he brings home the offering. He asks Clayton to count it. Clayton sits on his bed, watching the coins tumble through his fingers. He counts the money several times to give an accurate account.

Clayton receives an orange for Christmas, as do his brothers and sisters.

It is so cold and stormy out that snow seeps through Clayton's upstairs bedroom and onto his bed.

Homer investigates the boys' windowsill. He wonders aloud why the windowsill is rotting. Clayton looks to Kenny. Kenny looks to Clayton. They stay silent. When Homer leaves the room, Kenny asks, "Should've we told him that we pee out that window all the time?"

Clayton responds, "Do you want to get killed? Of course, we shouldn't-a told him!"

The winter sledding adventures have been upgraded. Today, Clayton and his siblings go to the much larger Menno Lehman farm hill. Sledding is much faster and more daring. Clayton laughs and has the unfettered energy to drag the sled back up the steep ridge.

Clayton begs to go sledding again after church. Homer tells him emphatically, "No! Elno and Marion wouldn't do that. They don't waste their time with such nonsense on the Sabbath."

> Margin notes: *How does Clayton feel about being compared to his older brothers Elno and Marion all the time? Surely, it doesn't motivate him, right?*

The Steiner children do not enjoy the comforts of a heated brick at the foot of their bed like their father has in his bed. Instead, Clayton and his brothers devise what they think is an even better contraption—a light bulb in a wood-framed box that they place under the covers. They don't concern themselves with the fire hazard because this invention keeps their feet warm.

Homer entrusts his children (shocker of shockers!) to make the weekly visit to Dorothy without their parents. She is now enduring her second bout of tuberculosis at a sanatorium near Mount Vernon, Ohio, (a little closer to home). Marion and Roy share driving responsibilities, while Kenny, Normie, and Clayton sit in the back.

They pick up Dorothy and give her a scenic view of the area from the front seat. Even though they are just creeping along, they admire the view a little too much, and they end up in a ditch and are stuck. It's a head-scratcher as to what to do.

It just so happens that twelve prison-striped inmates are cleaning the roadsides and stumble upon them. One of the inmates says, "Hey, we can help you out." Marion gets in the driver's seat and all the inmates, Clayton, and his siblings push the car till it spins out of the ditch. Other than some dirt on the bumper that can be rubbed out, nothing noticeable appears damaged.

On the way home, Kenny asks, "Should we tell Dad what happened?"

In unison, the other car mates say, "No!"

Clayton talks to Bertha as she grades eggs. He corrects her a couple of times when discussing how some church members are connected to one another. At age twelve, he understands more of the genealogy of their acquaintances than even his mother does.

After his father's boring and demeaning (of his mother) devotions this morning at 6:20, Clayton watches his dad eat his breakfast and study tomorrow's devotions till 6:30. Homer then turns on the radio to listen to the daily news for ten minutes. When Homer leaves to go to his job at Smucker's at 6:40, Clayton sighs. The quiet house is mysteriously noisy and full of positive energy when his father is out of earshot.

Clayton continues to stutter more and more, in and out of school.

> In the margin: *Is this poor boy regressing? Do his dad's demeaning remarks have something to do with his stuttering? How will he ever be a hero if he can't even talk right?*

After their chores, Clayton and his brothers and sisters and some neighbor boys play a little softball before supper. Homer sees their raucous behavior and tells them they must not have worked hard enough at their chores if they have the energy to play softball.

Goodbye, Tom and Dull (the workhorses). Homer buys a tractor and the necessary accessories to replace the animals. Clayton and his brothers will no longer need to contend with the horses or the difficult farm work that was associated with them. But now, the boys must accomplish more.

Clayton drives the 1943 Ford-Fergusson tractor, pulling a trailer, home from the Menno Lehman hill. He decides to let the rig coast in neutral to see how fast it can go. Near the bottom, the tractor rattles, shimmies, and wobbles, and the trailer appears to try and pass the front end. Wildly pumping the ineffectual brakes, Clayton tightens his grip on the steering, realizing he has lost control. His life is in the hands of the farm machinery.

Somehow, he survives the terrifying ordeal without overturning either vehicle. Clayton lays his head on the now motionless steering wheel, his heart racing.

> Beemer writes in the margin: *Surely Clayton feels fear here. Was he afraid of losing his life or displeasing his father? Was that feeling of being out of control a microcosm of what he feels like being under Homer's rule all the time?*

While their parents are away visiting Dorothy, Clayton and his brothers take their Allis Chalmers tractor and chain it to their neighbor's Oliver 77 tractor for a chain duel. Both drivers floor the gas to see who can pull whom. Clayton stands next to Roy on the tractor and cheers him on. The chain snaps. No one goes home with bragging rights this day.

Homer asks how the chain broke. Clayton says, "We had to pull the neighbor's tractor out of the ditch."

... Clayton gets the day off school to help with the annual paper-drive fundraiser for school. He is granted permission to drive his tractor and two-wheeled trailer to school (though he's only in sixth grade). Then, unprecedentedly, he is allowed to drive the tractor on the road. His classmates ride on the trailer to pick up the bundled used newspapers in front of people's houses.

Clayton makes his friends in the back laugh as he wildly drives from one side of the road to the other, jostling his riders. When he gets to the top of a notable hill, he decides to show them the time of their lives. He places the gear in neutral, evidently forgetting his last near-death experience with a downward tractor in neutral. The tractor gains speed—rapidly. Halfway down, the tractor rattles, shimmies, and wobbles. The heavy trailer, laden with students and newspapers, begins to fishtail. Clayton tries to compensate for the twisting by pumping the worthless brakes and steering away from the melee. His efforts have little effect. The tractor's and trailer's destiny are out of Clayton's control. Disaster looms as they approach a one-lane bridge at the bottom of the hill.

Mysteriously, the trailer decides to center its way through the middle of the bridge, just missing the sides. The girls scream, angry at Clayton's daring. Some of the boys laugh. Clayton's heart beats fast. He does not laugh or cry. He drives back to the school slowly and safely. *He nearly killed his classmates!*

When he arrives back at the school, Clayton's teacher tells him his tractor driving is over for the day. Some people had called in about his reckless driving. Clayton gives no resistance to the order.

> Beemer's margin notes to the editor: *Whoa! Clayton just about died because he was showing off. I could have been out of a job just like that. And Clayton's life would have been a dud before he made anything of himself. I'd better come up with some good themes or something to make his life seem valuable in case he pulls some foolhardy thing like this again. And I'd better do something about the negative effects his dad is obviously causing.*

As Beemer spewed his fears onto the margin notes, the chief editor took a deeper dive into the Master Log. He saw his rookie reporter was falling into an all-too-common and alarming trend. He sighed and closed his weary eyes. *Beemer, you're going too far.* It was time for a visit.

6

WHO ORCHESTRATES CLAYTON'S LIFE?

Chief found his junior reporter writing in his biographic book near the twelve-year-old subject's bed.

"How's the novel coming?"

Beemer jumped, then he scrambled to his feet in a panic, dropping the book to the floor. "Oh! It's you, Chief. It's going well, thank you."

Chief shook his head sardonically. "You're not, you know."

"No, I'm doing pretty good. Really!" Beemer picked up the invaluable book from the floor.

"No. I mean, you're not writing a novel. You're writing a biography."

Beemer's eyes darted around the room; he was trapped. "Right. Sorry. I didn't catch that."

"Beemer, are you shooting straight with me?"

"What do you mean?"

"Are you writing truth or fiction?"

Beemer hesitated too long. "Ah … truth."

The chief sighed and glared his patented *don't-give-me-that* stare. With his sturdy glasses at the end of his bulbous nose, he lifted and opened the big Master Log from Beemer's hands and said, "It says here that the dad, ' … whips his kids every night before they go to bed.'"

Beemer's rapt eyes didn't blink.

The crusty teacher turned a page. "Here it says the dad, '… goes out drinking every night and comes home an angry drunk.'" He lifted his trained eyes from the page and homed in on Beemer.

Beemer couldn't meet his super's gaze and looked to his feet.

"Beemer, you said earlier in your account that the dad is a teetotaler. Which is it?"

Swallowing hard, Beemer said, "Ah … well, he doesn't actually drink exactly. But his presence seems to have the same effect. I figured adding that … er… added bonus would explain the dad's demoralizing dominance."

"So, you think the dad's leadership makes Clayton feel … what, beat up?"

Beemer nodded enthusiastically. "Yes. He never hears any encouragement from Homer. Only discouragement. How could he feel anything but degraded around this shame monger?"

Chief squinted his leery eyes. "Explain."

"Well, it makes sense. Clayton's been stuttering; he always remains silent when Homer speaks lies against their angelic mother, and he never gets physical affection from this disciplinarian dad. Homer must be a tyrant. How else would I explain Clayton's need for attention to go off and nearly kill his classmates in that insane tractor stunt? It's got to be Homer's fault."

The old chronicler let out a smirk. "Stop trying so hard to rationalize all your subject's miscues. These are humans we're dealing with. They're flawed. Get used to it. They can make bad choices without any discernible reasons sometimes. They learn best from mistakes.

"Whether the dad was being too much of a disciplinarian has anything to do with Clayton's behavior or not, you can't just make stuff up. We don't tolerate liars around here! You can write only what you know. You got that?"

Beemer gulped, then nodded.

"What's that? You're a reporter, not a dummy."

"Yes, Chief! Sorry, I just … " Beemer shook his head as if to toss the thought aside.

"No, speak your mind, boy. Now's the time to ask, when I'm here and your subject is dormant."

"Well, it's just that, it's a little confusing because last time you told me my writing was too drab. I was just trying to spice up Clayton's boring story a bit. Like you always did."

The chief smacked his forehead with the butt of his palm. "I never concocted stories! Or … at least not when I became a Full Fledged Chronicler. The point is, Son, your *writing* was boring, not the story. None of THE BOSS's children are boring!"

"But, at this rate, because of his dad's verbal abuse, Clayton will probably turn out to be either a cowering pushover or a mean-spirited bully like his dad. Why would THE BOSS want to read about that? And you said that sometimes greater lives come from rougher times. If I show how tyrannically awful the dad is now, I figure Clayton can't help but land in a better situation by the time he's an adult. Might as well find the silver lining in his cloudy life while we can."

The editor stared, unblinking, over his reading glasses at Beemer.

Beemer said, "Do you think maybe I should make things seem even worse?"

"No! Just stop!" Chief massaged his brow. "Look, Beemer, you're a reporter, not a political campaign manager. You report *his* choices. You don't orchestrate his story to make yourself look better. That's narcissistic subjecting. You're employed to be a benevolent projector."

Beemer donned the proverbial deer-in-the-headlights pose. "A what and a what?"

"I thought you mastered language." The editor paused, taking a full breath. "In simple terms—this job requires chronicling about THE BOSS's prized child, not demonstrating your clever writing. STOP MAKING IT YOURS AND MAKE IT THE BOSS'S!"

Beemer dropped his pen and stepped back. "Okay, okay. I won't be so artful. But I'm afraid Clayton is afraid of his dad."

"What if he is? Respect requires a parcel of fear after all."

Hesitant, Beemer said, "But what if Homer is the terrible tyrant that I painted him to be?"

"That's another chronicler's worry. Your job is to chronicle about Clayton, not the dad."

Beemer frowned. "But I still think Clayton will turn out bad because of his dad's cruel manner. I think he's bound for an empty life."

"Beemer, stop your negative forecasting!"

Beemer sighed and closed his eyes.

The editor breathed out as well. "When you know what Clayton feels and thinks, you're free to write that. He may be afraid of his own dad. He may have some terrible negative emotions about Homer, but you must wait to write about that until you *know* his feelings. THE BOSS will not be happy with misrepresentation. And neither will I." He closed his eyes and forced a compassionate, fatherly smile. "Don't force me to find another chronicler to finish this book."

Beemer opened his eyes and swallowed. "Uh … I can do this right. Just tell me what to do."

"I have been." The chief blinked morosely, twice. "Concisely, conduct an investigative case study while simultaneously administering a continuous exploratory evaluation of his emotional system."

"Huh?"

"You're limited to write what he sees and does until you can write in terms of his *emotions*, *environment*, and *experiences*. Remember the *Threeseez*?"

Beemer stared with his mouth hanging open. "Ah uh."

With a knowing grin, the chief said, "Great! And remember that it is not up to you to make his life *seem* valuable. Clayton *is* valuable to THE BOSS. That's all that matters. You don't need to make him seem in any way different than he is. He's THE BOSS's prized creation. His life is in no way a *dud*, no matter what you think."

Beemer sat motionlessly.

"Now, to settle your margin notes." The editor continued his training. "You've asked many excellent questions pertaining to Clayton's emotions. Bravo to you! Continue this habit. Each question will bring you closer to the answers. Soon, you will be a soul-buddy with your subject, and you will know what he's feeling."

"Soon? Like any day now?"

The wrinkled editor cracked a wry smirk. "Don't get overzealous, kid. You're on schedule. Keep at it, and you'll understand your subject at the appointed time." Seeing the unbound eagerness on Beemer's face, he added, "Usually happens by the time the subject reaches early adulthood. Keep working."

Beemer's hopeful gleam fizzled.

"Regarding the question of whether Clayton is questioning his dad's love for him or not, we partially just answered this, as you clearly don't know what he's feeling yet. But, speaking from experience, a child naturally trusts those in authority over him until something occurs to shake that loyal trust. At that point, the child's trust is granted in degrees rather than in totality, depending on the severity and frequency of the offense as well as the child's tolerance.

"You'll have to take copious notes to determine what kind of tolerance Clayton has for a deriding father who always provides for his physical needs but never for his emotional needs. It's a dichotomy, to be sure. He likely respects and loathes his father but is not mature enough to recognize the tenuous position he is in. Expect inner conflict when he realizes that he has been put in such an unfair predicament."

Beemer asked, "So, what if he can't handle his dad's meanness before he can process it good enough? What if he's a total mess before he even leaves home?"

The chief folded his hands on his ample belly. "Then you write about it. THE BOSS will be just as interested in him whether he triumphs over his dad's derision or falls because of it. There will always be a path to redemption. Don't second guess THE BOSS's plan.

"The problem, I think, that Clayton must contend with is that Homer gives off the strong impression that a person must always be in complete control of their actions and their temperament. He not only wants his kids to be strong, he wants them to be seen by everyone else as strong. This is a plan bound for pain and failure. Though it appears to display integrity, it, in fact, is disingenuous, fake, false. One can't pretend to be strong, noble, or courageous when one is not. Or at least, not for long. The building crumbles to rubble at some point. Even Homer, as strong a personality as he is, will likely fall at some point by exalting control and one's standing above all else. People are fragile. That's a truism Homer is trying to scorn but will one day surely be scorned by.

"You asked if Clayton will ever learn to feel the emotions THE BOSS gave him when those around him don't show theirs. That's an excellent question. I'd say he's in an uphill battle. He's starting out at a disadvantage in that regard. But I have seen far worse cases learn to be emotionally whole.

It will all depend on the leadings Clayton follows. THE BOSS will always give him a way out.

"Next, I notice you asked questions regarding prayer and THE BOSS's part in them. Though we are *Heaven's Chronicle* employees, I'm afraid we aren't granted access to THE BOSS's rule book on prayer. We, like the people on earth, don't fully understand how all that works. Certainly, THE BOSS answers prayer on occasion. But when and why remain somewhat of a mystery.

"You can be certain that THE BOSS cherishes Clayton. Clayton may have found that dollar bill at the end of the driveway through answered prayer. Then again, it may have been a coincidence. We can't know for sure. Clayton can't know for sure. That's the beauty of faith. THE BOSS drops enough breadcrumbs along the way to draw a person in, so after a while, it doesn't matter which situations THE BOSS orchestrated and which THE BOSS didn't. What matters is that the person finds meaning and purpose in the searching and the finding. That's how THE BOSS set it up.

"In the end, it is up to Clayton to decide how involved he feels THE BOSS is. Keep watching for signs of how guided he is by his faith, knowing that THE BOSS is interested too."

"Does his faith just come from his feelings," Beemer asked, "or is there more I should be looking for?"

"I won't lie. Faith is complicated if you try to figure it out. It not only deals with emotions, but cognitive apprehension, the will, intrinsic desires, intuitive perception, and on and on. Yet, if the subject is in tune with THE BOSS, it is the most simple and pure practice humans can know."

Chief looked at Beemer's helpless return gaze. "Don't get overwhelmed. Baby steps. Keep concentrating on his emotions first. The rest will follow in due time. You'll be fine.

"And lastly, 'Did THE BOSS stop the tragedy of the tractor and trailer running into the bridge from happening?' We could hypothesize and philosophize about THE BOSS's methods all we want. But in the final analysis, THE BOSS does whatever THE BOSS wants. I look at it like this: THE BOSS created everything, including time, space, and nature. Whether we perceive events as random or ordained is inconsequential. If they happened, they were part of THE BOSS'S plan.

"Clayton was lucky, granted. But the important matter, again, is—how will Clayton view it. He's welcome to place it on his faith platter, or he could see it as arbitrary luck. Which will benefit him more? A life-and-death experience like that is awfully hard to denounce as random or forgettable. Maybe THE BOSS did orchestrate the whole thing just to open Clayton's eyes. Is it worth it to Clayton to shrug that possibility off? Observe and report.

"Let Clayton decide these things in his own time. You are not his author. Remember?"

Beemer sheepishly nodded and looked to the floor.

"What's that?"

"Yes, Chief."

"Any more questions?"

Beemer looked back, transfixed by the wise editor's aura. "No, Chief."

And, with the student having been schooled by the teacher, the editor left his young chronicler in the Steiner home to observe, learn, and understand the unfolding life of one Clayton Steiner.

7
TEENAGE YEARS
EXPLORING CHOICES

The editor in chief found the time to sit down and scan over Beemer's biographic book of Clayton's teenage years, skillfully overlooking the non-essential parts, making sure Beemer wasn't espousing his opinions. He read the following:

Clayton continues his daily chores of milking, retrieving and spreading straw, and pitching manure. Farming life never ceases.

While Kenny is pitching manure, Clayton sneaks up on him and throws a pail of water on him. Kenny, though three years older, cannot catch the faster twelve-year-old Clayton to punish him for his mischief.

Clayton attends the annual Wayne County Brunk Tent Revival meetings. Nearly five thousand people are in attendance. Clayton plays out in the parking lot with other boys his age. After the meeting, Homer tells Clayton that he is of the age to join the church.

The Lehman cousins join Clayton's family for dinner after church. Jay announces that he plans to go overseas to fulfill his voluntary service for the church with an organization called *Pax*. Clayton shows rapt attention to his cousin's anticipated adventure.

Clayton again plays in the parking lot during the revival meetings without his dad's knowledge. But this night during the altar call, Clayton follows his second cousin, John, whom he appears to admire, into the massive tent and down the daunting aisle, up to the intimidating preacher, George R. Brunk, who had given the invitation. Brunk's helper, Rev. Mumaw, takes each of the youths (there are ten total) individually behind the pulpit. In turn, Clayton diligently follows this learned man's every instruction. He kneels, says he's sorry for his sins, and asks to become a child of God.

Rev. Mumaw then instructs Clayton to go to the pulpit and confess his sins in front of the church. Clayton's heart is beating fast and his hands are quaking. He looks out into the terrifying crowd and stammers, "Ah, I confess my ... all of my sins." Clayton looks to Brunk.

The preacher says, matter-of-factly, "Do you want to join the church?"

Clayton says out loud, "Yes, I want to join the church."

The evangelist beams, shakes Clayton's hand, and announces, "You are now saved!" He prays over all the new converts and exhorts them to inform their bishops of the decision they've made.

Clayton looks to find the faces of his mother and father in the sea of people before him after the prayer but can't spot them.

> Beemer made a note to the editor in the margin: *Did Clayton do this from a sense of genuine need and desire, or did he do it to please his parents? Does THE BOSS care about his motive? Will his salvation stick if his motive was impure?*

The first catechism class begins tonight. Clayton attends the meeting with the other twenty-nine students around his age. The jolly, respected Bishop Reuben Hofstetter teaches how important it is for them to follow the Mennonite doctrines because that is God's plan for them. They will all be learning what God expects of them now that they've asked God into their lives and committed themselves to him.

Clayton and Kenny work at their chore of getting the twenty-foot stack of straw down from the second floor to the first floor. Kenny uses a straw hook connected to a long rope from below, while Clayton guides the hook to the highest straw so Kenny can pull as much straw down as possible. They've done this hundreds of times. Today, Clayton takes an armful of straw and throws it on the unsuspecting Kenny below. Kenny hollers, "What are you doing?" and steps away like a wet cat trying to shake off the dusty mess.

Clayton giggles uncontrollably and says, "Sorry, didn't know you were there."

In catechism class, Clayton learns that the man should be the head of the household.

During devotions this morning, Clayton's father reminds his children that they should not be like their mother, who "likes to be lazy." As Homer drones on, the family eats their favorite breakfast, fried mush—painstakingly made by their mother, who cooked the cornmeal into mush the night before, cooled it, dried it, then fried it early this morning. As a special treat, Bertha made sugarcane molasses from the sugarcane that is grown on their farm to pour over the crunchy mush morsels.

In catechism this week, Clayton is told that women are to obey scripture by covering their heads out of respect for their husbands.

Clayton asks his mother if she has always worn her head covering (for he has never seen her in public without it). She tells him that she has worn it in submission to God ever since she became a member of the church.

Reuben Hofstetter teaches that the Bible is inerrant and infallible, which, he explains, means it says exactly what God means. God's people should not ever doubt it but should obey every part of it.

In catechism class tonight, Clayton learns the importance of honoring one's father and mother.

In-between trips of loading the manure cart, which hangs from an over-head rail and is pushed over to the manure spreader and dumped, Clayton convinces Kenny to push him inside the cart for a fun ride. Homer sees the shenanigans and scolds, "Why don't you do what I tell you? If you are like this, you won't amount to anything!"

This evening, Clayton beats his dad and brothers to the barn and decides to impress them by preparing the barn for milking. He lets in all the cows. But he forgets to fill their stalls with feed prior to their entering. The hungry cows go crazy, looking for the reward due them. One particularly frustrated Holstein turns into the annoying boy who is watching the parade (this would be Clayton), knocks him down, then steps on him. The wind is knocked out of his lungs, and Clayton finds it difficult to rise and escape the melee.

Homer rescues his foolish son, saying, "You should have known to feed the cows first! You deserved to get stepped on."

Clayton tosses and turns in his sleep. He groans and mumbles, "Oh! No! Kenny, I'm sorry. Please, get better."

> Margin notes: *What kind of nightmare do you think Clayton is having?*

Clayton learns about nonconformity to the world. Reuben Hofstetter teaches that, "We are in the world, but not of the world." They are not to follow what other people do who are not part of the church. Such rebel-liousness is considered *worldly*.

Clayton joins in with the other boys on the bus and shouts outrageous claims at the bus driver. The final blow comes when he says, "Hey, there's a fire back here!" The bus driver stops the bus and walks to the back of the bus where Clayton sits with the other grinning boys. He then grabs Clayton by the upper arm and hauls him off his bus. Clayton walks the remaining mile to school.

Reuben Hofstetter informs his catechism class that God does not like war. Jesus was the shining example that one should not fight back when attacked. The admired bishop reads Matthew 5:38-39, where Jesus says, "Ye have heard that it hath been said, An eye for an eye, and a tooth for a tooth: but I say unto you, That ye resist not evil: but whosoever shall smite thee on thy right cheek, turn to him the other also" (KJV). Nonresistance, Clayton learns, is how God wants his children to respond when people harm them in any way.

Clayton again dumps straw from above on his unsuspecting brother Kenny. Red in the face, Kenny responds by casting his straw hook directly at his laughing little brother above. The hook latches onto Clayton's foot, sinking a good inch into his flesh. Clayton flops onto the floor and cries, "You got my foot!" Kenny lets go of the rope and runs upstairs. Together, they pull the straw hook out of Clayton's foot. Clayton takes his shoe off. The sock is drenched in blood. Light-headed from the scene, but knowing the bleeding must stop, Clayton stands and hobbles down the stairs to find a dirty rag to wrap his wound. He gingerly puts his shoe back on. They finish dispensing the straw and go inside. Clayton tries his best not to limp or show any signs that he is injured.

In a fitful sleep, again Clayton mumbles, "I'm sorry, Kenny. It's all my fault. Please don't die!"

Clayton carelessly dumps some of the milk out of the water cooler as he hastily pulls it out to the road on their two-wheeled cart. Homer witnesses the waste and says, "Why can't you do better than that? Elno or Marion would not do that."

Bertha serves wheat pancakes for supper. Everyone eats their fill in silence, as usual.

The preacher of Kidron Mennonite Church, Isaac Zuercher, conducts the baptism ceremony today. Clayton, having graduated from catechism class, kneels with the other newly saved youths in front of the church. One by one, the preacher pours a special pitcher of water into the cupped hands of Bishop Reuben Hofstetter that he holds over each candidate. Then, the bishop releases the water onto each head, allowing it to cascade down to the candidate's shoulders, as he declares, "By the confession of your faith in the presence of these witnesses, I baptize you with water, in the name of the Father, Son, and Holy Ghost." Clayton giggles when he feels the water go in his ear and drip onto his shoulder.

Upon watering each student, the bishop goes back to the first baptizee, and repeats, in turn, the next ritual to each. He raises his outstretched hand and says, "Upon your confession of faith, rise. I welcome you to the body of Christ." Clayton, like those before him, rises to his feet. Clayton is now officially a Mennonite, though nothing changes in his appearance. However, the girls must now wear head coverings. Clayton finds his parents sitting in the congregation. His mother is smiling.

> Beemer's margin notes: *Did Clayton get baptized for himself or for his parents? I can't read him yet, but he doesn't act like this is a life-changing moment for him. Should we be worried about his status with THE BOSS?*

Since it is summer, Homer has his boys digging up thistles in the cow pasture. To pass the boredom, Clayton rubs a thistle on Kenny's arm, as Kenny is digging another up with a pitchfork. It not being the first time Clayton has pulled this prank, Kenny evidently has had quite enough. He swings the pitchfork like a weapon and stabs Clayton in the finger. The wound looks pretty gruesome, and Marion suggests Clayton go wrap it. Clayton, trying his best not to look at the poor finger, finds an old rag in the barn and wraps the finger as tight as he can. He continues pulling weeds, mostly with one hand.

Clayton cannot hide his gnarly middle finger at the supper table. He tells his parents what happened. Homer tells him to stop giving Kenny a hard time. His mother has him place his hand in a jar of kerosene.

After pitching the first cartload of manure, pushing it along the rail, and dumping it onto the manure spreader, Clayton convinces Kenny that he, on account of his injured finger, should have the honors of driving the tractor and spreading the manure. Kenny finishes cleaning up the rest of the manure out of the barn.

Clayton wakes at 5:00 a.m. to milk the cows on this below 0°F morning. No smiling from anyone.

Clayton tends the living-room woodstove throughout the winter.

Hurrying home from school, Clayton flies through the door and asks if his sister Viola is home. She just recently informed the family that she is engaged to be married to a D. Stanley Kuhns. His mother smiles and tells him Viola is home from Hesston College and is upstairs in her room.

"When will she be down?" Clayton asks.

"I don't know. You should go up and tell her you want to see her."

"Really?"

"Yes. It's okay."

Clayton paces back and forth in the kitchen a while before taking his mother's advice.

Viola snickers at his awkwardness and acts delighted to see her little brother.

Normie, age fifteen and two years older than Clayton, stays home from school because she is not feeling well. Clayton goes to school without her. He comes home from school to find that she has been taken to the hospital because she had become unconscious. "But she wasn't that sick this morning," Clayton protests. "How bad is it?" But no one knows much.

That evening, Homer comes home from the hospital and tells the family that Norma Jean is in a coma and the doctors don't know what is wrong with her. Clayton's eyes widen, and he looks to his other family members, who don't have much to say.

Homer goes back to the hospital this morning and returns home a few hours later to report that she is still in a coma, and the doctors say she may die. He directs the family to gather around the woodstove in the living room to pray. D. Stanley Kuhns, who had arrived just the night before for the wedding, prays a strangely bold and ardent prayer for Normie's healing, causing Clayton to open his eyes to watch this brother-in-law-to-be pray.

This afternoon, Homer comes home from the hospital to announce that an outside doctor diagnosed Norma Jean with a disease called *sugar diabetes*. Normie is now doing better as the doctors know how to treat her ailment.

> Beemer makes a margin note: *How is Clayton feeling about this strange turn of events? Does he conclude that THE BOSS answers prayer? Will this likely influence him when life gets confusing, or will life weigh him down so much that he forgets this beautiful moment? Maybe he'll become a faith healer when he gets older, you think?*

Normie comes home after just a few days in the hospital. She looks fine. Everyone treats her like a queen, bringing her breakfast or asking her how they can help her.

Clayton watches his mother use the scales that Normie brought home from the hospital to weigh her food to make sure she doesn't have another coma. Clayton also looks on and stiffens as Normie plunges a needle with stuff called insulin in her own leg. He is told she will need to do this every morning for the rest of her life.

Viola and Stan come in the door, laughing. They tell how their car got stuck in a snowdrift a couple of miles away on their way home from their honeymoon. When Vi and Stan are in another room, Clayton asks his mother, "Do honeymoons make getting stuck in the snow fun?"

Bertha stifles her laugh.

Time to *open the cornfield* again. This means that the boys chop down the outer two rows all around the cornfield so the big machinery can get into the field to harvest the corn without trampling good corn.

George, senior to Clayton by ten years, pushes the cart full of corn home (backward) with the tractor in full throttle, something none of the other brothers can do.

Clayton tries his hand at pushing the cart home today. The cart buckles whenever he goes fast, causing him to stop, back up, and start the two-car train again. He takes much longer than George to get home.

Lo and behold, Clayton (unlike any of his brothers or sisters) is given Homer's permission to play Little League baseball! The coach, a local veterinarian whom everybody likes, trains Clayton to play catcher.

Now in high school, Clayton can walk to nearby stores over the noon hour. The non-Mennonite kids often congregate at the popular Brownies, which has a pool hall in the back. Today, Clayton and his Mennonite friends go to the less popular store across the street to play pool. Clayton must borrow a quarter to get an ice-cream cone. Clayton's Sunday school teacher and preacher have often spoken of the evils of playing pool.

A Mennonite boy, whom Clayton doesn't know well, asks Clayton who he's taking to the hymn sing next month.

Clayton says, "Taking? I don't drive yet. I'll probably go with some friends or have my dad take me."

The other boy laughs. "I mean a date. Everyone takes a date to them things. You don't want to be a loser and go by yourself, do you?"

Clayton shakes his head, then nods, then smiles awkwardly.

Clayton's dad has Clayton stay home from school today to assist him in building the tiled garage on the farm.

After three weeks of working on the tiled garage, Clayton finally goes back to school. Though he is behind in his schoolwork, no teacher questions his excuse or offers to tutor him on what he's missed.

While Clayton's older siblings continue to leave home by way of mission programs through the church, employment, or further education, George remains home. George is different. He's a dependable worker but doesn't figure things out well on his own.

Today, Clayton comes home from school, and he owes a quarter to his friend. He finds George's secret, green safe. While George is working in the field, Clayton figures out how to open the locked box and helps himself to some of the cash stashed there. He relocks the box and places it back where he got it.

> Beemer writes to the editor in the margin: *I thought Clayton was saved. Isn't he supposed to be a new creature?*

Today, Clayton chooses to stay after school and play basketball with some friends, though he tells his dad he stayed to do homework.

Clayton's task this cold winter is to keep the woodstove and the cookstove supplied with wood. He chops wood late tonight, and his fingers lose their feeling. When he finally hauls the wood inside, he removes his gloves and holds his hands over the stove to thaw.

For no reason, Clayton hits Kenny in the head with a snowball and laughs. Though eight-teen years old, Kenny cannot retaliate in like manner because he is not as accurate as Clayton, and Clayton is too quick of foot.

Clayton hears other boys at school talking about their dates. A popular boy asks one of the Mennonite boys if he "got a piece" with his date last night. The Mennonite boy blushes and says, "No, she is too nice a girl for that."

The popular guy says, "There's no such thing as too nice if you make them want it." The boys hanging around this boy all laugh. "Let me know when you're man enough to go all the way." More laughter.

Clayton doesn't say anything.

After church, at the dinner table, Clayton makes a comment about the *boring sermon*. Homer is on that comment in an instant. "We will not talk bad about the preacher in this house!"

Clayton does not talk back or mention that Homer talks bad about others all the time during his devotions.

The corn is planted and school is out! Homer is working at Smucker's Apple Butter. George, Kenny, and Clayton spend many summer days picking stones out of the cornfields, "So the expensive picking machines won't pick them up and get ruined," their dad tells them.

George is having trouble backing the four-wheeled trailer up the barn bank. Clayton, though ten years younger, orders him off the tractor. Clayton labors at the task also, but he finally manages to park it, though it is not straight.

After days of practice, Clayton manages to master backing the four-wheeled trailer up the bank every time. Now he is practicing backing the four-wheeled trailer with a two-wheeled baler in-between the trailer and the tractor. This is a challenge that none of his brothers have accomplished nor any farmer that he has heard of. He spends hours practicing.

Today, Clayton backs the tractor/baler/trailer combo up the barn bank three times in a row. Are medals given for such achievements?

Kenny is now working outside the house, doing masonry work for Clarence Sommer like his brother Roy did. The chores are now up to George and Clayton.

Clayton sleeps past his mandatory 5:00 a.m. wake-up time, leaving George to do the milking. A rude rap on Clayton's ankle startles him awake, however. Homer tells him, "You'd better get out there and do your part. Don't be lazy like your mother."

As he pulls his clothes on, Clayton hears his mother singing "Amazing Grace" in the kitchen, no doubt making grape nuts.

He finds George slowly dispersing the straw. "You're slow as molasses. Give that to me." Clayton grabs the pitchfork from George's hands and spreads the straw wildly.

Clayton comes home from school in time to witness his dad yelling at George. "How could you be so damn stupid?" Clayton has never seen his father turn beet red like this or heard him swear before. "How could you drop a hammer into the chopper? Why can't you do better than that? You ruined it! Now, who's going to pay for it? I am, that's who. I've got to pay for your damn stupid mistake because you're a fool! Why didn't you do as I told you?"

George says nothing. After Homer steams off, George remains standing next to the barn, expressionless, alone.

Clayton helps his mom grade eggs tonight. They discuss favorite hymns and which Zuerchers are song leaders in the area.

Tonight, while getting ready for bed, Clayton hears his dad having another yelling tirade downstairs. This time, as so often happens, Homer is dressing down Clayton's mother, telling her how lazy and worthless she is. "You Zuerchers have never amounted to anything. And now, our kids are not amounting to anything. All because of you! You're supposed to honor me. Instead, you disgust me!"

In an unprecedented move, Clayton bounds down the stairs, opens the living-room door, and tears into his accusing father. "What are you doing, yelling at my mom? She hasn't done anything wrong. You can't just yell at her because you're mad. That's not right. You're being mean, and it better stop!"

Clayton looks at his defeated mother, then back to his suddenly silent father. He turns and slams the door behind him and marches upstairs. Finding it hard to breathe, he sits on his bed and stares at his closed door. The imminent footsteps up the stairs never follow. Clayton lies in bed, restless for half the night, before falling asleep.

Clayton has managed to avoid eye contact or talking to his dad since the confrontation in the living room. Now, three days later, Homer corners Clayton in the feedlot in the barn. Clayton's body becomes rigid. He looks toward the only exit, which is behind his father. Though he may expect a physical lashing, his dad only piles on the typical verbal assault. "What you did the other night was not right. Why can't you be better than that? You won't amount to anything. Good boys do not do that."

Homer exits the barn. Clayton is shaking.

Clayton and his pals have a plan for visiting their usual store during the lunch hour. One friend stands between Clayton and the store manager. When his buddy nods, Clayton knows the manager isn't looking and puts a candy bar in his pocket. The boys leave the store and share the candy bar on the way back to school.

> Margin notes: *Such behavior is becoming a habit. Is he trying to prove that he is a bad boy? I hope he stays lucky and turns things around soon.*

It's been a couple of days since Homer cornered his son in the barn. He calls for Clayton to join him in the living room. "I want you to know that I would give the shirt off my back to make your life better."

Clayton shows no emotion and utters no response.

Supper is ready. Homer leads the smaller family (only Dorothy, George, Kenny, Normie, and Clayton are still home at this point) in his boring and uninspiring devotions. He mumbles grace before they eat in silence.

Clayton wins a farm raffle! The L.E. Sommer Feed store sponsors a drawing for a baby heifer, and Clayton wins it. Now he can participate fully in Mr. Scott's agriculture class because, with the heifer to raise, he has the required farm project.

Clayton nervously informs his dad about his good fortune. Homer does not make him refuse the gift. He asks his son how he will pay for the feed this animal will require. Clayton admits he doesn't know. Homer says Clayton can use his feed, and they'll settle the matter later.

After chopping wood in the cold, Clayton checks in on his little heifer, making sure it has plenty of straw to insulate it through the long night.

At 5:00 a.m., Clayton rises in time to milk the cows with George and checks on his heifer, who made it through the cold night.

Homer buys a new chopper implement for the tractor. This tool will enable George and Clayton to manage all the crops since Homer now works full-time at Horst Machinery. Homer asks Clayton to read the instruction manual and figure out how to operate it. At age fifteen, Clayton is managing the day-to-day operations of the farm.

Clayton's best friend, Daniel Lehman, now has a car. He is in Normie's class and two years older than Clayton. Daniel drives them to the hymn sing without an adult. Clayton sees that most of the nearly four hundred teenagers in attendance are coupled with a date. They are some of the last to leave the event because they don't have to be rushed by parents picking them up.

Clayton is ankle-rapped out of bed by his dad again this morning. Bertha is grinding grape nuts and singing "Up From the Dead He Arose."

Clayton goes to his Lehman cousins' home after church to celebrate Jay's return from his Pax overseas service. Jay answers many questions, and everyone treats him like a movie star. He seems so much older and wiser now. Most of Clayton's brothers volunteered to serve their alternative military service through the church, but none had gone overseas like Jay.

While Clayton reads up on the upkeep of the new machinery his dad bought, he also looks at other paperwork in the maple secretary in Homer's bedroom. While he snoops, he finds Homer's tax statements and how much Homer paid for the latest Allis-Chalmers tractor, the Holland Baler, the big manure spreader, the International chopper, and the International combine. The cost is beyond belief. And, in a drawer below the one in which he found that information, Clayton finds some cold hard cash—more than he has ever seen! Leafing through another stack, Clayton finds his father's present wages at Horst's, and he even finds records for wages that go back to Homer's employment at Smucker's, Orrville Tile, and Orrville Body. Homer started out at thirty-five cents an hour in 1941 and now, in 1956, he's up to a dollar thirty-five an hour.

Adding the numbers on a piece of paper, Clayton knows the mere wages are not enough for the new, fancy farm equipment. Clayton knows full well that each child, after high school, was expected to work a full-time job outside and relinquish all their earnings to their dad until they were twenty-one. The wages from his own children have to be how Homer paid for the machinery!

Clayton has lived poor all his life. He had thought his dad barely made ends meet. Now, he finds out that Homer is relatively rich! And Clayton is the only one that knows how to use all the equipment. Not even Homer can operate all of it. His dad asks questions about *what* the farming schedule is but has little to do with *how* it is done. And he always demands the schedule be done to his satisfaction.

Clayton hears his dad's car coming down the driveway. He frantically slaps the cash and pay stubs back in the drawer as if he'd never looked.

> Beemer's margin notes to the editor: *Does Clayton see the wrongness of this unfair compensation? Or is he too afraid of what his dad will do if he gets caught spying on his dad's records? He is running his dad's castle but making nothing for it. Homer has made him live like a pauper all these years only to find out he was part of a scheme to make the king rich. Will he rebel and never again trust authority?*

"I'm starting to feel kind of dumb," Clayton tells his sister Normie. "Everyone's dating, and I don't know what I'm doing." Normie gladly schools her little brother on dating etiquette. She even suggests which girls he should ask out.

Clayton discusses his dating plan with Daniel.

In the evening church service at Kidron Mennonite, the females all sit on the south side, while the males sit on the north side. After the worship service, the women and girls exit out their south door, and the men and boys exit out their north door. Once outside, while the girls talk among themselves and look interested, Clayton and Daniel eye their targets. They make their move at the same time. Clayton walks up to a girl, and Daniel walks up to a girl. Just as Normie told him, Clayton says, "Would you like to go to the hymn sing with me?"

Her eyes widen. She smiles crookedly and responds, "Ah … sure."

"Great," says Clayton. He turns to find Daniel and his date looking back at him. "Um … we'll go in Daniel's car." Clayton heads for the car, turning back now and again to make sure his date is following him.

When they get to the car, Clayton opens the back door for his date to climb in. Daniel does the same for his date in the front seat. They close their respective doors, look at each other, smile, and walk around the car to get in the opposite doors.

Their conversation consists of *the nice weather* and *the good sermon*. When they arrive in the parking lot, each boy exits the car and walks around the car to open his date's door. (Thank you, Norma Jean, for all your instruction!) They walk side by side with their dates to the entrance of the church, open the doors for the ladies, and stride in together, allowing everybody to see whom they are paired with. They sit next to their dates and watch to see who else is walking and sitting next to whom.

When the hymn sing is over, Daniel and Clayton drive each girl home. A fun time is had by all.

Clayton sneaks into George's stash of money in his little green box again. He takes a wad and closes it up as if it hadn't been touched.

Because it is mandatory for Clayton to tell his dad where he is going, he tells him that Daniel will pick him up to go to the monthly Mennonite Youth Fellowship (MYF) gathering. They actually go to the movie theater instead. Clayton sees quite a few Mennonite friends there and many more other students from school, just as he was told he would. During the movie,

Clayton closes his eyes during the romantic and violent scenes. He even falls asleep during a kissing scene.

> Notes to the editor: *How could Clayton fall asleep watching something he has never before seen and that is no doubt tempting to his already raging hormones? Plus, it seems like he'd be too uptight to sleep, knowing how evil his dad and the church have pronounced the movie house to be.*

Clayton and Daniel each choose a different girl from their church to go with them to the hymn sing at 9:00 p.m. at another of the five area churches. No major mishaps occur.

In a baseball game, Clayton wears shin guards, a face mask, a chest protector, and a big glove behind home plate.

Clayton tells his dad he is going out for a sundae, but Daniel drives Clayton all over the county just to see what's going on this Saturday night. Not much. They park outside the popular Postscript Restaurant. They observe who enters and exits with whom. They talk about dating, marriage, and someday having families. They wonder if they will ever get out of Wayne County and be important. Clayton tells Daniel that he should probably get a little more serious about who he dates and pick girls that may be more suitable in the long haul.

Clayton arrives home after midnight.

On a Kidron Mennonite MYF retreat to Niagara Falls, Clayton asks a girl named Ruth Geiser to go on a walk with him around the scenic trails. She accepts. It just happens to be Clayton's sixteenth birthday. They walk for hours, talking all the while.

School begins another year. Clayton is now a junior, an upperclassman. He still walks to the corner of Zuercher and Baumgardner Roads to catch the bus. He still tries to sit with the popular kids and not with those who aren't.

Waking at 5:00 a.m., Clayton's sleepy eyes and sleepy ears are pleasantly opened by the sound of his mother singing "When the Roll is Called Up Yonder," in the kitchen while she faithfully grinds grape nuts.

For morning devotions, Homer warns against being worldly like the Zuerchers with their desire to be seen by everyone for their singing. Clayton glances at his mother who doesn't react. He looks sternly at his father before looking back down at his grape nuts. He says nothing.

> Beemer writes in his notes: *Does Clayton believe these lies his dad tells about his mother and her kin? He's heard them all his life and still respects (or at least fears) his dad. But a lie is a lie. How does a kid, though sixteen already, handle such conflicting information?*

Homer gives Jim Eberly, Normie's boyfriend, money to drive Normie, Clayton, Kenny, and Dorothy to represent the family at Roy's wedding in Oregon. Clayton sees the western United States for the first time. Roy and Vesta look happy and grown-up.

This is a big day for Clayton. His agriculture teacher, Mr. Scott, inspects Clayton's farm project. Clayton receives a B for the heifer's overall appearance—a high grade compared to his other classes. For once, he has a reason to feel almost smart.

The heifer goes to slaughter. Homer actually gives Clayton a large chunk of the proceeds—fifty dollars!

Clayton chops wood well into the night as he has fallen behind, and the woodpile was nearly empty. He beats his hands together occasionally, so they don't go completely numb in the 6°F temperature.

For his new agriculture class project, Clayton uses some of his fifty dollars to get five little pigs.

Homer asks Clayton why he is feeding his pigs differently. Clayton tells him that he has read that they will grow stronger this way. Homer allows him to feed all the pigs this way, but he tells him that Clayton will be paying for the feed.

Homer spreads out his tax papers on the living-room table and asks Clayton to "organize this. Add up the numbers and get the forms ready to mail."

Clayton works diligently at this request (or command; it is unclear which) until he completes the task. No signs of appreciation or pride are exchanged by either party.

The high-school track coach tells Clayton that "farm boys make good athletes because they're strong and have good endurance." Clayton takes the coach up on his invitation to join the track team. He stays after school to practice long jump, high jump, throwing the discus, and running the mile.

The coach takes him and some other Mennonite boys home after practice.

Daniel and Clayton decide to live large and go to the huge Holmes County hymn sing. They ask girls they don't know out for sundaes afterward.

Clayton competes in his first track meet. He finishes third, fourth, or fifth in all his events.

Clayton comes home to dry devotions on Leviticus, his dad mumbling a prayer, and his mother's mush. His mom comments that he "sure does eat a lot lately."

Clayton and Daniel devise a plan. They ask a girl with a reputation of being *easy to get* to go on a ride with them. She agrees to go, and they take her down a secluded lane and stop. Daniel and Clayton look at each other. They turn to the *loose* girl. She immediately says, "I know what you guys want." She folds her arms. "Well, you're not going to get it. I expect more out of you guys. Grow up."

Clayton looks wide-eyed at Daniel. Daniel swallows hard. "Right. Sorry, we'll take you home."

After they drop her off, Clayton says, "I wouldn't call her easy."

During the school lunch hour, Clayton deposits his dad's milk check, which has been in his pocket all day, into the bank.

Though Clayton is saddled with more and more responsibilities around the farm, he is not paid anything for his work. He steals from George's private stash again. George either doesn't notice or chooses not to do anything about it.

Clayton buys an ice-cream cone and a game of pool during lunch.

The devotions tonight are about not stealing. Clayton looks over at George, who eats his pancakes in silence. His sisters, Dorothy and Norma Jean, and brother, George, are Clayton's only siblings still living at home.

Clayton feeds his pigs before supper. He tells George to finish the milking on his own.

Clayton doesn't read an assigned book in English. He agrees with his buddies that school is boring.

The school report card is out. Clayton receives mostly Cs and Ds. His only B is in agriculture.

> Beemer notes: *Won't these poor grades affect Clayton for the rest of his life? How will he ever live down such a poor showing?*

Homer yells at Clayton for not doing all his chores on time. "Milking cows need to be milked on time! Why can't you be better than that? You're lazy like your mother."

> Margin notes: *Clayton is a teen, and he's making some foolish choices. But even though much of his life looks like it's falling apart right now, he still does some things responsibly like running his father's farm for him. Why does Homer never compliment Clayton or offer any encouragement? Surely Clayton*

*can't turn out well when all he ever hears from his father are
the mistakes he's made and how disappointed in him his dad is.*

At Wednesday night MYF tonight, the youth minister, Bill Detweiler, encourages the youth group to take God seriously. Clayton pays close attention.

As he has for the past couple of weeks, Clayton reads his Bible before he goes to bed. Tonight at 9:30, he drops to his knees, looking to make sure no one is in his room and the door is closed. He says, "God, I am a sinner. I want to be your follower. I want you to direct my life."

He squats on his haunches in silence as if waiting for a response. After several long minutes, Clayton sighs and looks around the room again. He goes to sleep looking troubled.

> Beemer's notes: *Did what I just think happened, happen?
> It sounded a lot like Clayton was asking THE BOSS to take
> charge of his life. Is he serious about making THE BOSS Lord
> of his life? Does he think he needs a reply? Does he need one?
> Will his life be forever changed from this moment forward?*

Clayton wakes up on time this morning. He milks the cows, feeds the pigs, and pitches the manure before breakfast. As he enters the kitchen, he hears his mother singing "Blessed Assurance, Jesus Is Mine."

Clayton applies himself in each class at school.

In English class, Clayton follows the prompt to "write a story that isn't true. Use your imagination." Clayton writes about a man that thought so deeply that he struck water.

The note on his paper when he received it back said, "Well done. Keep writing." Clayton has never gotten positive feedback in English class before.

Clayton's accounting teacher sends Clayton and three other students to the district bookkeeping contest. Clayton receives an honorable mention at the district bookkeeping contest on behalf of his school. His fellow students are amazed.

Mr. Scott's yearly inspection of the agriculture projects has arrived. Clayton receives an A for the outstanding growth and health of his well-fed pigs. The teacher tells Clayton, "Your dad should be proud of you." Clayton smiles as if his dad did say it.

The pigs go to slaughter. Homer tells Clayton that most of the profit will go toward the feed he used.

Clayton doesn't miss out on taking a date to a hymn sing throughout his senior year. He even asks some girls to go with him to MYF. He has more dates with Ruth Geiser than any other girl.

Clayton graduates from high school. He gets all As and Bs on his report card in his senior year and is on the honor roll. Now, he knows that he must find a job and still do his chores and work the farm in his spare time. Congratulations, graduate!

Clarence Sommer hires Clayton to be a part of his bricklaying crew, as he did with Clayton's brothers Roy and Kenny. Roy still works for Clarence as a full-time bricklayer.

Clayton works hard as a *hod carrier*, mixing mortar and carrying bricks. He hands his handsome paycheck over to his dad each week.

Clayton sets his sights on serving his two years of alternative military service through the Mennonite Church. In a bold move, he tells his father he wants to serve his time in mission work overseas as soon as he can. To do this, he informs Homer that he will need some money to prepare and support himself while he is away.

His dad points out that his brothers and sisters never left home this early, but says he will consider it.

Beemer to the editor: *I bet Clayton cannot get out of here soon enough!*

Beyond all expectations, Homer allows Clayton to begin keeping his own paychecks at the age of nineteen, so he can save until he goes into Voluntary Service (VS) through the Mennonite Church.

Now that Clayton has some money of his own, he sneaks into George's green box and replaces a portion of the money he has taken over the years.

Clayton hits the pillow. He is exhausted from working his demanding masonry job and then teaming with George to run the farm.

Finally, Clayton pays back all the money he stole from George. George, it still appears, is none the wiser.

8

THE VASTNESS AND INTRICACY OF THE BOSS'S PLAN

The old editor in chief of *Heaven's Chronicle* sat back in his office chair, hands clasped around the tuft of hair that framed his bald head, and contemplated Beemer's manuscript.

He had not been forced to intervene in Beemer's chronicling for the past seven years. But if Beemer was to grow as a chronicler and make Clayton's biography the quality THE BOSS required, Beemer needed to realize some concepts.

The editor transported to Clayton's bedroom to find Beemer writing in his biographical book. "Hi, Beemer."

Beemer jerked his head around. "Chief." He turned on his seat to face the editor full-on. "Uh, what brings you here? Am I being too creative? Not technical enough? Not emotional enough?"

"Relax. It's just time for a checkup. You've been riding solo for quite some time now. I thought you'd like some company ... maybe discuss some of your questions."

Beemer's eyes darted this way and that while the rest of his body remained motionless. "Okay ... "

Clayton stirred.

Editor and employee looked over to his bed.

"He's probably dreaming again," Beemer said. "Why do humans have dreams?"

"Well, humans are given innumerable senses to govern their faculties. They know far more than they comprehend. Their minds are always trying to figure out their world. But while they are awake, they can assess their environment only through limited means. Their dreams help them make truth of all the hidden information that is stored in all their cells, not just their cognitive receptors."

"But I thought dreams were made up. How can they be about truth?"

"Sometimes, there is more truth in story than in fact," said the salty wordsmith. "THE BOSS made life so mysteriously vast that they can't possibly know everything. They learn best from the stories they've witnessed or been told. For all the infinite things they don't understand, dreams (which are made-up stories) offer possible insights to their fragmented data."

"So, why did Clayton keep having that weird dream about his brother Kenny?"

"Why do you think?" Chief clasped his hands around his belly.

"I don't know. It was like he dreamed that Kenny was in a really bad way. Like he was convulsing and contorting or something, and Clayton was really beat out about it. But that doesn't make any sense because Clayton was always taking advantage of his older brother, and as far as I could tell, it never really hurt Kenny."

"Really?" his manager said with obvious sarcasm.

Beemer nodded.

"Kid, you've got to start using the vocabulary of a chronicler and stop using 'really' every other sentence."

"Really?"

The editor in chief's sardonic smirk conveyed his irritation.

Beemer reddened.

The chief went on. "Was the way Clayton treated Kenny right?"

"No," Beemer admitted.

"Do you think Clayton should have felt bad about that?"

"Well, yeah, but he never acted like it bothered him. Of course, he still tends to shy from most emotions, I think."

"Now remember, THE BOSS makes these humans with emotions and a thing called a conscience. If the conscience is not acknowledged, emotions will have to come out one way or another."

"So, you think that Clayton actually did feel bad about bullying his brother, and his dream was showing him that?"

The editor nodded. "I can't say for sure. But that's how THE BOSS's plans often work. In Clayton's awake life, he convinced himself that he could and would dominate Kenny. But he was ignoring his teaching of being loving and respectful of others as Jesus was. He neglected to allow THE BOSS's seed in him to look out for Kenny's well-being above his own."

"Yeah, about THE BOSS's seed business," remarked Beemer. "Was Clayton really saved, and did he receive THE BOSS's seed, or did he just want to please his parents and follow peer pressure?"

"Clayton was born with THE BOSS's seed."

Beemer furrowed his brow. "Okay. But what about the sinner's prayer and salvation and all of that?"

"'All of that?' You're so eloquent, Beemer."

Beemer bit the corner of his lip.

Chief said, "Clayton has life because of THE BOSS. If Clayton decides to acknowledge and dedicate his life to that truth, celebration is in order. A good thing just got better."

"So, what you're saying is that it doesn't matter if his profession of faith was genuine or not."

"Oh, it matters. THE BOSS cares. But THE BOSS's plan is bigger than that."

Beemer said, "Well, I think it's pretty obvious that his first conversion experience was a fake."

"And what makes you say that?"

"Because after his supposed salvation experience he stole from George's green box. Then he stole a candy bar. What kind of a *new creation in Christ* does that?"

"He's not perfect, Beemer. Having THE BOSS's seed does not mean he'll always make good decisions. THE BOSS didn't make robots. He made people. People are messy. Recognizing, accepting, and committing to THE BOSS's beautiful gift is only a beginning. It's not magic. Neither germination nor metamorphosis happens instantaneously."

Beemer frowned with an open mouth. "Huh?"

The chief grinned his little perturbed grin. "Growth and change, Beemer. It takes time to mature into the being THE BOSS planted in him. Clayton is learning to be his own person as THE BOSS created him to be. To figure that out, he must toy with rebellion by crossing the established line of acceptable behavior now and again. It's all part of the maturation process ... as uncomfortable as it is to observe for parents and us onlookers. And besides, you don't think he fell asleep at that tempting movie theater because he was sleepy, do you? His conscience was in full-aware mode, trying to protect him from his sorry actions."

"So, THE BOSS wasn't mad at him? Or holding Clayton's poor choice against him until he really committed his life to God for real?"

"Really?"

Beemer stopped himself from taking his manager's bait this time. "Sorry, Chief. Just trying to keep it ... um ... real." His eyes wandered off before they settled on his inescapable feet.

"THE BOSS is not mad at Clayton, Beemer. This commitment, or salvation, that you're so determined for him to establish, is not for THE BOSS anyway. It's for Clayton. If Clayton is *all in*, his life will have more meaning and purpose. It doesn't miraculously change THE BOSS's love for him."

"Hmm ... I thought it did."

"It's best to stick to the basics. THE BOSS loves Clayton. And Clayton must filter through his environment to learn that."

"What exactly do you mean by his *environment*?"

"Ahh, now that is the question. Environment is the second required element in the *Threeseez*. You are learning how Clayton's individual emotional makeup is vital to understanding him. Now you must learn the significance of his environment.

"Without getting too technical, environment is basically the person's family, the groups they associate with, the sources that inform and teach them, and the physical area they reside in—all the outside things that shape how they view the world.

"And while they are young, their environment is especially important. For how they are nurtured during their upbringing molds their character."

"Great," said Beemer. "So, Clayton's dad is involved in molding his character? If Homer's nurture sticks, Clayton will never amount to anything."

"Now, hold on. There are other ingredients in the environmental equation, remember. His mother not being the least. She held him when he fell, heard his cries, smiled at his wonderings, supported his ambitions, listened to his music, and showered him with motherly love. For whatever nurturing Homer lacked in giving, Clayton's mother excelled in providing."

Beemer shot back, "But Homer practically ripped that away from Clayton through his ridiculous rants of how awful she was. Do you think Clayton believes him about his mom being so bad?"

"Part of him probably does because his father said it. But there's THE BOSS's seed in him that I'm sure doesn't believe it. The question is, will Clayton be able to pull that truth out when he needs to?"

"I sure hope so," Beemer said. "Otherwise, his father's role will win out, and Clayton will be a loser for the rest of his life."

"Now, don't forget that his father has done *some* good for his character."

"Like what?"

"Like clothed and fed him and taught him how to be a faithful and tenacious worker. Not everyone in their world has that going for them. And the negative aspects that Homer brings to the table are a double-edged sword."

"What? You mean there's a good side to being degraded all his life?" asked Beemer.

"Homer's litany of discouraging comments and total dearth of verbal support could devastate Clayton's future, certainly. But such extreme opposition can also serve to clarify and direct one's life as well."

"What do you mean?"

"When Clayton's environment changes, when he leaves his father's home, he may find encouragement from other sources more readily. His thirsty soul longs for the uplifting words that he never got from his dad."

"Really?" Beemer bit his lip. "I mean, he's pretty slow in processing things sometimes. I'm thinking his dad's unfair belittling treatment has something to do with that."

"True as that may be, he'll develop the tools to adjust soon enough when he sees through different environments. There's a great chance, too, that memories, like Norma Jean getting well after being boldly prayed for, will remind him to employ his faith in THE BOSS's higher authority, rather than in his earthly father's offensive one."

"The rougher the start, the greater the life?" Beemer remembers.

"Yes. But don't get too excited and go overboard like the last time we discussed this. We will have to wait and see how Clayton reacts and responds to new environments. You have no idea how much a human can endure. THE BOSS has equipped them with remarkable stamina."

"But pain is … painful."

"Yes, it is. But where the struggle is great, the victory is greater."

Beemer nodded. "Clayton has struggled to get good grades in school. Can we expect his poor early showing to affect his future?"

"Likely. A person must always contend with his own actions, especially the regrettable ones."

"Great! Then Clayton's likely to be dealing with being a slouch the rest of his life."

"Not necessarily. His script is still far from written. His dismal early education presents an uphill climb, but there is still a path toward learning. You never know, he may end up being known as a lifetime learner."

"Hmph. Right." Beemer looked at the sleeping Clayton and shook his head.

"Hey, you're talking about a child of THE BOSS here. Whatever ineptitude Clayton may exhibit, remember, THE BOSS is more than capable of overcoming."

"Well, of course. THE BOSS can overcome anything. But we're talking about Clayton here."

"Did Clayton not commit his soul to THE BOSS?" asked the supervisor.

"So far as I know, I think he did … at least that second time when he was seventeen."

"And did he not miraculously turn his grades around after his vow to *take God seriously?*"

"Well, yes. That was a head-scratcher."

"Miracles don't just happen, Beemer. THE BOSS isn't idle."

"You mean, THE BOSS changed Clayton?"

"I mean, THE BOSS has a plan. Like Clayton learned when he was younger to team the horses to plow the fields, so THE BOSS's restorative, redemptive, and purifying seeds must team with Clayton's motives, efforts, and commitment. It's a team effort. THE BOSS doesn't move any other way."

"Hmm. An amazing plan, actually."

The old editor nodded. "That's why we're all doing what we're doing. Your part will be to figure out how the environment THE BOSS gave Clayton to work out of plays into how he understands the world. Eventually, you'll be able to assess his feelings and thoughts with confidence."

A smile crossed Beemer's face. "Oh, for that day!"

"Any other concerns before I leave you?"

Beemer thought. "Other than the girl, not really."

"The girl?"

"Yeah. Ruth Geiser. I've got a funny feeling about her. No," Beemer reconsidered. "It's more that I've got a funny feeling about Clayton's feelings for her. I'm not sure, but he seems to be a little irrational about her. He acts like he's in love and wants a real relationship with her. Is it normal for a young man to go ape over some girl that treats him nice?"

"Oh, you don't know the half of what THE BOSS has planned for these humans. *Love* changes everything for them. Especially young, romantic love."

The editor in chief's eyes wandered beyond the reading glasses on the end of his nose into space somewhere. He rubbed his chin. "How did I miss this? The workload must be getting to me."

"What?"

The chief wagged his head. "Nothing. Just talking to myself. You do that when you get to my age. So, you think he's serious about this girl?"

"Serious? I wish I knew. I think he's goofy about her though."

With lips pursed, the old editor nodded his bald head. "I'll have to go back and read through the Master Log on all that you've written about her. Meanwhile, stay on this. This could be the scoop of his life ... of your life."

"Huh?" Beemer's mouth predictably dropped open.

9
ROMANCE YEARS
LONGING FOR LOVE

The editor in chief sat at his desk, shaking his head. How could he have missed the girl thing? His professional skimming never missed those potential life-changers … well, rarely. Though, they were occurring with greater frequency lately … probably a side effect of those confounded transports.

If this was a genuine romance, Beemer's subject was about to make some irrational choices and, likely, throw the novice chronicler for a loop about the strange phenomenon. This meant Chief had better explore this whole situation before his editing duties exploded.

He found Beemer's biographic book of Clayton on his Master Log and looked back as far as necessary to find mention of Ruth and the Geiser family. They did, in fact, go to the same church as Clayton—Kidron Mennonite. And each could view the other's farm from their own homesteads over Kidron's rolling hills. They lived just three miles from one another.

At the Kidron one-room school, the nearly 160 students were divided into four, two-grade groups, which meant Clayton and Ruth would have been in the same group every other year.

The two rode the same bus to school for Clayton's seventh and eighth-grade years but did not go out of their way to sit with each other. They were bused to the 350-student Dalton High School separately.

It was in his sophomore year when Clayton noticed Ruth "in her tight white sweater." The editor read this a few times and shook his head, wondering why he hadn't caught this obvious physical interest.

And *retreats* were, no doubt, a rare and special occasion for the youth group of a farm community that didn't get out much. Chief could just imagine the anxious exuberance abounding on the bus and motel they stayed in during their trip to Niagara Falls. It was a gutsy move for a shy guy like Clayton to ask a pretty gal to walk with him in such a majestic, foreign place. He expected there was likely more here than mere teenage lust.

Embarrassingly, the veteran supervisor had failed to realize in his first perusal that the distinct majority of Clayton's dates in his junior year were with one girl—Ruth Geiser. He took her to the monthly church MYF gatherings and hymn sings in their county as well as to hymn sings in Holmes and Stark Counties. By January 9, 1958, seven months after their first date around Niagara, they had accrued twenty-nine dates. Chief whistled to learn this.

Often, he noticed, they double-dated with Daniel and Elaine, Ruth's best friend. Sometimes, they doubled with Normie and her boyfriend, Jim, too.

But then, he paused when he read that Clayton and Ruth had mutually decided to,

" ... not go steady," on January 26, 1958. Yet, they dated several more times in the months to follow, and ironically, the affection displayed showed anything but tapering down.

The editor found that this friendliness must have concerned Clayton because he sought advice from his brother, Marion, on his feelings toward Ruth. Since Clayton was only sixteen years old, Marion advised that he slow down and maybe even back off. He needed to have more experience under his belt and date other girls because he was too young to settle down.

On June 6, Clayton received a postcard in the mail from Ruth that said, "Dear Clayton, no matter what I do, I'll never be able to forget you, nor do I want to. You've been wonderful. Thank you for everything. Love, Ruth."

Chief scratched his head. He reread the intriguing phrases—"I'll never ... forget you," "wonderful," "LOVE?" Was she saying, goodbye, or don't leave me? If he, an old reporter who'd seen it all, was confused, what must Clayton have been? *No wonder Beemer hasn't a clue.*

He read on.

Two days after the strange postal note, a day after Clayton's seventeenth birthday, Ruth and Elaine both told Clayton and Daniel respectively that they were breaking up with them. Though Daniel acted shocked, Clayton appeared to expect and accept the announcement.

However, Beemer reported that Clayton always found out when Ruth went out with other guys. And evidently, she must have been popular as she went out often. Clayton seemed particularly observant when she went out with Robert or Russ, the boys with whom she competed for the highest GPA for their class.

The editor squinted at this detail and recalled that Clayton had improved his grades about this time (when he dedicated his life to THE BOSS). *THE BOSS works in mysterious ways*, he thought.

Ruth began working at the Town and Country grocery store in Kidron where Normie also worked. Clayton saw that they became close friends, and he often asked Normie how Ruth was doing. Normie always obliged by telling him everything she knew about Ruth's goings-on. In December of '58, Jim and Normie set Ruth up with Samuel, a guy that Clayton knew and liked.

On February 26, 1959, Ruth's family's barn caught fire, invoking the Kidron community to jump into action. The Kidron fire sirens alerted Clayton and Homer to the ominous smoke that was billowing from the Geiser farm. They hopped in the car and raced to the scene. The advanced fire was too explosive to tame by the time they arrived, though neighbors frantically joined the bucket brigade to ease its fury. Clayton sought out Ruth in the melee, though he appeared to have questioned the appropriateness of such an action. She immediately hugged him. He held her as they watched the hungry flames engulf the sentiment-inducing building, then eventually die out, leaving only a smoldering skeletal structure.

Clayton remained by Ruth's side the rest of the night. Hand in hand, she took him to the house, where no one else dared intrude, to find her father, Lester, bawling over the overwhelming loss. The scene was heart-wrenching.

Over the next couple of weeks, Clayton dropped in to visit several times to assist in any way he could. He even skipped school to help on the day of the community barn raising.

Clayton took notice and showed visible signs of concern when a *Glen* started dating Ruth and was obviously trying to make an impression on her. In Clayton's discussions with Daniel, it was clear that Glen was known to be *fast*—something a Mennonite girl would certainly frown upon … one would think.

Meanwhile, Clayton dated a similar *loose* girl named Carolyn during this time. Though likely tempted to take her up on her advances, Clayton talked to Bishop Reuben Hofstetter about whether he should continue dating her or not. Oddly, or perhaps wisely, the bishop did not give strong-handed advice. Instead, he asked questions and allowed Clayton to come to his own conclusions. Clayton ended the relationship shortly after. The editor noted that Clayton's father also weighed in on his involvement with Carolyn, telling him, "You should drop Carolyn and go back to Ruth, who is a better fit and from a good family."

Beemer had asked in the margin notes: "Why is his dad so consumed with appearances?"

Chief chortled. *Why indeed? Why do humans want other humans to think they are flawless? It's certainly not because they are flawless.*

That fall, Clayton dated Ruth's younger sister, Irene, a couple of times.

The chief editor smiled to find that Clayton asked several pointed questions about Ruth on the dates. He learned that Ruth was busy her senior year with maintaining top grades, babysitting, singing in a quartet, helping around home, attending church youth meetings (meetings Clayton was now too old to attend), and still dating regularly.

On August 3, 1960, after Ruth graduated from high school as the salutatorian, Clayton took her and four of her friends to Chippewa Amusement Park. The expected *fun time was had by all* did not apply. The old, paunchy editor guffawed as he read Beemer's rendering of the excursion.

Clayton had coolly and bravely traversed the giant Ferris wheel with the greatest of ease … until his head began spinning like the ride he sat upon and his stomach started arguing with the foreign movement. By the top of the adventure, his face was ashen. Sudden and utter lack of control spewed the day's hotdogs out of his mouth and onto Ruth's friends below. So much for exhibiting calm confidence!

Somewhere between the pallor of green, blue, and gray, all dignity went the way of the hot dog for Clayton. Ruth stayed by the sick boy for the rest of the day, while her friends cleaned off the upchuck as best as they could and enjoyed the many remaining rides. *That must have been a fun drive home,* the editor mused to himself.

Meanwhile, as this embarrassing misadventure unfolded, Samuel called the house for Ruth three times. Ruth's mother informed her of his request to urgently call him back as Clayton dropped her off at the door. Upping the stakes, as Clayton later found out, the charming suitor invited her to a Cleveland Indians Major League Baseball game, unheard of for young Kidronites. Ruth accepted the once-in-a-lifetime offer, and they went two nights later.

The next night, August 6, Clayton dated the surely worn-out Ruth again; evidently, he was now taking the competition with the respected Samuel seriously. Clayton took her to visit his brothers Roy and Lee and their families the following night to total their dates at an even fifty, though Clayton likely had no idea of the unbelievable count.

On these dates, Clayton shared personal details concerning his dad's exasperating ways—a theme Beemer reported often. He freely shared his frustration with his dad's boring devotions, degrading comments of his mother, constant comparison to Elno and Marion, lack of appreciation for anything Clayton did, and snatching his paycheck from his full-time job every week. Homer micromanaged everything Clayton did, despite Clayton basically running the farm for his dad. Their constant bickering over Homer's *right ways* exhausted Clayton more than the work itself. Ruth always listened without judgment, or so it appeared.

On their next date, Clayton and Ruth talked about their mutual desire to do mission work someday. On the following date, August 17, Ruth finally discussed her complicated feelings regarding Clayton and Samuel. Clayton, according to Beemer's biographic reporting, seemed uptight and at a loss for words.

Ironically, Clarence Sommer sent his bricklayer, Al Newman, to Ruth's family to construct a chimney onto the back of their house on August 20, 1960. Clayton was his assistant. At 10:30 in the morning, Ruth came around back and asked to speak with Clayton in private. Clayton climbed down from the scaffolding, and they walked around the corner of the house.

Ruth said, "Samuel asked me to marry him last night." Clayton looked stunned. "Relax," Ruth quickly went on. "We stayed up till 1:30 last night, talking. I told him no, Clayt. I want to be with you." She locked eyes with the even more stunned Clayton.

Ruth went on, "You came to our house when our barn burned down (now a year and a half ago, Chief realized) and stayed with me all evening in my time of need. Samuel was hanging out at the barbershop that night, unconcerned about me. You have always shown me care and concern, Clayton. And you have strong spiritual values and understanding." She held his dirty hand and pecked his sweaty cheek. "Just wanted you to know. Sorry to take you from your work." With that, she let go of his hand and walked back into the house.

Ah huh, the editor thought. *Of course, these two are an item. Clayton's not going to let her go after this!*

He read on, just to make sure the volatile teens hadn't somehow sabotaged the relationship.

They dated eight times in the next couple of weeks, including a romantic hayride. On September 7, they loaded Ruth's belongings into her parent's car. She was going to Goshen College in Goshen, Indiana, over four hours away. Clayton had known about this move all along; Ruth had always shone as a student and wanted to share her gifts as a teacher. To celebrate her departure, Clayton took her to his house for homemade ice cream that evening.

When he brought her home, they looked over information in a Voluntary Service (VS) manual for the opportunity that Clayton was interested in pursuing. Then they went on a walk and talked well into the night. Clayton confided that he'd gotten his dad's unlikely approval to join a VS program soon. He said, "I just want to go somewhere far away from my dad and do something great ... for God. My brothers all served the church, but I want to go even further."

To end their affectionate time together, they prayed that God's will in their lives be done.

Oh, my! The editor transported himself back to the Steiner farm.

"Beemer."

Beemer turned from his writing. "Chief. Is something wrong?"

"Kid, I know you're new to this human stuff. And especially new to this romance stuff. But I just wanted to let you know that this love situation between Clayton and Ruth is serious."

"It is?" Beemer contemplated that. "What does that mean, exactly?"

The editor looked over his glasses at his pupil. "Well, we don't know. It could be anything. But from what we know of Clayton, I'd suggest you plan for his plans to revolve around her."

"But isn't he a little young for that?"

"Yes."

"Ruth's going away to college, and Clayton still hasn't served his two years of alternative military service. I figured it's just too impractical to take seriously. Isn't it?"

"No. This kind of love can make a man do some mighty impractical things."

"Well, what should I do about it?"

"Report it. Honestly."

And so, Beemer did. Honoring his profession, Beemer commenced writing about Clayton's every move, hoping against all odds that Clayton wasn't making a major mistake. For a blunder on Clayton's part this early in his life, Beemer figured, would surely decrease his biography's acclaim and not impress his accomplished editor.

After a few months, as the busy editor in chief skimmed Beemer's thorough report, he read the following highlights:

Clayton sits alone in his room late at night, writing a letter to Ruth: ... *My dad keeps telling me how to do things. He doesn't even know how the farm implements work... I'll be so happy when I get out of here and he can do all his work on his own. And George.*

I miss you. I wish I could hug you in my arms.

Clayton goes for his first visit to Goshen to see Ruth.

"Is everyone here as smart as you?" Clayton asks Ruth.

"Clayton, I'm not that smart. I just want to learn. And you're not so dumb. You could be here too if you wanted."

Ruth comes home for the weekend. Clayton spends as much time as he can with her. They go out to eat Saturday night. They talk about her professors and her writing assignments.

"How can you write that much?" Clayton asks. "Don't you hate it?"

"I don't hate it, Clayt. Sometimes, it's hard. But writing helps me understand things. It helps me voice what I see and who I am. Do you hate writing to me?"

Clayton blushes. "No. I love writing you. It's the closest thing I've got to being with you."

"Maybe someday, writing will be something that helps you be closer to life."

Clayton writes to Ruth: *I thought about you all day. Mixing the mud (mortar) for the fireplace we built today, I thought of how the dry cement, lime, sand, and water by themselves are not much good for anything, but how together they make this strong bond. I had to wonder, is that like what we'll be someday? I hope so.*

Lonely without you, Clayton

Clayton takes Ruth to his sister Arlene and Irvin Nussbaum's in the evening after visiting Elno and Mabel's during the day. They enjoy playing with Arlene and Irvin's six children and talking to Arlene and Irvin late into the night.

On the way home, Ruth tells Clayton how much she admires Arlene. Clayton smiles and returns the sentiment, "She's always been like a second mother to me."

On her second visit home, Clayton asks Ruth how many friends she has at Goshen.

"I don't know. A lot."

"How many guy friends do you have?"

"Some. But they're just friends. Clayt, I'm not dating anyone else. You know that, right?"

Clayton nods. "Yeah. Just wondering. There's probably lots of great guys there, is all. I mean, I'm not exactly the smartest guy around."

"Clayton. Don't say that. You are too smart. You're going to serve the Lord. That's more important than going to school anyhow."

"Really? You think so?"

"Yes, I do. I wish I could go with you."

"Me too."

> Beemer writes in the margin to the editor: *Ruth sounds firm in her resolve to stay true to Clayton, but let's be realistic here. He can't possibly think that a beautiful, smart girl like her, who surely has many guys knocking on her door, will stick with an uneducated guy like him, who is also living somewhere else for two or three years. Is he about to get his heart broken?*

On Clayton's third visit, Ruth is busy studying for her finals, so Clayton walks around campus on his own much of the time.

Clayton writes Ruth: *...Getting cold here. My fingers are freezing at work when they get wet mixing the mud. Then I scraped them on a cinder block and it bled all day. Now they are cracking. When I get home I have to grab onto those dumb milkers. Then Dad tells me how I should be doing it faster. I'm going crazy.*

Maybe I'm just crazy for you.

Christmas is almost here. This year, all I want for Christmas is you.

December 16, 1960, Ruth is home for Christmas break. Clayton greets her at her home late at night, making it their seventy-seventh date. They talk past midnight until Ruth is so tired that she can't keep her eyes open.

Since it's Saturday, Clayton works only his farm chores and spends the rest of his time with Ruth. They walk, drive, go to the store, get a bite to eat, and talk in her living room. They are inseparable.

It's Thursday night and Clayton should be completely tuckered out from his two physically demanding jobs and spending time with Ruth every night. But tonight, they are embracing on her living-room couch, talking till 2:00 in the morning. "I can't let you go," Ruth tells him.

Clayton has trouble staying awake on the less than three-mile drive home.

On Christmas, Ruth smiles broadly, jumps up, and embraces Clayton. "Thank you! It's beautiful." She holds her gift, a small, wooden chest, out to admire; then, in front of her parents, she kisses him on the cheek.

Today, December 29, Clayton receives a letter from the Mennonite Central Committee under the program, Pax (which means "peace" in Latin). Clayton is going to Algeria to serve!

On their date tonight, Ruth giggles. "Oh, you've got to hear this. I saw Mom's best friend, Freida, today. She told me how they were at their monthly sewing circle at Kidron Mennonite. Freida asked Mom what the name Clayton means. Mom said, 'I hope he means business!'" Ruth cackles, bobbing up and down, imagining the anecdote.

Clayton smiles and silently reddens.

Ruth cries as she says goodbye to Clayton on New Year's Day, 1961.

Clayton begins orientation for the Pax Volunteer Service in Elkhart, Indiana, fifteen miles from Goshen on January 2, though school has not yet resumed for Ruth.

Clayton receives word on January 10 that the door to Algeria is temporarily closed due to the war for independence from France. Instead, he is to work, right away, with the VS unit in Hesston, Kansas, until Algeria opens up.

Clayton and Ruth drive back to Kidron on January 13 right after Clayton finishes orientation, marking their one hundredth date.

In an awkward, but affectionate, farewell, Clayton says goodbye to Ruth at the Wooster train station today, January 14.

> Beemer's margin notes: *I wonder what Clayton's feeling and thinking? Does he wonder if he'll ever see her again? Seems he's pretty naïve. I mean, he's never lived in a different environment before. Is he scared? Or excited? How can he handle all this newness all at once?*

Clayton begins working for the VS unit in Hesston to help construct the Showalter Retirement Community today.

Clayton writes a letter to Ruth tonight: *I finished my first day on the job. It's nice to be good at what I'm doing. I'm doing most of the same things I did for Clarence the last couple of years. Lots of brickwork needed here. I'll have plenty of work for a while ...*

Clayton writes the next night: *I have the first roommate I ever had. Well, at least the first one outside of my family. His name is David Summer. I think we'll get along swell. There's other VSers here too. It's kind of fun learning to know people from different places. Of course, it's nothing like a big college like Goshen. But I'm learning new things at least.*

The next night, Clayton writes: *Work is hard. But when it's over it's over. I sure don't miss Dad's farm. It's nice not having to be told what to do all the time. After supper we sit around and talk awhile then I have the rest of the evening to myself. I miss you. I usually go on a walk through this wheat field behind our unit and pray under this clump of trees near a fence.*

Just like almost every night since he's been here, Clayton writes to Ruth: *I've been here for two weeks now. I'm known as the garbage pie eater. When we have pie, everyone eats at least one piece. If there is some left in the pan, I eat it clean. This pie is good! No use letting it go to waste.*

Time to go on my walk and pray. I'm getting used to where God has me.

After his customary walk through the wheat fields, Clayton spends a longer time praying than usual tonight.

> Margin notes to the editor: *I sure wish I knew what Clayton was praying. He spends quite a bit of time there. And he never looks particularly happy on his walk home. It's like he's frustrated about something. Is he homesick? Or Ruth-sick? Is THE BOSS telling him something that he doesn't want to hear? Is he asking for something inappropriate? Whatever it is, I'm pretty sure he's not enjoying his prayer time like he makes it seem in his letters.*

Instead of writing a letter, Clayton records himself talking to Ruth on a cassette tape tonight.

Clayton says to Ruth: "*... Seeking God's direction when I'm done with VS and Pax. Lots of different options. I'll keep praying. Maybe God's leading me to mission work like we've talked about. That would be pretty great to serve God full time. But it would have to be his will for sure.*"

A letter arrives from Ruth's parents, which tells Clayton about their plans to visit their son, Carl, and daughter-in-law, Elaine, who are working at a retirement home with VS in Eureka, Illinois. Ruth will be with them.

Clayton writes back to them saying he would indeed like to try to surprise Ruth with a visit.

On Friday, March 31, Clayton and a fellow VSer, Sam, cut out from work early to drive all night to Eureka. The trip is on the way to Goshen, where Sam also has a girlfriend who he plans to visit.

Somewhat abreast of the sleeping arrangements, upon his arrival at 6:30 a.m., April 1, 1961, just as the sun is dawning, Clayton goes into the room where he hopes to find Ruth. Two women lie asleep on the bed in the dark room. Fairly certain which one is Ruth, he gently places a kiss on her cheek.

She awakes, squinting. "Clayt?"

"Good morning. Are you up for a visit?"

"Of course!" They embrace.

Beulah, Ruth's roommate and brother's sister-in-law, quietly leaves the room.

After breakfast, Clayton and Ruth go on a little walk. Ruth says, "I can't believe everyone but me knew you were coming."

Clayton grins.

… They sit on a stump. Breathing uneasily, Clayton finally says, "Ruth, will you marry me?"

"Yes!" She swallows him in a big hug. He answers in kind. The world sits still for a long moment.

The beaming couple sits down for lunch with the Geiser family. Neither tells what just happened.

Before they part ways today (Sunday), Clayton and Ruth discuss how they plan to keep their engagement to themselves until Clayton returns from Algeria.

Ruth is grateful to be engaged, she tells Clayton, because now she can concentrate fully on her studies, and she has a good excuse for turning guys down if they ask to go out with her.

> Beemer notes to Chief: *They can't be serious. These two young, naïve kids are going to keep a secret promise for over two years? Is this even possible? I know this is supposedly romantic, but is it wise? There are so many ways their immaturity could*

destroy these plans. Will this scheme ruin his next two years of adventure away from home? He finally has the opportunity to be like the famous William Clark of Lewis and Clark, and now, he might botch the whole thing for a girl.

The old editor sat back and took a long, deep breath. There was so much his young apprentice did not yet know about humans. He could let Beemer figure out how they operated in their world all on his own. But that would lead to mistake-ridden assumptions. Assumptions which he, the editor, would need to painstakingly weed through to edit.

No, if there was one thing he had learned from his years of chronicling experience, it was that new writers always benefited from foundational teachings of how humans operate. People are all quirky, to be sure, but THE BOSS imprints an insatiable yearning to pursue joy, hope, and love into them. It doesn't matter how impractical or trouble-inducing their yearnings—they are drawn like thieves to a treasure. And romantic love was perhaps the most sought-after (and confusing) treasure they pursued.

It was time for another lesson for Beemer.

10

THE AMAZING DEPTH
OF HUMANS

The plump editor watched Beemer watching Clayton sleep. "What are you thinking?"

Beemer jumped. "Chief!"

"Relax." The mentoring reporter raised his hand to indicate he didn't come for a battle. "I'm just here for a little chat."

Beemer wearily sat back down, slowed his breathing, and looked back to his slumbering subject. "Why does he have to sleep? I mean, it seems like such a waste. He could be so much more productive if he didn't spend a third of his life sleeping."

The editor smirked, then considered. "These creatures' experience is much more invigorating and powerful than ours. So many stimuli easily overload their system. Sleep restores perspective and their brain's ability to focus."

"Hmm. It doesn't seem like Clayton feels all that much. It's like he's so consumed with what he *should* be that he doesn't feel things naturally ... or fully. It's almost like he's afraid to be himself. Is that a thing with humans?"

"Keen observation, Beemer! I think you're catching on."

Beemer beamed.

The salty advisor continued, "Yes, humans do that often. They project their ideals. Many get stuck presenting an image they want to be instead of living life honestly—especially young people of Clayton's age."

"Great, so he's pretending to be someone he's not."

"Relax. Most of his *best-side-forward* presentation is likely just human immaturity. He is beginning to be honest with that one girl, after all."

"Ruth Geiser. Yes, about her. You don't think that maybe he's setting himself up for a big fall? I mean, if he opens himself up to her any more and she dumps him, where will that leave him? He'll never trust again. And worse, all the negative digs his dad has fed him will be reinforced. He'll think he's a worthless, no-good twit."

"A twit?" Chief wagged his head, ill-humoredly. "If he gets hurt by being disappointed, he gets hurt by being disappointed. I've certainly seen people come back from far worse. He'll just have to pick himself up and head in a different direction. THE BOSS has unlimited paths to hike out of turmoil."

"But that would sure be a hard hit to his pride. Would he ever be able to trust again?"

"Good question. Do you think Clayton trusts now?"

Beemer scrunched up his face. "Well, he trusts his mom. And he trusts the church, which for him, means he trusts THE BOSS. But his dad is still a bit of a wild card. I think Clayton reveres Homer, but I don't think he trusts him enough to share himself with him. I'm not sure, but could fear be getting in the way of his trust in his dad?"

The chronicling tutor nodded knowingly. "Another good question. You're getting the hang of this biography business. What might be some reasons that Clayton would fear his dad?"

"Well, first off, Homer's a very my-way-or-the-highway kind of guy. If Clayton doesn't do it Homer's way, Clayton pays for it, usually in the form of a demoralizing tongue-lashing. Homer nearly always finds something to disapprove of in Clayton's work, responses, and general character. Though Clayton respects his dad as his authority figure, I don't think Clayton thinks Homer's fair. It's hard to trust someone who always makes you feel bad."

The editor's eyes widened and he peered over his reading glasses. "Beemer! Did you just figure out something Clayton was feeling?"

Beemer's leery and confused glare slowly turned to an inquisitive grin. "Maybe."

"Go on. What else does Clayton have to fear in his dad?"

"It's hard to put a finger on it, but there's something about Homer's miserable devotions that's scary. I'm not sure what it is, but that man somehow casts an oppressive blanket over the whole family when he rants about scripture. Every time, he takes a little truth from the Bible and twists it into his dreadful philosophy."

"And what might his philosophy be?"

"Well, his favorite theme is to make an example of how terrible someone is by referring to their actions or perceived sinful character. He does this with Clayton's mom, their neighbors, relatives, and church members— pretty much anyone but the preacher or the bishop. They're untouchable for some reason."

The chief editor nodded again. "Interesting. So, Clayton's been fed all his life that if a person doesn't do it right, look right, believe right, or be thought of right, that person is in bad standing with THE BOSS. Is that right?"

Beemer took his turn to nod.

"If that is true in Clayton's mind, what do you think that he might think other families might be discussing in their devotions if he steps out of bounds?"

Beemer's face lighted. He turned his head to Clayton who was sleeping on the bed. "He's afraid that if he doesn't act like a good Christian boy should, he'll be chewed up and spit out like gristle at their tables too. Homer's judgmental devotions have essentially taught Clayton to be so concerned with appearances that he's totally shut down his feelings so those uncontrollable things don't make him look bad. He's afraid his inner world will sabotage the outer world he sees and wishes for."

Chief gave mock applause. "Well said."

"It's rather obvious now that I stop and look at it. Why didn't I see that before?"

"For the same reasons Clayton can't see it yet. You're young and caught up in doing everything *right* instead of letting life flow and being the being that THE BOSS has created you to be."

"Okay," Beemer went on. "Clayton wants to do what's right, so he doesn't look bad. Then, why is he moving so swiftly with this Ruth? Doesn't he see the risk of looking really bad if it goes wrong? It's like he's throwing caution to the wind and logic out the window."

The grizzled editor choked a chortle. "Yes, well, we heavenly chroniclers don't have much use for the illogic of love. But these humans seem to need it. It's the one time that they can sell out to their emotions and wishes. And sometimes, it pays off a hundredfold. It's a remarkable plan, actually."

"I think I'd prefer logic."

"Spoken like a true novice."

Beemer cringed.

"Trust me," the editor promised. "This will make much more sense when you become Clayton's soul-buddy. THE BOSS makes them googly-eyed for a reason. It's just not a rational reason.

"Let's move onto prayer again," Chief said. "This is another apparently illogical concept that you are obviously struggling with. But it is one we must pay credence to. What do you think Clayton was praying about when he prayed under the grove of trees?"

"Well, I don't know. He could've been praying about anything. Direction, discernment, understanding, help, peace, strength, hope, justification, proof ... anything."

"Whoa!" the editor interrupted. "Of course, it's confusing when you begin to question *everything*. Let's start with the basics. What is the purpose of prayer for Clayton?"

"I don't know. To get what he wants?"

The chief sighed and grimaced. "That's certainly the indulgent side of it. But okay, let's hold that premise. Whom is Clayton expecting to provide for his ... let's call them *needs*?"

"THE BOSS."

"Okay. So, he's praying *to* THE BOSS. He's not just praying to himself. Correct?"

"Correct."

"So, is he essentially talking to THE BOSS?"

"I think so. But he's not talking out loud. I think it's all in his head."

The editor winced. "Let's hope it's not all in his head, but genuinely through his whole being. So, could his silent talking be construed as a conversation?"

"Yes." Beemer thought for a moment. "Assuming THE BOSS is listening and responding."

"And it would also imply that Clayton expects a response from THE BOSS, which is an innate desire THE BOSS has planted in each human."

"Are you suggesting that maybe Clayton isn't receiving the response he's wanting?"

Chief looked over his glasses and tilted his head as if to consider the possibility.

The gesture piqued Beemer's curiosity. "Or, he's not getting a response at all. That would explain his forlorn reaction after each prayer session. Maybe he's asking and not receiving answers even though he's been told he will receive whenever he asks." Beemer looks to his shrewd mentor, who gives the slightest of nods, spurring on the young apprentice. "But if he is asking and he's not hearing, does that mean the Bible is wrong *or* that THE BOSS is snubbing him for some reason? Or is Clayton doing it wrong?"

"How about … life is complex? We don't know all THE BOSS's ways, just that THE BOSS is complete and these humans are not. I suspect that if Clayton is not hearing from THE BOSS or is not getting the answers he thinks he should, it's the human element that is clogging up the works, not the perfect one."

Beemer nodded.

Chief asked, "What do you think Clayton is specifically praying about that he may not be getting a response to?"

"Probably that Ruth doesn't change her mind or that he can live up to her expectations. Maybe that he will be able to provide for her."

"Very good," the chief confirmed. "I'm sure he's prayed all of that. How do you think he will provide for her?"

"I have no idea."

"Do you think Clayton has any idea?"

Beemer thought a moment. "Probably not. Guess that would make him worry. And if THE BOSS was silent on the matter, it's hard telling all the worrisome thoughts he's fighting off: 'Does THE BOSS not care?' 'Is there something wrong with me?' 'What will happen if I fail to be the provider?'"

The editor nodded. "Now you're connecting the dots. Clayton has a humongous burden on his shoulders, and the most powerful resource in his world is apparently mute to his dilemma."

"Wow," Beemer pondered. "So, if Clayton is in such a tizzy over this, why doesn't THE BOSS just speak to him? Tell him what career path to take? Or touch his human emotions … or instincts … or psyche … or whatever mindless part of him that senses THE BOSS's presence in his life? Then, he would at least know experientially that the relationship is alive and real."

"That's the mystery, isn't it? I don't know, Beemer. Maybe THE BOSS is simply communicating to Clayton in a way Clayton is not aware of. Often, I have found that THE BOSS's voice is imperceptible to the subject because the subject is bent on hearing it in only one way. THE BOSS often speaks through small, still means, like a caring neighbor's smile, a beautiful sunset after a trying day, or a flat tire that causes one to meet an informative stranger. But I do know one thing—THE BOSS will never give up on Clayton."

"What's Clayton to do then … if he doesn't hear what THE BOSS is telling him?"

"It's a long life, my friend. THE BOSS will consistently speak his pearls of wisdom to Clayton. Know that. Eventually, Clayton will have the spiritual ears to hear. Until then, well, don't expect him to lie in a bed of roses. Or, if he does, expect the thorns to make rest fitful at best."

"So," Beemer concluded, "what you're saying is that his frustration with prayer and the mysteries of his relationship to THE BOSS are likely to continue for a while?"

"Likely. To make this relationship between the human and THE BOSS all that it can be, struggle is always in the equation for the subject. For some reason, THE BOSS seems to require that the subject earnestly search, empty, and alter before the relationship can be all that THE BOSS intends for it to be."

Beemer exhaled a deep breath and nodded once. "Okay. I guess I'll just observe this masterful plan and write."

The old editor in chief smiled. He clasped his hands over his generous belly. "Well said, my boy. Such is the duty of a chronicler—observe and report. I'll leave you to it then. Keep those margin notes coming. I'll be back when I need to."

With that, the wise old chronicler was gone.

All in all, Beemer was pleased to be living the dream of writing for THE BOSS under his hero chronicler's tutelage. Now, if he could just write something incredible to get their attention.

11

MISSION WORK
SERVING, LEARNING, SURVIVING

The *Heaven's Chronicle's* editor in chief sat back and mused over his novice chronicler Beemer's recent trouble in assessing his subject's romantic exploits and dissatisfied prayer life. It was time to go beyond merely skimming the Master Log on Beemer's biographic book. He began his deep-read where Clayton still assisted a masonry crew in Hesston, Kansas, in April 1961.

In Clayton's letter to Ruth, he writes: *I just got a letter from Mennonite Central Committee's Pax program today. They told me Algeria has opened up and I should be prepared to leave Hesston on May 1st. That's in just a few weeks. I'm pretty excited! And a little scared. Guess I'll just trust God to take care of me. It will be neat to do his work.*

Curt Nussbaum will be joining me. It's crazy to think that of all the people teaming up with me, your neighbor and Normie's classmate will be my partner overseas.

May 7, 1961. In a nice service at their home church, Kidron Mennonite, Clayton and Curt are dedicated for service to Algeria. Ruth attends, though she hastily hugs Clayton farewell afterward and travels back to Goshen College.

Clayton is packed and ready to head to New York City on May 10 to catch a ship to France, the first leg of his journey to Algeria. A strange episode occurs as Clayton says goodbye to the life he's known for nineteen years. From a family that doesn't show much emotion, Clayton's mother cries helplessly and achingly. Clayton has never seen his mother cry before.

He awkwardly embraces her and says, "I'll miss you, Mom. Thanks for all you've done for me." She tries to smile through the tears, words evidently too difficult to speak.

Homer looks more perturbed at the situation than anything. He says, "Serve the Lord good," then he heads out to the barn before Clayton leaves.

After arriving safely at the New York train station, Clayton and Curt find the ship dock and deposit their luggage. Clayton strains his neck looking up at the tall skyscrapers.

May 12. They board the SS *United States*, billed as "the fastest ship to ever cross the Atlantic." Clayton and Curt look around the ship in awe. The ship is bigger than downtown Kidron by a long shot!

Clayton embarks on his first ocean voyage. His seasickness is uncomfortable but tolerable. He can't imagine this five-day trip being the fastest crossing to anywhere.

On their last day on the ship, their older roommate, John, shows them the thousand dollars he's hidden in his shoe. He explains his intent to find excellent French prostitutes when he lands. He expresses, in detail, his previous encounters with such beauties.

Clayton and Curt say nothing in response.

Beemer notes to his editor in the margin: *Clayton has never heard of such exploits. It's his first time in foreign territory, and right away, he gets slapped with stories he's likely never even imagined. Will such information tempt or appall my naïve subject?*

Clayton disembarks in La Havre, France, on May 17. It is eerie how Clayton is among so many Americans on the ship one moment, and the atmosphere suddenly changes to *foreign* the minute he walks off the ship.

"Do you see signs for the train station?" he asks Curt.

Curt takes in the vast dock with people walking everywhere. "No. Maybe we should ask someone." He walks up to a young man who is adjusting his luggage. "Excuse me, do you know where the train station is?"

The man looks at him, confused. Then, he speaks in some other language and waves his hands like he doesn't know what Curt is talking about.

Clayton has a similar experience. Helplessness appears to be their mode of operation today.

They eventually talk to a man who tells them in broken English that the train station is *that way* and points. They walk in that direction with their luggage, and they eventually find a sign with a train on it, which provides further directions.

At the train station, communication is wanting. They pay for tickets to Paris … they hope.

The train finally stops in Paris … they think. They get off and retrieve their luggage.

"Now what?" Clayton asks when they set foot inside the terminal.

"I don't know. Look like we're Americans in desperate need of a ride?"

A young man approaches them and asks, "Are you looking for Bob Witmer?"

"Yes!" they say in unison.

"Great. I'll take you to him. I work for Bob with Pax."

The boys shake hands, smiling their obvious relief.

Mennonite missionary, Bob Witmer, shows his guests the setup in his home where he works with handicapped children.

Clayton and Curt help with maintenance around Bob's residence in exchange for room and board and sightseeing opportunities.

After twelve days at the Witmers', it's time to depart for Algeria. "Are you ready to be real missionaries?" Bob asks as he drops them off at the train station.

The boys nod, trying to look confident.

Bob laughs. "You'll do fine. Stick together. You'll figure it out."

The train takes Clayton and Curt to Marseille, a port in Southern France where they find the next ship on their voyage.

"Not quite as opulent [a word he learned from old John] as the SS *United States*, is it?" Clayton remarks to Curt.

"Not exactly."

They view the rust, the absence of rooms to sleep in, and the abundance of travelers on such a small ship.

"How bad can it be for twenty-four hours?" Clayton asks.

The first hour or two feel like a child's carnival ride as the little ship gently dips and rises with the timid swells of the Mediterranean Sea. However, the closer they get to the middle of the journey, the more exaggeratedly the boat sways. Glasses of water do not stay on the table. The chair Clayton is sitting on becomes too uncomfortable for him to remain in. Many passengers, he notices, lie on the floor, though it is not yet night. Others drink beer, something Clayton has witnessed little of previously.

As Clayton's stomach begins to feel queasy, he too finds a place on the deck to lie down. But, as the ship sways from side to side, the beer bottles all roll from one side to the other, clanking an obnoxious tune.

Clayton can't sleep. He heads for the outer, open deck, stumbling over a rolling bottle as he does so. Trying to steady his unpredictable gait, he grabs an unoccupied chair that does not hold his lopsided weight. On all fours, he inches his way to the side rail.

Clayton decides to traverse the stairwell to the upper deck, hoping to find nirvana from his nausea. He staggers upward. Things look worse up here.

He smells vomit. Puke from the other passengers who are leaning over the railing sprays him before he can return the favor. When he finally relieves his knotted gut, relief instantly turns to disgust when the howling wind throws the full force of his own barf back into his face.

Clayton throws up for the sixth time in four-and-a-half hours. No rest for the weary, bleary, or teary.

Clayton and Curt timidly leave the old sea bucket without looking back on May 30, 1961, when they arrive in Algiers, Algeria. *Good Riddance!* their stomachs shout.

Their new host, Mennonite missionary Robert Stetter, greets them, "How was your trip?"

Clayton and Curt look at each other, then back to their supervisor as if he is speaking in French. Bob chuckles. "Sorry. The old tin bucket is never very obliging. But the good news is, dry land cures seasickness every time."

Bob drives them to his upstairs apartment, where he, his wife, Lila Rae, and their three daughters reside, at 52 Rue Richard, Maguet, El Biar, Algiers. "This," he informs them, "will be your home base."

Clayton writes Ruth in a letter: *We finally arrived in Algeria! Curt and I are settling into the Stetter home. I think we'll be here a few weeks before our first assignment.*

Tonight, I am sitting on the third-floor open-roof balcony (called a terrace), which is as large as the Stetter's second floor. It overlooks the city of Algiers. It's amazing watching the huge city peacefully go to sleep. I'll be dreaming of you tonight…

Clayton sleeps in the lower bunk bed. He places a picture of Ruth in the webbing of the upper bunk, so he can gaze at it before drifting off to sleep.

Clayton and Curt both get sicker than dogs, complete with vomiting and diarrhea, after just two days in the new land. "This is pretty common for foreigners," Bob informs them. "It's probably just till you get used to the food and water."

To his parents and family, Clayton writes: *This morning we are eating fresh, warm French bread with jam from a bakery below the Stetters. It is so good! They also gave us coffee au lait, which is hot milk and coffee. I kind of like it ...*

We have met two fellow Pax men, Emory and Stanford. They seem like really nice guys. There's also this Mennonite missionary across the hall from the Stetters named Marion Hofstetter. She's already taught us some basic French.

Yesterday we explored the town a little and I bought a French Bible and dictionary, got an international driver's license, and started French classes from a French Mennonite named John. We will be doing maintenance for the Mennonite mission while we're here...

June 18. John Aseltine, head of the Brahim Plage Baptist Missionary Camp, picks Clayton and Curt up to take them to his camp, which is four hours west of Algiers. On their way there, he explains their task of building the camp.

Two hours into the journey, a French military checkpoint stops them. They are told that the boys do not have the necessary paperwork. They must return to Algiers.

John explains that Algeria is in the middle of a civil war. France controls the country, but some Algerian rebels want to overthrow the government. "France isn't about to let the peace they enjoy be lost. So, they're making sure no one is aiding the ungrateful Algerians. We just need to do whatever the French authorities tell us, so we can reach these poor lost souls for Christ."

After the boys retrieve the necessary paperwork, the French authorities allow Clayton and the group passage. They arrive late this evening, June 19.

To Ruth, Clayton writes: *We're staying with John and his family. Grace and him have 3 girls. They're a lot of fun to be with. Very kind. They rent this house about 100 feet from the Mediterranean Sea. After work every day we swim and bathe in the sea! It's refreshing since we get so dirty pulling weeds and bushes all day.*

The house has this big open ceiling and a tile roof. Every night we fall asleep hearing the waves. Tonight it's lightly raining. I hear the pitter-patter on the roof. Oh, I wish you were here to enjoy it with me ...

After choosing the lower bunk bed again, Clayton falls asleep, as he gazes at Ruth's picture above him.

Clayton writes in his diary: *After three weeks of clearing the land we're finally going to build something. A French barrack.*

In a letter home, Clayton writes: *We just completed the barrack. It's like a big shed. People will be able to sleep in it and they'll probably have meetings and things in it. We're preparing to pour the floor and put in a toilet with a septic tank.*

Camp finally begins. Clayton records in his diary: *We are having camp for ten students. We all eat, sleep, have classes, and prepare classes in the barrack. Quite a bit different than how we would do things in the states. We are never alone here...*
I'm teaching a Bible class...

Clayton's diary, August 4. *I have lots of time to pray in the evenings. Though I'm not sure it's doing any good.*

Another evening is spent writing Ruth: *Back in Algiers at the Stetters resting up. Doing maintenance again here. I am enjoying the French bread and coffee au lait every morning!*
Can't wait to get back to teaching Bible at camp...
I miss you.

Clayton journals: *Curt and I in Brahim Plage put up some tents today while the camp was going on. We're supposed to clear more brush the next week or so to prepare for next year's camp...*

Clayton gives his testimony to the campers tonight while John interprets. Clayton tells how God gave him a good home where he learned the truth from the Bible and how, when he was a teenager, he got off track and was making a mess of his life. So, he accepted Jesus into his life, and now things are so good that he wants to spend the rest of his life serving Him.

Clayton writes in his diary: *God, if you're listening, please let me know somehow. I feel like I'm doing this on my own and I'm running out of strength.*

> Beemer writes a note to the editor in the margin: *Which is it? Is he in good with THE BOSS or not? Or is he just trying to impress people and prove to himself that he's on the right track? I hope he doesn't make his relationship with THE BOSS about status.*

In a letter home, Clayton writes: *Camp is over. We're just closing things down and preparing it for next year...*

On our last Sunday together the staff had a church service together. Curt and I were in charge. I gave the sermon. It went pretty good ...

September 4. Clayton travels to Mostaganem Reformed Church Mission to help Rev. Lopez build a barrack.

Rev. Lopez speaks to Clayton in French and points to some supplies.
Clayton looks to Curt. "Do you know what he just said?"
Curt shakes his head.
There are no fluent English speakers in camp.
Clayton uses what little broken French he can muster to follow Lopez's orders. They are learning French much faster here.

Clayton observes Rev. Lopez smoking and drinking alcohol in the evening.

In his diary, Clayton writes: *I have been offered cigarettes and wine from two different French pastors now. The other day I saw a French pastor passing out clothing for Mennonite Central Committee (MCC) to some Muslims. Hard to swallow.*

> Beemer's margin note reads: *Some blatant proof that Clayton is more concerned with looks and dos and don'ts than inward value. How will he ever learn that THE BOSS cares for all people and what's inside them, not just their appearance, superficial actions, or religion?*

After two weeks of not getting any mail, Clayton receives a backlog of letters from Ruth and his family when he gets back to the home base in Algiers. He reads the five letters from Ruth first, as if he is starving for her attention. Then, he reads letters from his mom, Dorothy, and Arlene.

In his diary, Clayton writes: *After an hour and a half bumpy bus ride through the Kabylia Mountains we arrive at some small town about the size of Kidron in Les Quadhias for our next assignment. We're supposed to build some additions onto a building...*

To Ruth, Clayton writes: *Curt and I hiked in the beautiful mountains today. Wish you could have gone with us...*

Clayton goes back to the Stetters' by train after finishing the building on October 20.

Clayton and Curt are teamed with two other Pax men, Stanford, and his brother, Muriel. They are given orders to go to Yachir, a small village that is up a three-thousand-foot mountain and thirty miles from the nearest town on a steep, winding, narrow road. Clayton understands that they are to build some buildings for some refugees there, but he doesn't know much else about the operation.

The Mennonite Mission supplies them with a four-wheel-drive Jeep which they are happy to navigate like a ride at the fair. But their ideas of a picnic adventure are quickly thwarted when they are required to be escorted by a French military convoy. The convoy consists of a heavily armed Jeep that leads the procession, the pacifist Pax men, and a large truck that carries armed French soldiers.

When they ask why they need military assistance, they are told, "The FNL will attack anyone. They can't be trusted!" The FNL (National Liberation Front) is an Algerian liberation group that is known to use guerilla warfare.

Humor is kept to a minimum as the Mennonite boys traverse the heavily forested mountain. The going is slow!

Suddenly, they hear gunfire! The Pax men look around and can't see where the attack is coming from. Their armed escorts fire back.

"What should I do?" Stanford yells. He is behind the steering wheel, but he ducks down like the rest of his cohorts.

"Drive!" shouts Curt.

Stanford inches his way to catch up with the French truck that is firing in front of them.

The hostile exchange eventually subsides. No one in the Mennonite Jeep says a peep.

Fifteen minutes after the attack, they arrive at the fenced-in village of Yachir. Three injured soldiers are quickly hauled away from the truck in the rear before the Pax partners can see the extent of their injuries.

They unload their gear upon arrival into a twelve-by-twenty-one-foot barrack that has two bedrooms on one end, a kitchen on the other, and a dining room in the middle. There is no electricity, running water, or bathroom.

In his diary, Clayton writes: *I can't believe it. We were shot at today. We could have been killed. It scared the living daylights out of us. I miss Ruth more than ever.*

There are approximately five hundred displaced Algerians here that the French picked up in the surrounding mountainsides. Most of the refugees are farmers. The French do not want the FNL infiltrating their farms, so they brought them here for safekeeping. No one is allowed to enter or leave without going through the French checkpoint. The French give them food and water, and a seventy-five-by-one-hundred-foot plot of flat, open ground 150 feet from the camp to use as their restroom.

Clayton and his crew are charged with building two houses for these residents. The French military pays for all the costs of supplies, food, and necessities. It supposedly protects the Algerians with guards that are constantly around the premises, keeping a watchful eye for any movement outside the camp and keeping track of all who reside inside.

Clayton writes in his diary: *No electricity. Which means I'm writing by candle-light at my bedroom desk tonight. We have a gas lantern and cook with gas too. The real fun thing though is finding the hole in the back of our barrack to take a crap. At least we don't have to go in the public field all the refugees use. I used that once. It's a minefield trying to dodge all the piles of crap all over. To pee, we just do it wherever a good place to pull down our zipper is. Reminds me of being on the farm.*

In a letter home, Clayton writes: *We are having a ball laughing at each other's cooking and washing. I'm getting really good at Rook. We play it all the time.*

Clayton journals: *I still find my prayer time about every night. My work here is pretty good but I still am trying to get some direction from God. He doesn't seem to be listening. I hope I hear him or sense him before I get back home. Maybe I should just call the whole thing off with Ruth since I don't know what I'm doing. Frustrating!*

It's 1:00 in the morning. Clayton stirs and fumbles his way in the dark room to head to the potty hole. As he opens the door to step outside, he hears guns cocking. Suddenly, instinctually knowing guns are trained on him, he shoots his hands in the air. Now wide awake, he stammers, "I'm just going to the bathroom."

The soldiers lower their weapons and allow him to pass. The crap is successfully scared out of him.

To his family, Clayton writes: *We are nearly done with our first house. We had to dig out the floor with a pick and move the dirt with a wheelbarrow. The floor is dirt, the inside walls were smeared with mud. The outside walls are made of rock covered with cement. My work with Clarence Sommer is paying off. The roof is tin on wooden rafters.*

Some of the guys aren't feeling well. They stay in and do our cooking.

Clayton writes to Ruth: *I stayed home today. Looks like I finally got what everyone else has had. I'll prepare the meals. Guess it's pork and beans again.*

We've almost finished the first house. Won't it be nice to someday be in our own house? Hope you can wait on me.

November 10. Clayton is so sick that he must leave camp and go down to see a doctor in Algiers. The doctor diagnoses him with yellow jaundice. He must stay in isolation at the Stetters' and receive a shot of penicillin every day for a week because the disease is so contagious.

Clayton journals: *I don't feel so good. And I don't mean because I'm sick. I just read a letter from Ruth. She was asked to go out on a date. I knew it! She said she turned him down. But how long before the next one? And how long before she forgets about me and says yes to one of them? I pray God won't let that happen... If he cares.*

Walking for more supplies back at Yachir, Clayton hears a loud noise. He immediately hits the dirt. Then the next explosion jolts the airwaves. Clayton runs to his friends inside the building they are working on. No one knows what to make of it. The refugees, Clayton notices, are just as terrified, if not more so, as the missionaries. But the refugees have no building to hide in.

Clayton writes in his diary: *We found out from one of the guards that that explosion we heard the other day was a cannon they fired over our heads from one mountainside to the other, scaring the Algerian refugees in case they considered leaving the camp. The guard telling us this had a big grin on his face.*

In a family letter: *On New Year's Day we played football with the French Army...*

The Pax men, having completed the houses, wind back down the mountain seamlessly. But when they find the main road, the Jeep dies on them. Hard telling what would have happened to them had it stalled midway down with FNL guerillas in hiding.

The journey back to the Stetters' that should have taken one day takes four.

Clayton and Carl again settle into maintenance work and French lessons back at the Stetters'.

In an unprecedented letter to his dad, Clayton writes: *Dear Dad, Because of all the mission work we've done for the Lord, Pax is giving us the opportunity to take a tour of the Holy Lands where Jesus lived. I really want to join all the other Pax men. The only problem is it costs $375 to go. I don't have the money because I'm not working for myself but God. Could you please loan me the money? I'll pay it back as soon as I get back and get a job.*
Clayton

The two Pax men are assigned to the edge of the familiar Kabylia Mountains again. They go to Mission Rolland to help with maintenance and learn French from the hospitable Rolland family.

Clayton writes in his diary: *The Rolland family is very nice and easy to work with. But they don't speak much English. It's helping me to learn French quicker but I'm pretty slow at the process compared to some of the other Pax men. It's a little frustrating. I wish God would help me catch on better.*

In a letter to Ruth: *I can't believe it. This has got to be the first time ever. My dad sent me the money for the three-week Holy Land tour. I don't think he's ever given money to any of my brothers and sisters. I get to go to the Holy Land! I only wish you could go with me.*

February 22. Clayton writes in his diary: *... even a worse trip across the Mediterranean than the first time. They need to make these ships larger or something. I felt like Jonah, almost wanting to be thrown off the boat.*

By train, Clayton and Curt travel through Thessaloniki to Athens, Greece.

Clayton takes a stroll around the unfamiliar city of Athens this morning before they are to head to the airport. His curious adventure disorients him, and he can't find his way back to the hotel. He doesn't ask for directions, since their language, "is all Greek to him."

As he is sweating in his lostness, a bus beeps its horn and pulls up next to him. The door opens, and the driver, in a Greek accent, asks if he's going to the airport with the Pax tour.

When Clayton gets on the bus and finds a seat, the tour leader tells Clayton that, after waiting for him at the hotel, they finally decided to leave without him. Had they not found him walking aimlessly on the street, he'd have been forced to fend for himself and been sent home.

Clayton gulps. His walk was a near regrettable blunder.

> Beemer's margin notes: *Where else is Clayton headed in his life without a clue about where he's going? One minute, he's mindlessly traveling down a road he fancies; the next minute,*

117

reality hits him like a bus. I hope his preposterous walk to the unknown with Ruth turns out this fortunately.

In a postcard to his family, Clayton writes: *I had my first plane ride to Cairo, Egypt. The pyramids are impressive!*

In his diary, Clayton writes: *I got to see Jericho Road today where the Israelites walked around the city and the walls came a-tumbling down. This was one of the best days of my life.*

At Jacob's well, where Jesus met the Samaritan woman, the tour guide asks if anyone has any questions. One guy asks if that story really happened since it is not in the original manuscripts. Another guy asks why Samaritans were considered taboo. Clayton has nothing to ask.

Clayton confides in Curt, "Some of these guys ask the strangest questions. I'd never think of such things."

Clayton's diary: *March 11 — Best day of the trip yet. I saw the Garden Tomb and Golgotha, the Valley of Kidron, the Golden Gate, the Gate of Stephen, and the Stone of Agony.*

In a hotel in Jordan, Clayton meets a Jordanian about his age. When Clayton realizes the Jordanian speaks good English, they strike up a conversation. It turns out that the young man has also been to Algeria. They exchange information and impressions. This is the first Muslim Clayton has struck a chord with. Then, the guy tells Clayton about his poor family and his great need to pay for medical care. He asks Clayton if he could spare some money.

Clayton hesitates; then, Clayton tells him that he is a Christian. "I don't have any money to give you, but if you accept Christ into your heart as I have done, you'll be saved from sin and death." After an awkward pause, they part ways.

Clayton writes in his diary: *I've been looking for the opportunity to witness to someone ever since I left home. I finally got to share Christ with a guy from Jordan I met at this hotel. It went pretty good. I don't think he accepted Christ into his heart. But at least a seed was planted.*

> Beemer to the Editor: *Really? He's barely talked to or acknowledged any of the Algerians he's supposedly serving since he's been here. Now, he's Mr. Evangelist? Does he really think that saying some magic words will make more of an impact than loving people through loving relationships? If he truly came to "witness," why doesn't he ever write about the people he's here to serve, instead of always writing about his girlfriend, his worries, and wondering where God is?*

After a thirty-hour train trip back to Salzburg, Austria, Clayton writes in his diary: *I'm exhausted but renewed. We got to stop off at the concentration camps in Germany. Not quite as encouraging as the Holy Lands.*

While they wait for their visas to be renewed at the French Mennonite headquarters to re-enter Algeria, Clayton and Curt work maintenance in a Mennonite Children's Home.

Visa papers finally arrive, and Clayton flies from Paris to Algiers on March 31, avoiding the awful Mediterranean voyage.

April 1, 1962. Clayton writes Ruth: *Happy anniversary! Hard to believe it's been a whole year since we got engaged. Can't wait to tell the world!*

In Clayton's diary: *Today I felt a big need to remember Ruth in prayer because of the upcoming Goshen Spring Fest and all the new opportunities it presents. May this next year pass faster than the last year for Ruth's and my sake.*

The War of Algerian Independence is heating up. Both sides are becoming more aggressive.

To Ruth, Clayton writes: *In the evenings, from the Stetter's third-floor terrace, we've been watching flashes of light from bombs going off in various parts of the city followed by loud booms. It's really something to behold. Tonight, we saw ten explosions. It's kind of like fireworks...*

Clayton pens in his diary: *...Tonight a bomb came just a few blocks from our place. This isn't fun anymore. This is scary!*

Today, on his walk to the local grocery store, Clayton hears gunfire echoing off the tall buildings that surround him. Clayton slows, looks around, and tries to discern which direction the evil intent is coming from. Cautiously, he negotiates the next corner only to find men running past bloody men lying on the street. Obviously, they have just been shot!

Realizing he's an open target, he makes a run for it ... to where, he is unsure, but hopefully away from the carnage. As he flees, he sees a man pull one of the lifeless bodies from the street.

More shots are fired! Clayton takes a sharp left at the next cross street and keeps running. When he finally recognizes an area, he is hypersensitive to the environment and jogs cautiously until he lets himself into the Stetters' abode. Tragedy avoided ... at least for him.

Clayton writes to his folks on April 11, 1962: *... The gutter was flowing with blood.*

Clayton's diary: *Not the best day I've ever had. Last night I read long into the night reading, "Mission to the Headhunters." It hit me hard. I like the book.*

With the influx of new Pax men, Clayton learns he will now partner with Dan Beachy from Hartville, Ohio, instead of being with Curt.

Clayton writes in his diary in March 1962: *I'm not sure why Algeria was granted independence, but they were.*

> Beemer's margin notes: *Clayton doesn't seem to grasp the Algerians' predicament. Considering everything he's written and the way he's acted, you would think he believes what all of the non-Mennonite missionaries have told him—that the colonizing French should be in control of the country and the inferior Algerians are ungrateful rebels and bad for wanting their independence. Does he not know that THE BOSS's heart is always for the oppressed and not the oppressor? Why must he always side with the given authority?*

En route to their return destination of Brahim Plage, where they are to erect a second barrack, they are stopped by the FLN fourteen times in a forty-mile stretch. Clayton tells Dan, "It's hard to tell who's manning these checkpoints or why."

In his diary, Clayton writes: *I finally got my long-awaited birthday card from Ruth (two weeks late). I'm now 21, legal age. Wish I could celebrate with her.*

To home, Clayton writes: *July 4th, They're having their first Independence day here, the same day as the U.S. It's really interesting to see how they celebrate. They march the streets, dancing and shouting. Most everybody wore green to celebrate the end of the long seven-and-a-half-year war. I heard that of the 10 million Algerians, around 970,000 were killed. And something like 32,500 of the French died trying to keep them in line. It's good it's over.*

August 11, 1962, Clayton is deployed to Marengo Hospital, which is an hour and a half west of Algiers. The 275 beds it holds are usually full. Only two doctors are on staff—a German and a temporary Mennonite volunteer named Dr. John Kraun from Canada. On his first day, Clayton is given the tour and meets the six-foot, five-inch Dr. Kraun in the operating room

(OR) while he is operating on a patient. Clayton quickly exits the OR, queasy at the sight of blood.

Because he needs help, Dr. Kraun takes on Clayton as his assistant. On his first day on the job, Clayton assists the doctor in stitching up a man and in delivering a baby.

On his second day, Clayton helps put on casts...

To his sister Norma, Clayton writes: *I got to give some shots to some patients today. It helped to watch you give yourself shots so often.*

Clayton assists in the OR and does not pass out!

A badly burned girl enters the hospital today. Dr. Kraun must give her a skin graft to help her survive. Clayton is needed to hand him the appropriate surgical tools at his prompting. Clayton gets nauseous and light-headed from the skin removal and seeing blood everywhere. He tells the doctor that he needs to leave. The doctor emphatically tells him, "No, you can't go!" Clayton, nevertheless, drops the medical tools on the table and beelines out of the room before he faints.

Clayton gets a drink of water after lying down for a while. Afterward, the doctor, surprisingly, does not reprimand Clayton for his disobedience. Instead, he compassionately tells Clayton that he needs to "get over seeing blood."

Dr. Kraun and Clayton are together 24/7. They eat together and even sleep in the same room at the same time. Kraun's bed requires an extension so his legs don't dangle off the end. Clayton even interprets for him when the German doctors aren't available to translate French for him. In many ways, Clayton is Kraun's seeing (or hearing) eye dog, assisting his every move.

Waiting for Kraun to tend to a needy patient, Clayton watches the life go out of a patient he is holding in his arms. Clayton lays him on the bed and stares at him for a long moment. Alive one moment. Gone the next.

The girl with the skin graft dies today …

> Margin notes to the editor: *These deaths have got to be affecting Clayton. What do you think he's feeling? Is he seeing the preciousness of life with gratitude, or is he feeling more pressure to hurry up and decide what he's going to do with the rest of his life?*

Dan joins Clayton at the hospital.

Today, they hear gunshots not far off. Several minutes later, an ambulance unloads nine wounded soldiers for the hospital's care.

Dr. Kraun quickly assesses each case and determines that two of the nine require immediate intervention. Clayton is holding up one of them. He is a French soldier, and his guts are literally falling out of him.

The doctor decides an Algerian (of less importance to the French-run hospital) must be attended to first if he is to survive.

Clayton asks, speaking about the guy with his guts hanging out, "What should I do here?"

Kraun, on his way to the ER, says, "Shove it back in." Then, over his shoulder, he adds, "I'll need you in here."

Clayton watches the doctor and the Algerian patient disappear through the door. He looks at the terrified man in his arms, then down at the man's protruding intestines, then back to the injured man's face. "I'll be right back." He lays him down and leaves to help Kraun.

By the time Kraun comes back to the French soldier who needs abdominal surgery, the soldier is nearly gone. But, with Clayton's assistance, the doctor does his magic and gets him through the night.

> Beemer's margin notes: *Is Clayton getting this? Does he have any idea how much a risk the doctor just took to work on an inferior person from Algeria before a Frenchman? The doc may be thrown out of the country for his action. Yet, he chose to make an insignificant life matter as much as any French one. Will Clayton ever see this the way THE BOSS does? … that one*

race or people group isn't superior to another just because of their skin color, heritage, or belief system?

In a letter home, Clayton writes: *The soldiers were butchered like a cow.*

Clayton is shell-shocked and unaware of hospital protocol much of the time. Except for two exceptionally kind Algerian nurses, most of the staff are too busy or disinterested in Clayton's plight to recognize his bumbling ignorance in so many areas.

In Clayton's diary: *I'm so tired I can hardly write. Today, I got three letters from Ruth after no letters for three weeks. I miss her.*

August 29. Dr. Kraun's term here is up. He leaves. The hospital administration does not discuss Clayton's options with him. They detail him to the cleaning crew with Daniel. He now scrubs walls and mops floors all day. Unlike when he assisted Kraun, Clayton's new role is boring, unvalued, and deprived of people.

Unaware of (or disregarding) hospital protocol, Clayton decides to go to the *women's ward* to find a woman from Algiers that he and Dr. Kraun had treated. She knew of the Mennonite mission, and Clayton wants to encourage her.

Clayton gets a call from Vern (his new boss), who says that the hospital administration called him and are demanding that Clayton leave the hospital for good. Clayton has no idea why. Vern tells him that it is because he went into the women's ward without a doctor.

Vern picks Clayton and Dan up from Marengo Hospital on September 19 and takes them back to Algiers. Dan tells Clayton on the way back, "Well, at least we don't have to clean anymore of those dumb walls."

Clayton writes in his diary: *Last day at Morengo Hospital, and a long day it was too. I will leave with a lot of new and mixed feelings. I will never forget its experiences.*

I wonder why God didn't help me stay when I was trying to witness to that gal? Sometimes I feel all alone in my faith.

A two-week vacation comes at just the right time for the disheartened Clayton. He and Dan devise a plan to get to the European Pax Convention in Bienenberg, Germany, the following week. They plan to hitchhike and sleep in sleeping bags after sailing across the Mediterranean in the old sea bucket.

The first night, they get no takers on their stuck-out thumbs. They decide to call it a night and to sleep in a field. At 9:00 p.m., they decide it is too cold and the ground is too hard to sleep on. They walk to the nearest hotel where they pay for a room and sleep.

On this, the second day of their journey, the two hitchhikers again get no bites. They agree to change their tactics and to travel by train or rental car from now on.

Through parts of Switzerland, they travel through the Sonnenberg mountains and valleys. Clayton has heard that his ancestors have some connection to this area, but he is not interested enough to alter their travel plans and explore his roots.

The conference serves around fifty Pax men, many of whom Clayton remembers from his Holy Land trip that he took months earlier. Clayton soaks in the music, sermons, workshops, and fellowship.

To Ruth, Clayton writes: *It's like being in a big family here. I only wish you were here.*

On October 5, Clayton excitedly shares his experiences at the conference with all his associates back in Algiers. Meanwhile, the Mennonite Mission has changed its name (and function). It is now called Christian Committee for Services in Algeria (CCSA).

As CCSA personnel arrive, Clayton helps prepare office space.

Peter Dyck, the director of the Mennonite Central Committee (MCC), which is in charge of Pax, arrives. He explains that now that the war is over and France has pulled out, there is great need in Algeria. Pax, who Clayton answers to, will now fall in line with relief efforts through the World Council of Churches (WCC), which consists of various countries and churches. Their most pressing matter is to restore the forests, which were burned down to prevent the FNL from hiding and attacking French troops.

Dyck confides with the Pax men, "We Mennonites will be developing a demonstration farm. I can't wait to get started!"

The demonstration farm sits on sixty acres and boasts a huge house. The site is located near the city of Ain-Kercha.

Clayton's diary: *When five of us Pax men first arrived, we had to stay in the Social Center even though WCC owns the huge house in the middle of where the demonstration farm is to be. It was occupied by the local mayor and his family as a favor to him for his help in ending the war. As the senior Pax man, they asked me to tell the mayor he had to move so we could live in it. I didn't really enjoy the experience, but I did it. The mayor didn't want to leave and told me all the reasons why he needed to stay. I tried to be nice about it because I was told we would be needing his assistance and the support of his followers in the community (whom we're here to serve). It was tricky business.*

In the end, he left the house, and we moved in. I think he'll still work with us. I hope.

Clayton chooses a bottom bunk again. He tucks Ruth's picture safely above his bed.

Clayton and the crew begin to clean the rustic mansion on the farm. They work to get the electrical system and plumbing in working order. Clayton goes to local stores to buy furniture and necessities for incoming Paxers, who are arriving daily. The house will hold fifteen Pax men and six support staff (European Mennonites). It is nearly full already.

Clayton writes in his diary: *In my home church, I grew up trusting people named Amstutz, Gerber, Hofstetter, Zuercher, and Steiner. It was common knowledge that Mennonites from the neighboring liberal Salem Mennonite Church with names like Sprunger and Wyss were off target. I therefore find Mennonite names like Dyck, Ginter, Bontrager, Swartzentruber, Schumacher, Friesian, Bartel and others also suspect. But here they are working side by side doing the same thing I am. I'm here to serve the Lord. I wonder if they are too?*

> Beemer notes: *Finally, Clayton sees that his narrow view of how THE BOSS works is not the only view. Will he ever shake the* us *and* them *thinking in his Christian faith?*

When the relief wagon comes around, Clayton helps hand out powdered milk, MCC blankets, and clothes for the adults. Many of the locals are hungry and out of work. Clayton runs out of supplies and tells those still in line that he is sorry. Clayton watches the dejected stragglers disperse.

> Beemer to the editor: *What is Clayton feeling? Surely, the obvious need, the joy of giving, and the frustration of running out of life-sustaining supplies have stirred something in him! But will it change him?*

In a letter home, Clayton writes: *In Algeria right now they say that 5,000,000 people are hungry, which is half the population. This spring and winter, the World Council of Churches hopes to give out 46,000 tons of wheat, 19,500 tons of powdered milk, 2,000 tons of cooking oil, 1,500 tons of sugar, and 486 tons of soap to Algeria. Along with this, they want to give out 650,000 blankets and*

1,300 tons of clothing. Reforestation is another project. 21,000,000 trees are to be planted in our area, planted by Algerians themselves. MCC will be responsible for the welfare of 7,000 people living within five miles of the farm.

Clayton folds up the brochure he is copying this information from and prepares his letter for mailing.

November 11. One of the Pax men, Ervin, has yellow jaundice and is sent back to Algiers.

Gene now has yellow jaundice. He is isolated from the other staff in a room. Because Clayton has had yellow jaundice already, he is Gene's roommate. They talk to pass the boredom that Gene is experiencing.

The most talked-about topic is their girlfriends. Both girlfriends attend Goshen College and both young men left for Pax promising to stay true to their love. Gene's girlfriend, however, recently broke off the relationship with a Dear John letter. Gene is crestfallen. He wants to go back home to rectify the situation but is obligated to fulfill his Pax tour.

This is the third Pax man that Clayton has talked to about receiving a Dear John letter.

> Notes from Beemer: *I'm only guessing, but this knowledge has got to scare the wits out of Clayton. Is it any wonder that he writes Ruth so often and journals about her in his diary? He's afraid she will do the same thing, which will leave him even more directionless. I wish she'd just get it over with already and dump him, so he can start concentrating on why he's on this mission—to serve the Algerian people.*

The MCC Christmas bundles arrive! Each bundle contains a toothbrush, toothpaste, a notebook, pencils, soap, a washcloth, underwear, a shirt, and pants, all wrapped in a towel marked boy or girl, or male or female. Mennonites from all over North America paid for and prepared each bundle.

Clayton and Gene help hand out the Christmas bundles and blankets. When the bundles arrive, the village congregates in one spot and gets unruly, pushing, and demanding. Fortunately, the mayor is there and disperses the crowd. He organizes a method where only three at a time receive the bundles.

A letter home from Clayton: *I found 3 bundles from Kidron Mennonite. I got to help distribute them. We ended up handing out 12,000 blankets worth $10,000. Give my thanks to the Church.*

Two tractors arrive—one for the fields and one to till the garden. Clayton and the project leader, Al, ordered them a few weeks prior to their arrival. The villagers and the staff gawk and ogle!

In Algiers, Clayton picks up a brand-new Peugeot 403 pickup truck to take back and use on the farm. It's over a five-hour drive, so he knows he must hurry if he is to get back before dark. About an hour before the farm, Clayton is going too fast to negotiate a curve and rolls the new truck over the embankment into a field. Clayton maneuvers his way out of the upside-down cab and sees that the roof above the driver's side is severely crumpled. He feels a small scratch on his forehead. How did he escape with nothing more?

Clayton walks to the nearest town and tells the police department what happened, adding, "The road must have been slanted the wrong way." They understand his broken French but can offer him only a cold, hard floor to spend the night on because there is no phone at the farm to call.

> Beemer's margin notes: *Clayton's lucky he didn't get killed. Do you think he's thinking about his brother Lee's similar accident where someone was killed? He must be feeling lots of strange emotions lying all alone on the police station floor.*

The police awake Clayton at 6:00 a.m., and Clayton takes a taxi to the farm.

Right away, he finds Al, the project manager, and tells him what happened. Al says, "But we need that pickup for the farm."

Clayton takes in a deep breath, exhales, and looks down.

Al continues, "We wondered what happened to you. I'm glad you're alright."

In his diary, Clayton writes: *Sunday, January 6, 1961 ... Didn't feel like much. Kept thinking about the accident two days ago.*

Monday—Clayton and Al get the pickup towed to a garage in Constantine. The repairs will cost $1,200.00 and take three months.

Clayton's diary: *This was a bad day. Al called me into the office to tell me we couldn't afford to fix the pickup. I cried like a baby. I ruined a brand-new truck for nothing!*

> Notes to the editor: *Am I hearing Homer's voice condemning Clayton here? What makes him not want to give up?*

Clayton writes his folks: *...One of the buildings I helped build with the home-made bricks I made will be an auto shop. Turns out taking apart the '38 Dodge behind the toolshed paid off. I'm going to teach auto mechanics. I think it's more because I know more French than the others than it's about knowing about cars.*

I have five different engines that we will be working on plus rear ends, transmissions, generators, starters, and what-not. I also got some tactical instruments for measuring. I'll probably learn more than they will.

The work of the farm is divided into different areas. Some Pax men work on improving livestock because the local livestock leaves much to be desired. Many cows raised for milk produce only enough milk for their own offspring. The farm, therefore, brings in heifers from other countries and makes them available to local farmers in exchange for giving offspring to neighboring farmers. Another way to help the farmers is to breed the local cows with bulls from abroad. This helps build up the quality of the cows in the local community and thereby supply milk for their families. Other Pax missionaries hatch and raise top-grade chickens that are made available to the community, thus upgrading the health of the community with protein from eggs and chicken meat.

A letter to Ruth: *Ruth, I just found out my term will be over May 1! I'll be home with you in a few short months!!*

At supper, Clayton sneakily pours water over the edge of the table on the unsuspecting thirty-year-old Liz's lap; she is an elder Pax employee. The few laughs he receives from this prank are short-lived. Liz stands, rubs at the water, walks around the table, and yanks the chair out from under Clayton. Clayton falls to the floor like a sack of potatoes. The ensuing laughs are loud and widespread. Clayton smiles, but his red face betrays his enjoyment.

In a letter to Ruth: *I'm on my third roommate here. The Pax guys come and go. I can't wait till I get to "go" and be with you.*

I clean my room, do my own laundry, and even help the gals with the meals sometimes. In the evenings, the twenty of us enjoy eating together and goofing off. We joke around all the time. My favorite thing to do is play Rook.

Then we wake up and do our jobs as unto the Lord.

Miss you, Clayton

February 1. Clayton's long-anticipated first day of teaching auto mechanics is a flop. No students show. Clayton talks to the mayor about recruiting students for his class.

Four students attend Clayton's class. He uses three-by-five-inch note-cards to spell the names of the parts he cannot pronounce in French. Communicating his limited knowledge is a chore. He uses an abundance of layman's sign language, like shrugging the shoulders.

To Ruth, Clayton writes: *This weekend we hiked up the small mountains just south of us. The view of our farm at the top is gorgeous. It would be romantic if you were here to join me...*

A new set of shop classes begins today, March 4. Eighteen guys show up! Some struggle with loosening a nut. Some take a whole engine apart with ease.

March 7. Because the demand is so great, Clayton begins a night class. Seven more locals show up.

Clayton receives a letter from Ruth: *I received the cuckoo clock you sent from Germany on March 11. Thank you so much! It's perfect! Someday, we'll hang it on our wall.*

Clayton writes in his diary on March 19: *Had four classes today. I am beginning to enjoy them.*

April 1, to Ruth: *HAPPY SECOND ANNIVERSARY, HONEY DEAR!*

A letter to Ruth: *A few of us Paxers took several days off to go to the Sahara Desert. What an eye-opener to see the desert towns of Biskra and El-Qued. How does anyone survive in such a hot and dry place? Between those two towns we saw beautiful clean sand dunes. We had to be really careful to stay on the roads because the sand drifts often cover them. If we were to drive off the road into the sand, we would have easily gotten stuck, which would have been awful in a desert!*

Every once in a while, we would see an oasis. A welcome sight for us thirsty travelers. I can't help thinking how my dry and thirsty soul will soon find my oasis when I see you soon!

I love you more than the ocean, Clayton

May 1 finally arrives. Clayton says his goodbyes and finds his way back to Algiers. He says to Dan, "I can't believe it's been two years. I wonder if my family even remembers me or cares what I've been doing."

In the two years since Clayton has left the States, air travel has become more common. He flies from Luxembourg to New York, avoiding traveling the Atlantic by ship again.

Clayton's brother Lee and his young family of six children greet Clayton at the airport.

Clayton says, knowing Lee has taken over the family farm, "I can't believe I'm home. Thank you for taking time off and coming all this way to pick me up. I know gas isn't cheap."

Lee says, "We wanted to be the first to see you."

"Well, it's good to see you." Clayton wipes his tear-filled eyes and looks away. "Excusez-moi. I've got to use a toilet that flushes." He heads for the restroom, knowing at least some of his family still care about him.

12

THE CORNUCOPIA
OF EXPERIENCES

A couple of years had passed since the editor in chief had visited his apprentice chronicler, Beemer. The busy manager figured it was probably time for another visit at this pivotal time as Clayton transitioned from Algerian missionary back to home life in the States.

All in all, Beemer had done a great job describing Clayton's diverse encounters abroad, despite the unimaginative chronological format he used and recording every incidental event. The chief sensed, however, that Beemer was unsettled and possibly on edge regarding his upcoming progression from outside reporter to intimate soul-buddy.

He transported down to Clayton's room in his parents' new house some one hundred yards from the old house, which was now occupied by Lee's family.

The editor observed Beemer concentrating on his writing as Clayton slept.

"What are you thinking about, Beemer?"

Beemer turned his head at the sudden emergence of his supervisor. He sat in stunned silence for a long moment, not knowing whether to be alarmed or relieved. He settled on nonchalant paranoia. "Hi, Chief. I didn't expect you."

"Well, that wouldn't be any fun, now, would it? Coming only when you expect me. Unpredictability is in my job description. Sorry. You'll have to get used to it. I've found chroniclers write best when they're on their toes."

Beemer stirred in his chair.

"No, sit. That was just a figure of speech. You don't need to salute me. I just thought you could use some cheering up."

"Cheering up? I'm not sad."

"No? So, you're enjoying the frustrations of not understanding your subject, are you?"

Beemer's return stare at the master chronicler's knowing inquiry lasted only a second.

Chief nodded. "I thought so. You've amassed quite the collection of questions from Algeria. Are you ready to learn and grow?"

They both looked over at Clayton sleeping.

Beemer nodded, his cocky demeanor melting away. "Yeah. He's got me baffled in some ways, I've got to admit."

The busy editor called Beemer's reluctance. "Such as?"

"Well, for starters, I don't get his fascination with this Ruth. He's thousands of miles away on the adventure of a lifetime, and he can't stop thinking about the girl."

"And how do you know he can't stop thinking about her?"

Beemer hesitated. "Well … because he wrote about her in his diary more than anything or anyone else. And he wrote her a zillion letters. And every night, he looked at that picture of her before he nodded off to sleep … "

The chief smiled.

"And you should have seen him when he got her letters," Beemer went on. "You would have thought it was his first Christmas every time."

"So, you know what he's feeling now too?"

Beemer scrutinized his mentor's strange retort. *Was he sarcastically doubting him or playfully complimenting him?* "On this thing, yeah. His joy was uncontainable."

"And his enthrallment with this gal concerns you, why?"

"He could have been the next William Clark of the famous Lewis and Clark on this Algerian expedition, and he completely blew it, preoccupied with his hometown sweetheart."

The chief let fly an uncensored laugh.

Incensed at missing the joke, Beemer sat in baffled silence.

After the editor in chief composed himself, he said, "Beemer, you've got a way to go. Your writing has improved, but the child in you still wants the recognition of a successful subject, as if it is your responsibility. I remind you—it is not! THE BOSS defines a subject's success in their unique *being*, not their acclaimed *doing*. Your job is to show his fascinating journey, not guide his path like an expedition."

Reproved yet again, Beemer humbly said nothing.

"Romantic love is something THE BOSS invented, not humans. Why do you insist that Clayton's desire for Ruth is of his own making and not THE BOSS's gift to him?"

"Well, because it seems like he's worshipping this girl instead of THE BOSS."

"Love is not selfish. Clayton can love Ruth *and* THE BOSS, you know."

"Yes, but Clayton tends to focus his attention on one thing to the exclusion of the other. I'm not convinced he can think clearly about anything else when his mind is on the girl."

The editor's big belly jiggled as he chuckled. "You say that as if it's a curse. THE BOSS has designed these humans to crave such romance. Even if it makes them silly, they need this starry-eyed love."

Beemer shook his bewildered head. "Whatever. I guess I just don't understand human love then."

The chief smirked. "Don't feel bad. Even humans don't understand it. This kind of love isn't supposed to be understood so much as experienced."

Beemer's head wagged, stupefied all the more.

"Which brings us to the final lesson of the *Threeseez*—*Experience*. You've learned the importance of the human's peculiar wiring of their *emotions* and the *environment* they grew up in. But, sometimes, to corral unruly emotions and overcome unhealthy training received as children, humans must turn to *experience*."

Beemer nodded, unsure.

"Now, as you've noted in your ubiquitous margin notes, Clayton was exposed to many new emotions and placed in a foreign environment while in Algeria. But his only way of processing this new adventure was through the emotions and environment he grew up with."

Beemer's expressionless nod gave him away.

"Okay. This will all make sense to you later. I'll make it simple. Clayton will only reach the potential THE BOSS made him for through his experiences."

"So, Clayton will only be as great as his experiences?"

"No!"

Beemer jumped at the rebuff.

"The experiences don't make the man. It's his response to the experiences that mold him into the being he's meant to be."

"And what were his responses to his experiences in Algeria?" asked Beemer.

Chief pursed his lips. "That's the question, isn't it? That's what a good chronicler could answer."

Beemer cleared his suddenly parched throat. "Yes, well ah ... one would think these experiences have affected him profoundly."

"How daringly noncommittal of you, Beemer." The chief's eyes rolled. "Just as you assumed Clayton could only love Ruth *or* God, so humans often tend toward a binary system that says all choices must be right or wrong, whereby demonizing any view they don't hold to be true. Though this works well in some environments where all agree, it wreaks havoc when opinions differ. For whatever reason, humans gravitate to the simpler task of categorizing things as black or white instead of through the often-messy grayscale or, what I like to call, *the rainbowed cornucopia* that life frequently nestles in.

"Did the environment Clayton grew up in, heavy on the pronouncement of right and wrong, lead him to fall into the binary trap in Algeria? Did he display prejudice?"

Beemer thought. "Now that you mention it, he did automatically judge smoking and drinking as wrong."

Chief nodded. "Such actions didn't fit his environmental views. He was forced to either judge the people doing the wrong behavior as bad or consider that maybe his environmental values were wrong."

"That makes a lot of sense now. Clayton was having to process a lot of uncharted experiences through the lens of the only environment that he previously knew—his home upbringing."

"And what other possible skewed views might Clayton be wrestling with?"

Beemer rubbed his chin. "Well, because he thinks he has a firm grasp of right and wrong and THE BOSS's plan for humankind, he tends to look down on anyone not following that plan—like the Algerian people, in general, and Muslims in particular."

"So, how did Clayton treat them, then?"

"Well, he didn't become good friends with any of them, that's for sure. And he tried his hand at evangelism only once. For most of his time in Algeria, he seemed more concerned with looking the part of a Christian role model than authentically living the part." Beemer's head wagged. "Very disappointing."

"Just who's doing the judging here? Clayton of the Algerians or you of Clayton?"

Beemer's eyebrows furrowed. His mouth hinged open.

Chief said, "You're being too hard on the boy. He's learning. Remember, he's an emotional being. When his heartstrings are plucked, it reverberates throughout his whole body. It's hard for a human to concentrate on anything else when their whole being is doing a concerto in the key of *Love Major*. What do you think it did to Clayton when he heard of three different Paxers getting Dear John letters?"

Beemer closed his eyes and shook his head. "It made him worry to death that Ruth might do the same thing to him. Which devoured all his focus away from THE BOSS."

"Yes, but you see, the thought of losing Ruth gripped him emotionally. He couldn't free himself from that any more than he could stop growing the hair on his head. THE BOSS made his emotions this way. He's got to go through these experiences if he's to learn, mature, and navigate his emotions."

"But at the expense of hearing and following THE BOSS?"

The old chronicling mentor sighed and scratched his bald head. "Did you not say that Clayton has been seeking THE BOSS's direction?"

Beemer harrumphed. "Yeah, but he's obviously not finding it. He wants THE BOSS to answer all his prayers like a magic genie. I'm not so sure he's asking for THE BOSS's direction so much as he's trying to direct THE BOSS's action. I think he thinks that he deserves to be given direction because he was serving THE BOSS as a missionary."

"And is THE BOSS responding?"

Beemer's bleary eyes dropped to half-mast. "How should I know? It sure appears like the prayer pipeline is clogged. Clayton keeps coming away from his personal prayer time like a beaten puppy. I think, after pleading with THE BOSS, he thinks his requests are unimportant and himself not worth answering. That's an eerily similar reaction he displayed in his relationship with his earthly father not so long ago, come to think of it. Clayton must not be praying right or something," Beemer surmised.

"You think THE BOSS should embody a formula that if Clayton follows just *right*, THE BOSS will respond. I'm telling you that THE BOSS does not follow our rules. THE BOSS's plan is more extraordinary than we can fathom. Trust THE BOSS!"

"So, what, is Clayton just supposed to go around blindly until THE BOSS inexplicably decides to reveal the plan?"

"I'm saying he doesn't need to explicitly know THE BOSS's plan. He just needs to know THE BOSS's character and learn to know that voice."

Beemer furrowed his brows. "How is Clayton going to hear voices all of a sudden that he couldn't hear before?"

"Oh, he's heard. He's just not attuned to listening."

Beemer looked at his master like he'd grown an extra head.

The mentoring chronicler went on, "You assume Clayton's pipeline to THE BOSS is vertical. What if THE BOSS flows as much (or more) through horizontal pipelines?"

Beemer rubbed his chin. "You mean, maybe THE BOSS is not up in heaven?"

"I mean, maybe THE BOSS speaks through nature and the other fascinating people on earth."

"Like the missionaries, priests, teachers, and pastors?"

The bushy-browed editor nodded. "Like pastors, prostitutes, Muslims, and atheists."

Beemer lowered his chin, keeping his eyes trained on his hero chronicler who may have just misspoken or finally passed into dementia. The term blasphemy came to his mind, but he dared not say it. Instead, he weakly sputtered, "What? Why would THE BOSS be shamed like that?"

"There is no shame in any of THE BOSS's creation! They are all incredible wonders."

"But prostitutes? Atheists? Next thing you'll say is that THE BOSS speaks through criminals and murderers."

"THE BOSS could! And does."

"What?"

"Look, you're making the human mistake of equating a person's bad actions with bad worth. No matter how bad a human acts or how poor, handicapped, or marginalized a person is, he or she is still of great value to THE BOSS and worthy of love and pride. THE BOSS delights in using them to speak to others. Take those Algerian refugees Clayton handed out food and bundles to, for instance. They were about the lowest rung on the human social ladder. I'm sure Clayton felt superior to them in about every way. Then, when he ran out of food, do you not think that the look in their eyes of utter disappointment and despair spoke to Clayton?"

"Well, I hope it did. I wasn't sure, to be honest."

"Trust me, an experience like that changed him. Seeing their great need and hopelessness spoke to his soul. No doubt about it. The pious confidence that religion offers does not speak to the heart like seeing a fellow traveler desperate in need and grateful for the help. Now, what Clayton does with that is another matter."

"Hmm. So, an experience can change a person without showing any obvious outward signs?"

"That's right. And it can even change a person without them knowing it right away."

"That's pretty cool. I'll have to look for that."

"Let me ask you this, Beemer, do you think Clayton still sees the Algerian people as wrong, inferior, and insignificant?"

"Well, you know, though he first bought into the bill of goods the non-Mennonite missionary leaders sold him that the Algerians were rebellious idiots, I think, by the end, he saw the error in the French thinking that they had some God-given right to rule Algeria. I think maybe (I hope) that stint in the hospital with Dr. Kraun showed him just how valuable all lives are, not just those that supposedly are on the right side of thinking and believing."

"Why do you think he bought into believing what the French and those missionaries sold instead of buying into the Algerian's great need for independence? I mean, you stated it well; ultimately, THE BOSS is always for the oppressed, not the oppressor, after all."

Beemer thought about that for a moment. "It must stem from Clayton's understanding of authority through his Mennonite heritage. Clayton learned as a teenager that his church, Kidron Mennonite, regarded the local Salem Mennonite Church as disobedient because it split off from the initial Sonnenberg Mennonite Church in the 1870s. Kidron humbly boasted of following God's laws *to the T* and cited scriptural texts as the basis for their heavy emphasis on obedience. Ironically, however, Kidron had also splintered off from the mother Sonnenberg church (in the 1930s), choosing a more liberal approach. Though, in the world's view, all three churches were considered conservative for their staunch adherence to scripture, they applied their strict obedience differently from one another ... which, in the final analysis, came down more to dress, other worldly issues, and teaching styles than objective scriptural laws. Evidently, their hypocrisy never weakened their creed to obey authority.

"Basically, Clayton's earlier environment taught the importance of *always* obeying authority to the extent that disagreeing with authority was always wrong. So, he probably figured if the French (who were in authority in Algeria when he arrived) and the Christian missionaries in charge of the Algerians' spiritual well-being said the Algerians were peons, it must be so."

Chief agreed. "Yes, what a dangerous undertow that duality construct—that authority is always right—is! Obeying trusted authority is a valuable tenet to adhere to, but, oh, the dire consequences when that authority misses the mark. What an excruciating lesson to learn! Do you think Clayton learned it?"

"Well, maybe. But maybe ... probably, he'll learn it even better when he experiences something like it again."

"Touché! That's how it works—learning from experiences."

"So, it sounds like THE BOSS uses experiences and people more than interpersonal prayer," said Beemer.

"Sometimes. But don't limit THE BOSS. Prayer is by no means off-limits. THE BOSS uses whatever is best for the subject. Let THE BOSS be THE BOSS. You just observe and record."

"So, since THE BOSS is the ultimate authority, earthly authority must be kind of unnecessary. Is that right?"

"Oh, no. Earthly authority is necessary. Essential even. But THE BOSS can just as easily speak through the lowly. Keep an ear out for THE BOSS speaking to Clayton through his horizontal human peers (expert or amateur), even if he's not listening just yet."

PHOTO COLLECTION
PART 1: 1932–1963

Bertha (Zuercher) and Homer Steiner in 1932 as the parents of six of their eventual twelve children.

The 1952 Steiner homestead in Kidron, Ohio, where Clayton grew up and where Beemer searched to find his first biographical subject.

Sonnenberg School #10, the one-room school attended by Homer and all his children. When Clayton was in first grade, five of his siblings also went to school here, making up nearly a fourth of the total number of pupils.

The Homer and Bertha Steiner family in 1944 at their homestead in their Sunday best. Clayton is the youngest in front center. His parents are in the back row.

Ken, Clayton, and Roy on their way to school. As nobody else among them had their own bikes, sometimes the Steiner siblings would ride four to a bike. Clayton is on his bike that was later stolen.

Clayton in his bedroom at the desk where he surrendered his life to Christ as a junior in high school.

*The photo of Ruth that Clayton kept
above his bed while he was in Algeria.*

*The Mennonite Pax family in Algeria in 1963. This humanitarian alternate
service met the government's military draft requirements as Clayton was
a conscientious objector to war. Clayton is in the center of the back row.*

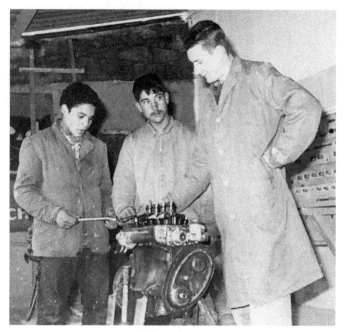

Clayton teaching auto mechanics to young Algerians during his time with Pax. He wasn't sure how to say vroom *in French.*

Clayton showing Algerian picture slides to Homer after returning to Kidron.

PART 2
GROWING

13

BECOMING ADULT

MARRIAGE AND THE NEXT STEP

Beemer thought a lot about the editor in chief's advice. If what he said was true, and Beemer had no doubt it was, then THE BOSS was likely speaking to Clayton regularly through people and situations, horizontally, and not just vertically through prayer, scripture, or a spiritually-sensed pipeline. But Clayton, ill-trained and too immature to recognize THE BOSS's voice, probably didn't have the ears to hear it yet.

How could Beemer write Clayton's full story when he didn't know THE BOSS's nudges any more than Clayton did?

To add to his worries, the first objective goal of any aspiring chronicler is to become a Full-Fledged Chronicler (FFC) by "exemplifying literary mastery of the subject," as the Chronicler's Manual reads. But Beemer was getting bogged down trying to remember everything from Clayton's past to clarify his present story. He could only manage so much. Maybe he was fooling himself. Maybe he wasn't cut out to be a chronicler. *I wonder how Chief kept it all straight when he wrote all of his famous biographic books.*

After his two-year hiatus in Algeria, when Clayton arrives at his parents' new little house on the farm on May 3, 1963, at 8:30 p.m., the first thing he does is call Ruth, who is home on a Friday night for the weekend from Goshen College. She drives over right away.

After some pleasantries with Homer, Bertha, and Dorothy, Clayton and Ruth politely excuse themselves. Finally, the estranged couple is reunited, alone!

They hold hands; they smile; they kiss; they laugh; they talk; they interrupt; they apologize for interrupting; they hug; and they talk some more … The evening is charmed, interwoven with the familiar and the new, overflowing with promise and hope.

At this point, Beemer wondered, *Did I just romanticize this romantic scene? Maybe the only reason their reunion appears successful is because they've been apart for two years and have longed for this meeting every day of their separation. Maybe they're in love with the romance and not with each other. Who am I to discern their romance?*

Beemer's exuberant trust in his writing prowess dropped off the map. And he didn't know why. His writing seemed directionless, hindered for some reason.

Clayton talks sweet to his mom, but he doesn't share himself in a vulnerable way like he naturally did as a youngster. His demeanor is now guarded. He does, however, still greedily chow down on her fried mush.

Homer asks him questions about Algeria. Clayton answers "yes" or "no," avoiding any lengthy conversations. No longer required to work his father's farm, Clayton acts more like a boarder than a son.

After a hard day's work for Clarence Sommer, Clayton is content to stay in his room after a silent supper. He writes a letter to Ruth, who is in Goshen for her junior year of college. Perhaps the only thing still familiar to Clayton since Algeria is this separation from Ruth.

May 10. Clayton finds his way to Goshen College to be with his main squeeze for the popular *College Spring Fest*. The hectic festivities and ever-present friends and family give the young couple little time to themselves. They make the most of their time, bonding in unfamiliar ways, like introductions and reminiscing Ruth's past with her parents.

Hearing Ruth introduce Clayton to her friends as *her boyfriend* sounds foreign to Clayton, though he automatically smiles. When Ruth and her parents speak of how the *Spring Fest* reminds them of the state fair they once went to, Clayton asks questions like a curious outsider.

Sunday evening, before Clayton and Ruth's parents must travel back to Kidron, Ruth finds a quiet moment alone with Clayton. "So, are you ready to tell the world about us?"

The broad smile on Clayton's face tells her all she needs to know. But he quickly adds, "For sure!"

"I was thinking June 7th would be a good day to have an engagement party. What do you think?"

"That's my birthday."

Ruth giggles. "I know."

"It's a date!" They hug, full of expectation.

June 3rd arrives, and Clayton finds himself at Lester and Grace Geiser's living room. "Ah, I would like to ask for your permission to marry Ruth."

Grace looks at Lester. Lester looks at Grace. They look at the nervous young man in front of them. They smile.

After some questions, clearing of throats, and timid answers, there's an awkward hug and a handshake. Clayton passes the test.

On June 5th, Ruth relays the comment back to Clayton: "They told me they didn't know 'who they'd rather give me to.'" With a grateful tear in her eye, she adds, "You're part of my family now, Clayt."

They embrace. Ruth says, "I'm needing this lovin' so much! Two years was a long time!"

The formal announcement of the June 7 engagement get-together in Clayton's parent's basement reads, "Each for the other, both for the Lord. Time and space may do their best to keep some hearts apart, but God kept the faith and we replied—Unite our souls, ourselves, and our hearts." Parents and local siblings attend. Clayton gives his bride-to-be a watch as a token of his timeless love.

On June 13, Clayton drives Ruth to Ocean City, New Jersey, to work for Sharp's Restaurant as a hostess for her second summer. He sticks around for a few days as she settles in.

Before Clayton leaves this morning, Clayton sneaks into Ruth's room to give her a tender *good morning* kiss, a repeat performance of her awakening in Eureka, Illinois, before he had left for Algeria. "This is the best ever," she whispers into his ear as they hug.

Clayton, in his solitary room, writes to Ruth: *Life without you is boring. Work is fine, but time just seems to drag on. I sure wish we could be together.*

I'm glad I don't have to work the farm anymore. I paid Dad back for the travel money he sent me in Algeria already and I'm paying him rent. But it still feels like he thinks I owe him something. I will look forward to getting out of here so I don't have to hear his awful devotions and all the bad things he says about everybody ... especially Mom.

Sure am hoping to get into Goshen this fall. That rejection letter I got from them really got me. I won't lie. Sometimes I wonder if I should go to remedial school this summer like they told me I should, since my high school grades weren't good enough and I don't catch onto things real quick like most people. But I've got to work to get some money to my name. I hope my appeal letter and your mom's good words will change their minds. She sounds confident. We'll see. I can't see living at home here much longer. Though Mom is as comforting as can be.

Love, Clayton

In another letter to Ruth: *I sure am loving all your letters. I'd be a mess without them.*

Guess what? I just got my acceptance letter from Goshen College! The admittance officer, Mr. Shenk (who has family in Kidron), said that your mom's letter of endorsement and some other person's letter convinced him to admit me. My Pax time must've paid off! I'll have to be on parole, however, which means I can't drop below a certain GPA. That's kind of scary, since I've never gotten too good a grades before. I hope I'm doing the right thing ...

Clayton receives a letter from Ruth: *...That's great news! I've always known you're worthy of college. You can do it! You just have to stay determined. I'll help you know the ropes...*

A letter to Ruth: *It's lonely without you. I can't believe I'm having to be without you again. It's just like being in Algeria...*

Ruth finally returns to Kidron on August 26. Clayton greets her with a big sappy smile, as if he'd been on a deserted island for a few months. She returns the exuberance, though early in the evening, she says, "I wish this night would never end, but I'm exhausted. I've got to get to sleep since I've got to leave for Goshen first thing tomorrow."

Clayton sighs. "Oh, yeah. You're starting your student teaching at Riverdale, aren't you? I'll be a shrimpy freshman, and you're already starting your profession."

"I'll be learning my job, and you'll be learning yours. That's the way we should look at it. We're both starting out. No one is dumb. We're just new to our field."

Classes start hot and heavy for Clayton on September 8, 1963. His homework is more than he ever had in high school. He *burns the candles at both ends*, as his mother used to say, to keep up with his studies.

At a dorm meeting, Clayton must turn down an opportunity to go on a weekend retreat because he lacks funds and time.

Clayton talks with other students in the dorm about classes, teachers, and the cafeteria food tonight instead of putting his nose in the book all night. He finally excuses himself to "get back to the books, so I won't be sent back home."

Clayton finds Ruth in the lounge of her female dorm, Kulp Hall. Like most evenings, Clayton studies, and Ruth grades her papers. They catch up on their days and hint about their future.

"I can't believe all the writing I have to do," Clayton says. "Especially in English. I have to write a few paragraphs a couple of times every week."

"Clayt, that's not that much."

"Yeah, but it gets graded. You wouldn't believe all the red marks I get on them. And the worst thing is that Rhoda grades them."

"Rhoda? Our friend, Rhoda from high school, is an assistant teacher this semester? Wasn't she kind of your girlfriend there for a while?"

Clayton reddens. "Well, not for very long. It's humiliating to have her read my stuff and mark the tar out of it."

"I can help you. Let me see one."

Clayton hands her his latest war-zoned paper. Ruth reads it. She nods. "It needs some work. For starters, don't start your sentences with 'And.' Professors hate that."

Clayton is reading faster and retaining more of what he studies now, thanks to some tips he learned from his roommate and classmates. Writing continues to be a chore, however.

Ruth helps him with his grammar this evening.

For breakfast, Clayton meets Ruth in the cafeteria, as usual. "How'd you sleep?" Ruth asks.

"Not great. I'm studying for finals."

"Now that's one thing I don't have to worry about. But I remember when I did. You need to get your rest, Clayt. And trust yourself. You have been very diligent. It will pay off. You'll see."

"I hope so."

Clayton tries to retire early on the eve of his first final. Unfortunately, the dorm is wide awake. He hears a debate in the hall.

"They still don't know who did it?"

"Now, they're saying it may have been a conspiracy."

"What, the Republicans did it?"

"I heard some of the Democrats might have done it."

"No way! It was just one nutjob that did the whole thing. You guys are buying into sensationalism."

Clayton does his best to ignore the chatter but does not sleep soundly.

Beemer read over what he had just written, questioning the inclusion of such a trivial occurrence.

> He wrote in the side margin: *Chief, I'm not sure what's going on, but all of a sudden, I can't figure out what all of Clayton's life to include. How will I know if the parts I'm including will end up being relevant to him or not? If I don't include some small event and it turns out to be life-changing, this biography will be faulty. But if I include every little thing, I'll be so busy I'm sure to make the thing choppy ... or boring. Help!*

Up to his squatty neck in paperwork, the editor in chief got an alarm notice. He looked up past the reading glasses on his bulbous nose to the big Master Monitor on the wall in front of him. A flashing (and annoying beeping) Master Log coded RED across the screen.

The old chronicler frowned and furrowed his already wrinkled forehead. "What now?" When he saw where the alarm originated, he sighed and nodded, perhaps not surprised, but concerned. *Heaven's Chronicle* could not afford to lose a promising chronicler.

In answer to Beemer's emergency call, before Clayton awoke, Chief transported down to ease his young apprentice's escalating tension. "Don't trick yourself into thinking you're not up for the challenge, Beemer. You were made for this. That's why we picked you."

"But how do you know I'm ever going to get this? What if I end up being a big screwup?"

The old reporter eyed Beemer carefully. "We all have our bad days. Even us word jockeys. I once called a bassoon a baboon. I said, 'He played his baboon with eloquent ardor.' My editor asked if my baboon would someday be the orchestra conductor.

An involuntary chortle escaped Beemer's nostrils. "Did the bassoonist beat his chest when he was done?"

"That's funny. Your writing could use a little humor like that."

"I'm too busy trying to figure out why my biographic book is so scattered to write any humor. It's all I can do to make a cohesive story. I have no time to be playful or winsome. All my creative potential is under arrest."

"Let yourself go a little. Be the pen in the hand of THE BOSS."

Beemer considered that. "Maybe I'm not the man for this job. I'm floundering."

The wise teacher sighed. "If you were not our man, you'd pretend to be good at what you're doing and think THE BOSS is pleased with whatever you pen."

"I doubt THE BOSS is pleased with anything I'm writing these days."

"But THE BOSS is always pleased with you, regardless of your output."

"But how could that be?" asked Beemer.

"I don't know. It's just the way it is."

"Then, why am I even bothering with any of this if THE BOSS doesn't care?"

"Oh, THE BOSS cares. It matters what and how you write because you are writing about one of THE BOSS's prized children. Getting it right matters."

Beemer squinted. "And if I mess it up?"

"THE BOSS will still love you the same."

Beemer shook his head like an angry terrier. "That makes no sense. Then, how will this biographical book be made if I fail?"

Chief said, "Oh, THE BOSS will find a way. Trust me on that one. Most likely, I'd have to can you and either find another chronicler or write the rest myself. Not something I'd be terribly fond of, but I'd manage."

"Hmm ..." Beemer mused.

"But THE BOSS is a pretty good judge of character," said the editing expert.

"So, this isn't just *my* dream to write? THE BOSS actually thinks I can write good?"

"Well."

Beemer scrunched his face, waiting for more. "Well ... what?"

The editor rolled his eyes. "You can write *well*. THE BOSS thinks you can write well, not good. Come on, Beemer. Talk like a good chronicler even if you lack the confidence to be one."

"You really think so?"

The super frowned. "Think so, what?"

"You think I write well?"

Mouth pursed, tired eyes distracted, the editor in chief nonchalantly nodded.

Beemer beamed!

"That doesn't mean you can't fail or get your butt chewed occasionally," said the crusty *Heaven's Chronicle* manager.

Beemer's smile flattened. "So, my writing's still a bit drab?"

"Facts can be dry. One doesn't appreciate sand in a desert. It's the oasis or the concept of one that stirs the soul."

Beemer's smile resumed. "So, what? You're suggesting I dream up a mirage?"

"Of course not. What I mean is, you can't see the forest for the trees. It's time to back up and see the big picture. When a good chronicler approaches his subject's story skillfully, they can convey the tale from a distance as well as up close."

"Are you saying I can generalize?"

The editor paused for a long moment. "I'm saying a licensed chronicler can generalize when he sees fit, just as he can write topically, instead of only chronologically … when appropriate."

Beemer jerked his head to glare into his supervisor's eyes. "Wait. You said licensed." Beemer brightened like a Christmas light. "You mean? … " He waited for his mentor's completed lesson.

"Use words, Beemer. You're a chronicler!"

"Yes, sir … ah, Chief. Are you saying I'm now a Full-Fledged Chronicler?"

"That's what I'm saying," the chief said with no voice inflection. "Congratulations. Don't abuse the privilege."

Beemer jumped in the stale air and pumped his fist. "So, I can basically write anything I want now?"

"No," the stoic manager said. "I will still have the final say. If your product does not meet the muster, you're gone. With great privilege comes great responsibility. The rewards have increased, but so have the consequences should you depart from our teaching."

Beemer, wide-eyed, blinked several times, then swallowed as if to consume the dire message. "Okay."

The editor in chief's face never flinched. "Any questions?"

"Uh … So, I won't get in trouble if I don't tell the story exactly in order?"

The grizzled teacher closed his eyes before they customarily rolled in their sockets. "Don't think of it as telling the story out of order. Think of it as explaining the story through general truths. A wise chronicler will usually write chronologically; though for effective insights, he may choose to write topically at times to present the subject more fully."

"But what do I do with concepts that present themselves after I've written a story? Whatever I write goes directly to your Master Log, right? I can't get it back. I mean, in-the-moment reporting is all I was taught in training. I can't just rewrite the story with the different information, can I? That would be real rookie-ish."

"Rookie-ish? Only a rookie says that. Look, I'm not criticizing what you've been taught or your understanding. It was best that you be taught the chronological method in real time. A baby must crawl before she walks and drink milk before she eats meat. You've crawled through your training and drunk of your necessary experience. Now, it's time to spread your wings."

"Really?"

"Really. And you can close that gawking mug before one of these farm flies finds a new home."

Beemer snapped his jaw shut.

The wily editor explained, "As a Full Fledged Chronicler, you now have editing privileges. This means, like the chronicler for JFK, that you can tell your subject's story from multiple viewpoints. But it may take several edits before you grasp the true significance of all the circumstances and influences your subject evolved from."

"Who's JFK?"

"Oh, yeah, you were in Algeria when this all went down. John F. Kennedy was the president of the United States who got assassinated. They think they caught the guy, Lee Harvey Oswald, who shot him. But they never proved it because someone shot and killed him two days later. So, it's a big mystery. No one knows if he acted on his own or if one of the political camps hired him."

"Oh, yeah. Now I remember. Some guys in the dorm were trying to sort that out one night when Clayton was trying to sleep. Wow, wouldn't that have been the biography to write?"

"Famous people are no more valuable than unpopular people, you know, Beemer."

"A-hem. Of course ... I was just saying assassinations are rare."

"Sure, you were. My point is, a chronicler can use the bountiful dimensions of a subject in creative ways and from different angles like JFK's chronicler did.

"Your writing need not consist of objective facts from a single perspective. Instead of having frayed strands strewn over the pages, you can make a cohesive rope capable of holding many stories at once. Remember to utilize the *Threeseez*—Clayton's experiences, environment, and emotions—to build on the stories you're telling."

"But I don't know his emotions yet."

"Oh, yeah. You're not a soul-buddy yet. Well, keep observing. You'll get it one of these days. In the meantime, try writing about different aspects of Clayton's journey topically instead of through only in-the-moment reporting."

"So, what all does editing entail?" Beemer asked.

"Now you can add, change, erase, whatever you need to do to produce quality results. Nothing is etched in stone."

"Which means, I don't have to write about everything as it's happening?"

"Which means, you now can practice patience. You don't need to write down every action you see or thought in your head. Prudence is your new template. Take copious notes, study all responses and patterns, and tie as many experiences and emotions together as you can."

Beemer sighed and smiled contentedly. "Thanks, Chief."

"You earned it. But if you get a little complacent or think you've *arrived*, you can kiss this job goodbye. Diligence got you here, and diligence will keep you here. Got it?"

"Got it, Chief!" Beemer was all grin.

The chief turned to leave.

"Does this mean I won't see you anymore?" Beemer asked.

The *HC* manager turned back around. "Oh, no. You're not that good. You'll see me when you least expect me. I'll be reading *all* of your stuff now."

Beemer winced as subtly as a rookie FFC could.

After the editor in chief left, Beemer kept shaking his head, as if to shake all the reverberating marbles into some semblance of order. *Wow!* he thought, *now I can write whole chapters of Clayton's life after they've occurred, so I'll already know what's important about them. I feel so ... empowered.*

Holding off writing the play-by-play of Clayton's everyday theater did several things for Beemer. First, it calmed him. He no longer felt the stress of writing every minute detail down. It also afforded him the primary purpose of keen observation. He couldn't believe how vivid his understanding of Clayton's actions was now. Where once he had seen Clayton's studying efforts as part of normal college life, for instance, now he saw the fear-based diligence behind his fervor. Clayton was obviously fighting as if his life depended upon good grades. There was no plan B. And Beemer now understood that Clayton's meetings with Ruth nourished his dry soul and were not a mere childish need to be liked as he had previously supposed.

Beemer noted all the cafeteria meals Clayton and Ruth ate together, the numerous Saturdays they spent at the popular Goshen Dam, all the

Sundays they attended his brother Elno's church (Olive Mennonite) out in the country, and the occasional visit to his sister Arlene's church (Benton Mennonite) that her husband, Irvin, pastored. But he waited to write about each experience until they had been established as significant patterns toward Clayton's married-life journey.

Well after Clayton and Ruth got married, Beemer wrote the following of 1964, the winter before they were to marry:

For a time, Clayton and Ruth taught Sunday School at Olive Mennonite, allowing them the opportunity to experience teamwork—a necessary tool for marriage. They also found they enjoyed spending time with the seven (Arlene and Irvin) Nussbaum children, no doubt spurring their desire for an enriching family.

As spring of 1964 approached, they happened to pass a mobile home for sale. After looking over the trailer for several Sundays, they plopped down their twenty dollar deposit and soon borrowed the rest of the $1,200.00 needed for its purchase (which Clayton repaid later that fall).

On March 19 of Ruth's senior year, she signed a contract with West Goshen Elementary to be their first-grade teacher that fall. She would make $8,500.00 next year. The guaranteed wage was so beyond their recent earnings Clayton and Ruth rejoiced like they had won the sweepstakes.

On top of the rigors of college courses, Clayton and Ruth added another course to their busy lives. The college offered a non-credit, six-week marriage course for engaged couples. Their enthusiastic participation was highlighted by individual and couple sessions with the teacher, Harold Bauman. Because their marriage endeavor was such a serious venture, they were neither too prideful nor too naïve to seek advice and training. This attitude and action may be the strand that holds their marriage together someday.

Clayton landed a job making lids for hog feeders for the summer of 1964, between his junior and senior years, with Star Tank in Goshen. Elno, the company's part-time department foreman, went out of his way to get Clayton the job. Irvin worked with them as well. It seemed many of Clayton's role models were hardworking pastors.

In step with this camaraderie, Elno married Clayton and Ruth on July 11, 1964, and Irvin shared a short dedication.

Clayton and Ruth were hitched without a hitch. The only disappointing exception to their united bliss came two days after the wedding, when Ruth discovered she had lost her ring after washing in a public bathroom. She pleaded her sorriness to Clayton, who readily consoled her and bought her a new ring on July 17, the same day they opened a joint checking account.

Their transition into married life was remarkably seamless. On their first stop back from their three-day honeymoon from Kidron to Goshen, they dropped in on the Nussbaums. Arlene wisely shooed them off to spend more time by themselves. They modestly took her advice and walked to the nearest park and picked mulberries, which ended up being a story in itself.

While Clayton was at work the next day, Ruth took it upon herself to make a fresh pie out of the mulberries for her newlywed husband. The pie, however, flopped, and by the time Clayton got home, his new bride was in tears, again apologizing for disappointing him.

Clayton obviously was not nearly so concerned about the pie as she was. He held her and said it was no big deal. "There's plenty of time to make good pies in the future. I bet you Arlene would know what you did wrong."

So, Ruth called Arlene, sobbing about her failure. Before she got off the phone, she was laughing with Arlene at her silly round with the mulberry pie.

Clayton appeared to have adjusted to all facets of married life—the physical intimacy, the sharing of possessions and debt, the standing firm through a partner's weak moments, and working for his young family of two. This marriage matured him beyond his years.

> Beemer wrote in a margin note to the editor in chief and to his editor-self: *Don't worry, I'll change this last paragraph if Clayton doesn't turn out to be the thriving husband that he's starting out to be.*

14

EARLY RELIGIOUS YEARS
SORTING OUT OBEDIENCE AND TRUTH

With the pressure of writing chronologically eased, Beemer finally enjoyed his job. What could be better than writing for THE BOSS about one of THE BOSS's children?

Writing about a famous person who made a huge positive influence on the world like Chief did, he couldn't help thinking.

Clayton still might become that person, though the chances were dwindling, Beemer knew. To nevertheless prepare for that unlikely event, Beemer decided to write his first topical chapter about Clayton's "Early Religious Journey," making his best guesses at Clayton's emotions, knowing he could now go back and change it at any time. The freedom he felt was huge!

Beemer summarized Clayton's spiritual life to the present as best as he could.

In a word, Clayton was *faithful*. Early on, he followed his parents' lead, prayed, listened to devotions, went to church, and walked down the aisle at that big tent revival. He learned how to be a good Mennonite.

Then, at age seventeen, in his lonely room, he began to take his faith seriously, asking Jesus Christ to be his Lord and Savior. Disappointed at the lack of observed fruit in the moment, Clayton told Ruth years later, "I remember not feeling God's presence like I thought I should that night. I was disappointed, even angry, and worried that this big *trusting in God* thing was just a religious hoax." But things did change.

For the first time, for instance, he gave genuine effort toward his schoolwork. And, for the first time, he reaped good grades! But Clayton's faithfulness did not always reap immediate rewards. Sometimes, his commitment to remain faithful was difficult, confusing, and even painful.

> Margin notes: *Of course, I'm taking my liberties here since I don't know what he's feeling yet. But if need be, I'll go back and change things when I become a soul-buddy.*

For example, when Clayton chose the more challenging overseas mission option for his mandatory alternative military service, his life became complicated and dangerous.

Earlier, though the strict demands and demoralizing impact of his father's instruction frustrated him, Clayton never rebelled, at least not outwardly. And with obedience as the basis of his Christian commitment, Clayton dealt with apparent inconsistencies—or dare he admit, contradictions—in his faith. Perhaps the simplest teaching Clayton struggled with was Jesus's promise in the Bible that said, "Whoever asks, receives; whoever seeks, finds; and whoever knocks, the door is opened to him."

When Clayton naïvely, dutifully obeyed this truth in Hesston, he fully expected to *receive* answers to his prayers; *find* strength in God's presence; have the door of the future *open* to him. Instead, he didn't hear answers; he didn't feel God; he had no idea where he should be heading. The fruit of his obedience appeared barren. He later told Ruth he felt "totally demoralized."

To his credit, Clayton did not abandon ship when his stormy sea made visibility next to nil. He continued to go to church, pray, and read the Bible, and he ignored his emotional angst of not feeling THE BOSS's presence, his distaste for his dad's spiritual devotions, and not experiencing a sense of direction from On High.

Margin notes: *Again, I'll correct this entry if I'm wrong about any of it.*

One of the most confounding elements in Clayton's religious outlook was the peace, love, and fruit he saw in others outside his close-knit circles. He could not understand how Mennonites with names associated with the wrong kind of Mennonites could serve the Lord in Voluntary Service (VS) with every bit the same fervor and joy as he did, if not more. He couldn't understand how Muslims could be so devout to their God that they publicly prayed faithfully four times a day. And how, he wondered, could many of these Muslims treat him and others with such warmth and care? They weren't even Christian, yet they loved like Jesus would, caring deeply for others' humanity.

Witnessing the Muslims' authenticity impacted him so powerfully that Clayton considered looking into their religion as a better way to live out his faith. But in a talk with the Goshen College campus pastor, Harold Bauman, he realized that Islam was more a works-based religion; it was not grace-and-love-based like Christianity. He preferred to count on love over deservedness, so he stuck with his Christian faith.

Perhaps the biggest stumbling block to Clayton's faithfulness came through the unlikely source of that pillar in Mennonite education, Goshen College. More accurately, it was the theology department that rocked his simple-faith world.

Clayton took his first Bible class his freshman year. At least one Bible class a year was mandatory at Goshen College. From numerous situations in Algeria that left him thinking he was far too ignorant of his faith, he eagerly anticipated learning from the *experts*.

His first course did not disappoint. The beloved J.C. (no physical relationship to Jesus Christ that Clayton knew of) Wenger taught New Testament Studies. J.C. was Elno's bishop and highly esteemed in all of Mennonitedom. For the first time, Clayton learned the background of the New Testament. He ate up Wenger's solid teaching.

But the second year couldn't have contrasted more. Dr. Willard Wirtz taught Old Testament Studies. Clayton's understanding of the Bible was quickly and utterly challenged. Wirtz exposed that Genesis had two different creation stories, which came from two different oral traditions that did not include Moses's rendering. Prior to this class, Clayton thought that Moses had written most of the Old Testament. This professor said that the Old Testament was not to be taken literally, word for word, but was subservient to the New Testament, meaning readers must read the Old Testament only through the interpretation of the New Testament. Wirtz even went so far as to say that some books in the Old Testament, like *Job* and *Jonah,* had never even happened: "Some Old Testament books aren't to be taken at face value, but rather as myths, legends, or poetically written for the believer's insight."

Time and time again, Clayton left that class stunned. Dr. Wirtz's teaching flat-out contradicted what Clayton had learned at Kidron Mennonite where he was taught that the Bible is infallible, inerrant, and completely inspired by God. Every word was true!

Poor Clayton just wanted to obey and believe. But now, he had to choose between the teaching he had placed his full confidence in all his life or this completely combative, seemingly sacrilegious, and possibly blasphemous, new teaching from a so-called expert Mennonite leader. He desperately wanted, needed, to have confidence in his faith. But how could he have confidence in his faith if what he believed in was not true?

Clayton was forced to seek Truth. Instead of childishly believing all he was taught as a youth, he now had to search the unknown. Instead of trusting those he knew and admired, he had to open his isolated heart to new possibilities. This painful journey required evaluating new data, to be sure, but it also required exploring the depths of his own heart. He did not know what possible sin and sludge he would find there.

In the process of this tumultuous dilemma, Clayton's junior year began. Unknowingly, he stepped into the dragon's lair by taking the Biblical class entitled, Protestant Christianity, taught by Dr. Norman Kemper. Kemper was known to pick a fight just to get a student to think differently, to provoke the status quo, and to reach for the possibilities, however outlandish they might be.

After just a couple of classes, in Clayton's mind, Kemper was maniacally out to destroy his faith. Confused and losing his footing, Clayton worried that the contentious professor might succeed. It was as if this mad doctor of ill repute splayed Clayton's simple faith on the table and dissected it piece by piece with little effort or concern.

Exposed and helpless, Clayton didn't know what to do. Discouragement and depression knocked on his door regularly. Occasionally, he let them in.

> Side margin notes: *I'm making this assumption about his emotions, based on his low energy. I'll have a lot to change if I'm wrong.*

Kemper taught that "Catholics, Lutherans, and Reformed Churches all have something to teach us." By so proclaiming, he essentially declared that Mennonites do not have all the answers. Clayton nearly lost his faith over such a ludicrous presumption. If he was not holding onto the absolute Truth (by way of the Mennonite Church), what was he doing? Living a lie? Clayton's world suddenly got infinitely bigger, and he got infinitesimally smaller.

Beemer worried that Clayton's thin walls of blind obedience were beginning to crumble. He feared the professor's new views would destroy his subject.

Oh, if only Clayton had checked out the validity of his environmental information sooner. Or had not been exposed to the wiles of this shapeshifting college and been content to rest on the laurels of his upbringing. But those options were gone. Life had gotten messy for Clayton, and now, it was sink or swim.

Beemer hoped Clayton could keep his head above water and somehow swim to a hopeful shore with a safer harbor. The fact that Clayton was now married only increased the need to anchor his floundering faith. And the conceivable prospect of Clayton's great adventure coming to a halt terrified Beemer. He imagined someday writing about Clayton on a trashy street corner, destitute, possessing nothing, not even faith.

Knowing how busy the editor in chief of *Heaven's Chronicle* was, he dared not ask him to come down. That would sound too much like another emergency.

Beemer decided to write his questions and concerns through long-form in his margin notes. He hoped the editor in chief would appreciate this unconventional (and less confrontational) approach.

Hey, Chief. Had some questions. I'm concerned that Clayton's religious stability is breaking down. Don't get me wrong. He's a great kid. Very faithful to THE BOSS (or as he calls him— God). But what should I expect if some of his flimsy reasoning gets the heave-ho? Are we looking at a possible meltdown here?

Let me explain. Clayton is in a very vulnerable spot right now. He's a young man trying to carve out his place in the world. He wants to lead his newlywed wife to spiritual maturity. But his early environmental religious foundation now seems unsteady after being shaken by the Bible classes he's taken. Couple that with what I suspect is his poor self-image, and I think he's headed for disaster.

See, I don't think he really knows THE BOSS yet. I think he only sees THE BOSS through the narrow lens of what his church taught him. Now his beliefs are being challenged by educated men whom he thinks he should respect.

Up to this point, Clayton has staked his faith in obedience. But is obedience always good? What of obedience to bad instruction? Is a person applauded for obeying the instructions to murder or following an evil cult? What if Jesus had obeyed the laws of his day and not healed on the Sabbath? It would have suppressed his ministry and left many lives untouched. The full story of Jesus would have been blunted. Blind obedience to inflexible rules can't be good, can it?

There is a purity to Clayton's simple obedience. His compliance with authority is commendable. But what will happen when simple turns to horror? When authority is found to be on the dark side? Will Clayton flip out? Will I soon be writing about Clayton's group sessions in a mental ward?

And though his compliant faith is admirable, it is also boring ... and unimaginative. By putting THE BOSS in a box, just think of all the fabulous places he's limiting THE BOSS to taking him. Surely, there's a way out of this dangerous rut! Is there not?

Please advise.

And oh, please don't take all this to mean that you need to come down here in person. I'm just curious about what I should expect. You can just jot down your response in this biographic journal … if you have time … if you want … no pressure.

The editor in chief responded to Beemer's petition in written form (to Beemer's surprise and delight) later that same day:

Always glad to answer thoughtful questions from an earnest chronicler. I am pressed for time, so I will give only succinct answers here.

While human authority is necessary for the hierarchy of their species, no earthly authority is perfect. No person or group of people can know THE BOSS perfectly. Only through continual and thorough checks and balances can such authority be wholly honored.

If Clayton realizes that his relationship with THE BOSS is more mechanical than life-breathing, his eyes may open. He may be drawn to, not repelled from, life's possibilities because of such confrontation. Of course, he may, as you fear, *flip out*. But these humans are, by and large, resilient creatures. For, whatever shattering his firmly held beliefs undergo, he likely will re-establish a firmer structure, though the time frame of such a journey varies.

Living in a snug, comfortable hut is nice until the outside storms ravage and expose its vulnerable structure. Clayton is sheltering his given values as best he can. I would expect that he will no longer cling to the straw hut when the storm blows it down, bringing in its wake, new, stronger building supplies. Altering foundational beliefs will shake him, to be sure. But I would wait till the storm has passed and he has time to assess the damage and reconstruct new convictions. Be patient. Time repairs many collapses.

While obedience is basically good, as with most things, taken to the extreme, blind obedience is bad, foolish even. You want a young child to obey her mother and not cross the busy street unattended. But if an adult is told to never cross that street and she blindly obeys, she may be forever stymied, deceptively sheltered from the possibilities of life.

Seeking Truth, therefore, is a greater virtue than blind obedience. If people only follow and never question, danger lurks. Think of how Hitler persuaded his obedient followers to go along with massacring thousands of Jews. Because Hitler was guilty of heinous crimes of genocide, so were all his obedient followers.

A good seeker asks questions first, so he knows what and whom to follow. Obedience is always at least second on the to-do list.

Truth and meaning requisitely need to be wrestled with before they can be found. Truth is not meant to be followed through someone else's (however heartfelt) conviction.

Rules, laws, and doctrines are there to protect people. THE BOSS wants people to be safe. But, just as fervently, THE BOSS wants them to live! To live curiously while honoring one's neighbor fulfills THE BOSS's purpose. Life is an adventure, not a prison.

That being said, sit back and allow Clayton to learn these lessons. Record his account and be amazed at how THE BOSS tailors his story to experience such life. We never know for sure, but reading your annals of Clayton's emotions, environment, and experiences, I'd venture to say that the character he's developing will learn soon enough that compliance alone is unsubstantial.

Beemer loved the idea of this potential growth and adventure! He always remembered the thrilling adventures of his man, William Clark, in his timeless Lewis and Clark Expedition. Poetically, Beemer's adventure was writing Clayton's chronicles. And though Clayton didn't exactly live recklessly, probably due to figuring out how to obey *just right*, he was nevertheless acting out his great adventure. And Beemer would be there recording the whole thing!

15

COLLEGE GRADUATE

IN TUNE WITH TRUTH

Beemer, reveling in his newfound FFC privileges, penned his next chapter a short time after the events took place.

Clayton's day of triumph arrived. He stood on the Goshen College lawn, donned the black gown and mortarboard with its dangling tassel, and proudly held his certificate next to his already-graduated wife and his in-laws, Lester and Grace. Clayton beamed the broadest smile imaginable. And who could blame him for his self-respecting joy?

The little farm boy, unexposed to the ways of the world, disinterested in school most of his life, and treated like a dumb failure by his most influential authority figure, has conquered all the odds. Clayton has graduated!

Though his parents did not make the four-and-a-half-hour trip to attend the service, surely even his dad would be proud of Clayton's feat. Egged on throughout his bumpy college journey by his dad's hair-raising charge to "be more like brothers Elno and Marion," Clayton never buckled under the pressure.

After the fun, chaotic dorm life of his freshman year, he and Ruth moved into the trailer he purchased in the Goshen College Trailer Court at the edge of campus. They enjoyed the camaraderie with their neighbors, especially Ron and Judy, all three years.

The time-consuming complications he shed by leaving the dorm were replaced with time-consuming, fulfilling relationships with three other young couples from church. Together, Ruth and Clayton attacked all that life threw at them. Enriched by their encouraging friendships, Clayton gained an insatiable hunger to learn.

Elementary Education became his major, more through default than from passion. Ruth was already leading the way in that field, and job security held great appeal for a man coming from little and uncertain of his plan. His other considerations, Accounting and Bible, held too many insecurities and too little promise.

During his senior year, 1967, Clayton completed his student teaching by instructing a fifth-grade class in Middlebury, Indiana. His classmate, Ellis Bontrager, and fellow church member (and principal), BJ Miller, encouraged him along the way, as did a couple of standout teachers. An A was granted to him for his student teaching, and in April, he signed a contract to teach fifth grade at Rensberger School in Goshen, Indiana, to begin teaching in the fall of 1967.

Looking back at Clayton's rise to success, his difficult journey was nothing less than incredible. With his theology in shambles after his wrecking-ball Bible courses, the religious challenges continued. A glutton for punishment, some might say, but curious to learn *real* Truth, Clayton took another, elective, Biblical class during the second semester of his junior year. Bible and Philosophy was taught by Dr. Marlin Jeschke. Perhaps because this professor resembled Clayton in appearance (people had stopped Clayton to say, "Hi, Dr Jeschke"), Clayton was much more receptive to Jeschke's considerate approach than he had been to his predecessors, Wirtz and Kemper. Jeschke challenged Clayton to reconsider his faith platform, claiming there need not be a conflict between the Bible and science or between Christianity and other religions and philosophies.

Later, in his senior year, Clayton took Biblical Studies, which roused him to dive even deeper. Slowly, Clayton became a thinker. He came away from his college experience with a much more, tried-and-true, mature faith—an honest faith he could call his own, not one he had borrowed or mimicked from someone else.

He learned that Truth is not stagnant. Becoming the man that THE BOSS wanted him to be meant he must continually grow. He was no longer stuck in binary, black-or-white thinking but realized that the world is a big place. No one person or group of people can know all the right answers. One can gain wisdom along the way if one asks the right questions.

Now, Clayton thirsts for spiritual knowledge and insight. He knows that all the answers aren't handed to him from a doctrine or book. He's a seeker. A lifetime learner. Instead of being duty-bound and governed by impersonal rules, he now determines Truth through the eyes of Jesus, imagining how Christ himself would see the world.

He knows he will still make mistakes in the future. He will not always make the best decisions or hold to the best understanding. But through patience and continual seeking, he has hope. Compassion and empathy are now driving forces in his relationships because he is open to seeing the world through another's eyes. His is a fluid, alive faith.

The theological storm from his agitating professors, which had threatened to blow his faith away, has strengthened Clayton. He's now prepared to take on challenges progressively and practically.

Clayton is perhaps the best example ever known to man of trusting THE BOSS and never giving up, even in his bleakest hour.

Here, Beemer paused. That last sentence would have to be edited. His inexplicable exuberance had gotten the better of him. But this new, tingly perception he felt demanded expression. He suddenly, impulsively, understood with clairvoyant insight the depths of Clayton's struggles and triumphs. With a lust he neither expected nor imagined, he yearned to shout his sharp awareness.

Unaccustomed to such vivid passion, he feared losing control, a trait all good chroniclers must maintain. And so, not wanting to set into motion the inevitable, but realizing the emergency this new passion mustered, Beemer called down the busy editor in chief.

In just a few minutes, the bald, bulbous-nosed editor, disheveled notebook paper in hand, arrived at the foot of Clayton's bed in the middle of the night. His grave expression told Beemer, *This better be good.*

Beemer swallowed, then blinked several times. "Hi, Chief. Ah … I've got a bit of a crisis here. I, ah, I must be losing it or something. I'm feeling … I don't know … emotions of some kind. I might be going crazy. I just want to write the most impassioned things about Clayton. I don't know where it's coming from. It's absurdly ridiculous! But so amazing!"

Beemer forced his dreamy gaze back to his supervisor. "It's scary. Like I'm—losing control." Beemer willed the chief to prove him wrong.

The exalted chronicler maintained his expressionless, steady stare. He nodded three times. "What kinds of things are you wanting to write about Clayton that you suddenly *know*?"

"Well, Clayton began with this awkward, impractical, impersonal faith from his initial environment. Then, it was put through the wringer, and now, his faith is this beautiful, glowing thing that THE BOSS is totally blessed by." Beemer swallowed hard and caught a glimpse of the editor, then Beemer looked away, knowing such presumption about THE BOSS was playing with fire. He nervously went on. "But see, the thing is, he could've so easily abandoned his faith altogether and said, 'Forget you. I'm not believing in this confusing God.' But he didn't. He stuck with it. He allowed the painful bending and twisting and reshaping of his faith. And when he entered THE BOSS's new castle of hope, I feel I entered it with him. At once, I felt his agony and joy."

"You felt it," Chief repeated flatly.

"Yeah, he was a deer in the headlights there for a while. It's tough when the walls you count on for protection and warmth collapse."

Beemer rambled on, "Well, anyway, like Clayton, I couldn't help seeing that the Truth is not about facts and finite conclusions. Truth is more of an art. It's amazing, profound, uplifting, rare, and highly coveted. And it takes a true seeker to find it. Clayton has become such a seeker. He's come to realize that THE BOSS's Truth is personal. It is not given to authority alone, and no authority has a full grip on it. And I am flooded with awe and inspiration by his transformation."

Beemer rubbed his chin. "I think I'm seeing all of this as Clayton is seeing all of this. But can I rely on this intuition I'm feeling? It doesn't feel terribly logical. I'm aching to express it in the biography, though. But writing from my hunches goes against everything I was taught in training."

The *Heaven's Chronicle* editor stared at his employee. "Is that a question?"

Beemer cleared his throat. "Um ... right. Ah ... the question is, Can I go ahead and write all this irresistible insight? Is that acceptable?"

The editor in chief peered gravely over his thick black glasses. "You called me all the way down here to ask me that?"

Beemer's eyes became full-moon wide. Words did not come forth.

The tired manager rubbed his wrinkled face. "You're asking me if you're going nuts."

Beemer's wide eyes darted around the room.

With a hint of a rare, wry smile, Chief said, "The answer would be, No. You are not going crazy. You are experiencing what we call in the biz, *transfixatia*, which means you are transfixed by Clayton's transformation."

Beemer waited for the other shoe to drop to determine if this was a good thing or a bad thing.

"This is the chronicler's bar mitzvah you've been waiting for, Beemer," the editing manager said.

"Wait. What? You mean ... "

"Use words like a good chronicler, Beemer."

"Are you saying I'm now a *soul-buddy* with Clayton?"

"That's what I'm saying. You can now feel everything Clayton is feeling."

"You're kidding!" Beemer's mouth hung open.

"Beemer, why would I kid? I don't particularly enjoy viewing the inside of your mouth."

Beemer shut his mouth. "Sorry. I just can't believe it. I've worked so hard at trying to figure this guy out. I just figured I might never make it. Now, all of a sudden, *Boom!* I'm his soul-buddy."

The head journalist cocked one eyebrow up. "Congratulations." Deadpan.

"Thank you!" Beemer's smile ripped open his face. "Now what?"

"Now what, what? You observe, and you report, just like you always have."

"But what about my superpower? Can I use it at will?"

"If Will was your subject, you could. But since Clayton is your subject, you can only use it when necessary."

"When necessary? What does that mean?"

"It means, you're given this gift to more accurately express Clayton and how THE BOSS has made him, not to indulge in *your* sleuthing philosophy."

"But of course."

The chief unloaded a knowing stare. "Do you think you can distinguish Clayton's feelings from your presumed insights?"

"But, of c ..."

Chief cut him off with one finger in the air. "Be careful. Don't be so eager to share your novice ignorance."

One corner of Beemer's lip curled. "Well, I guess I have no idea."

"It is paramount that you write what you know and not what you expect."

"Okay. So, should I write about Clayton's genius?"

"What do you mean, *Clayton's genius?*"

"Well, only a genius could have overcome all he had to deal with and graduate, right? I mean, not only did he contend with familial, social, and scholarly deficiencies but he processes concepts really slowly. I didn't realize before how much of a handicap he's been dealing with."

Chief said, "Genius is a relative term, which is doled out by those who are incapable of fully seeing. THE BOSS gives all people some genius in diverse ways. Don't over-praise Clayton just because you can feel his accomplishment so profoundly now."

Beemer nods. "Okay. Well, what about all the amazing encouragement he got from all the right people at just the right time? Was it just luck that all of those people showed up when he needed them, or was it Clayton's skillful acceptance of such timely assistance?"

"Yes."

"Huh?"

"It was both. Certainly, not all people have as many encouragers as Clayton had. He's had an element of privilege, to be sure. But he has wisely entertained new ideas and followed good counsel as well. Some must find their mentors to be liars before they can find hope and success."

"Whoa! That's terrible."

"Yes, it is. Every human faces a myriad of difficulties in this life. It's fascinating how THE BOSS orchestrates their paths through those troubles."

Beemer raised one eyebrow. "Glad I don't have any troubles with difficulties."

The salty editor grimaced. "Now, be careful."

"Oh, I'm just joking around, Chief."

"It's your attitude I'm worried about. Your impending fall will be harder the more unbridled your cocky optimism."

Beemer's playful snigger slowly ceased. "Wait. What impending fall?"

"I've seen it a million times. It comes with the territory. Novice makes Full-Fledged Chronicler. FFC becomes soul-buddy. Empowered chronicler falls. Write it down. It's like clockwork."

The pleased expression on Beemer's face disappeared. He squinted and furrowed his brow. "No way. That's not happening to me. I'll only write what Clayton feels and does. Dutifully."

"Uh-huh. Well, we'll see, won't we?"

Beemer frowned at his supervisor.

Chief stared back blankly.

16

DWELLING WITH THOSE IN NEED

INTENTIONAL NEIGHBORS

A fter graduation, Clayton felt on top of the world!

Beemer had always wanted to say that—to express Clayton's feelings!

With a wife at his side and a degree in his pocket, there was no telling what Clayton could accomplish.

Graduating meant moving off campus and out of their trailer. Fortunately, parents of a friend were assigned a Voluntary Service year in Puerto Rico, leaving their Indiana house available. Clayton and Ruth rented their house, which worked out well because it was near Clayton's new employment at Rensberger School.

Conveniently and remarkably, Clayton's mentor, BJ Miller, and his wife, Carolyn, lived catty-corner to their new abode. Clayton admired and wanted to emulate BJ, as he confidently lived out his faith to love others through understanding and action. Often, his spiritual wisdom, Carolyn's nursing experience, and their fine listening skills helped Clayton and Ruth. (Once, Carolyn rescued Clayton's hair from an abominable haircut from Ruth.)

Proud to don his first career hat, Clayton quickly applied himself to being the best fifth-grade teacher he could be. He studied his requirements, planned lessons, and asked Ruth, fellow-colleagues, and his principal plenty of questions. When he put all these necessary ingredients into action, he felt that he fulfilled his duties responsibly. The principal agreed ... save for one incident. Once, when the class became unruly and Clayton felt his control ebbing, he mildly slapped one of the agitators to restore order ... and to be taken seriously. He confessed this lack of constraint to his principal before the parent reported the case. Clayton agreed with the principal that he needed to be more careful. He was let off the hook and invited to teach the next year.

Clayton wavered on the idea that teaching was his calling, though another opportunity in early childhood education soon presented itself.

After Clayton and Ruth married in 1964, they endeavored to find a church home where they could immerse themselves. Some friends introduced them to a new mission-oriented church in a poverty-stricken area of town. Six families from a large Mennonite church north of town had started the church plant. Clayton and Ruth, convicted to serve an active church as a couple, fell in love with the idea of living and dwelling on the mission field, being the hands and feet of Jesus, and loving those in need. After a couple of visits during which they heard the church's vision and received a warm acceptance, they eagerly joined Walnut Hill (WH) Church.

With the burden of full-throttle commitment toward graduating behind him and with a baby on the way (yes, their dream of a family was coming true, too) Clayton and Ruth felt compelled to put their exuberant youthful idealism into action by fully involving themselves with Walnut Hill and the community. They served in any way they could.

From a survey of the 190 homes that surrounded Walnut Hill, the church discovered that there were sixty-one single-parent households, sixty-three children under the age of six, and twenty homes that had registered a need for childcare. These eye-popping numbers led the church to appoint three couples as a committee to implement a plan to operate a daycare center in North Goshen. Clayton and Ruth, along with their mentors, BJ and Carolyn, were on that committee.

The church took seriously the recommendation of the committee to aggressively move forward on initiating a daycare facility, but it did not want to move forward without a church-wide unanimous consensus. Clayton was one proponent of this consensus approach. He liked certainty.

After many long church meetings, on June 2, 1968, the membership finally agreed to borrow $20,000.00 to build a daycare facility since the small 1957 church structure they currently used was inadequate. Two dissenting families left over the decision, and each remaining family pledged sixty-five dollars a month to pay off the loan.

Later that summer, Clayton and Ruth decided to put their money where their mouth was even further by following the pastor's lead to be intentional neighbors; they became the second family to purchase a house in the Walnut Hill community. They borrowed most of the $8,500.00 investment from Ruth's dad, Lester.

Their first child, Kevin, was almost a year old when it became clear that the $20,000.00 for the building project would not be nearly enough. Through arduous, lengthy meetings, the church agreed to borrow $40,000.00 more, increasing the monthly fee by $267.00. Another family left over this commitment to debt.

On the positive side, several new families joined the church, offering their full involvement; these additions brought the total to thirteen families who were now active members. Despite the growth, it became obvious that fulfilling the daycare mission was too large for their small group to handle.

So, Clayton reached out to his oldest brother, a pastor in the community. Elno helped appoint a larger community board of directors from the greater Goshen area that oversaw the daycare operations. This new board was called the Goshen Daycare Board.

After raising money for operations, the first goal on the board's agenda was appointing a director of operations.

Unsure of whether to return to teach at Rensberger in the fall of 1968, Clayton threw his name into the hat of possible daycare directors, knowing that he had no preschool education experience and that the modest income would tax his young family.

Low and behold, he got the appointment and was named the new director of the Walnut Hill Daycare Center!

Clayton felt excited, scared, honored, and driven to become just as successful as his brothers Elno and Marion; hopefully, he would achieve even more than they had, proving his worth through that base standard that his dad had thrown in his face as he was growing up. Deep down, he imagined his father's pride at this appointment.

Wasting no time, Clayton jumped right in and wrote out a philosophy statement and the daycare's goals, which the board approved. Next, he set up his salary and personal guidelines, a sliding fee schedule for the students, the first budget, and hired his first employees—a teacher and an aide.

Because the facility was not yet built, the daycare opened in a makeshift classroom in North Goshen Mennonite Church on September 7, 1968. Expecting the daycare to be overflowing with toddlers, the meager seven students sorely disappointed Clayton. The common practice in their society, however, was for the mother to take charge of her own children during the day, not cast them off to others. Though the need for many mothers to work was great, many refused to give in to that need, opting instead to stay at home and hope welfare, friends, family, or churches would help them survive. Walnut Hill, Clayton realized, was fighting against culture to meet the needs of young families.

His first year as director challenged Clayton's novice skills throughout the year. If he wasn't putting out fires, he was searching for better methods and direction for the center. The inadequate facility generated daily challenges.

On November 29, 1968, they finally moved to the long-awaited new Walnut Hill building with twelve students. Not quite meeting the needed capacity of twenty students, the financial shortfall became a daily drain on operations and Clayton's outlook.

To top off the hectic environment, Clayton and the teacher did not see eye to eye. Both felt they needed to be in charge: Clayton because that was the role of a director, and the teacher because she led their precious commodity, the children.

In the spring of that stress-filled year, the Daycare Board asked Clayton to lead the program for another year. The teacher found another position elsewhere. Clayton accepted the charge, breathing a sigh of relief, quickly followed by a deep breath of anxious determination.

He and Ruth knew that if the Daycare Center was to survive, drastic measures needed to occur. Together, they discussed and concluded that the best way to assure its success was to decrease the salary expenses. Clayton would forego his salary and volunteer his time for the next year. Though the selfless consideration was a ludicrous idea for his personal budget, they decided to lay their lives on the line and allow God to meet their personal needs.

The board paid Clayton a stipend to cover his family's basic needs. Ruth's parents graciously agreed to pick up the mortgage on their house as Ruth had baby Kevin to care for and no longer held a paying teaching job.

With their bare necessities covered, Clayton again immersed himself in the monumental task before him. He tirelessly set up speaking opportunities at churches and community clubs, asking for financial support. Slowly, support came in, including from the Elkhart County United Way. By the end of the 1968–69 fiscal year, the daycare reached its capacity, finally paying its fair share of the expenses.

Clayton's family was above the poverty level when he again received wages, which began in the 1970 fall school year. By 1971, the daycare had a waiting list, so WH remodeled the original church to accommodate more students. This move allowed their daycare capacity to be thirty, which they quickly filled. By then, Clayton had staffed two teachers, three aides, and a part-time secretary, cook, and custodian. The business side, though still charging a low sliding scale for low-income families, was suddenly booming.

With the influx of students came unavoidable needs. Sixty-five percent of the mothers were single parents, often with twice the stress. To assist them, the WH Daycare Center housed an office for both the Elkhart County Counseling Center and the Oaklawn Psychiatric Center (for a time) in their building. Through these professional resources, a part-time social worker offered free counseling for parents, single-parent therapy groups, and parenting classes. They also counseled teaching staff on problem children.

Clayton opened and closed the Daycare Center daily at 6:30 a.m. and 5:00 p.m., respectively, often taking a long break midday. He also attended about one board meeting a week for either the church or the daycare.

Along with his many tasks, Clayton also became the proud father of two more children—Duane in 1969 and Bruce in 1972.

By 1974, the wait-list became so long that Clayton recruited two local mothers to provide licensed childcare in their own homes. These satellite locations served as an alternative to the main daycare and offered childcare to more families. Walnut Hill Daycare Center had become a beacon for how to start and run a daycare center as heralded by local newspaper articles and TV news spots. Political leaders took notice, applauding its success. Goshen's Mayor Schenk asked Clayton to accompany him to the capital city, Indianapolis, to ask for state support. The United Way referenced the daycare as a model non-profit organization.

Beemer beamed with pride over his subject. Clayton, from his vantage point, had sacrificed his livelihood to save the Daycare Center and dedicated his time and energy to make it prosper. Was there no end to what this determined, thirty-three-year-old man could do? And to think, not too long ago, this supposedly *slow* kid had zero interest in learning, had no idea what THE BOSS wanted, and had no conception of what a good leader was.

Beemer was so excited to be chronicling this annal for THE BOSS!

On the community front, trying to shine their light of hope to the lost, Clayton and Ruth worked tirelessly at getting to know their neighbors, sharing their lives as open books, helping those in distress, lending a hand when needed, and making friends with people out of their normal sphere. Most of their neighbors did not attend church, though some gave it a try when their children wanted to attend. Fortunately, many church peers followed Clayton and Ruth's lead and moved within walking distance of the church.

Rubbing elbows with their poorer neighbors sometimes produced fruit. At other times, it caused complications and stress. On one such occasion, Clayton and Ruth learned that their two oldest, Kevin and Duane, had gotten into trouble with the Travelle and Connolly kids. To remedy the problem, they had their boys make a poster to give to their fighting con-spirators. This bad fruit turned good when they began to see more and more of the Connollys from then on. The two families even planted and worked a garden together.

Clayton and Ruth began supporting their neighbors in emotional and spiritual matters as well. On September 19, 1973, a tragic accident took the life of a father in the neighborhood. Claus Mueller, roughly the same age as Clayton, was working under his car when the jack slipped, crushing his head. His wife, Erna, discovered the tragedy some hours later. Their oldest boy, Mark, was Kevin's buddy, and he had a sister, Monica. Several years later, the mom, Erna, died of cancer. Kevin and Mark's kindergarten teacher took custody of the children, and Clayton and Ruth helped as best they could under the horrendous circumstances.

At one point, a staff member named Debra was reeling from her husband leaving her. Clayton and Ruth counseled her in her grief through many hours of listening and support. The relationship was well worth the effort but was emotionally draining. The two had little energy for anything else after sessions with Debra. She eventually moved to her hometown in Illinois but kept in contact with them for years after that.

In 1975, an unhappy couple named Henry and Hilda began coming to Clayton and Ruth for counseling and prayer. Henry had an unconquerable wild streak and led a controversial, but popular, Goshen College rock band after he wrote a popular Mennonite hymn. When Henry went on tour with his band and got involved with his female singer, his marriage finally ended. Disheartened by this sad situation, Clayton and Ruth continued their nearly daily contact and support of Hilda for many exhausting months. The emotional investment took a huge toll on Clayton's stamina.

While the daycare job and community involvement spent much of Clayton's energy, he was also still part of the leadership team at Walnut Hill Church. This meant not only attending Sunday morning, Sunday evening, and Wednesday evening services, and twice-a-month business meetings (usually on those busy Sunday afternoons), but he also had to be totally engaged in those meetings, constantly assessing what improvements needed to happen. The involvement was invigorating when harmony flowed but taxing when necessary changes bore disunity.

Sundays were a dichotomy of nourishment and energy depletion. For every encouraging sermon Clayton took in, he also heard of a disgruntled parishioner's take. For every new attendee that was blessed to join a church service, there was another that required extra attention to accommodate.

Saturday was not Clayton's day to rest either. Generally, Saturday was his family time, the day he catered to his family's needs. But inevitably, church and community opportunities presented themselves. Invoking the spirit of *community*, Clayton tried as best he could to incorporate his family into that mission.

So, when a neighbor needed a fence mended or a room painted, Clayton took his whole family to help (or to witness him helping when the kids were too young to actually help). When the church organized a community work project or seminar, Clayton's kids were always in tow, whether they added joy or stress to the situation.

Though the family had their fun outings, like bike riding and trips to the park, they also worked hard to maintain their property and sustain their well-being. They always grew a large garden in the summers, tilling, planting, weeding, watering, and harvesting. Then, they canned. Not stopping at their own garden's vegetables, they also bought produce locally and often brought home fruit to can from their family visits to Ohio. Canning was not an exercise for the faint of heart!

One way the family participated in the church was the Summer Bible School. Clayton and Ruth helped lead the preschool class, which perennially enrolled twenty children. The Steiner children joyfully took part. One year, the class boasted twenty-five preschoolers. The church sure knew how to have babies!

The enchantment of communal living pulled at Clayton's heartstrings. Like the disciples and their followers in the biblical book of Acts, Clayton yearned to be a part of such a bonding existence. The pinnacle of this dream came when friends shared their international Mennonite community experience in Evanston, Illinois, where they shared resources among themselves at a place called *Reba Place.*

Clayton viewed a property across the street for sale as an ideal location for such a communal building. Charged with the idea, he approached some WH friends one Saturday morning to see whether to proceed. Surprisingly (to Clayton), they shot down the extreme measure, citing that the church was already giving its soul to the community.

Beemer felt Clayton's determination to radically live out the biblical *Great Commission*. He knew Clayton saw some good fruit from his and the church's efforts but longed for more.

Beemer hoped that, above all else, Clayton would be compensated for his dutiful efforts. Surely, THE BOSS would recognize the purity of his actions and the determination in his heart. Then again, he worried that maybe THE BOSS would see some chink in Clayton's armor and deny him his deserved reward. The unfairness of such a thought was more than Beemer cared to consider.

But he remembered his editor's words. Something about how hardship is always a necessary ingredient of the human experience to give them much-needed character. *Why would Clayton need more character when he's giving of himself 24/7?* Beemer wondered. *These human lives are a mystery.*

One Sunday afternoon at a church business meeting, the open discussion centered around discipline.

"But what do we do with them?" one member said. "It's fine for us to spank our own kids if they misbehave, but we can't hardly take these neighborhood kids, *out behind the woodshed*, as they say, can we?"

"Why not?" commented another. "Maybe that's what most of them are lacking. A little slap on the fanny might do them some good."

"We're asking for a lawsuit if we go down that path," another said.

"So what, we're just supposed to let them get away with insubordination?"

"Well, we can try to talk to them."

"Good luck with that. They'll walk all over you."

"Under the circumstances, there's not a whole lot else we can do."

"But what does this show our own kids? They'll think they can be rebellious and get away with it too."

Clayton said, "We'll just have to trust our kids to be the examples we've taught them to be. You know, let their little lights shine."

By the end of the meeting, everyone agreed that they needed to show love to all the neighboring kids, no matter their behavior. They spent considerable time praying that the Sunday school teachers would have wisdom for each unique situation and that God would shine His light through their children.

After the meeting, the babysitters approached Clayton and Ruth. "We had some problems tonight."

"What problems?" Clayton asked.

"Well, Kevin and Karl were bullying the other children. When we asked them to stop, they ignored us and acted like they were in charge. We can't babysit anymore if this kind of thing continues."

Clayton closed his eyes and breathed out his nose.

Observing the ironic scene, Beemer took a deep breath. Maybe Clayton's determination wasn't as pure and almighty as he thought. Maybe (here Beemer gulped), though Clayton's heart was wide-open to outreach, his eyes were not as open to seeing the needs of what he professed to place first—his family.

To clarify Clayton's past and present parenting ideals, Beemer thought he'd better devote the next chapter to Clayton's entire parenting experience, starting from the beginning. Beemer sighed. He was thankful that he had the liberty to write out of chronological order.

17
PARENTING YEARS
FAMILY OR SUCCESS?

To Clayton, family just made sense. It wasn't a truth that needed to be proved or even sought. Family was natural. Normal. Of course, there were good families and bad families, and he wasn't gullible enough to think that good families happened by accident. A good family required hard work. Understanding. Love.

Clayton's dad had taught him the value of hard work. But Homer had been so lacking in understanding and love! Clayton did not want to lead his family down that same path of confusion and resentment. If it was the only thing he did in his life, he wanted to be a better father than his own had been! Frankly, raising that bar would not be difficult. In fact, though Clayton placed much value on being a better father than his own, it was so obtainable that he easily took small family matters for granted, much like one does a beautiful sunrise when one is busy.

Clayton figured that if he loved God, loved the church, and loved his wife, his offspring would just be a natural reflection of that love—a love, if he'd stopped to think about it, his dad also claimed to possess, though *he* came up woefully short. But such psychological realities did not present themselves early on to Clayton. His goal was simply to fulfill God's natural plan—to have a family to love—a family that would, in turn, share God's love to a needy world.

This plan began on October 4, 1967, when Ruth awoke to a wet bed. Alarmed at the strange occurrence, she called her nurse friend, Carolyn, who informed her that her "water broke," and it was time to get to the hospital.

Clayton dutifully drove her to Goshen Hospital, where they waited to be admitted into a labor room. Once admitted, Clayton held Ruth's hand and witnessed his lovely wife endure the agonizing pain of labor for three hours. He felt helpless and distressed.

When Dr. Troyer finally informed them that Ruth was ready to deliver, he guided her to the delivery room and Clayton to the waiting room. Or, as he felt, from one torture chamber of witnessing to another one of imagining. For over an hour, he sat there alone, hearing the unearthly sounds of her groans from the labor room. When the noises ceased, his mind went wild. *Was her life in danger? Was the baby's? Why was he not being told anything?!*

When the doctor finally entered the waiting room, Clayton burst out asking, "Why has it taken so long? Is there something wrong?"

Dr. Troyer grimaced his regret. "I'm sorry. I had to deliver another baby first. Your wife and baby boy are both fine!"

"A boy?"

"Yes. You'll be able to see them in a minute. Just have a seat, and a nurse will get you when they're ready."

So relieved, excited, dazed, and ... relieved some more, Clayton couldn't hold his river of tears after the doctor left. One minute he had imagined his wife and baby in mortal danger; the next, he was a father of a healthy boy!

In step with the morning's affairs, Clayton waited another hour to see his new family. When he finally saw his beloved holding little Kevin Lamar, his heart erupted with joy. Family suddenly meant more to him than ever before—a feeling he reckoned would guide his life forever forward.

Though Kevin came with no instruction manual, Ruth and Clayton soon figured out how to care for an infant and even used the same cradle that Ruth had slept in as a baby.

The teachers at Rensberger Elementary, where Clayton taught, made a huge sign in celebration of Kevin's arrival. On Clayton's first day back, his fifth-grade class threw him a party.

Ruth's parents and sister, Pearl, came out to visit and help out on October 15. That Christmas, they introduced Kevin to the rest of the Geiser family and the Steiners in Kidron.

The summer of '68, when Kevin was approaching his first birthday, Clayton routinely took Kevin with him to work at the church on Saturdays. They did not pause their lives to raise a baby, but rather included baby Kevin in all their duties and dreams. But on one particular day, Clayton's attention wandered, and he lost his grip on the squiggly boy in his arms. Before he knew it, Kevin wriggled from his arms and landed on the concrete floor. Kevin's face bled a little from the impact, and he ended up with a nasty bruise. The terror Clayton experienced from that near disaster sobered him. This was not a toy. This was his live son. No other responsibility could be as important!

Clayton enjoyed including Kevin in their annual Christmas vacations to Ohio each year, especially appreciating the special attention Ruth's parents, the Geisers, showered on the little boy.

In May 1970, Kevin contracted chicken pox. His concerned parents had their hands full, keeping the active toddler from scratching the pox to prevent permanent marks.

A month later, his continuous vomiting and abdominal pain concerned them even more. After a trip to the doctor, it was quickly diagnosed that Kevin had a hernia. Dr. Minter performed the successful surgery, repairing the hernia on June 22. A year later, he repaired a hernia on the other side after the child suffered the same symptoms. Minter said such a development in young children was unusual but, "it happens."

Wanting to blossom their family unit, Clayton and Ruth read up on when the best time would be to have another child. They determined that two years apart was the ideal age gap. So, at the appropriate time, they scrapped birth control and became pregnant again, just as they had hoped. Clayton was fond of telling close friends, "I just put my shorts on the hook and, 'bingo,' we were pregnant."

> When Ruth became pregnant, Beemer wrote a margin note to his editor: *Is it normal for people to conceive whenever they want to?*

The editor in chief responded with a note: Not hardly. Without preachifying spiritually or scientifically, I'd say they got lucky. You wouldn't believe all the couples out there that cannot conceive according to their plan or at all.

The due date of baby number two was September 12. Knowing more about what to expect from the first pregnancy, Clayton and Ruth did not stress nearly so much over every unidentifiable sensation Ruth felt. The labor, the birth, and the wait all seemed to go much smoother the second time around from Clayton's perspective. They decided on the name Duane Harley (Harley being Clayton's middle name) as Clayton expected this would likely be their last son.

Ruth and Duane were released from the hospital three days later and wheeled to the family's car, their Volkswagen Beetle (aka the VW Bug). Clayton called ahead for the daycare to be the first to see baby Duane. The teachers had all the children lined up by the fence for the big reveal. In step, Clayton pulled up just outside the fence and brought Duane out of the car to show all the wide-eyed faces that were abounding with excitement and wonder. A week later, this visit was reciprocated by the daycare kids walking to the Steiner house to greet Duane.

After getting home from the hospital, they moved Duane into the same cradle Ruth and Kevin had used. Curly-haired Duane was a happy-go-lucky baby who was not hard to please.

Before Duane was a year old, he sat in a carrier placed on a deep freezer in the dining room. Kevin, curious as to Duane's outlook way up there (or perhaps he just wanted to play), once reached up and pulled the carrier to the floor. The loud impact startled Ruth in the kitchen, and she ran to her crying baby. Other than the obvious start, Duane, because he was strapped in, did not appear to be hurt. Whew! So many things could go wrong! Clayton and Ruth found that taking care of two children more than doubled the potential danger.

As the boys grew, Kevin and Duane mostly played well together—except when Duane did something that was not to Kevin's liking. In that case, Kevin pulled rank and put his younger brother in his place.

In 1974, when Duane was four, he got to spend part of the summer with his Geiser grandparents. Two separate incidents landed him in the bathtub for his grandma's scrubbing. Once, the wobbly-wheeled tricycle had a mind of its own and led him down into a ditch and into some poison ivy. The other time, he squashed hundreds of tempting, heat-induced tar bubbles on the paved road, which resulted in a gooey black mess all over his hands, arms, and knees.

That same summer, Clayton built an outdoor fireplace for the Geisers, an art he had learned during his days with Clarence Sommer.

When Duane was five, in September 1974, he stayed at the WC Daycare three times a week, allowing Ruth to teach part-time at the Daycare.

Once, when Duane's married cousin, Dean Nussbaum, and his wife, Bonnie, were babysitting, they played a chasing game outside. Duane inexplicably ran into the corner of the house and hit his head, insisting, "The house moved." He wound up in the emergency room where he received several stitches.

All in all, this family venture was turning out well. Clayton felt good about his place in his church, his job, and the direction the daycare was heading. He also was content with his role as a caregiver and role model to his kids. Adding another arrow to his quiver seemed the right thing to do. He and Ruth decided that a girl would round out their family nicely. Students that they were, they studied up on the best ways to conceive a girl, then pursued that plan with vigor.

> Beemer sent a margin note to the editor: *Is this possible?*
> *Can they really tilt the likelihood of a girl by trying when*
> *Ruth's temperature is the highest?*

> The salty editor replied: Stranger things have happened.
> But, to my knowledge, only THE BOSS is in charge of
> the sex of a newborn.

Ruth conceived in the summer of 1971, almost two years after Duane was born. On St. Patrick's Day, March 17, 1972, Ruth felt the birth process begin at about 5:30 a.m. Though the waiting game played its part in Kevin and Duane's birthing stories, this third child was playing another game—one called, *Ready or Not, Here I Come.*

Ruth bypassed the labor room and went directly to the delivery room. For the first time, Clayton was welcomed into the room with her. All he had to do was thoroughly wash his hands and wear a surgical gown.

Clayton and Dr. Troyer (who didn't even have time to put shoes on) entered the delivery room at the same time. The doctor said, "Okay, now you can push."

In no time, at 7:06 a.m., Clayton witnessed the miracle of birth and excitedly cut the umbilical cord. Ruth immediately said, "Here's our Bruce Alan." Before he could assess his volatile emotions, Clayton was ushered into the waiting room while they cleaned the eight-pound, eight-ounce, healthy boy and checked his vitals.

> Beemer wrote this side note to his editor: *Uh, oh! A boy was not what Clayton was hoping for. I guess luck goes both ways. I hope Clayton has it within himself to love and bond with this child as much as with his other children. How much love is one man capable of?*
>
> Chief replied: You'd be amazed at just how much a person can love. It's uncanny sometimes to see how much of THE BOSS is in each person.

When Clayton had waited for Kevin in this same waiting room over four years previously, fear and hope had raged in him. Now, joy and disappointment warred within him. Fearing danger in the midst of the unknown is understandable. But unfulfilled expectations in the midst of joy are just downright confusing.

Twenty minutes later, when Dr. Troyer met with Clayton, the excited papa burst out saying, "We wanted a girl!"

To which the doctor jokingly replied, "Well, we can put him back in."

After talking a bit more, the doctor placed a hand on Clayton's shoulder, looked him in the eye, and said, "Give yourself some time. You will bond with this child even though it is not a girl." The sobering comment finally shook the shock of the failed expectation off. Clayton's plans, he was learning, instead of shaping reality, sometimes got in the way of it.

Just a couple of hours later, Ruth was nursing Bruce, and both parents got to hold their amazing child. Bonding officially began on day one, and Clayton somehow became totally entranced with his third boy. They arrived home to a couple of excited brothers, and Bruce soon became a true part of the family.

The three boys all lived in the same room. Kevin slept on the top yellow bunk bed. Two-year-old Duane slept on the bottom bunk. Bruce slept in the same reliable cradle that his mother and brothers had all grown out of. Grandma Geiser gladly watched over the older brothers while Ruth and Clayton adjusted to their newborn.

Clayton was proud to compare his family to the famous TV show, *My Three Sons*. The love he felt for each of them continued to grow—even for his youngest, whom he had thought would be a girl.

> Beemer wrote to the editor: *You called it again. I'm amazed at how this guy can love so many, so much. What could possibly stop him?*

> The chronicling editor wrote simply: Probably not a question you need ask.

Bruce was easy to love. It didn't take him long to sleep through the night, which was divinely helpful for Ruth, who, for the past few years, had been taking courses from *South Bend Indiana University* whenever she could fit them into her schedule. This meant Clayton had double duty with the kids when Ruth was in class. Ruth received her master's degree in *Elementary Education* on May 17, 1972, two months after Bruce was born.

Likewise, when Clayton was finishing his master's from the same institution with the same degree (and a minor in *Early Childhood Education*) later that summer, Ruth double-downed with her parental role. He graduated on August 31, 1972. Thankfully, before tackling this epic goal, they had paid off their college debt. Their further education would not weigh them down.

Clayton and Ruth truly loved their three boys. Nevertheless, a yearning neither one could quite express nor overlook—to add a little girl to their fold—cried out to them like a foghorn in the night. Neither one was willing to let this dream go. Both wanted a girl, but both no longer felt the odds of naturally birthing a female child were in their favor or discretion.

Less than a year after Bruce's birth, on February 23, 1973, Ruth turned down a time-consuming opportunity to lead her city's *Bible Study Fellowship*, a nation-wide organization that she believed in. She refused the role on the grounds that they were considering enlarging their family through adoption.

Clayton and Ruth got favorable reviews on the adoption idea from Elno (Clayton's brother) and Mabel Steiner, and Jim and Norma (Clayton's sister) Eberly, both of whom had adopted children themselves. They also asked questions of several acquaintances, who had adopted internationally, about their experiences. On September 22, they spoke with a family who had adopted a child from Costa Rica. This family explained all the considerable hoops they had to jump through to make their adoption a reality. The inevitable contingencies were daunting! But still, Clayton and Ruth pressed on. Their heart was to go beyond the relative prosperity of the United States and adopt where the need was the greatest, even though the out-of-pocket expenses would also be greater.

Led by Ruth's urge to move forward, on December 13, 1973, their research led them to choose *Holt*, an adoption agency out of Eugene, Oregon, that specialized in international adoptions. They mailed in their application form that day and soon learned that they would need to be processed and approved by their local Elkhart County Welfare Department's adoption division. Adoption agents told them the process would take thirteen months.

Applications, endless paperwork, a couple of interviews by local social workers, and more paperwork ensued before they were approved.

It was a long summer in the *wait* department at the Steiner household. Consumed with anticipation, on September 26, they finally called Holt for an update. Holt informed them that they would likely have a child to place with them in November. Clayton and Ruth were so glad they had called. Rejuvenated, they praised God.

On October 4 (Kevin's eighth birthday), a gal from the Elkhart County Welfare Department called, inviting the whole family to come in to discuss the girl that Holt had found for them. Excited as popcorn in the frying pan, the Steiner family hopped on over to her office that very day. The agent showed them pictures and gave them specific information about Kim Mee Sook—their soon-to-be little girl! Kim Mee Sook had been born on July 10, 1974. Her place of birth was unknown.

When asked, "Are you ready to accept her as your daughter?" Clayton and Ruth said in unison, "Yes!" Leaving that office, pictures in hand, they could not wait to tell their friends and family her name would be Kimberly!

The next day, they began a new cluster of paperwork. After a couple of weeks, they learned that, due to Korea's notoriously slow processing procedures, they could expect to wait up to another three-and-a-half months!

Clayton built shelves and painted the large bedroom for Kevin and Duane to move into. He painted their old bedroom yellow for Bruce and Kimberly to share. They hung pictures of Raggedy Ann and Andy on the wall and a fish-themed mobile on the light. Ruth made a kitten pillow and placed it in Kimberly's cradle. A dressing table, chair, and cedar chest filled out the ensemble. Ruth told others that all these preparations made her feel pregnant again.

In the excitement, two-year-old Bruce attempted to say his sister's name, "Kimberly Joy," enunciating each syllable carefully.

On November 20, a blow to their anticipation came when they found out that Ruth's fingerprints would need to be reprocessed. It was as if a tricky salesman kept adding contingencies to the deal.

The waiting became so oppressive that, on December 16, Ruth wept after another—*these things take time*—phone call. Nearly in despair, she finally realized this situation was all out of her control. All her wishing for Kimberly to come to the US quickly would not change things. She prayed with Clayton, and, together, they released the circumstances to God, opting instead to stay busy and to trust God to figure everything out in His timing. "And thank you, God," they celebrated, "for all the people involved in this process with us. Please guide them to make the best decisions!"

Instead of putting their life on hold, they put their faith into action, fully participating in the rich traditions of the Christmas season—the new life story of Christ. On December 24, they headed out for their annual visit to Ohio for a scheduled five-day trip, without their new little girl. They shared their hopes and dreams of Kimberly's place in their lives with friends and family on Christmas Day. The next day, the 26th, they exchanged gifts at the Geisers'. At 4:30 in the afternoon, Clayton got a call from Grandma Bertha (his mom), saying she had gotten a call from their pastor at Walnut Hill, instructing Clayton to call Holt.

What? To call over the holidays must mean something important! Clayton felt a sense of dread and possibility simultaneously. *Were forms filled out incorrectly again or something?* Heart racing, Clayton dialed Holt's number, taking one deep breath before they answered on the other end. The agent on the other end said matter-of-factly, "Kimberly will be arriving on Northwest Orient Airlines flight number 6 at O'Hare International Airport on December 28, 1974 at 6:54 p.m. Can you be there to pick her up?"

Clayton's heart stopped. He blinked. His eyes widened with delayed comprehension. He looked at Ruth.

Ruth asked, "What did they say?"

Clayton relayed, "Kimberly will be here December 28th. Can we pick her up?"

"Yes! Of course!" Ruth nearly shouted.

"Yes!" Clayton repeated.

They hugged. Cried. Laughed. It was their most joyous Christmas to date without a doubt! And they shared it with family.

They learned that Holt had a difficult time contacting them. They finally got someone to pick up the Daycare Center phone. The janitor had just happened to be cleaning there, so he answered the call and told the pastor, to whom Clayton had given his parents' number in case of emergencies.

They canceled a few get-togethers and then headed home the next day. They discussed Kimberly's arrival nearly the whole way home with their boys. *What would it be like to have a baby girl in the house?*

That night, Clayton and Ruth slept fitfully at best. Five-year-old Duane woke them early the next morning saying, "Today is Saturday. It's Kimberly Joy's day!"

Before loading up the family in their compact VW bug and heading out, Clayton realized he had locked his keys in the trunk the night before. With the family waiting around the car, he had to run back into the house to get Ruth's set of keys. On their way to Chicago, they dropped off young Bruce to stay with friends.

At the airport terminal, excitement hung in the air for all six families that were waiting to see the eight adoptees who would soon arrive. Cameras were cocked and ready to shoot. The Holt greeters entered the plane and returned with one child at a time. The first child was a crying mess. The greeter handed her to Ruth. "No, she belongs to the Myers family," one of the other Holt officials said and lifted the screaming infant away from her. "Your child will be the last one off."

Finally, the greeter came holding little Kimberly. Clayton unknowingly held his breath. The greeter placed her in Ruth's welcoming arms. To Clayton, she was, without a doubt, the prettiest, quietest, and most contented of all of the newly arrived children. Tears of joy flowed relentlessly from mother and father as they gazed at their enchanting little daughter.

As if aware of their delight, the sleeping Kimberly suddenly opened her eyes and smiled at her new family. They laughed and gazed and cried some more. Not only were they joyfully adding a girl to their contented family, she, it appeared, was adopting them!

Papers to finalize the exchange (and the adoption) were signed and processed in an adjoining room. There, they spoke with the children's escorts, who informed the parents that the babies each had traveled the eighteen-hour plane trip remarkably well. Each Steiner family member took turns holding Kimberly. When she was cleared to leave, fully in their custody, they changed her into a beautiful white dress.

The ride back to Goshen seemed extra-long; all of their energy was spent. They picked up the sleeping Bruce late in the evening and piled him into the crowded VW. With all *four* kids in their beds, Clayton and Ruth talked long into the night about all the momentous details of the day.

The next morning, everyone in the household awoke to the gleeful Bruce announcing at the top of his lungs, "Kimberly Joy is here! Kimberly Joy is here!"

Exhausted, but unavoidably full of joy, Clayton and Ruth smiled at the ensuing mayhem. Their family of six. Nothing could be finer in Clayton's mind and heart. A wholesome pang of rightness infiltrated every fiber of his being.

Kimberly was so peaceful that morning that they took her to church and eagerly shared her with their friends.

Though the house rivaled Grand Central Station the following day with all the visitors showing up, Kimberly slept serenely much of the day. Though her days and nights were mixed up from jet lag, by January 5, she was sleeping through the nights, usually between ten and twelve hours. Not bad for a less-than-six-month-old.

Holt Adoption Agency held a special gathering in Gary, Indiana, on January 20. Ruth attended the meeting with Kimberly in her arms. As a special treat, Ruth and Kimberly got to meet Grandma Holt, the founder of the program.

Kimberly was dedicated at Walnut Hill Church on February 2.

Many diverse sources commented on how beautiful and contented Kimberly was. Nearly all who met her were transfixed. She definitely captured her family's heart; Bruce and her dad were particularly enamored by her. The older the kids got, the more Bruce took her under his wing, helping her navigate this dangerous world. She, in turn, reveled in his attention. Clayton, too, fell seamlessly into his role. She was Daddy's girl from day one!

In the meantime, Clayton's job as administrator of the Daycare Center was in full swing. The preschool childcare business was bursting at the seams. Clayton not only had his hands full with managing his staff, but he also dealt with the many issues low-income families brought to the table. The mission, after all, was to provide more than a mere thriving business. It was to help and share with those families as Jesus would. Many situations called for relationship. And relationships took time—often time out of Clayton's family's busy schedule.

Having kids did not slow Clayton's goals for the daycare project. If anything, his family helped him permeate deeper into their neighbors' lives, enabling him to relate to and inspire them authentically. After all, children are the universal currency in building trust and hope in a community.

It was common, therefore, to share their kids with their friends in the community. Often, Clayton and Ruth's kids spent time at a friend's house after school, after church, summer days, or for weekends. The Steiner family reciprocated, entertaining their children's many friends and establishing a network they could trust.

Family. Community. They melded together in Clayton's mind. It was all part of the mission to live out the neighborhood church that God had called them to.

But lovingly adding families to the fold required effort, resources, and time. And it was often a one-way venture. Clayton and Ruth frequently gave to their neighbors without receiving a *thank you* or a desire to reciprocate. Loving the unlovely, the down-and-outer, the mentally unstable, the unmotivated, the careless, the messy, the smelly, the crass, the hateful, the meager, the uneducated, and others as Jesus would was no small task in many instances. Clayton and Ruth grew through their failed attempts as well as their successes. They were becoming God's dependable servants, living sacrifices for the kingdom of God.

Of course, meeting the needs of others does not diminish one's own needs and weaknesses. In Clayton and Ruth's case, showing kindness and inviting neighborhood kids to church did not mean their own kids were problem-free. Oh, no! Their kids were kids in every sense of the word. They were not always the little angels that church kids were thought to be.

Kevin and his friend, Karl Brugger, along with bullying the church kids on occasion, one time decided to up and walk out of church. When it was discovered that they were missing, a mad search ensued with all the ladies in an uproar. "Were they taken?" Canvassing the neighborhood, they finally found the boys on the Bruggers' porch, waiting for their mother to open the door to let them in.

Once, Kevin found a container of paneling glue in the bathroom. Curious, he opened it. He then got the bright idea to coat his arms, face, and clothes with the smooth, thick substance. He presented himself to his parents like a smiling ghoul. They were mortified! His smile was wiped off his face when they had to wipe (and scrub!) the sticky mess off his sensitive skin with kerosene.

Another time when Kevin was at a neighbor boy's birthday party, Kevin covertly approached the boy and asked him for the dollar he had received as a gift. The boy complied and handed his precious commodity over to him. Later that night, the parents of the crying birthday boy came over and asked

Kevin to return their son's present. Kevin ashamedly went to the backyard and dug up his hidden treasure to return the dollar to the boy.

As Duane grew old enough, he found ways to get himself into trouble as well. While riding his bike with Kevin, they decided it would be cool if they could touch their front tires as they were riding. After many tries, they successfully accomplished said aim—to Duane's undoing. He got a nasty gouge on his foot when it got mangled in the tire spokes.

One rainy day in his kindergarten year, Duane was driven to school and dropped off across the street. His mom told him to cross the street safely where the crossing guards were. When he did so, the crossing guards seized their moment for fun by carrying the scared civilian across the street over their heads. The principal had his hands full trying to calm the confounded crying lad.

As their own children multiplied and grew, Clayton and Ruth became busier and busier as they continued to lead the daycare and to actively fellow-lead the church. And as they kept up with their responsibilities, a disturbing pattern arose with their children. Apparently, their children did not appreciate inconvenient instruction or corrective discipline, and they often would not cooperate with authorities. And even when they did cooperate, their poor attitude begged their parents' judgment and intervention. Discipline issues became commonplace, which wore the overextended parents out. Something was amiss, Clayton feared.

Beemer scratched his head, pondering over Clayton's feelings and options. He was as perplexed as Clayton. He asked if maybe the editor in chief might be able to come down and square some matters for him.

The squat journalist appeared with a reddened hue to his pallor. He didn't look happy.

Beemer tentatively greeted his supervisor. "Chief, is everything okay?"

The editor took a deep breath and closed his eyes for a few seconds. "I'm fine. These transports aren't getting any easier. One of these days, I'm going to fall over from all the excitement."

Beemer gulped, dumbfounded.

"What do you need?" asked the sickly editor.

Beemer tried to remember. "Ah … Clayton is feeling kind of blue about his kids acting up."

The editor looked blankly back at his subordinate, waiting for more. When none came, he said, "That's what kids do."

"Yes, of course. But Clayton is seeing that he's been a little too preoccupied to deal with them properly."

"Preoccupied, meaning with his job and the church?"

"Yes. Which is crazy because he's doing THE BOSS's work really well. The daycare is flourishing. What could be more important than that?"

"I'd say preparing the next generation is about the most important aspiration one could pursue."

"Exactly!" Beemer reconsidered. "You mean, the daycare kids, right?"

"I mean his own kids. Clayton set out to serve and love his family, did he not?"

"Yes, which he's doing by providing for their needs like food, clothing, and shelter."

"What about their emotional and spiritual needs?"

A corner of Beemer's mouth puckered. "I think that's what Clayton's worried about all of a sudden."

"He's got a lot going for him, your subject."

Beemer smiled as if it was his compliment. "Yeah, I think he's a great dad, too."

"He's right to question his parenting efforts."

Beemer stilled, his unblinking eyes alert.

Chief asked, "Why do you think he's so *preoccupied* with work and church?"

"'Cause it's so stressful!" The young chronicler blurted, then he winced and quickly added, "And it's THE BOSS's calling for him."

The old chronicler closed his eyes in lieu of rolling them. "He's not even enjoying the job?"

"Not really the day-to-day."

"Are his giftings in line with his job?"

"Umm, not so much. That's why it's so exhausting, I imagine."

"Beemer, you're his soul-buddy. Other than obediently serving THE BOSS, what's really driving him? Be honest."

Beemer looked sideways and dipped his head a little. "Well, he cares about the community."

Nonplussed, the editor stared back. "What else?"

Beemer reddened. "Ahh ... he likes completing tasks." His eyes darted around the room. "And he likes being in charge. He started this daycare thing from ground zero, and now he's successful. I'd say that's something to be proud of." Beemer turned his smile back on, tickled with his impromptu answer. Then he thought about it more and added, "You know, it's funny, that slow dumbness that he's always felt about himself kind of leaves him when he's in charge of something and people look up to him."

"So, what you're saying is that Clayton takes so much pride in successfully doing THE BOSS's work, he's willing to neglect his own kids."

"No!" blurted Beemer. Then he thought a moment. "I don't think so, anyway. Do you?"

"I don't know. Go back to his frame of reference, his initial environment. How's he defining success and family?"

Beemer rubbed his chin. "Well, to be a success, I guess he thinks he must be in charge and have things turn out like he wants. And family ... well, I'd say one that isn't beaten down at every turn but is loved."

"So, he's leading without disciplining, is that it?"

Grimacing, Beemer said, "Well, I don't know about that, but he loves them. He's just really busy—doing THE BOSS's work."

"Could Clayton be leaning too heavily on his construed duties for THE BOSS, for which he may not even be made for, so he doesn't have to place his weight on the messy business of family needs?"

"Hmm."

Beemer hoped Clayton would attend to this festering sore spot.

When the Steiner children's behavior became unmanageable (especially in public), Clayton and Ruth sought help. They enrolled in an eight-week parenting class that was based on the work of Alfred Adler. His approach was to identify the goals of the children and teach them to use proper methods to reach those goals. It became clear to Clayton and Ruth that Kevin and Duane were misbehaving to get attention. Children need attention, Adler taught. But receiving that necessary attention through negative means was counterproductive. So, Clayton and Ruth devised a plan to ignore negative attention-getting ploys such as crying and whining, and instead they gave positive reinforcement by way of attention when the children obeyed. When they picked up their toys or helped a family member, their parents showered them with compliments and praise. When they cried at not getting their way, their antics were ignored. There was a lot of crying in the Steiner household for a while. They seemed to be slow learners from Clayton's perspective.

As parents, they had much to improve upon, but at least Clayton had a plan now. The feeling of his kids being out of control had been unbearable. Clayton felt best when he was in control and in a controlled environment. Though the temptation to resort to his dad's method of demoralizing the kids through shaming rhetoric to control them presented itself regularly, he refused to stoop to such harmful means (unless his temper slipped, which rarely happened).

Still, family was of utmost importance to Clayton and seeing his off-spring's disobedience bothered him. Their wayward behavior in church was particularly humiliating. He was a leader in the church and the community. His example spoke volumes, he knew, of his priorities and character. Was he a failure as a dad? Was he preaching one thing to the community but living another? And, perhaps the worst torment of all, did he, like his dad, somehow not love his children properly? The thought was horrifying!

18

FAMILY OF ORIGIN TRAIL

LOOKING FOR NURTURE

Clayton was a good dad. But as is the case so often in this complicated world, he sometimes fell short of his ideals.

His marriage was one such sensitive area. Relative to the rest of the population, one could argue that he had a fine marriage. But was it all that it could be or should be? Clayton wondered. Though he easily recalled those early blissful years of romantic passion and ease, the partnership felt different now.

Instead of the children joining them more closely together as they had expected since before their wedding day, petty arguments, unresolved disagreements, and unkind judgments often festered and divided the lovebirds. They could have easily resolved many of their disputes had they taken the time to carefully discuss their issues. But, they hadn't the time, or so they assumed. The practicality of raising four complex, needy consumers, maintaining the daycare, being sunshine to the darkness in their impoverished community, and fully participating in a young, hands-on church made time scarce. And their lack of skill to tackle relational conflict during these draining activities left them feeling out of touch with one another.

Clayton's insecurities regarding his manhood, which stemmed from his dad's open disgust of anyone acting like Clayton's mother, haunted him more than he cared to admit. He wondered if his innate soft nature was too much like his mother's. And because his dad never affirmed him, Clayton sought affirmation from his job, the community, his church, and his wife. Like affirming his kids for their good behavior, he figured he deserved positive feedback whenever he was in the right, which was partly why he tried so hard to prove he was right so often.

He often tried eliciting responses from Ruth by saying things like, "That was pretty good, wasn't it?" "See, I told you that would work," or "Why don't you ever tell me I'm doing a good job?"

Growing up in her straight-forward, autonomous household, Ruth did not see the need to pamper her husband. She often quipped, "I need affirmation too," or "Take care of yourself," or the real zinger, "I am not your mother."

Such words, carelessly flung like feed to the swine, hurt Clayton. He soon developed the pattern of sulking and withdrawing whenever he felt he deserved positive feedback but didn't receive it. This behavior was followed by the temptation (which, he felt he nearly always heroically resisted) to act like his dad; Homer lambasted his wife for not being the submissive wife that the Bible commanded. When Clayton's willpower wore thin and she questioned his anger, he inevitably heaped the blame on her plate, saying things like, "It was your fault," "What did you expect after being so unkind?" and "You started this."

When he got particularly adamant, she threw the final dagger that always pierced his heart—"Stop being like your dad!"—the thing that he tried to avoid more than anything else in the world, hurting those closest to him like his unrelenting dad had.

The irony of counseling their neighbor friends, Henry and Hilda, was not lost on Clayton. Their relational issues and marriage collapse were stark reminders to Clayton that separation and divorce resulted when the partnership was not handled well.

Though Ruth was of the mind that their marriage (Ruth and Clayton's) would work its way out, Clayton knew that there were things deep inside him that she could not help him with. He needed outside help or, he feared, they would end up like Henry and Hilda. Or worse, he would become like his dad.

The Goshen College community generally endorsed professional counseling, much like they did medical care and financial advice. If one needed help with emotional or relational issues, they taught that one should seek counsel from those in the know! But such dogma opposed the thinking of most Mennonites that Clayton had grown up with. His upbringing taught him to "trust God, and He will help you in your time of need." Indirectly, Clayton knew, this meant relying on outside help was suspect at best.

After talking to his brother Marion, who was in the social-work field, Clayton felt led to find a counselor. He did not tell Ruth.

The counselor quickly identified that he needed to deal with his family of origin. As it turned out, Clayton held some anger toward his dad *and* an overattachment to his mom. The latter was an eye-opener to Clayton. He had always focused the confusion of his identity and dysfunction on his dad's demeanor and shaming words. Now, one of his fears of being too much like his mother (like his dad warned against) felt like it was being waved back in his face.

Clayton learned that he still expected to find the acceptance and comfort he had felt from his mother when he lived at home, and he projected that expectation onto Ruth. He subconsciously expected her to soften life's harshness for him as his mother had. When she did not, he felt ripped off. Ruth was supposed to confirm his manhood, not undermine it. He needed, his counselor told him, to recognize he was the man God wanted him to be without needing others to convince him of that fact.

Slowly, Clayton found some hope through his counseling sessions. He eventually told Ruth he was seeing a counselor and invited her to join him on some occasions. She hesitantly agreed. They both learned, grew, and changed many of their unhealthy attitudes. Their behavior toward one another gradually became kinder and more thoughtfully intentional, an ongoing process that they endeavored to commit to. They did not get well overnight, and sometimes, Clayton felt that they grew angrier before they became more forgiving and accepting.

One thing they did to rekindle their embers was to stay overnight at a friend's cabin out in the country on occasion, just the two of them. These rare rendezvous transformed their marriage, if only for a short season.

Though these few and far-between getaways were encouraging times of renewal for them, Clayton wanted to speed the eternal bliss process up a little. Over and over, his counselor took him back to *his family of origin*. His history, he came to find out, profoundly impacted his internal views. What if he were to research his family history in-depth? Perhaps such insight would heal his psychological wounds faster and strengthen his marriage. He had always enjoyed genealogy and history. Maybe now was the time to indulge his childhood interests.

The dream was born.

Meanwhile, Ruth's father, Lester, had a massive heart attack in 1975. At age sixty-six, his farming came to a temporary end. Only if he regained a semblance of his former health could he ever farm again.

To cover his immediate incapacity, Clayton and his family came to the rescue in July 1975 for twenty-three days. Clayton and Ruth helped with the farm work nearly every day. Clayton enjoyed the unpredictability and imperative nature of farming to a point. Every day felt like it could make or break the family business.

In a front-porch discussion with the supervising Lester one day, Clayton asked his father-in-law if he thought he (Clayton) could handle taking over the farm. Lester wisely counseled that Clayton's many interests and abilities would not lend themselves fairly to the steadfast nature of farming. That sage advice hit Clayton profoundly. Just because one could do something, did not mean one should. Clayton couldn't help applying the same insight into his employment at the daycare. *Should early childhood development really be my vocation?*

Along with his marriage contentions, children's behavioral lapses, and work disenchantment, Clayton also realized that his church participation was weighing on him. Where he had once enjoyed instigating change and vying for solidarity, the impact of his passionate leadership input now often left him and the group stuck.

The humble pastor of Walnut Hill Church had fully endorsed the church's foundational mission of reaching the poorer community around them from its inception. That vision had spread throughout the many young, inexperienced, ambitious laypeople who now comprised the church. However, Clayton found the pastor's tentative leadership style weak. He found he enjoyed pushing his own opinions across and dominating the pastor like the younger brother he had never had. Unfortunately, as time dragged on, their mutual respect waned. At the height of Clayton's dedicated directorship of the successful Daycare Center, for instance, the pastor gave him an *average* review, a grade Clayton felt like a slap in the face. Subsequently, right or wrong, Clayton was one of the main instigators to remove the pastor, in favor of a more aware and capable leader. In the end, Clayton won out. But disharmony with many of the other members resulted from the departure of their beloved pastor.

Perhaps even a greater burr under his saddle was Clayton's insistence that the church board meetings come to a unanimous consensus when they made decisions. They had used this criterion for years until the board members became so bedraggled from the exhausting, never-ending impasses, that they finally dumped Clayton's ideal for the much more practical Robert's Rules method of conducting meetings. This left egg on Clayton's face. But worse than his personal feelings was that all the time they had wasted in arguing, trying to convince one another that they were right and the other wrong, had caused discord. The whole mess was a bitter pill for Clayton to swallow.

After going to counseling, Clayton realized he was stuck in old patterns, mindsets, and attitudes. He needed to change. He needed a change. As a result, on April 16, 1975, Clayton contacted the *Mennonite Board of Missions* for a possible job change in Elkhart County. They sent him an application, which Clayton and Ruth sent back five months later, in September.

Over Christmas that year, Clayton and Ruth looked into options for taking a year-long sabbatical from the grueling demands of the daycare. They visited college friends in Harlan, Kentucky, for a possible temporary voluntary position. They also visited the Voluntary Service (VS) unit in Canton, Ohio. Neither seemed a good fit.

In March of 1976, Clayton was granted a year sabbatical by the Goshen Daycare Board that would begin that summer. Clayton and Ruth then inquired again of the Mennonite Board of Missions, but this time, they were looking for possible year-long voluntary placements. The Elkhart office, in charge of VS assignments all over the United States, notified

Clayton that they had a possible position for him in Champaign, Illinois. After expressing interest, Ruth and Clayton were quickly offered the job of supervising a VS Unit. They accepted the VS position, sight unseen, on March 17, 1976.

Now that the weight of the next year's daycare duties was off the table, Clayton felt energized to work on the project he longed to tackle—a book about his genealogy. He spent much of his free time that spring researching data through libraries and interviews. He made several trips to Ohio, interviewing his aunts, uncles, siblings, parents, and anyone who might have information about his ancestry. Collecting accurate data energized Clayton like nothing before. The more he learned, the more he wanted to find out. He was thrilled to think the finished product, which would allow them to know their heritage, would bless his family as it had him.

Specifically, though it was never verbalized, Clayton hoped to impress his dad by chronicling both of their broader stories. Spending hours asking his parents questions, Clayton learned many of the details surrounding their earlier lives. Homer's dad had died of Bright's disease, a kidney ailment, three days before his fiftieth birthday when Homer was eleven years old. Though Homer's brother, Lloyd, was a year his senior, Homer took charge as the man of the family, shouldering the responsibilities of all seven of his siblings, the farm, and his mother. Early on, authority became Homer's legacy.

Homer did not question Clayton in his efforts of writing the book, entitled *From Switzerland to Sonnenberg*. But neither did he express obvious appreciation or praise for Clayton's work. Homer did use a large eraser toward the editing when asked to read over the first draft. He did not approve of anything that showed him in a negative light. Thus, the flavor of the book took on only positive tones.

Along that positive vein, Clayton held a breakout meeting for his book at Norma (his sister) and Jim's house after church on July 10, 1976. His parents and siblings attended the momentous event along with many nieces and nephews.

Marion (Clayton's brother) opened the meeting, reading Isaiah 53:3-5 from the Bible, which suggests "through Jesus' death, sinners may be healed and find peace."

Elno (Clayton's brother) prayed, "Dear heavenly Father, we thank you for being the father of our ancestors who loved the Lord. We pray that we, the present generation, might continue to live and pass on the good news of the gospel to the next generation. We ask that you bless Dad and Mom as we descendants offer support, hope, and encouragement."

Marion then mentioned how much he liked these family gatherings as they provide a time to reflect on how the good things from their past have enriched their lives. He conveyed that history gives them a glimpse as to how they became who they are today, so they can make informed decisions for tomorrow. Thanking Clayton for all the hard work he put into this book, he asked others to show their support. They applauded.

Clayton graciously opened, emphasizing his desire for everyone's participation in the meeting as they had all had such an important part in its compilation. He talked in-depth of the various contributions, which he nicknamed *the four Ss*, that their ancestors from Switzerland had brought to this family: The Lehmans, Bertha's maternal side, were known for their *singing*, as their mother was still known to all of them. Bertha's paternal side, the Zuerchers, by and large, had a *stick-to-it-ness* nature. Their Christian fervor was particularly admirable. The Amstutzes, Homer's mother's side, were considered *solid* in their work and their faith. They valued living orderly lives through sound doctrine. The Steiners, on Homer's dad's side, were from Alsace-Lorraine on the German and French border. They had fled persecution from Switzerland, *sojourning* frequently. Their adventurous spirits had led them to move frequently and tackle new things. They also had a considerable number of preachers and teachers in their lineage.

Clayton ended his summary by saying, "With this kind of heritage, what more can we ask? Hopefully, this presentation and reading my book will help us know the positive things from our past and help us decide what we want to pass on to our children. We certainly have a godly heritage. We need to be grateful. Let's ask for God's blessing on our family."

Beemer paused here to write a margin note to the editor: *I'm hearing a lot of positive mumbo jumbo here. I'm not saying it's wrong or even inaccurate. But does Clayton, all of a sudden, forget the inexplicable pain he endured under his dad's unbearable scrutiny?*

From there, Elno led a song to the tune of "God Bless America," in which he changed the words to go with the God Bless Our Heritage theme.

Then Clayton said, "Now, we come to Grandpa and Grandma—Homer and Bertha. We have not talked about them yet. We have heard of our past, but we are living in the present. Let us start with Grandma Steiner. I would like to open this up for your input. I will start by restating the traditions she has given us. Our singing ability, stick-to-it-ness, and our need to do things well come directly from her and her ancestors. She has taught us well.

"What would you like to say about Grandma Steiner? Personally, I think that Grandma Steiner gave our home that extra personal touch. She mothered us; she loved us; she fed us; and she clothed us. She literally did everything that Grandpa could not do. (Laughter.) She did these things for us with grace, patience, and sincerity."

Elno mentioned how their mother taught them about God's love through her playing piano, singing, and teaching hymns. Then, he added, "While the kids stood around singing along, Dad sat there with us. He couldn't carry a tune, but he supported her in her singing."

Clayton said, "I will never forget the time Grandpa Steiner and I had a verbal fight. It ended with Grandpa telling me, 'If he could, he would take his shirt off his back to make life better for me.' I think that was true. Grandpa, you would have taken your shirt off your back if needed. Grandpa, you certainly taught us self-discipline, how to work hard, and how not be satisfied with just the status quo. You taught us to do our best and move on."

Beemer writes in his side notes: *Now wait a minute. Doesn't Clayton remember this 'take my shirt off my back for you' comment in context? It was right after he stepped in to stop his dad from verbally assaulting his mother and was then told, 'good boys do not do that,' as if good boys let their dads treat their mother like trash. I wasn't privy to his feelings back then, but from what I feel now, Clayton very much holds that exchange against his father. But he's using part of that conversation to make his dad look like the man of the year. What's with this overly optimistic bit? Isn't he lying by not telling the whole truth?*

And why did the conversation about his mom get taken over by so many compliments about his dad?

At this point, the forum gave way to open discussion. Many asked questions, and some made comments regarding their memories. Then, Clayton said, "I had a hard time appreciating my parents until I had children of my own. I am sure many of you can relate to that. It is hard to raise kids these days. They raised eleven of us, and I believe Mom and Dad did the best they could. We children made mistakes growing up in how we related to our parents, just as our parents made mistakes. Now, we have made mistakes with our children. But as you look around this room, our parents' success is evident. You have to admit Mom and Dad did a darn good job. (Laughter, probably from the near-swear word, darn.) They did the best they could, even if it did not always feel that way. We siblings have turned out well."

Elno said, "In addition to teaching us to put God and the church first, I thank the Lord that Dad taught us honesty and clean language. I can't ever remember Dad using cuss words or any foul language of any kind."

"That's quite a testimony," Clayton agreed.

Ironically, Homer, now seventy-seven years old, shared a rare moment of humility, admitting his imperfections. "I never felt I was capable of raising children. I always felt I fell short and was incapable. For some reason or other, everyone here loves the Lord. You all have had more schooling than I had or ever will have. But the point is, I did many things wrong, and I realize that. For some reason or other ..." As he searched for his words, all waited patiently. "I was going to say something, and now I cannot think of it."

Bertha then mentioned how she wished Kenny could be there. "He's an important part."

Homer interrupted and began again, "Yesterday, I was thinking of a sermon I heard. I cannot give chapter and verse, but it was very good. It reminded me that my ways are not always so good. I often make a mess of things and ..."

Elno cut in and said, "I often thank the Lord that he takes us as parents just the way we are. We don't feel adequate. We fall short. But he takes us just the way we are. Dad, your heart was in the right place. You had a good attitude."

Beemer notes to his superior: *Really? Is everyone else buying this? Why doesn't Clayton speak up?*

Someone read aloud a Psalm from Scripture. Several people, including Homer, commented on it, declaring God's wisdom and "our" inadequacies.

Marion said, "I am not a theologian, but sometimes we get carried away. The central message of the gospel is that we can forgive each other. We are not here to lay blame or find fault. The message of the Christian faith is one of freedom, joy, and creativity. We are sojourners with power and stick-to-it-ness. I liked Clayton's presentation this morning. I thought it was fantastic to hear what we can learn from each of our ancestors. I think one of the things Mom was concerned about was Kenny not being here. And now, I see, he has arrived. It is like Mom to always think about the other person."

Clayton expressed his sorrow that his brother Roy was the only sibling who could not attend as he was tending a new business in Oregon. Clayton also acknowledged several others for their invaluable service toward the book. Niece Rhoda helped with indexing. Sister in-law Mabel proofread the manuscripts. Nephew Ray made it possible to bind the book. And sister Arlene was especially thanked for lending her diary as Clayton's top resource.

Marion announced the cost of the books at six dollars apiece and encouraged all family members to recognize the hard work and love Clayton had put into the project. Then, he wondered if they could take up a love offering for Clayton. Elno concurred, citing the $500.00 in travel and other costs beyond the printing. Each sibling bought multiple copies of the book to share with their families, allowing Clayton to break even on the book's cost. The group collected an offering for Clayton, which covered his other, related expenses.

Many family members hung around well after the meeting adjourned. All in all, Clayton felt the event was a huge success. He was pleased with the turnout, support, and enthusiasm he received. Absent from his bucket list, however, was his dad's acknowledgment and appreciation. With all the positive banter thrown around the room, Clayton expected that his dad would feel so honored that he'd helplessly express his admiration for his son and the massive undertaking that writing a book of their heritage entailed. But such a response did not occur.

To Clayton, his father's silence made it seem as if he'd never written the book. It appeared that his dad did not like the book, did not care, or purposely refused to affirm his son regarding it. Deep down, Clayton was hurt by his father's lack of response, though he could not identify the emotion or the reason for the pain. The (unattended to) offense, over the years, slowly turned to a festering cauldron of anger, a subject to be discussed with a counselor some other day.

At this point, before chronicling further, Beemer tried to assess all that had taken place at the book reveal. His confusion stymied his progress. Reluctantly, he broke down and again asked to speak with the editor in chief.

The round-nosed editor, a little woozy from the transport (as usual), shook off the unwanted effects and faced his young counterpart. "A little frazzled by your subject's positivity?"

Caught off guard by his mentor's accurate and concise probe, Beemer said, "Ah … yeah. Clayton's suddenly over the moon with his happy upbringing. Is it common for humans to lie about their experience to somehow change their reality?"

The old stone-faced journalist dropped his weary eyes a moment, then reached Beemer's eyes again. "It's complicated." He drew a deep breath. "Perhaps they're merely emphasizing the good to encourage more of the same," countered the old journalist.

"Is that how it works? They just talk about the good things, and the bad things go away?"

"Not exactly," admitted the chief. "The negative things need to be dealt with at some point, or they will grab their host and never let go. But even if he didn't quite step up to the plate on this one occasion, he'll have many more opportunities."

"What?" Beemer wrinkled his nose. "How will he ever accomplish great things if he can't even conquer a minor thing like telling his dad off?"

"You think telling his dad off is a minor thing?"

"Well, that mean old man deserves it. It would be truthful to tell his dad that he is the cause of so much of Clayton's ineptness and cowardice. Wouldn't that truth set Clayton free?"

Chief's wry grin spoke before he did. "So, you think if he'd shared that in front of the whole family, their undoubtedly mixed reviews and the father's angry response would not affect Clayton negatively? You don't think Clayton would need to navigate through a whole new emotional turmoil that might set him back even further?"

One side of Beemer's mouth scrunched. "I guess I didn't think of that. But surely everyone saw the elephant in the room. Why didn't anyone speak about the dreadful part of their childhood? His oldest brother, Elno, practically delivered a sermonette on Homer's wonderful kingship, while Marion, the other brother that Clayton wants to be like, was selling Clayton and his book like he was the undeniable prince, walking in the royal highness's footsteps."

"Perhaps the success of the book will encourage your subject. It may be a necessary step toward the confidence he desperately needs."

"Maybe," Beemer admitted, still troubled. "I guess I wish he'd just hurry up and get on with tearing out the root of his instability."

"Which is ...?"

"Well, I don't know exactly. But it's got to do with his dad somehow. Being continually made to feel deficient and never validated by one's father for all of one's life has got to breed confusion and hopelessness, doesn't it?"

The old editor bobbed his round head. "Very good, Beemer. You're learning. So, based on your research, what does your subject want from this toxic relationship now?"

"Good question! I wish he'd just throw it in the ocean. But it appears as though he is determined to still gain his father's love and admiration. I don't see the old man changing. Why would Clayton?"

"Because THE BOSS made them for nurture. They aren't robots. They're living beings that require love for their sustenance."

"But he got nurture from his mother. In fact, now he's finding that he was over-nurtured by his mother."

"Was he over-nurtured, or is Clayton still craving that nurture so much because the masculine side of his environmental equation shut that need down?"

Beemer's frown softened as he pondered.

Chief continued, "If humans don't get the love they require, their needs often become insatiable. Those that don't dedicate their lives to denying those needs often turn to absolute dependence on substances, mind power, physical pleasure, emotional nirvana, or a host of other addictions."

"Whoa! Clayton craves that nurturing love so much because Clayton's dad basically robbed him of it when he routinely bad-mouthed his mother."

"That's right. And ignoring that need doesn't make it go away."

Beemer said, "That's why it dumbfounds me that the whole roomful did not acknowledge the toxic negativity the dad smeared all over them. I mean, from what I witnessed, he was the master at convincing them they were mess-ups."

"Are you saying their dad's goal was to mess them up?"

"Well, no. But, regardless of his goals, that was the net result."

"True enough."

The editor in chief nodded imperceptibly. "I think you're onto something, Beemer. Keep probing and writing. And don't give up on your subject. He may not receive the healing boost he imagined from this genealogy book, but he's likely to learn far more about his dad, and, in turn, himself, than he expected to before it's all said and done."

19
VOLUNTARY SERVICE
MORE THAN A JOB

A headline in the Goshen newspaper on June 5, 1976, read, "Clayton Steiner Granted Leave." The family moved a month later, leaving their furnishings as their house would be rented the next year by nephew Dean and his wife, Bonnie Nussbaum.

Kevin was eight and entering third grade; Duane, at six, was entering first grade; Bruce was four; and Kimberly was almost two. The kids adapted to the new adventure in stride.

As they entered the foreign, bustling, disorderly metropolis of Champaign after their four-hour drive, Clayton and Ruth looked at each other as if they were in a sci-fi movie. Clayton thought, *What have we gotten ourselves into? Will we survive this dangerous move?*

But the quaint property where the two *Voluntary Service* (VS) houses were located dispersed their fears when they drove into the complex. Their single-family dwelling, at 303 West Beardsley, was a stone's throw away from the single's larger VS house, which was found at 305 West Beardsley. They received a warm welcome from the other VSers and ate their evening meal together. The next night, they met with the VS support group, which consisted of dedicated members from the three local Mennonite churches, *First Mennonite, East Bend,* and *Dewey,* and they immediately felt welcomed and accepted.

They quickly began to get settled and to adapt to their new surroundings. On Thursday, they held their first VS unit meeting with the ten young, single VSers that they would be shepherding. It went splendidly well from Clayton's perspective. During the next day, they enrolled Kevin and Duane in the local school system. The first couple of months held plenty of uncomfortable, humbling moments as they adjusted to the new roles, met many new people, and developed new skills.

Clayton's job description included maintaining the two houses, paying the bills, keeping the lines open between the Elkhart office and the three sponsoring churches, reporting to the local VS support group, meeting the needs of ten to twelve fellow VSers between the ages of eighteen and twenty-two, and finding meaningful work assignments for each of the VSers. Occasionally, when he was needed, Clayton joined the home repair crew.

Ruth's assignments included relating to the local community and school, preparing the weekly meal schedule, and buying the groceries. Ruth soon became busy planning getaways with Clayton, providing emotional support for the VSers, and getting involved with *Bible Study Fellowship* through the First Mennonite Church. She was not one to let the grass grow under her feet.

Each evening, Clayton and his family joined all the single VSers at the 305 West Beardsley house around a long table that was spread out in the living room for supper. Clayton looked forward to the faithful gatherings where they unwound, shared the goings-on of their days, played tricks on one another, made announcements, and laughed at some of the meals the male VSers made, as each person took their turn preparing and serving the meals.

Clayton's first meal prep was August 2. Not quite catching the gist of *each* person taking their turn at preparing the meal, he did little in the kitchen other than bring out the delicious dishes that Ruth prepared. He gratefully accepted the compliments on the *great meal*. Ruth did not correct their misguided appreciation.

It was not until he saw some of the other males struggling with their meals that he recognized his deceit. He regretfully realized that he had expected Ruth to do the job his mother had always thanklessly done while he sat and ate, like his dad had always done. But this unit was based on *everyone* chipping in for the benefit of the group. Not only was he lying, he realized, but he was also not doing his part to live as a community.

When Clayton finally owned his responsibility to feed his crew, he often made his favorite dish, Fruit Storm with Swiss Cheese. This classic Swiss Kidron, Ohio, specialty consisted of fruit, milk, bread, and sugar, mixed like a storm. The cheese completed the meal … lest anyone feel the need for a main course. Most of the group said they enjoyed the fruit soup, a term of mixed endearments the VSers coined, though after dinner, they usually sought the leftovers from other meals that Ruth always made available.

They established Thursday nights as the unit meeting time. During these meetings, Clayton and Ruth managed grievances that inevitably came with living so closely together, handled VS business, planned future events, took turns sharing their spiritual journeys, and established prayer partners for the coming week. This precious time enriched Clayton and Ruth as they developed friendships, enjoyed comradery, and supported the others.

An unexpected benefit was the VSers' involvement in the Steiner children's lives. The kids were welcomed into the VS family as graciously as Clayton and Ruth were. They soon looked at the VSers as older brothers and sisters, relishing their attention. Some VSers gladly babysat on occasion, allowing Clayton and Ruth to go out on evening dates. Once, the men even took the boys on a weekend camp out at a nearby park, an event the boys never forgot.

Clayton and Ruth managed the daily care of their young children jointly. Also together, after the kids were put to bed, they lent their ears to the VSers in the evenings, availing themselves for counseling and resolving conflicts among the younger VSer housemates. They soon found these vulnerable, one-on-one meetings life-breathing—to themselves as much as their mentees. Where months earlier Clayton had found his job tedious, insignificant, and draining, he suddenly found purpose, significance, and life in his position as Papa Caretaker. The concept that he was gifted as a nurturer, like his mother, never presented itself to him as such. What kept Clayton going was his drive to do his job well—as good or better than his brothers Elno and Marion would have.

Clayton and Ruth found their nurturing efforts to cultivate health, growth, and harmony rewarding and unifying. They hadn't healed all their relational issues or arrived at *eternal bliss* just yet, but they felt healthier as they worked toward mutual goals together. And because Clayton felt harmony in his marriage and saw harmony among the VSers, he felt good about himself as the one in charge.

In the March–April 1977 edition of *The Agape*, a publication representing Voluntary Service, Clayton wrote "October 3, 1976, was an important day in Champaign County VS history. It was the day that thirty-three leaders from the three sponsoring churches met to review and act on the proposed papers on the mission and by-laws of its VS program."

The proposed papers were a seventeen-page document about the goals of the Champaign unit that Clayton had spent hours constructing after talking to many church representatives and coordinating their input. The board approved his proposal, praising and supporting the direction. Clayton's first objective task was a success, which made him feel good. Of course, things in Champaign were not always this easy or successful.

A large portion of the challenge in managing the VS unit was the transitory nature of the beast. The one constant Clayton could count on was that each VSer would arrive and leave (usually on a one-year term) at differing times, which always jostled the group dynamics.

A month before the Steiners moved to Champaign, a VSer named Lars had moved into the 305 house. Lars, a non-Mennonite, was friendly, had some college background, and though somewhat elusive and quirky, generally endeared himself to the other VSers. A month after Clayton's family settled in, Lars was picked up by his girlfriend, May (the daughter of a prominent Goshen College professor). They left, going to an undisclosed location for six days and leaving Clayton to scratch his head, not knowing how best to handle the untoward situation.

Another bone of contention with Lars' behavior was his excessive phone use. One month, he accrued over a hundred dollars of long-distance calls to his family and girlfriend, which he couldn't pay.

Meanwhile, his place of employment had begun to call Clayton, complaining about Lars' inconsistent management of his position. When he was asked about his spotty attendance, Lars always gave a plausible alibi, giving Clayton little to reprimand him about.

Soon after another of Lars' rendezvous with his girlfriend, Clayton and Ruth confronted him on his poor work performance, which he acknowledged and pledged to improve. The next day, his place of employment called Clayton in an uproar that Lars was late in preparing a meal for his dependents.

Clayton and Ruth met with Lars and his employer to resolve the conflict. A couple of months after that and after more one-on-one meetings with Lars, Clayton finally gave him an ultimatum of shaping up or shipping out.

Reluctantly, Lars finally resolved to resign. The sad ending took a month to transpire, but Lars finally left the cozy confines of 305 Beardsley.

One of the young VS housemates later shared the following story about Lars and the unusual phone call she had received in the middle of the night when everyone else was sleeping. "The lady on the other end told me in no uncertain terms that she needed to talk to her husband. I told her that she must have called a wrong number because no one at this house was married. Agitated with that notion, she said, 'That's because he didn't want anyone else to know he was married.' I then realized the gal on the other end was obviously inebriated. 'Is this May?' I asked her. She said it was, and that she needed to talk to Lars. I then knocked at Lars' door and let him talk to her.

"The next day, curious as all get out, I interrogated Lars about the incident. He told me May was calling from New Zealand and had no idea what time it was here. He told me she gets 'really flighty when she's drunk like that.' About the being-married part, he admitted to it and told me they just needed some time apart to work on things. I agreed, for some dumb reason, not to tell anyone about the conversation."

Somehow, Lars's marriage had slipped through the VS system undetected for nearly eight months! He had gotten married a month before his VS arrival. Clayton couldn't have dreamed up such an encounter had he tried.

The beauty (and the challenge) of running a VS unit corresponded to the unique story and personality that each individual brought to the table. The diversity each radiated colored Clayton's world. Working through their differences, to Clayton, was like weaving a needle through a multipatterned quilt. The labor was strenuous and tedious, but the result usually crafted each piece into the whole wonderfully.

Clayton and Ruth's most accurate title could have been *sounding board*, as the mere act of listening to their boarders reaped bountiful harvests. Often, when a complaining or injured party in the busy VS household felt heard by their leaders, whatever problem they voiced worked its way out. However, not all problems worked out with a positive result. For instance, one young woman was so attached to her parents that she could not cross the hump into independent living. Clayton and Ruth sympathetically granted her wish to return home.

Sometime after their stint in Champaign, Clayton and Ruth learned that two residents under their watch had been involved in a little hanky-panky without their knowledge. But Clayton and Ruth were not their boarders' consciences, policing everything they did. The VSers were adults—Clayton and Ruth were their guides, confidants, and older siblings in a way, and there for support. These roles Clayton and Ruth embodied fluidly.

Another VSer had a romantic struggle that was outside the unit. She felt she needed to cut her boyfriend out of her life. He did not agree. Afraid of hurting the boy who *loved her so*, she lacked the moxie to sever the relationship decisively. After months of half-hearted attempts to end things and a third *Dear John* letter, her boyfriend called the unit to inform his fair maiden that he was en route to visit her. Clayton just happened to answer the phone. With more force than the girl had ever exerted, Clayton informed the hopeless romantic that his infatuation was sorely misguided, and she would not see him if he came. The disappointed suiter evidently got the message (finally) because they never saw head nor tail of the persistent lad again.

Another warm and affectionate young woman easily confided in Clayton and Ruth, so freely and often that they had to establish firmer boundaries, asking her to stay away for specific periods of time.

Many VSers opened up to Clayton and Ruth in matters they could not discuss with anyone else. One VSer shared his father's sudden declaration that he was gay—a shock the VSer was totally unprepared for.

Clayton sometimes had to discern if a VSer's ability and effort coincided with their employer's needs and then intervene if necessary. Clayton learned to treat such matters discreetly and compassionately, measures never shown to him by his demanding, callous father, but they were ones that Jesus graciously exemplified.

The pinnacle of challenging situations that confronted Clayton came when a local pastor had an inappropriate relationship with a female resident who was under Clayton's care. In counseling the girl, Clayton and Ruth learned that the affair was sexual, though the pastor, when confronted, insisted nothing more than counseling had occurred between the two. The pastor's wife knew of their relationship but not of its sexual nature. Clayton and Ruth encouraged the young woman to break it off, but she was too weak or befuddled to carry such action through. The problem continued and thickened to the point that Clayton finally stepped in and informed the pastor's denominational headquarters of the ongoing indiscretion. He included a written statement of facts of the whole mess. Eventually, after Clayton and Ruth left Champaign, the pastor lost his job and was not allowed to lead in any capacity within that denomination for several years. The victim, however, would carry scars from the ordeal for the rest of her life.

After being entwined in the rat race of working to get ahead and placing so much emphasis on the almighty dollar in Goshen, Clayton had resolved to *live within their means* at their new post in Champaign, just like the other VSers. This meant he would not dip into their Goshen bank savings for their day-to-day living expenses. This idealistic theory worked fine … until Christmas rolled around.

The family ventured out on a vacation to Kidron over the holidays to visit both sides of the family though their car needed repairs, their threadbare clothes needed attention, and they had no money for presents. Never had they entered a Christmas or their families' homes with so little. Ruth prayed that the gifts their family would give them would be clothes, not toys. On Christmas Day, when the offering plate was passed around at church, they contemplated over being a faithful steward with the remaining two dollars in Ruth's purse or saving it for themselves. They decided to honor their commitment and to return a tithe, plopping the coveted two dollars into the offering plate.

Here, Beemer wrote in his margin notes: *What, are they nuts? Why wouldn't they use the savings money (which they earned!) in their Goshen account? How does being a pauper help anyone?*

The editor quickly wrote back: Sometimes THE BOSS honors such upside-down principles. Watch and learn.

The next day, as a Christmas gift, Clayton's sister Vi gave him seventy-five dollars that she had saved in her alabaster box. Tears rolled down Clayton's cheeks. He and Ruth joyously went to the clothing store the next morning and bought overalls for the kids, jeans for Clayton, and underclothing for Ruth. Never had they rejoiced so bountifully on Christmas.

Beemer wrote back to his chief editor: *Hmm. I guess having less helped them appreciate their gifts more. What a strange world this is.*

In a May 1978 article entitled "VS Can be Hard on a Father's Ego" for the Mennonite family magazine called *Christian Living*, Clayton wrote "It was late fall of 1976, and I had just received my first Voluntary Service allowance—a total of $50.00 for my family of six. I felt like I was on welfare. The process of shifting gears to a life with few extras, though difficult, went rather smoothly."

In his side notes Beemer wrote: *Smoothly? Really? How quickly he forgets how bumpy the ride without regular income was. Why would he lie about his journey?*

His wise chronicling mentor wrote back: People often forget their struggles after they learn from them and move on. Plus, they have a propensity to present their best side, hoping to be worthy of love. Many never discover that THE BOSS loves and esteems them no matter what.

Beemer wrote back: *Well, I thought Clayton had already figured that out. I don't know why he keeps trying to prove his worthiness. I guess humans just need to keep learning and relearning some things.*

In the magazine article, Clayton undersold the emasculating feeling his ego underwent. In a strictly logical sense, he wondered how he could provide for his family. In a spiritual sense, he lived out his faith by trusting God to provide. He also neglected to mention in the article how his kids participated in the *free lunch* program due to their low-income status, and how their need for winter coats affected his pride. *All for the greater good*—he hoped.

Approaching their year commitment, the Elkhart VS office asked Clayton and Ruth to stay on for another year and take on additional leadership of four neighboring VS units. They counseled with trusted friends in February and prayed in earnest about their decision. After sleeping in on March 12 (a rare occurrence), they woke up and decided to commit to another year.

Action suddenly broke at breakneck speed. When they announced their decision to their kids on March 13, the kids responded jubilantly at the news. On March 14, Clayton wrote his letter of resignation (since they were only on a one-year sabbatical) to the *Walnut Hill Daycare Center* and shared it with the VS unit, who affirmed their decision. He met with five administrators of the Elkhart Missions Board on March 17 to clarify his next year's job capacity. On March 19, they went on a retreat with the WH church. Many people shed tears, but, in the end, all their friends were understanding and supportive, and even gave them a farewell gift of a hundred dollars.

In mid-April, Dale, the VS coordinator, visited and clarified Clayton and Ruth's new role as Regional Cluster Leaders of four neighboring VS units. There was no resting on their laurels. Though Clayton felt a twinge of concern for the possible time away from family that the extra responsibilities might cause, he mostly felt honored to be in leadership for an awesome organization.

Like all kids, Clayton's children went through their share of growing pains. Kevin enjoyed his freedom to roam around on his bike. From ages nine to ten, he found his favorite hotspots and frequented them at will—until he broke his parent's trust, which changed his roam-free status for a time.

One afternoon, Kevin forlornly entered the house and told his mother that someone outside wanted to speak to her. Ruth, bewildered, walked out the front door to find a car parked in the driveway. The man in the car got out and introduced himself.

The man explained to Ruth that Kevin had tried to steal some suckers from his store down the street. Aghast, Ruth looked at the sheepish Kevin then back to the store owner. She apologized profusely and thanked him for going to the trouble of bringing Kevin home, knowing he could have reported her son to the police. After lecturing Kevin for his disrespectful behavior, Ruth sent him to report his wrongdoing to his dad who was working at the 305 house. That night, Clayton and Ruth talked at length with him about the incident and prayed with him. As a parent, Clayton hoped Kevin's apparent remorse was genuine.

Kevin had another, quite different, adventure one cold, wintery night. On this occasion, the front doorbell rang after the family had readied themselves for bed. Wondering who on earth would be calling on them at that hour of the night, Clayton robed himself and meandered through the dark house to the front door. When he opened the door, to his dismay, barefoot Kevin stood there in his pajamas and wanting to go to his warm bed. He didn't remember how he had gotten there or what he did while he was outside. Clayton deduced that Kevin had sleepwalked out the back door, woke in the cold, realized he was outside his own house, and rang the doorbell when he discovered the front door was locked. They had found him sleepwalking in the halls before but never outside the house. Alarmed, they lodged a chair in front of his bedroom door for a few weeks after the incident to keep him from harm. Eventually, he grew out of this bizarre habit, though he did walk in his sleep one other time that they knew of. On that occasion, he walked out into the hallway, pulled out a drawer, peed in it, and went back to bed.

The boys were a distinct white minority in school, but they had to learn how to navigate in the school population. On the way to school one day, seven-year-old Duane got in a fight with a boy named Benji for which he was sent to the principal's office. Later, at home, he asked his parents, "But what's wrong with calling a black boy the N-word? That's what we called them in Goshen." Clayton winced at his son's insensitive perspective. He vowed to help him change. That, however, was not the last time Duane found the principal's office. He learned best, it seemed, by first acting on his impulses and saying what he thought and then dealing with the repercussions.

To help the family appreciate what a big city had to offer, they toured Chicago after attending a VS orientation. They came home to discover that Kevin's bike had been stolen. He was heartsick over the ordeal. He used that bike to go to the city pool (which the boys loved), the library (which Kevin thrived on), stores, and other kid-friendly hideouts. To be without his bike was like ripping his heart out.

However, the next day Kevin came barging into the house, ecstatic. "I found my bike!" He had spotted the bike about a block away, so Clayton followed him to verify his findings. They decided to share the misdemeanor with the police instead of taking the matter into their own hands. Soon after, a police officer visited their house and asked Kevin how he knew it was his bike. Kevin demonstratively said, "That's easy! It has a little Goshen license plate on the back." Sure enough, the officer returned the stolen bike to Kevin later that day. Clayton worried that one of the boys who lived at that house would threaten Kevin at school the next day, but no retribution occurred. Other than the swashes of black that had been spray-painted over the areas identifying its make and model, the bike was no worse for wear.

Another day, Clayton and Ruth heard some crying in the other room. Scrambling to find the source of the noise, they were horrified to find little three-year-old Kimberly stuck in a cold-air register. Though her two oldest brothers said that she *fell in*, Clayton sleuthed the truth out of them. They had purposely put her in the cramped duct to see if *she'd fit*. They ended up getting the worse *end* of things; their dad made sure of that!

All in all, the kids' positive behavior far outweighed the bad. And living in a university city (the University of Illinois at Urbana-Champaign) allowed the family to find opportune and innovative ways to complement their financially limited lifestyle. For instance, they had unparalleled access to the university's functions and free activities. The kids enjoyed the free gymnastics, computer classes, and outdoor swimming (which was even available in the winter under a unique dome-shaped, air-filled canvas). In addition, Kevin and Duane loved being in a play called *Zach Jr.* at First Mennonite Church, which they performed several times around the area with Kevin proudly playing the lead role. A conglomeration of stores, which came to be known as a *mall*, opened not far from the VS unit, and the family enjoyed visiting it too. Clayton even audited a public administration class.

The unit had a monthly budget, which afforded the group to go to a festive event about once a month. They used the allowance for things like college basketball games, movies, and cultural events like The Ice Capades and The Harlem Globetrotters. They often celebrated birthdays and going-away parties for departing VSers at one of the city's many classic restaurants.

The kids also enjoyed occasional excursions outside of the city like the biannual VS family retreats. In the Ozarks, on one such occasion, an odd hippie couple oversaw the kids while the adults attended classes and seminars. The kids enjoyed the primitive aspect of no running water or electricity and the freedom to roam around in the woods. Clayton never knew exactly what all went on, other than a rattlesnake was killed, and Duane screamed when his parents plucked a tick off his scalp. The kids sure did enjoy the wilderness experience though.

Back at the unit, from Clayton's family's perspective, there was never a dull moment. At least one, if not all, of the VSers always had time for the kids or was up to something unusual or intriguing. One of the ladies, Barb, had a soft spot for Duane, who absorbed her gentle attention like a sponge.

One time, when the family came back from an Ohio trip, Clayton and Ruth found their bedroom filled, floor to ceiling, with crumpled-up newspapers. Another time, upon returning from a family outing with the kids, Ruth opened their bedroom closet and screamed. Clayton observed four still bodies, faces smeared with red ketchup, lying on the floor. When he and Ruth saw the staged corpses start to move, they laughed and laughed. Clayton interpreted the practical jokes by their young housemates as gestures of acceptance and friendship. One cannot have too much family.

Throughout their time in Champaign, Clayton felt constant support from the three Mennonite churches and their pastors. He felt particularly drawn to Jim and Ann Dunn, pastors of First Mennonite Church, and he even preached one of their morning sermons. That same spring, he was instrumental in restructuring the church, a role he delighted in.

Irvin and (Clayton's sister) Arlene Nussbaum, pastors of *East Bend Mennonite*, often invited them to their home, filling Clayton with that grounding sense of family he craved. Clayton had many stimulating personal conversations with his sister. He considered this sister and her husband his substitute parents.

Feedback from the VSers fueled Clayton's sense of worth. Upon departing, VSers often wrote letters back to Clayton and Ruth or left cards with sentimental regards. One VSer wrote, "I am giving thanks for the relationship which I had with you, for your giving and caring commitment. You have helped me through some *rough spots* in the last several months. Thanks for the many, many long hours of listening and sharing … for holding my hand—both literally and figuratively." Another VSer wrote, "Ruth and Clayton, I want to thank you ever so much for how much both of you have meant to me these past three-and-a-half months. You both show such a love and concern for everyone here in the unit, and that means a lot." A third VSer wrote, "Ruth, there have been lots of times when your good, encouraging words were a big help for me. I will always remember you," and "Clayton, I really admire your willingness to always be trying something new. You've got a beautiful family, and you're going great on life."

Such feedback was invaluable to Clayton. The raw emotions they produced within him affirmed and scared him. Humbled to be admired and appreciated, he longed for still more and deeper acknowledgment.

> Beemer wrote in the side margin: *It is almost earth-shattering to see Clayton's true emotions coming through. To think that I wondered if he even had emotions not too long ago. Now he feels so much. I can't help but think he's becoming the whole person THE BOSS made him to be.*

The editor in chief wrote back: Positive emotions are a good sign. Be on the lookout for his negative emotions too, for they also indicate how the subject is maturing.

Beemer scowled at the bizarre comment. Why should he focus on the negative? And besides, Clayton wasn't having too many negative emotions these days.

When 1978 rolled around, Clayton knew it was time to consider his family's next step regarding his employment as the Voluntary Service positions were generally not vocational, but temporary. His first choice was to go back to Goshen where his house, close friends, and home church were located and find employment with the Elkhart Mennonite Mission Board. With that intent, on March 23, Clayton interviewed with several administrators in that office, confident that his successful VS leadership resume would be more than enough to land him a significant position in the organization that had sent him on his VS mission. To his horror, no job openings were available nor would anything be available any time soon.

Dismayed and put off, Clayton, with the help of their friend, LV Mast, responded by putting his Goshen house up for sale on March 27. On April 28, 1978, the house sold for nearly three times what they had paid for it ten years prior, an indisputable sign to Clayton of God's will! But this sale also narrowed the slight chance of returning to Goshen.

What to do next? Clayton's second choice was to stay in the Champaign-Urbana area. He put out twenty to twenty-five resumes in the area. By the first of May, there were absolutely no bites. Uneasy, he doubled his efforts, knocking on doors and sending out thirty more resumes.

Meanwhile, the Elkhart office had hired a new family to take the Steiner's place, starting the first of July. Not only would Clayton be jobless, but the family would also be homeless if he could not figure out his future. He found an affordable housing arrangement in Champaign to cover his bases. By the first of June, still with no prospects or direction, he consulted a mentor from the First Mennonite Church. Clayton was encouraged by the mentor's optimism that Clayton's situation would surely be clear within twenty-four hours—until his prediction did not hold.

On June 24, the First Mennonite Church held a Steiner Appreciation Day, replete with special music, key speakers, open well-wishing, and the good, ole-fashioned Mennonite potluck that all fond farewells deserve. Blessed by their thoughtfulness, but embarrassed that he had no firm direction to head, Clayton learned of a slim chance that he could get on with a carpenter in Champaign.

Another possibility surfaced when the Elkhart office notified him in the eleventh hour that there might be an opening at *Laurelville Mennonite Retreat Center* in Laurelville, Pennsylvania. Clayton called Laurelville on July 3 as a last-ditch effort to secure a job. After no one picked up, he left a message with Tom Nofziger, the executive director, citing his credentials. Nofziger called back and asked Clayton to send his resume. Clayton did, and on July 8, Mr. Nofziger called again and asked if Clayton could come out for an interview. Clayton agreed and left for the interview on July 15. Before he left, Clayton moved all his family's belongings into the garage to accommodate the new caretakers who were moving into the VS unit the next day.

The interview for the job to serve as the business manager of Laurelville went surprisingly well. But the proper committees and boards would need to discuss and approve such a hiring. While waiting for their decision, Clayton's family stayed with Ruth's parents in Kidron. Finally, on July 19, they received an official invitation to work at Laurelville. Clayton eagerly accepted on the spot; he was so glad that the job search had ended!

That same day, the family traveled back to Champaign to join their VS family for one last meal together. They drove to Goshen two days later to tie up loose ends with the house sale, and they held a garage sale to sell off many of the items they had held in storage. What didn't sell, they sent to the dump. How does a family accumulate such junk?

In the 1978 July–August edition of the VS publication *The Agape*, Clayton wrote an article about his VS experience, which was also picked up by the *Gospel Evangel*, the official publication of the Ohio Mennonite Conference. The article was titled, "What is VS Doing to My Family?" People often asked him why he had taken a family of six into VS. He wrote in response, "Looking back, we can say that entering VS was the best decision our family has made." He continued, "Would I take my family into VS again? The answer is a strong 'YES.' We are a better family unit because of our experience. However, I would caution that our experience has not been without problems and that a VS experience for a family is only as strong as the family itself. For us, VS met our needs, and we are a richer family."

Beemer wrote to his editor: *It's obvious that Clayton has grown. In his last article, he did not entertain the realities of struggle. In this one, he recognized the struggle and credits the struggle for his growth and health. I'd say he's well on his way to success, fame, and wealth.*"

Chief wrote back: Be careful!

Beemer wrote back: *Why?*

The master chronicler swooped down (as close to swooping down as an old chronicler could) to Beemer's side in the middle of the night. Beemer jumped at his mentor's sudden appearance. "Chief! You scared me."

"We need to talk, Beemer."

Beemer's eyes widened. "Okay." He sat down on a chair.

The chief said flatly, "Don't lose your focus."

Beemer squinted and tilted his head.

The stodgy editor scratched his bulbous nose. "You seem to think your subject is deservedly on top of the world."

Beemer looked back at his demanding superior, and replied by saying nothing.

"Beemer."

The firm articulation of his name shook him out of his contemplation. "Uh, yeah. I mean, what, sir ... uh, Chief?"

"Tell me what you're thinking about your subject."

Beemer cleared his gravelly throat. "Well, I think he's doing extremely well. He had just come from a job and community where he gave his all but was depleted. Now, he's giving his all and feeling deservedly splendid about it.

"And their VS teamwork has done wonders for their marriage."

Beemer went on, "The uncomfortable and bewildering diversity that he and his family experienced here not only opened their eyes but strengthened their characters. They're now much more adaptable and capable of living out the golden rule of 'doing unto others as they would have others do unto them.'"

Not getting much of a reaction from the chief, Beemer said, "So, I think he's so sold out to following THE BOSS and serving others, he can't possibly get messed up now."

The editor frowned. "The growth your subject has made has been remarkable. I don't question the truth of your witness. However, to infer that all his present happiness is deserved and will last is taking the matter too far. There's a randomness and an unpredictability about life that only THE BOSS understands. We and humans can't know THE BOSS's absolute will through any formulaic understanding."

"What about reaping what they sow?" asked Beemer. "Isn't that a promise of THE BOSS?"

"It's not so much a promise as a principle. That general proverb is true. But to hold to that like a mathematical equation is not how THE BOSS set up the world. Glean truths, don't skewer them with a fork."

"Hmm. So, doing good won't always turn out good?"

The old journalist said, "Just because he's been rewarded with some relative success today, does not mean he will have enjoyable circumstances tomorrow."

"Well, that's a little unfair, isn't it?" Beemer asked.

The editor's bushy eyebrows furrowed. "Perhaps, relative to our understanding. But Beemer, now that you can feel his feelings, I suggest you feel all his emotions—even the ones he doesn't recognize or chooses to deny. If you don't, you're essentially falsifying THE BOSS's document. And I have strict orders to revoke your license and discharge you if you can't muster the reality of his negative emotions."

Beemer's jaw dropped. He swallowed hard. "That seems a bit harsh for overlooking a guy's ugly feelings."

"THE BOSS isn't into fake, Beemer. You share the truth about everything going on with your subject or you don't chronicle at all. It's that simple. Do you have the stomach to get dirty and grapple with *all* of this messy human's life?"

Beemer sat there stunned for a moment, realizing that his desire for a healthy subject might destroy his career. He nodded … repeatedly … in a daze. Then, he finally asked, "How do you know he has such hidden feelings?"

"I've been at this a long time, son. Humans stuff unwanted or difficult feelings (just like you want to). That's what they do. I'm not guessing. I'm saying, like all humans, your subject is stuffing some feelings and is not being completely transparent."

"Why would he do that?"

"Well, in his case, go back to his childhood. Was he encouraged to feel the whole gamut of emotions THE BOSS meant for him to feel?"

Beemer looked over to Clayton again and frowned. "Far from it. He was taught to feel pride in obedience and hard work, and shame about anything not living up to his dad's ideals. Any other emotion was as foreign to him as a snowflake in summer."

"There you go. He's trapped some keen emotions deep in his cellar."

"Are you saying he's not being honest?"

"Use whatever word you want. But until he finds the emotional fortitude to feel those hidden emotions, he can only fake integrity, which will leave him vulnerable to provocation and circumstantial attack."

Beemer's head jerked back. "Provocation and circumstantial attack? What does that mean?"

"It means things are going to happen to him that are completely out of his control. He's going to be attacked by his own conscience as well as by the world. Only when he can be truly honest with his inner emotions, will he be able to fight off the accusations of the enemies of his soul. But, until then, expect a rough ride."

Beemer's face flushed. "But things are going so well. He's not ready for a sniper attack."

"You'd be surprised what these humans can go through. But just know that he's going to face disappointment, heartache, and confusion. Happiness is not a solution. It's a fleeting gift, however coveted."

Just then, Clayton snored.

The editor said his farewell, leaving Beemer to contemplate the unexpected.

The young Chronicler shook his head. He sure hoped the old editor was wrong.

20
CAMP LIFE
EXPECTATIONS

Before Clayton's next employ in Laurelville, Pennsylvania, the Steiner family went to the tenth Mennonite World Conference in Wichita. Clayton made a family vacation of the trip by treating his family to a tour of the Gateway Arch in St. Louis, Missouri. Their steady *hand to the plow* and meager salary during the past two years had allowed for little vacationing, so Clayton wanted to hit as many memory-inspiring stops as possible.

Clayton's sister Vi and her husband, Stan Kuhns, in Wichita, opened their modest home to Clayton's family and two other related families. Clayton enjoyed the united family experience as much or more than the heralded conference.

While the adults listened to gifted speakers and teachers in a large round building with seven thousand others, the children experienced innovative ways of learning and interaction in their own age-appropriate group meetings. The boys ate this up! Kimberly, not so much. She preferred to stay by her mother's side, if not on her lap.

In the evenings, they all assembled to hear dynamic messages for all ages. Ten-year-old Kevin especially enjoyed donning the supplied earphones. He could hear the speeches in whatever language he wanted. Forget that he couldn't understand any of the non-English ones, it was cool to eavesdrop on a foreign communication like a CIA operative!

The sixteen thousand who attended the concluding meeting, which was the largest gathering of Mennonites in one place up to that time, gave Clayton a tangible sense of awe and togetherness with his fellow life-travelers. This experience grounded and inspired him.

After saying their sad, inevitable farewells, they headed to Ohio, stopping again in Champaign and Goshen along the way. Keeping in step with the *family* theme, Clayton took the boys camping in Benville (near Kidron), in the delightful, secluded backyard of a friend. The solitude of the outdoors and playing and roughing it with his kids helped unwind the built-up tension that was clinging to Clayton.

It was a busy, albeit fulfilling, month!

August 19, 1978, they wound up the narrow road, lined with striking rhododendrons, that was a third of a mile from the center of camp to their soon-to-be home, the Hi-Alps house. This was a much more rural location than the Champaign Volunteer Service (VS) unit. Clayton thought to himself, *This is a beautiful place to raise kids!*

After the massive unloading of two trucks and a car, they set up house. Friends showed up with their stored Goshen items a few days later. With ample room in the expansive three-story house, for the first time in their lives, storage was not a limiting concern.

They enrolled the boys at Norvelt/FDR Elementary School first thing. Four active kids who were raring to try out their new Huck Finn surroundings required plenty of patience from their parents. Though exhausting, the *settling-in* phase arrived surprisingly soon.

Unskilled, untrained, and ignorant of his new job duties, Clayton, of course, felt intimidated in the beginning. Expecting as much coming in, he was determined to *learn the ropes* and make an impact on the Laurelville Church Center (LLC). Knowing he had big shoes to fill from his position's respected predecessor added to the pressure he felt.

Fortunately, the staff graciously helped him navigate his new responsibilities. Tom Nafziger, his immediate supervisor; Dana Sommers, head of the maintenance department; and Suzie Bontrager, head of food services, proved especially patient and helpful throughout his training.

Clayton's job description included approving bills, signing checks, assisting his secretary to book groups, welcoming and billing groups who attended LCC events, balancing the books, and preparing for the various LCC Board Committees that came to the Center to do their work. The effort and commitment Clayton gave paid dividends in a few short months when Clayton felt he finally knew his employment responsibilities. Throughout the humble learning process, he met weekly with Tom, his supervisor, to stabilize his approach.

Early in the transition, Clayton had the privilege of sharing a speech with the LCC staff that he had previously given at First Mennonite Church in Champaign and at Walnut Hill Church in Goshen, which recapped his watershed journey. In it, he articulated his struggle and fear of *not knowing* what he was to do after the VS position ended and he had sold his house in Goshen. Though he expected God to honor his proven service record to the church, he admitted to feeling cheated and thinking "the world seemed awfully cruel" when no jobs showed up within his time frame.

He told them that "the harder I looked and tried to open doors, the harder they closed." Finally, when all hope appeared to be lost, the LCC job glistened in the rock pile, and they offered him the job. Though Clayton was skeptical from recent false hopes, his ten-year-old son, Kevin (out of the mouth of babes), said, "Daddy, don't you want the job? Why are we trying to dream up reasons not to accept it?" This query startled Clayton back on track, and life suddenly made sense again. He explained, "At no other time in my life have I felt the presence of God more than in the past several months and especially the two weeks before the end of my family's VS term. Indeed, God is real and personal. He is alive and doing well. He provides for his people in his own way and time."

Beemer hovered his pen over the side margin, poised to express his subject's faith-building testimony through triumphant comments such as "Clayton's trusting THE BOSS now!" or "There's no stopping this man of faith!" or "I told you he's on his way to fame and prosperity." But caution hedged his confidence. No one liked a gloater. Least of all, he suspected, his wily editor. He decided to hold off on his victory lap—for now. He'd let his subject's life prove his obvious accurate forecast. He couldn't wait to see the wise old chronicler's expression when he'd have to acknowledge his student's amazing insight.

The August 1978 edition of the *Laurelville Breezes Shalom Newsletter* announced the resignation of the former LCC business manager and the hiring of his replacement, Clayton Steiner. References to Clayton and Ruth included "solid," "mature," and "devoted."

The *Gospel Herald*, the official Mennonite periodical, wrote in their October 10, 1978 issue, "Clayton Steiner, Kidron, Ohio, assumed responsibilities as business manager at Laurelville Mennonite Church Center. Clayton and his wife, Ruth, come to the assignment from two years as VS unit leaders at Champaign, IL." Clayton's picture was posted next to the article.

More and more, Clayton felt significant and validated—things he had never experienced under his dad's roof. As much as he wanted to bask in that glory, he wanted more to add to the favorable identity he was gaining. This momentum meant he had to continue pressing forward and using the gifts God had given him to improve whatever God put before him.

To further that cause, Clayton and Dana Sommers drove to Hesston, Kansas, and Goshen, Indiana, where two Mennonite colleges were located, on a recruitment expedition to fill the summer staff needs of LCC. Clayton loved selling the attributes of the camp and interacting with the students.

While in Hesston, he and Dana stayed with Clayton's sister Vi and Stan Kuhns. Clayton stayed up past midnight one night talking to his sister, a rare intimacy that fed his hungry soul.

In the midst of learning his job well, Clayton also found great delight in his family and in the unique setting of their home. Their rustic Hi-Alps house rested at the foot of the beautiful Laurel Mountains. The family accepted the primitive condition of the house as part of its charm, despite its idiosyncratic flaws, including several steps that had to be traversed before entering the main entrance and a main bathroom that had barely any water in the toilet bowl. Additionally, all four bedrooms were on the upper floors, and the wood-burning stove that heated the house was located in the basement, so Clayton had to regularly traverse the rickety stairs to feed the beast.

Duane and Bruce shared the only room on the top floor. Kimberly's room was below theirs. Kevin's was on the same floor as Kimberley's, but it had the distinction of having an unusable fireplace and displaying three large, black snake skins that the boys had found in the attic. Rounding out this bedroom floor was Clayton and Ruth's room. They kept the only TV in the house in their room, so they could monitor its use carefully. This rule, Clayton later found out, was frequently thwarted when the parents stepped out of the house. At home, the kids enjoyed a sense of open freedom. They played around the house at will. The long rope swing that hung from a tree in their backyard, amidst the backdrop of the mountainside, provided endless hours of fun, as did Jacob's Creek, which bordered the camp.

The family frequently hiked in the forest at the back of their property to popular spots such as Lover's Leap, Look Out Point, Split Rock, and Sunset Hill. Once, they even took the long hike to Primitive Camp, which Clayton, Kevin, and Duane had previously explored together. One time on a family hike, Duane noticed his four-year-old sister poking at something off the path. When he made out what she was messing with, he screamed. Clayton and Ruth came running, just in time to see a venomous copperhead snake slithering in the other direction. The hysterical hug Ruth captured Kimberly in touched Clayton as much as it scared her rapt boys.

They often spotted deer in their backyard at dusk, eating the corn they left out for them. Their record sighting was thirteen! And in the winter, the kids loved sledding in the snow, their favorite spot being Motel Hill.

Lest his boys think life was only fun and games, Clayton had them help him gather firewood from the nearby woods throughout winter. He then sawed and chopped it to fit into their house-heating stove.

For Christmas, Clayton took his family to a local tree farm and dug up a live Christmas tree to display in their house. After the holidays, they planted it near the house, and Duane oversaw watering it. But it didn't survive. It was very difficult being uprooted and planted elsewhere … though Clayton believed he was the exception to the rule.

Part of what made the family experience so enjoyable was the freeing atmosphere. For one, Ruth was not bogged down with meal preparation. They ate the noon meal with the staff and their families, which was prepared for them by the food services staff. For breakfast and the evening meal, they had free access to the refrigerator, which was kept full of premade meals.

To better color in the Swiss Family Robinson way of life, Kevin needed a dog. He missed his Toby that he'd had to leave behind in Goshen. As luck would have it, he adopted a stray and named it Buster. They became the best of friends, just like in the movies. Similarly, the family also adopted a cat that had been left in their care by the kids' Aunt Pearl who was attending grad school and could no longer care for her. Blackie became Duane's responsibility. That was a match made for Hollywood, too.

Duane read twenty-seven books, more than anyone else at his school. For this accomplishment, he was given a free pass to attend a speech by Franco Harris, the famous Pittsburgh Steelers running back. It was an unforgettable experience for Duane and his mother to drive to Pittsburgh to see Franco up close. The family also took advantage of an opportunity to see the Harlem Globetrotters, again in Pittsburgh, proving they were not some unrefined hillbillies from the backwoods.

Clayton took on the big project of remodeling their kitchen, a similar feat to what he had accomplished in his Goshen house. He found old barn siding, which he used for the kitchen cupboard doors and for the dining-room walls. The evening project took about six weeks to complete, but the results pleased his persnickety eyes.

Clayton admittedly caved to peer pressure when he bought a Honda 275 motorcycle like the other staffers. With it, he often explored the many mountain trails with Kevin or Duane holding on for dear life behind him. It was all Clayton could do to stay on the winding trails much of the time. Though riding on the trails was dangerous, Clayton found a little more of himself on that thunder cycle.

Buying into his heart's desires, Clayton purchased his first new car—a 1978 Plymouth Volare. Perhaps the worst (certainly in the top ten) financial decision in his life, that bomb was a lemon from the get-go. It caused more havoc than it helped them.

One time, on the family's way back from Ohio on I-70 in a dark, cold rain, the Volare just up and stopped without warning, leaving them stranded on the side of a busy thoroughfare. Not knowing what else to do without a phone, they waited. After that got old (rather quickly), they prayed for someone to assist them. At least an hour passed before a highway mainte-nance worker pulled in behind them and asked if he could help. Clayton explained their pitiful predicament, and the man offered to look under their hood. He found a fried wire and then spliced, or overrode, or bypassed it ... or whatever a fly-by-night mechanic does in those situations. Voila—the gutless wonder started up. The good Samaritan then told them to follow him to his garage so he could ensure things were fixed properly. When he was satisfied with the repair job, he sent them on their merry way without, he insisted, allowing them to pay him a dime. As so many times before, when the chips were down and Clayton felt all hope was gone, a miracle had saved them. God sent the right angel at the right time. He was sure of it!

Beemer smiled. He looked over at the margin, closed his knowing eyes, and shook his head. He'd let the story speak for itself ... again!

Clayton and his family attached themselves early on to Kingsview Mennonite Church in Scottsdale, Pennsylvania, about thirty minutes from LCC. Clayton and Ruth especially enjoyed the small group they were assigned to because it had many relatable young couples with children.

One aspect of living at LCC was the frequent visitors they received. On November 16, Homer, Bertha, Norma, and Marion stopped at their house on the way to drop off Bertha at the Philhaven Mennonite Health Center, near Lebanon, Pennsylvania. Clayton's mom was obviously not herself; she could barely carry a conversation.

Prior to their move to Laurelville, Clayton and Ruth had noticed Bertha's deteriorating mental health. Clayton had surmised that it was likely a result of Homer's continual attacks on her humble and nurturing character. But after his parent's visit at LCC, Clayton felt guilt-ridden. *Was it his fault that his precious mother was losing it? Could he have prevented this if he had stayed and protected her from Homer's horrific character assaults?*

Clayton remembered learning from therapy years earlier of his obvious anger at his dad and overdependence on his mother. Learning these facts helped him put his unfamiliar, untouchable emotions on a grid and, like a good student, he had written his family heritage book to attack these problems. But he had also distanced himself from his mother, lest he be pulled into her enticing nurture still deeper. In hindsight, this impulsive decision seemed more cowardly than prudent. After all, it was *he* who had overly clung to his mother's love. Whether that was even a fault, it certainly was not his poor mother's fault. Yet, she was clearly the one being punished here; she was completely alone. She exemplified love. Clayton's genuine heart for people came from her. And he had shunned her because he had wanted his wife to be too much like her. It made no sense, now, looking back on it.

Clayton became detached. Worse, he resorted to his old trick of holding his feelings in. *What does one do with such guilt?* Surely, he could not retch it all over his blossoming family and the wholesome camp. For now, he could only fight back the tears and stay strong, ignoring the pain (his and his mother's) as best he could. It was a lonely battle.

Homer, oddly enough, went along with the psychiatrist's advice to admit his wife to the mental health facility. Even he, evidently, knew she needed help. *Where was this benevolence,* Clayton wondered, *all those years he verbally abused her?*

Philhaven Health Center administered shock treatments, the popular procedure at the time, to help Bertha release unwanted memories. On the elder Steiners' LCC visit after Bertha's discharge from Philhaven, nearly three weeks later, Bertha appeared revived, almost back to her old self. Clayton could only hope she would remain that way and that Homer had somehow learned his lesson and would now treat his wife with the respect she deserved. But, of course, predictably, nothing of the kind was ever uttered upon their departure.

Soon after, Bertha took a spill and broke her hip. While she was hospitalized at Akron General Hospital, Clayton took advantage of an opportunity to visit some LCC supporters in Wayne County. His co-worker Dana accompanied him, which allowed Clayton to visit his mother in the hospital. The guilt and pain finally overwhelmed him on their trip back to LCC. As Clayton shared his mother's plight with Dana, his hidden emotions bubbled out, and he cried like a baby, healing a small portion of his heart's pain … though it felt like putting a Band-Aid on a chest-sized wound.

Meanwhile, Ruth's parents were dealing with their own health issues. The heart attack had proved to take more from Lester's stamina than he willed. He became resigned to selling the farm and all its implements. Clayton and Ruth helped them clean out the farmhouse on October 24 and move into their new, humble retirement home on a corner of the property that they would keep for themselves.

Despite the separation from their parents, extended family continued to bless Clayton. Karen Nussbaum (Clayton's niece) became Tom Nafziger's and Clayton's secretary on February 13, 1979. Her parents, Irvin and Arlene, escorted her to camp because she had recently survived a car wreck and could not drive. Other than a noticeable limp, she came prepared to serve and please. Clayton glowed at her helpful disposition. Additionally, Curt (Clayton's nephew) and wife Carol Kuhns responded to Clayton's request to be the program directors of the vibrant summer children's camp. Their enthusiastic and devoted leadership was a breath of fresh air.

Filling out the Steiner ensemble were Clayton's nieces, Debbie Steiner and Bonita Kuhns, who were hired as kitchen staff. The dormitory-style living arrangement equipped them to have a ball, just like the campers did. Their lively presence added humor and excitement to everyone's lives.

Clayton's glorious sense of united family, through Ruth and the boys, his relatives on staff, and LCC's staff-at-large helped fill the void from his parents' dysfunctional tale. He felt so at home that he often shared commentary on the inefficiencies and dead policies LCC worked with. He was his job, and LCC was the family in his charge. His calling was to responsibly guide and encourage his employment family, just as he did his own family. If a wrong needed pointing out, he freely did so.

On March 19, 1979, Melton Thorpe, the LCC board president, pulled Clayton aside and asked him to express his evaluation of LCC in writing. Clayton found the encounter and request odd. He had sensed from their previous encounters that Thorpe was a man of stern beliefs and untrusting eyes. He got the idea that the calculating leader had never really liked him. But then, he figured that Thorpe was probably just one of those authority figures who kept their opinions close to their vest and never really showed their cards. Clayton didn't want to play too much into his limited appraisal. The man probably just wanted input on how to improve the place he was dedicated to.

So, rather than flippantly writing a brief paragraph or two, Clayton went all in, seeing the request as his opportunity to share his uniquely qualified perspective. Clayton proudly wrote a seven-page article entitled, *"LAURELVILLE — AN EVALUATION — A WORKING PAPER."* To the best of his ability, Clayton wrote a fair accounting of Laurelville Church Center, reporting how he saw each department functioning. He felt that he accurately, professionally, and skillfully provided both positive and negative traits and suggested how each could improve. In the interest of transparency, he even included his personal shortcomings of not remembering numbers well and needing more education in business administration.

On March 26, Clayton got his first whiff of peculiar goings-on. The executive committee of the board met, but he, the business manager, was not invited. He let the anomaly slide and proceeded with business as usual … for months.

In those following few months, Clayton began noticing a frustration— almost an inexplicable hostility—toward him in his weekly meetings with his supervisor, Tom Nafziger. Tom often made unsolicited comments such as "Your critical, disdainful attitude is hurting you and the LCC cause." Clayton saw this as proof that his evaluation of the needs for change were accurate, however unpleasant to his supervisor. He inwardly vowed to temper the harshness of his comments but not the truth of them.

On July 11, in the middle of the busiest season for LCC, Ruth commented to Clayton that "Something's afoot." Clayton felt it too. A few too many cold shoulders and instances of a lack in communication were occurring. A few days later, on July 17, Tom asked to come by the house for a visit after the kids were down for the night. Antennae out, Clayton wondered what Tom could possibly need to tell him at his home. *A raise? Was Tom leaving?*

Clayton and Ruth invited him into their cozy living room. With little chitchat, Tom plainly said, "Your contract on September 1 will not be renewed. Your services will no longer be needed."

Shell-shocked, Clayton's heart fell to the floor. He was being let go, fired in a sense. He didn't know how to respond. *Was this a joke?* "Was this your decision?" he finally asked.

"No. This was decided by the board," Tom responded without meanness.

When asked what their reasoning was, Tom told them merely that the personnel committee decided they needed "someone with better PR skills."

Clayton and Ruth sat on the couch, stunned.

"I'm sorry," Tom said softly. Then he ushered himself out.

Clayton and Ruth embraced. A torrent of tears fell from both. Together, they wrestled with the implications of it all.

Were they to blame for this? But they had helped this ministry so much! The staff loved them. The camp was flourishing! Why would God take them from this beautiful place?

The hardest accusation for Clayton to fight off was that his slowness in processing things had something to do with this rejection. He must be too *dumb* to handle things.

Beemer, in a rush, called his supervisor down. Forget the protocols. This was an emergency!

The editor in chief appeared, looking as if he had barely survived another spin cycle. He grabbed a bedpost to steady his wobbly legs. "Beemer," he said, holding his aching head and directing his spent gaze at his subordinate, "this better be good."

Beemer swallowed, hesitated, glanced around the bedroom where Clayton and Ruth slept fitfully, and quickly reconsidered his resolve. He cleared his throat. "Chief!" as if a cheery greeting would solve his dilemma. "Ahh ... no, this is not good. This is very bad!"

"Is your subject dying?"

Beemer looked over at the bed. "Well ... no, not exactly. But his old fear of being slow and dumb may ruin him."

The old editor rolled his already dizzy eyes. "Tell me what's going on."

Beemer gave him a quick synopsis of the night's events. "And out of nowhere, they fire him. Can you believe it? He's given his all to this place, and they turn around and can him. Is there no justice? And this is a Christian organization. They have ruined this man's life! And his family's! He was doing so well."

The chief slowly blinked. "He's not ruined, Beemer."

"Good. I was hoping you'd say that. So, how can he get his job back?"

The master journalist raised a bushy eyebrow. "That's not our job as chroniclers to fix or care about. Whether he gets his job back or not, he's not ruined. Life goes on."

"But he's invested everything into this job. He is this job. They can't just take it away from him. They can't just ... rip him apart like a rag doll."

"Why not?"

Beemer returned a dumbfounded stare at his mentor. "Why not? Seriously? Because he deserves better. He deserves to run this whole place as far as I'm concerned. Not get canned."

"So, what has he done for this place that's so incredible?"

A scowl covered Beemer's face. "Okay ... He started out knowing nothing about how this camp worked. But he diligently learned his job through humbly asking questions, reading helpful articles and past records, and applying himself. Now, he does his job admirably. And don't forget all the fantastic staff he hired; they all love him. He has made this place shine like the sun itself!"

The editor nodded imperceptibly. "Ahum. And what did he do that wasn't so good?"

"What? Nothing. His heart is in the right place on this. Trust me, I can feel it."

The old chronicler wrinkled his wrinkled forehead even more. "I know you can feel what Clayton is feeling. That's why you're so vexed. But it's not always a matter of one's heart being in the right place. Were his actions always perfect?"

Beemer was speechless—finally.

The editor went on, "Even if his actions were perfect (and I know they weren't because he's a human), life is a cornucopia of unexpected events. Only THE BOSS knows why things happen as they do." He looked over the reading glasses that hung over his bulbous nose. "Still, I'm guessing your subject's actions had something to do with this, even if it was a measly percent of the overall cause."

"No way! Things were going so well."

"Boom!"

Beemer looked at his chief editor. His hands were mimicking a huge explosion in slow motion.

"That's not funny!" Beemer protested.

"I'm not laughing."

"Then what are you saying?"

"I'm saying that when you feel you deserve prestige, power, and happiness, that's when it blows up on you. Life is a gift. It doesn't owe its members."

"But Clayton is seriously getting ripped off here. THE BOSS has proven to him in numerous ways—in miraculous ways—that THE BOSS has Clayton's back. He's here because of that leading."

"He probably *was* led here," admitted the chief.

Beemer shook his unbelieving head. "But why would THE BOSS allow this to happen?"

"I don't know. What does your subject still need to learn?"

Beemer squinted. "Huh?"

"What are some problem areas in Clayton's life?"

Frowning, Beemer said, "He doesn't have any. He's confident and knows his role—unlike a lot of the clowns down here."

The chief didn't move a muscle, then he said, "So, you could say his problem is being arrogant and unsympathetic, is that right?"

"What? No."

The editor in chief's cold stare and the raising of his already high forehead stopped Beemer in his whining rebuttal. Then, he remembered the firing consequences of not chronicling *every* truth that Clayton experiences. He gulped. "Okay. Ah … if I really stop and think about this objectively, yes, sometimes when he's really focused on a goal, which is an excellent trait of a great achiever, by the way …" Beemer cleared his throat. "Right … ah, sometimes when he's really focused on a goal, his empathy gene kind of disappears. He can forget about what others need. But that wouldn't deserve losing his job and throwing him out on the dung heap, and starving his childr …"

"Beemer," his mentor interrupted, "it's still not your job to make your subject a hero. Let him live his life as he will. Yours is to observe and record, remember?"

Beemer swallowed his remaining words. He cleared his throat and nodded.

The editor said, "Now, I suggest you adjust to this reversal of your subject's fortune just as he must—and sooner than later. Keenly observe how this situation will defuse his arrogance and recharge his empathy."

"Yes, Chief."

The chronicling guru looked at his beaten reporter. He sighed. "Is there anything you need to share about this situation while I'm still here?"

Beemer slowly lifted his chin. "Just that … well … injustice really hurts. How will Clayton ever move on?"

"I don't know. My guess is, if he's half the man you think he is, he'll survive. And because I've seen THE BOSS work wonders a million times before, I think your man, Clayton, will someday be even a better man because of all of this turmoil."

"I hope so." Beemer's scowl returned. "But I can't stand that Melton Thorpe. Just because he has the authority and he doesn't like Clayton doesn't mean he should have the right to destroy Clayton's life and deprive LCC of a wonderful future."

"Beemer?"

Beemer held his breath and sheepishly looked over to his chief officer.

The old chronicler said, "Be careful what you assume, son. If you throw your logic out the window, you'll start to write from a biased point of view, and THE BOSS will not be able to use your writing. Do you understand that?"

"Yes, sir... ah, Chief."

"Now, we don't really know much about this Mr. Thorpe, do we?"

Beemer shook his head.

"He's not your subject, after all. He may like Clayton and truly have LCC's best interest at heart. Maybe Clayton was getting a little too big for his britches?"

"How can you ..." Beemer blurted.

The editor cut him off with raised hands again. "I'm not saying that's true or not true. The point is—the decision has been made. Life goes on, and your subject will learn from the heartbreak—as will you."

Beemer said nothing for a long moment. "I know you're right. But why must these humans face heartbreak at all?"

"Without disappointment, mastering goals would mean nothing. If they could conquer anything they wanted, before long, they would cease to want. Desires, needs—these are what make humans human. Failure is the necessary evil of fulfillment."

"But failed expectations hurt so badly; I can hardly stand it. Can this really be overcome?"

The wise old chronicler took his turn to pause, then he said, "You know, there is a famous precedent for this. The early Christian Jews expected the Spirit of THE BOSS to establish His Kingdom here on earth. When the Jewish Temple fell in 70 AD—the very temple their living God constructed and promised to forever reside in and through—they were as crushed in their failed expectations as the fallen walls. They thought that would be the end of this marvelous *Son of God* Church where they had witnessed miracle after miracle. But look at Christianity today. The death of their temple did not kill the dream of their faith. THE BOSS still reigns in Christian churches all over the earth. If anything, their failed expectations solidified their faith. No longer seeing their God in a physical building, they were forced to trust in a God they couldn't see to the ends of the earth. Which do you think proved more powerful—hope in the building or THE BOSS Himself?"

"The one that required faith."

"Precisely. Now, the irony in this story is that this was not the first time their failed expectations doubled back on them. When Jesus, the man, roamed this earth, his followers expected him to reign and establish THE BOSS's kingdom here on earth. But that all fell apart the night Jesus was crucified on the cross. His followers scattered; his disciples fled; and his top dog, Peter, denied him three times. They weren't just disappointed. They were decimated. Their King died! 'Why would God do that?' they cried. It made no sense.

"But look how that turned out. Jesus rose on the third day, visited his disciples, deployed his Holy Spirit among them, and now dwells in his followers today. Now, you tell me, is THE BOSS capable of working through failed expectations?"

Wide-eyed, Beemer blinked and swallowed. "I never really thought of it like that before."

"Well, that doesn't mean all is rosy. I'm sure Clayton will feel his pain acutely, and so will you. It's all part of it. But it helps to have a heavenly perspective on the whole thing."

Beemer nodded. "Thank you, Chief."

The editor left Beemer to ponder his words and Clayton's predicament honestly.

The day after the surprising announcement from Tom, Clayton and Ruth met with their pastor, Rev. Alderfer, and his wife, from the Kingsview church. They were understanding and appalled. Clayton and Ruth cried unapologetically.

Tarrying at his job became intolerable. If he was not wanted, Clayton reasoned, working his job served no one's best interest. Two days after the dismissal notice, Clayton gave his letter of resignation, effective immediately.

Of course, there was a multitude of people affected by the turn of events, like Curt and Carol, Karen, Debbie, and Bonita, who were all engrossed in the jobs he had hired them for. Upon being invited to Hi-Alps to hear the news personally, they too were flabbergasted by the notice. Clayton felt as if he had let them down. He could only tell them he was sorry. Pointing fingers or pressing for reinstatement would only conflict the whole organization. He had to remain publicly silent. It was the noble, however painful, thing to do.

Fellow staffer Dana and his wife went out of their way to express their sorrow and displeasure of the current happenings. This dulled and added to the pain for Clayton, who loved this man like a brother and would miss him dearly.

On July 23, 1979, six days after the pseudo-firing, they removed their earthly belongings from Hi-Alps and loaded them onto Carl's truck. The emotionally wrenching scene of the normally stoic Kevin bidding farewell to his beloved dog, Buster, only added to Clayton's breaking heart. As they pulled away from the picturesque landscape, involuntary tears rolled down Clayton's cheeks. His wide-eyed children sat in amazement. They had never seen their strong daddy cry before.

With Ruth's parent's place as their home base, job hunting became the first item on the agenda. Two days later, they drove to Goshen, hoping against the odds that they could once again find a job there and call it home. Sadly, they had no bites.

They resolved to stay in the Kidron area, in large part because they trusted the school system there with their children. The high density of Mennonites was a huge draw as well. The other undeniable reason was that both Clayton's and Ruth's parents were experiencing declining health. Clayton did not want to disregard them—especially his mother!

On October 16, Clayton wrote a letter to Melton Thorpe and Tom Nafziger, asking questions and stating that he was still thinking about the happenings of the past year and struggling to understand it all from God's point of view. He wrote, "I continue to rest assured that God makes no mistakes and that he continues to follow one all the days of one's life." On October 24, Thorpe responded, giving no additional reasons for Clayton's dismissal, only reaffirming Clayton's belief that God knows what He is doing and that he anticipated seeing Clayton's family at future LCC events and annual meetings. Clayton found it extremely difficult to hold the letter in his hand, while trying to release the whole torrid matter.

21

WORKING FROM THE BOTTOM UP

IN SEARCH OF CONFIDENCE

Clayton awoke early. He sat at his in-laws' dining-room table vaguely looking over yesterday's Wooster newspaper. Gazing out the front window, he surveyed the healthy crops of soybeans and corn nearing harvest. The potential before him compelled him to take stock of his own harvest or, better stated, lack of harvest. The clean rows bearing fruit clearly contrasted with his situation.

Clayton inhaled deeply, then he let out all the stale and anxious air that was clinging to him like a leech. Or he tried to let it out. One sigh was not going to change things, he quickly realized. He didn't have a job; he didn't have a home; he didn't know where he was headed in his career or in God's plan; and his family depended on him to navigate through this rough patch.

He sighed again.

Though he was trying to remain positive, negative questions bombarded him. Namely, *Why? Why did all of this happen? Why did he lose the job he loved when things in Laurelville were going so well?* He fought off the familiar urge to blame.

He might never know the why, and searching for that answer was proving counterproductive. Perhaps he'd best follow the day's plans and stop questioning. He'd chase down some job possibilities and go look at a house for sale. *Surely, God,* he prayed, *something will work out in all of this. Please help me!*

Finding God's assurance was a daily grind. Sometimes, he found a motivating glitter of hope, and some days, he tarried as if he had.

Clayton and Ruth checked out a house for sale in Benville, a small community adjacent to Kidron. The owners immediately recognized Ruth as their former babysitter. Clayton and Ruth felt the house was ideal for their family, but they explained that they had no money and no job.

Clayton walked away from the pleasant exchange, discouraged. He knew of no one who could loan him that kind of money. *What's a guy just trying to serve the Lord, but with nothing to show for it, to do?*

Then, the unbelievable happened. On August 9, 1979, the Gerbers lowered their price to $50,000.00. For a farmhouse with five acres to flourish on, this was a steal! To sweeten the deal and because they *trusted* Ruth and Clayton, they said no payments would be required for two years. But after two years (here's where the teeth of the bargain sunk in), the full payment would be due. Clayton had no idea where that money would come from. But because the offer was so unbelievable and perfect for his family's needs, he felt he had no choice but to take the once-in-a-lifetime offer. Finally, something good was in motion. God was providing!

Through a connection with Ruth's sister-in-law, Elaine, Clayton landed a job with Wood Décor, a small but growing company that manufactured and sold inspirational wall hangings, furniture, and furniture accessories. Clayton made $4.25 an hour working on the assembly line—a far cry from what he had been making at LCC. This degrading drop in pay and the tediousness of the job roughed up his ego. Not only was he unfulfilled, but he was not adequately providing for his family. The kids qualifying for reduced school lunches humbled him further.

Thankfully, Clayton was not the only provider in the family. With the boys in school, Ruth was again ready to take on the employment world and became a fifth-grade teacher at Kidron Elementary. To Clayton and Ruth, this was another obvious and timely miracle that God provided.

The only drawback to the convenient opportunity was the inconvenience of Kimberly needing half-day provision for her first year of kindergarten. Fortunately, in a home community, needs can always be shared and filled. Clayton's Aunt Lucille and Ruth's sister-in-law Gladys came to the rescue, assuring that Kimberly would be safely cared for.

In Clayton's own time, to make up for the shortfall in income, Wood Décor owner Peter Dunn, consented to Clayton manufacturing Homer's innovative marble tracks using Peter's business tools. Clayton sold about fifty of them through Lehman Hardware Store in Kidron before realizing the venture was financially imprudent.

Peter also contracted Clayton to custom-make a kitchen table with matching benches for Peter's home. Impressed with Clayton's work and seeing his creative eye-to-hand aptitude, Peter asked him to design new wood products for the Furniture Accessories department. Clayton enjoyed the new challenge and proved he was up for the task.

By the end of 1980, Clayton designed (with the help of his nephew Terry) twenty-two furniture accessories shown in a Wood Décor brochure. For his efforts, his salary increased to five dollars an hour, which Clayton appreciated but was still unimpressed with.

Nevertheless, Clayton pressed on, working diligently, as if he made fifty dollars an hour. In July of 1981, nearly two years after he started, an evaluation of Clayton gave him all high marks and said he especially excelled at special assignments and staying on task. Though this boosted his slighted ego, he still struggled to pay the bills and could not build a savings account.

The $20,000.00 they had loaned Clayton's friends for their Goshen house was finally paid back by the end of 1980. *But where would he ever get enough for the $50,000.00 due on the house come September 1981?*

In a panic, Clayton turned to his brother Kenny, the executor of their brother George's estate. George was alive and well but did not have the capacity to negotiate his finances. He had plenty and didn't need it all presently, but Kenny reasonably asked, "If I loan you George's money, what will I do if other siblings ask for loans?" Clayton had no answers.

After much thought, Kenny finally relented and loaned Clayton the money, enabling Clayton to fully pay off his debt to the previous owners of their home. Clayton, once eager to bully his older brother Kenny and steal (or borrow behind the lender's back) from his other brother George, now bowed to their generous benevolence. He would forever be grateful!

Beemer wrote in the side margin to his editor: *Was the house Clayton bought a bona fide miracle if he had to beg his brother for his other brother's money to keep the house? Or did he just want it so badly that he put THE BOSS's name to it?*

The editor wrote back: Sometimes, humans employ presumption when they think they're exercising faith. Sometimes their presumption works for them. Believing seems to often be the key ingredient in moving forward, regardless of whether THE BOSS was in it or not. But don't worry, Clayton will find his share of bad luck in future presumptions—especially when he believes something obviously contrary to THE BOSS's character. Just chronicle what you observe and don't worry too much about figuring it all out. You won't. THE BOSS always adds a touch of the unexpected, lest we think life can be figured out.

Clayton's creative genius continued. By the end of 1981, just after he began making his house payments, his boss gave him some deserved recognition in a letter. In it, Peter Dunn stated, "We want to express our appreciation for the new technique in edging you engineered. It has made a significant contribution to our production this fall! We want to give you a bonus of $100.00 as a token of our appreciation."

Clayton smiled broadly. It was nice to be noticed and appreciated!

Though Clayton had longed for these very sentiments from his dad all his life, he now realized that appreciation, in itself, did not complete him. He wanted more—more money, for one. Not providing adequately for his family ate at him continually.

To meet some of the financial burden that fall, Clayton became a chimney sweep after work hours and on weekends. He completed a course on paper, purchased chimney sweep equipment, had his nephew Jay make a logo that he put on the side of his large panel truck, and advertised in local newspapers and at Lehman Hardware. A second motive was providing his boys with the chance to work for the business and earn their own spending money. His boys soon learned that the dirty job of cleaning soot off dangerous, hard-to-get-to surfaces was challenging, and the job lost its appeal quickly. Clayton found that motivating them to stick with it was more of a chore than the work itself. Clayton made little after paying for equipment, advertising, and his kids' wages.

A year later, at the end of 1982, he faced the music. The Wood Décor job would likely never fulfill him or pay him what he needed or, if it did, the fulfillment and pay would not come soon enough for Clayton's satisfaction. So, despite being a loyal and hardworking employee, he began to look for other employment.

That search found him a job as the office manager for Energy Reduction Systems in Wooster at the beginning of 1983. Energy Reduction Systems manufactured and sold ceiling fans wholesale. Clayton was aware that the company had filed chapter 7 bankruptcy and downsized considerably. Inwardly, Clayton relished the opportunity to be the owner's (a Mennonite man) business savior. He felt that he could organize the books and straighten the company out with his leadership expertise.

Seven months later, while he was stopped at a stop sign on his way to work, a fellow employee informed him that the business had been taken over by the bankruptcy court, and the plant was bolted shut. He lost $500.00 in back wages. So much for his presence carrying the day.

Beemer wrote his editor: *Is this an unlucky hunch? Or was he just being slow and stupid?*

The editor's response: His arrogance likely played a part, but you can't blame him for his gumption. Better to try to improve and grow than to rot on the vine.

Losing the job that he was just gaining confidence in felt eerily similar to when he had been released from Laurelville four short years previously. This starting over again was becoming a pattern he cared little for. Was he destined to wallow in dead-end jobs for the rest of his life? The implications gnawed at him.

With his tail between his legs and after finding nothing else worthy of his abilities, he humbly asked Peter for his job back. Peter received him graciously but did not reward him with a pay raise or the same status as he had had previously. Peter gave him the only position available—back on the production line ... on the night shift!

Adjusting to sleeping during days came at a huge price. The family was coming when he was going and vice-versa. Communication faltered. Anxiety climbed. Anger infiltrated their disjointed existence. Much grace was required from all parties. Eventually, Clayton did get promoted to shift manager, but those nine months on the third shift felt like they lasted forever, and they nearly tore the family apart.

When he finally got switched to the first shift as the department manager, things started to gel. Being on the same schedule as his family helped all the members coexist, and Clayton felt more in control of his life and his future. Maybe he could survive in this small, but growing, company yet.

The owner, Peter Dunn, hoped so. As a display of good faith, Peter handed Clayton his personal credit card in 1984 to pay for gas during Clayton's three-week, family summer vacation out west. Diligence had its benefits!

"How's it going, Beemer?"

Beemer, who had been writing in his biographic book, bolted up and turned around. "Chief!" He stood, picking up his book that he had just dropped. "What are you doing here?"

The double-chinned editor in chief said, "Time for another random inspection."

Beemer gulped and looked around as if something needed straightening. "Is everything okay? Has my writing been satisfactory?"

"For the most part, yes. You're still adding plenty of needless details that I edit out, but, other than that, you're depicting your subject well. I'm not here to criticize, Beemer. Relax."

A smile blended with suspicion crossed Beemer's face. "Great to hear."

"This is more of a confidence review than anything else," said the sober elder. "Is your writing going as you want it to?"

Beemer thought of lying but knew he could not fool his teacher. "Well, Clayton's at a really weird place right now."

"You mean Kidron?"

"Well, yes, he's certainly having to contend with the smallness and staleness of this dinky little town. But I was referring to his emotions. He's at a weird place emotionally."

"Explain." The pudgy instructor clasped his hands around his substantial belly as if ready to stay put for a while.

Beemer bit his lip and took a deep breath. "Well, after the debacle in Laurelville, he felt discouraged, directionless, and humiliated." He cringed at his admittance. "But that was because he was so unfairly treated!"

The chief broke in, "Beemer, you're a reporter, not his savior. If he felt humiliated, he felt humiliated. You don't need to justify for him. Whether he was actually treated unfairly is not yours to prove. The question is, does he still feel humiliated?"

Beemer thought about that a moment. "Yes ... and no. I think he's still reeling from the sting of it all. He's got all these pent-up emotions going on, like embarrassment, shame, anger, resentment, hurt, sorrow, and guilt. At the same time, he's trying to be a good husband, loving father, and make a mark in the workplace. It's a bit much. But no one would suspect any of this because he's really good at presenting himself as a made man, covering the torrent of emotions going on under that cool façade."

"So, you're saying he's utterly miserable, but faking it?"

"No, I wouldn't say that. He really does enjoy his kids. And I think he has taken some pride in his work. Those furniture accessories he designed went over big. Finally working his way up to department manager was huge for his confidence. I think his church-life involvement has been a steadying force too.

"So, no, it's not all gloom and doom," Beemer continued. "But I'm afraid if he doesn't deal with these bottled-up frustrations, a firestorm may be coming."

"That's a concern," the advising journalist agreed. "Maybe you should be concentrating on the positives more, though. What else does Clayton like about life in Kidron?"

Beemer raised his brow and rubbed his chin with thumb and forefinger. "Hmm. He really likes the quality of education the kids are receiving. They're getting more than just textbook learning. They're learning how to be civil and respectful."

Chief nodded. "What else?"

A momentary frown flashed on Beemer's face because he expected to concentrate more on the annoyances of rural life. "Well, let's see. I guess he and his family feel more secure here. I don't expect they'll get their bikes stolen. Safety's a nice benefit."

"What else?"

Beemer rubbed his forehead and looked at the floor for more answers. "Ah, well … there are the values of morality, hard work, and integrity. The environment certainly encourages determination and fulfilling one's duties. I don't suppose that's second nature in a lot of urban cultures. They're also getting good teaching at church about THE BOSS—or God, as they say."

Finally, the steady editor raised his brow. "Beemer, I get the sense that you could go on all day talking about the value of living in this dinky little town." A wry smile flickered.

Beemer frowned at the sarcasm. "Yeah, well, I guess you've made your point. There's more to this place than the narrow-minded, ingrained thinking I'm worried about." He sighed. "I just … sometimes, it seems like if he was in a more *with-it* place he'd grow more and not have all these annoying, bottled-up feelings. He'd be exploring some new land or invention like William Clark did in his Lewis and Clark Expedition."

The chief closed his eyes before they rolled around. "Beemer, he'd just have that many more bottled-up emotions. Don't you think he has enough on his plate already?"

"Yeah, I guess. But he's not really addressing a lot of these feelings. Maybe moving somewhere more exciting would do him some good. You know, jostle the ole noggin up a little. Stretch his horizons."

The old journalist sighed and nodded. "Yes, he could do that. But why would greater opportunities be so important for Clayton?"

Beemer looked toward the ceiling. "Uh … because he'd feel more … you know, important." He turned, unsure, to his mentor.

The veteran reporter, shaking his round head in annoyance, said, "Don't you get it? You need to stop caring how Clayton's story is affecting you and start caring about how it is affecting him, like THE BOSS does. Clayton's not living here just for his own sake anymore or his wife's. He's living for his kids now, Beemer! So much of the inward struggles he's undergoing are the consequences of the war within—the war between doing what's best for his kids and that selfish, human pang of wanting to be noticed and admired."

Beemer thought a long moment, trying his best not to be humiliated. "That makes sense. Clayton's trying to be a protecting, encouraging father to his kids—something he never felt from his father. He so wants to be a strong father who deserves their love."

"Does THE BOSS love *him* because he deserves it?" Chief asked.

"No," said Beemer. "But what's he supposed to do when he's not feeling strong? Fake it?"

"What, indeed?"

"So, I'm confused. Is he to step back and let THE BOSS take care of his concerns, or is he to forcefully go for what he thinks THE BOSS wants, regardless of the barriers? Is THE BOSS teaching Clayton humility or courage?"

The chronicling guru nodded and opened his hands.

Beemer shook his head, frustrated. "This is tough! I'm feeling both sides of the coin really strongly here."

The editor finally jumped in. "There are no pat answers, Beemer. That's life for these humans. Truth is not handed to them on a silver platter. The answer to each conundrum may become obvious at some point. But it's the search for Truth that matters. For through the searching, they find meaning. And meaning is the hands and feet of Truth."

"So," said Beemer, "whether he understands Truth perfectly or not doesn't matter so much as him finding meaning in loving his kids and putting them first. Is that what you're saying?"

"Exactly! You'll understand these humans yet."

A corner of Beemer's lips rose into a smirk. "Thanks. But I think I have a ways to go. These critters are complicated."

The head chronicler uncharacteristically guffawed. "Truer words were never spoken. Observe and report, Beemer. Observe and report."

After the editor in chief left, Beemer wondered how uncomfortable Clayton would need to become before he searched with his whole heart.

22

THE FAMILY TRIP
UNFORGETTABLE MEMORIES

"Help!" Beemer screamed as loud as his heavenly voice could shout. He desperately looked for solace.

Seeing no evidence of support for his dire pleas, he looked back down at Clayton, attended to by unknown helpers and utterly alone on his sterile, transit bed. Clayton wept bitterly, pathetically.

Beemer's first case and he was losing his subject.

Running out of alternatives, Beemer strode to the sunlight, away from the frenzied commotion. Knowing he could not leave his subject—UNDER ANY CIRCUMSTANCES—he nevertheless looked away, searching the blue sky above, craning his neck heavenward. Frantically, he hollered, "Chief!"

"Never lose sight of your subject, Beemer." The pudgy editor stood before him stoically, if not steadily, after the transport.

"Chief! I thought you'd never get here." Beemer scooted back to the human activity once he realized a heavenly being was there to help him navigate the impossible scene. "He's ... he's ... losing it. I don't know what to do. Can they go into another dimension? I feel all his pain. Oh, the deep pain!" Beemer wrapped his inconsolable face with his hands. "He hurts so much! Make it stop. Make it stop!" Beemer sobbed wretchedly.

"Beemer, you'll be okay." The reliable mentor spoke in his grandfatherly tone. "You're experiencing his shock. You're not going crazy. This will pass."

Beemer looked back at his supervisor like a deer in the headlights.

Chief went on. "Be patient, Beemer. You'll remember your purpose in time. Right now, it's important to experience all that your subject is going through. Feel what he feels. Don't resist. Take it all in. In time, you'll be able to chronicle all of this seamlessly. You're a good chronicler, Beemer."

Beemer blinked and jerked his head back imperceptibly. "I'm a chronicler," he repeated, as if remembering.

"Yes, and a good one," his superior cajoled. "What are you feeling right now, Beemer?"

Shaking his head back and forth like a pendulum, Beemer said, "So many feelings just pounced all over me. I feel drained and out of sorts, like there's nothing firm to hold onto. The pain in his upper back is crying out for attention, though the medication they gave him has lessened that. Mostly, though, there's this heavy feeling of sadness infiltrating every pore of my body."

The bald journalist nodded. "That means he's coming out of shock. The day's memories will now be inundating his system. He's trying to make sense of something so far off his making-sense grid that it's caused a breakdown of his nervous system. While he's in the throes of all these flashbacks, don't let it derail you. You'll feel his emotions, but you must stick to your job as a chronicler. You must straighten out what really happened. This is why we hired you. Do you understand?" With one eye squinted, the old reporter held Beemer's stare.

Beemer gulped and nodded. "Yes, sir."

The old editor frowned. "Good. And you call me Chief, not sir. Now, as soon as your subject is resting, begin writing what you remember. You can always go back and edit it. But for traumatic events such as these, it's best to write raw emotions and reactions as they happen."

When the editor left and Clayton calmed, Beemer commenced to report all that had led up to Clayton's broken state.

For three years, Clayton had planned the ultimate vacation. He wanted to celebrate his family's time together while the kids were most impressionable and he was still young enough (at forty-three) to manage such an adventure. What better timing than to plan it around his and Ruth's twentieth wedding anniversary in July of '84?

Because funds were the obvious hindrance to such a plan, he and Ruth came up with the idea of committing a portion of Ruth's biweekly paycheck to the long-anticipated trip. Frugality, a practice he came by rightly, growing up in a large Mennonite family with little means shortly after The Depression, became the necessary glue of the project. He loved the process of making the goal a reality, and he loved passing the anticipatory joy to his children.

A month before the departure date, instead of skimping, which was his tendency (being a lifelong frugalitarian and all), he splurged on a '79 Chevy van that his nephew Roger had recently converted to a traveling van, complete with four captain chairs and a back seat that laid down into a bed. Weeks before they left, the kids hung out in the van after church, reading their Sunday school papers there instead of reading them in the living room as usual. The hype was definitely on!

The dream vacation began, as planned, on June 15, 1984. The triennial Homer Steiner reunion, this year at Temple Hills near Belleville, Ohio, was the first stop. It was always an enjoyable affair, and Clayton's family laughed and participated in the activities with their relatives, many of whom they saw only at these reunions. Bruce loved a trick his cousins did with a dollar bill. Clayton, known as the in-house historian of the group, shared his *joke of the year* and the latest stats of the family at large. Amazingly, other than a few infant deaths, no one from the Homer Steiner clan had died. Including in-laws; this family was now composed of nearly one hundred people over a span of eighty-some years! The group loved hearing these tidbits from Clayton.

From there, Clayton's family drove south and west toward the west coast. Clayton, Ruth, and sixteen-year-old Kevin shared the driving responsibilities. Early on, Ruth always brought up the tedious reminder of wearing seatbelts. The habit of wearing them was not a natural routine, and her demands slowly became nagging requests, a tension that seemed to inhibit family freedom and unity instead of enhancing it.

They picnicked, camped, and stayed with friends and family along the way, generally enjoying the sights and the freedom from job and school responsibilities. The highlights they beheld were the Carlsbad Caverns in New Mexico, dropping into Old Mexico, seeing old Native American ruins in Arizona, and experiencing the awe of the Grand Canyon.

In California, they enjoyed the countryside scenery and the huge Redwoods in Sequoia and Yosemite National Parks. They jumped on the iconic cable cars in picturesque San Francisco and drove the famous Golden Gate Bridge on their way north. Then, they wound their way up the scenic California and Oregon coastline via the renowned Highway 101.

They thrilled at joining Clayton's brother, Roy, and nephews, Ray, Dean, and Ted, and their families in Oregon. Ray took them to see Clayton's Great-Grandpa C.B. Steiner's grave marker. Over the 4th of July, Ray then treated them to a visit to the Oregon coast. The kids enjoyed exploring, shells, kelp, and other signs of marine life. Bruce especially delighted in making boy-made rivers in the sands of the Pacific shores. The boys bought some fireworks with their precious savings and set some off on the beach. Though Ray's kids were quite a bit younger, Clayton's kids got along well with them. Bruce enjoyed being the older brother for a change, sleeping with his cousins, Brian and Jonathan.

Clayton swelled with the glow of his family enjoying new adventures in new lands with extended family. This investment was proving beneficial beyond his hopes. As is common, however, the high of the trip made the prospect of their return trek to the mundaneness of homelife feel dreadful. But Ohio-bound they headed. And there were some further adventures. After leaving Ray's on July 6, they viewed the remains of the Mount Saint Helens volcano and the majestic snow-capped peak of Mount Hood on a crystal-clear day. Clayton smiled, recalling the family photo Ray had taken in front of their van before they departed.

They stopped off at the fascinating Bonneville Dam to watch the salmon resolutely climb up the fish ladders en route to the Columbia River to spawn, much like Clayton had pursued this family trip. Because Clayton's energy felt zapped (from the previous days' excitement or the miserable prospect of returning home, he didn't know which), he turned the driving over to Kevin.

Clayton figured he'd sleep off this vacation hangover (or whatever he was feeling) and proceeded to make his bed on the floor of the van as all other spots were taken. Ruth usually occupied the coveted front passenger seat because the air-conditioning flowed best there, but she gave up that luxury because the day was not exceptionally hot yet. They rewarded Bruce with his choice of seats for loading the van so helpfully that morning. He gladly sat shotgun! Duane slept in a captain seat in the second row, while Ruth and Kimberly snuggled in the back seat, now laid out into a bed. They each held a book, though Clayton realized they were sleeping even before he reached that solace. As Clayton drifted off, he glimpsed Bruce tranquilly reading his book, content with the situation, as usual.

In Clayton's sleeping state, he heard tires skidding on gravel, giving way to the normal wheels-on-highway sound. Then, before he could classify his unease, he heard a short screeching, followed by complete submersion in an upside-down, twisting world. Totally disoriented, he felt his back bang against a hard surface. Then, he slammed into a softer, but firm, object; then, the cycle repeated several times. This was either a scary nightmare or his life had literally just turned upside down. All he knew was that he was not in control of any of it.

The unknowable action stopped suddenly with a thud. Clayton landed, sitting on the inside of the roof next to Kevin. "What happened?" he asked his son who had, the last Clayton had seen, been driving the family van.

"I fell asleep," Kevin said. And with tears and more emotion than Clayton had ever seen from his normally stoic son, he said, "Dad, I'm sorry!"

Clayton immediately said, "It's okay." Still disoriented, Clayton asked, "Where are Bruce and Duane?"

Kevin didn't know but he thought maybe they were outside their imprisoning van. Desperate to cover his error, Kevin, more alert than his dad, quickly surveyed the outside terrain through the window. "I see Bruce!" he exclaimed and rose to somehow get to him.

Clayton, meanwhile, spotted his wife and daughter. They were not moving but were in the back of the van where they had been sleeping. Kimberly was beneath her mother, a suitcase, and the seat. Clayton called out, "Ruth?" No answer.

He crawled over seats and strewn luggage and tried to lift the seat off Ruth and nine-year-old Kimberly two different times, but he could not budge the thing. He spied Kevin crawling out a window. Excruciating back pain then clutched him with a vengeance, and he lay in a heap, helpless. Kimberly then came to. In a panic, she screamed, "Get Mommy off me!" over and over again. In agony himself, Clayton could do nothing but try to talk her down from her understandable claustrophobic fear.

Help arrived at the back of the van not a moment too soon. They pried the back door open and lifted the seat and suitcase off Clayton's cherished women. When they rolled Ruth off her crying daughter, Ruth awakened. In the mayhem, she asked, "What happened?" Clayton tried to explain what he knew about the accident, but he had a hard time expressing his thoughts, and she had a harder time entering back into reality. "What happened?" she kept asking.

A man spoke to them individually, introducing himself as Charles. He said he was a pastor and would help in any way he could. Clayton was glad for a calm voice of reason.

After slowly gaining her senses, Clayton saw blood running down Ruth's face. The sight was eerie. *Just how hurt was she?* He reached for her hand and held it. She held it back. Their future was totally unknown, but at least they would face it together.

Ruth asked about Kevin. Charles asked for his description. A moment later, Charles brought Kevin to his mother. Ruth had the wherewithal to tell him, "Kevin, I love you. It was an accident. Find someone to talk to. They might try to separate us."

Then Ruth asked to see Kimberly. Charles told her she was being held by some caring people, and it would probably be best to leave her be, but that she was fine.

Ruth asked about Duane and Bruce too. Again, Charles asked for a description of what they were wearing. After investigating, he came back and said, "They're doing all they can for them."

Clayton then heard someone, evidently new on the scene, say, "I know CPR! Does anyone need CPR?"

The distant reply came back, "We've been doing CPR for twenty minutes."

Duane's hysterical cries pierced through the air just then. His incoherent speech meant little, other than he was not happy.

When the distinct blare of a siren approached, Clayton's tortured heart raced. "Keep the family together!" he yelled to whoever could hear.

Still holding hands with his bride, Clayton eventually heard the siren leaving, not knowing which boy it took. The lack of information was infuriating.

Then, he heard the whirring of a helicopter. *Now what?*

Ruth was then pulled from the van, taken from his grasp. They said their goodbyes, perhaps the saddest farewell he had ever experienced. For now, he was alone—the last member of his wonderful family in the destroyed hull of their van. "Keep the family together!" he yelled … and then again when someone came to check on him. But, by that time, he knew his words meant nothing. No one was listening to him. He had no authority to lead in this jungle of fear and estrangement.

"Lay still," someone told him. "You don't want to risk a debilitating back injury by moving." *Too late for that.* Clayton had already moved and tried several times since. For all he knew, he was paralyzed. He knew he'd live … *but would I want to if I can't walk … and my family is …*

"We're going to get you out of there now," a medic told him. They meticulously checked him out and surrounded him with an inflatable body suit to limit his mobility. After sufficiently stabilizing him, they took him out of the van and placed him outside. Two unidentifiable men held a towel above him to protect him from the blinding, scorching sun. Clayton could not focus on anyone. To him, it seemed like an ant colony was overrunning his world, each fulfilling their own duties.

One face and voice he did recognize was that of Kevin, who came to his dad's side to make sure he was okay. This blessed Clayton to hear words of concern from one who loved him. Kevin again expressed his sorrow for the accident. They cried together.

The helicopter departed and another siren screamed its way to their proximity. Clayton learned, after asking, that Ruth and Duane had left on the helicopter. They then loaded him into the ambulance via a stretcher. Kimberly laid on a stretcher beside him. Kevin rode up front next to the driver.

The thirty-five-mile drive to the Hermiston, Oregon, hospital was no picnic for Clayton and his aching back. The excursion seemed to take forever. Clayton learned that Ruth and Duane (and probably Bruce, he imagined), went to another hospital in Richland, Washington. He hated this abysmal separation.

Upon arriving at the hospital, Clayton overheard a medical person telling someone about *the others*. Two were *medevaced*. Then he heard something about *DOA*. Danger infiltrated his system, but he didn't understand it. On the stretcher, as he was being wheeled to the entryway, he asked the doctor overseeing things about the rest of his family. He finally heard the accurate news. Kimberly and Kevin were fine. This he had surmised on his own. Ruth and Duane, he learned, were in intensive care but would pull through their injuries. "But Bruce," the doctor told him, "did not make it."

Clayton grabbed the bed rails tightly and wanted to rise but couldn't. His pulse quickened and his face flushed. "What?!" He was livid. "That's not true. You're lying. Why would you say that? That's not true." They assured him it was true. Clayton yelled and screamed! "No! How did you let that happen? What kind of hospital is this? You doctors are terrible! I need to see my son! Let me see my son!"

The staff recognized the acute traumatic outburst as shock and had to restrain him, which wasn't hard because his back didn't allow him to put up much of a serious fight. They brought him to his room, and the hysteria finally wore him out. The nurses eventually left him alone after checking him out and taking X-rays.

The shock was full-blown, and he lost himself for a time. But in the end, he had lost a son. Bruce was gone.

Beemer, after frantically recording the day's scene while Clayton slowly came out of shock, wrote to his editor: *Clayton's about as low as he can go now, at least emotionally. Feeling what he's feeling, I can't imagine him getting over this. What must happen for him to recover?*

The chief wrote back: It's not just one thing. Many things will need to occur for him to find hope again. Time will be the most important factor. I'd suggest you sit back and see how it all unfolds. I think you'll find THE BOSS's undeniable involvement uncanny.

Beemer did just that. He merely observed for the next couple of weeks, then he wrote the following:

Alone in that hospital room, Clayton had never felt such intense inner pain. Setting aside all the conflicting feelings that he didn't know what to do with, he easily focused on loneliness—an involuntary consequence that he wouldn't have wished on anyone. However, at 5:00 in the evening, about three-and-a-half hours after the accident, Clayton regained enough aware-ness to ask to see Kevin and Kimberly. A nurse brought them to his room.

Kevin explained how he sobbed in his room in front of a nurse when they told him about Bruce's death. Other than a cut on his forehead, he had no other injuries, likely because he was the only one wearing his seatbelt.

Kimberly had a cut toe, some scrapes, and a sore neck. Physically, she'd pull through just fine. She admitted to hearing about Bruce's death too, but she appeared not to know how to react to her best buddy leaving this earth. Bruce had always looked after her. From day one, he had helped her feel a part of their family. Clayton hurt for her nearly as much as he did for himself. But he didn't know how to convey that crippling feeling. So, they all just huddled together and cried, each with IV drips hanging from their arms.

Clayton was diagnosed with a bruised back. Nothing he'd die from, for sure, but the prognosis was vague at best. No paralysis, which was good, but would he have a sore back the rest of his life? The jury was still out, despite the doctor's tinny promises. But that was the least of his worries right then.

He had lost a son. Though the shock had passed, the anger had not. Slowly, his anger overtook the loneliness as his dominating emotion.

Beemer, feeling Clayton's intense anger at the time, wrote to his mild-mannered editor: *This is so unfair! He was just starting to see the true protection and provision of THE BOSS. Now, this harmony's been severed. Just like that! This feels so evil. So wrong! His earthly father's hateful criticism gave him good reason to be angry. Now, he's blindsided with an evil far worse than any hatred—death! He feels betrayed by the protector of his son. It's no wonder he's mad. He is angry! Shouldn't he be?*

The editor calmly, but firmly, wrote back: Anger is fine. But don't get so lost in your subject's emotions that you lose sight of Who breathed this life into being. Remember Whom you're chronicling for!

Anger is the by-product of disappointment. It helps them stay in the game instead of checking out and giving up. Clayton is fighting the only way he knows how to right now. He's angry. I doubt he knows that's a good thing at this point.

I think you're onto something regarding his anger toward his dad. Has Clayton ever made peace with how awfully his dad treated him in his youth?

Beemer answered back: *Well, sort of. He identified his anger through a counselor years ago. Then he wrote that book about his ancestry, which supposedly honored his dad. I think, in Clayton's mind, he did enough to deserve his dad's love and respect. But deep down, because his dad didn't even give him so much as an "atta boy!" I think he was just more disappointed than anything.*

Disappointed! That's it! He's holding onto anger in the form of unrecognized disappointment.

Do you think some of his anger now is residue of how his father treated him?

Chief replied: Without a doubt. A human cannot just throw aside such disturbing memories without becoming resentful. Other trauma usually triggers such reactions.

The anger is real and has a purpose. But because the heaviness of this event is so extreme and engrossing, it will likely take some time to unpack. Don't let the intensity of his anger distract you from your heavenly chronicling.

Beemer forced himself to take a deep breath and trust his superior's words that Clayton would somehow climb out of this awful pit within the bowels of his being. He hoped to see the hero emerge—eventually.

From Clayton's perspective, Bruce had that special sparkle in his eyes. Always eager to learn, he had found a divine wonder in life, like when he sang while mowing the lawn or when he made a candle holder with a dove for his fifth-grade teacher. He had taken life as it came and didn't try to be someone he wasn't. Bruce had rarely dwelled on excuses but endeavored to follow instructions. And this mischievous, fun-loving kid had admired his dad. Clayton had expected Bruce to do great and marvelous things someday.

It had pleased Bruce to please others. He had often empathetically held others' interests above his own … just like Clayton … just like Clayton's mom. Then, it dawned on Clayton, Bruce had died on his grandmother Bertha's eighty-second birthday.

Why did Bruce have to be taken? He showed so much promise, so much hope!

Beemer wrote a note to his editor at the time this incident took place: *This is a brutal obsession spinning through Clayton. Why doesn't he just turn it off?*

The editor in chief wrote back: Grief has no boundaries. Prepare for many irrational memories. When a human grieves, their world turns upside down. They fall into a dark pit and grab hold of despair as if it is hope. They cannot navigate fluidly. Expect a deadening of all positive emotions. Embalming with sadness is the only way they can heal from such trauma.

Later that evening, Clayton and his two fragile kids prayed with two hospital chaplains. Though sad, the experience was a bonding one.

Also helping to stave off loneliness, Clayton received phone calls from brothers, Roy, Marion, and Elno, nephew Dean, and his pastor, Bill Detweiler. Bill told him Ruth had notified him through the pastor that had ministered to them at the wreck. Bill, in turn, informed Clayton's family. This love and concern were a balm to Clayton's lonely soul.

Clayton called Ruth at Kadlac Hospital that night. They shared notes to try and grasp the whole mess. From talking to Kevin, Clayton learned that Kevin didn't want to wake them, even though he was getting tired as he drove. He had seen a sign for a rest area in eight miles and thought they could have lunch and switch drivers there.

Ruth called Clayton's niece, Kay, whom they'd just stayed with, to inform them of the accident. Roy and Dean both planned to drive to be with them the next day. Ruth called her brother as well. Others were slowly coming to their rescue.

Ruth basically felt fine when she arrived at the hospital. They ran their tests on her and cleaned her head wound. They were concerned about head trauma and so used extra precaution. She was hungry, so they gave her some red Jell-O, which she ate easily. Later, after an anxious visit with Duane in his room, her stamina waned, and she vomited up the Jell-O. She was told she had had a small seizure. Ruth thought the anxiety from the day and then seeing Duane finally took its toll on her body. Clayton could relate to the strange reactions one's body exhibits during extreme stress.

Ruth told Clayton of her once-in-a-lifetime helicopter ride, which she would never forget but never wanted to repeat. Duane was strapped into a stretcher above her in the compact helicopter cab. He was screaming and deliriously carrying on. She asked if the pilot or the assistant could help calm him. But they were too busy navigating and negotiating their arrival with the hospital. Duane's ranting became so intolerable that one of them finally asked if Ruth could try and calm him. She reached up to hold his hand and told him it was alright. She didn't remember what all she said but felt like God had given her just the right words to say. Miraculously, Duane calmed.

When she got to see Duane in his room much later, she told him the bad news of his brother's death. He acknowledged her message but made little reaction. Ruth was glad, after seeing his state in the helicopter, that he was back to, from her estimation, functioning normally.

The next morning, after a fitful night's sleep, a staff member informed Clayton that he was well enough to be transferred to Kadlac later that day, where Ruth and Duane were. Kevin and Kimberly would be released. They would need to be looked after.

The first physical piece of the out-of-control puzzle came in the form of Clayton's brother Roy and Vesta who had driven six hours to get there at 8:30 a.m. Never had Clayton been so glad to see a family member! His plummeted spirit lifted, if only a notch. They would take care of Kevin and Kimberly. Dean, Clayton's nephew, and Bonnie arrived shortly after Roy and his wife.

The invaluable presence of his relatives lightened Clayton's burdens considerably. They would look after details of hospital admittance, the location of Bruce's body, insurance matters, and the location of their van and belongings—a list with a large variety of tasks. *Thank God for family!*

After the noon meal, Clayton was transported to the other hospital. Clayton felt every bump and turn the whole fifty miles there. Still on his stretcher as he reunited with Ruth, they were informed that Duane was awake. Clayton excitedly asked to see his son! But to his dismay, by the time they arrived in his room, they found Duane asleep again. Clayton couldn't help but cry at the news, wondering if another son would soon leave him. Ruth's tears in her own bed across the room matched Clayton's, though the staff assured them that Duane's sleeping was normal and encouraged for such a severe concussion.

For the rest of the day, fueled by the other's torrent of tears, losing their son, and fear of the unknown, Clayton and Ruth talked and tried to comfort one another in-between a myriad of phone calls and visitors. They were forced to make decisions about funeral arrangements and medical matters as best they could.

Ruth told of her blessed encounter with her *night angel*, the night before. Her nurse worked only two nights a month and had just happened to be working on the night Ruth rolled into her shift. The caring woman shared her story of losing her own husband and daughter. Her caring ministry touched Ruth at just the right time and in just the right way.

A policeman came to visit Ruth as well. He, the pastor (Charles), and a doctor had all been off duty when they came upon the accident—all before the medics arrived. Without knowing it, the Steiners' physical, spiritual, and protection needs had all been looked after.

The policeman referred a chaplain, Jack Willis, to them. He pastored a small, local, Assemblies of God church called Bible Way Fellowship, which eventually adopted Clayton and his family as their own. Ruth and Clayton felt loved and cared for by Jack and his congregation even though the group had no Mennonite blood among them.

When Roy and Vesta brought Kevin and Kimberly to visit, Ruth asked Kevin if he had found someone to talk to at the accident like she encouraged. He brightened and said, "Yes, and they were Christians." When they asked how he knew that, he said, "They prayed with me all the time." He told of others—two truckers who befriended him and a roofer who had also prayed with him.

Kimberly told of some nice *Spanish* guy who held her. "He thought she was all alone," Kevin interjected.

"Well, I guess she kind of was," Ruth said.

"Yeah, but everyone kept asking if there was another car involved in the accident. I told them there wasn't, but I don't think they believed me."

Clayton's heart wrenched. He realized that his little adopted daughter was assumed to be alone because they saw no proof of her Asian family.

Ruth squeezed Kimberly's hand and gently clasped the back of her neck. "That must have been scary."

Kimberly nodded, nearly in tears.

That night, Kevin and Kimberly stayed in a motel with Dean and Bonnie. Clayton and Ruth, meanwhile, asked to have their beds moved together. They both were told not to sit up yet, so they held hands through the night, sharing notes on their many recent phone calls, the random accident-scene flashbacks they recalled, their present perspectives, and their recent memories of Bruce. Though Clayton longed to hug his wife, at least the wondrous touch of her hand alleviated his need to weep.

Ruth remembered Bruce's responses to some of the questions when they played the *Un-Game*, an interactive game that elicited honest replies to probing questions with (often) spiritual overtones. She marveled at how well the game had drawn out his personality.

She said, "Do you remember, when he was asked the question, '*When you are alone and no one else can see you or hear you, what do you like to do?*' he said '*Read.*' That was so like him, wasn't it?

"And when he was asked to *describe his favorite teacher*, his twelve-year-old-hands drew an hourglass to describe the beautiful Mrs. Augspurger." Ruth let out a stifled laugh.

"I remember when he was asked to describe a happy family, Bruce said, 'Christian.'" Ruth smiled, calmly. "Then, remember when he said that he wouldn't tease his brothers and sister so much if he had only a week to live? He had such a twinkle in his eye when he said it.

"I'll never forget when he was asked to *describe the ideal mother*." Tears flowed down Ruth's face as she recalled, "He said, 'Just like you, Mom.'" She sniffled and wiped her nose with a tissue.

"One peculiar thing, though, when he was asked to describe his life at age seventy, I remember him saying, 'I can't, Mom.' So, I said, 'Well, think of being a grandfather someday.' He said he'd never be a grandfather."

Clayton felt like Mary, Jesus' parent, when she found her twelve-year-old son prophesying at the temple and "pondered these things in her heart."

Yet, as profound as the nostalgic remembrances of his beautiful son were, Clayton could not elude the intense anger he felt. This pervading resentment came out in his speech, his defeated attitude, and his hopeless outlook. Ruth encouraged him to talk to their pastor, Bill Detweiler, as she had earlier in the day.

The next morning (Sunday), before Bill was to give his sermon back in Kidron, "Joy for the Journey" (inspired by their accident and the scripture in Isaiah that proclaims how God goes with his people no matter the journey), Clayton discussed his angry feelings with Bill. Bill told him, "God has big shoulders and can absorb your angry feelings. He knows how you feel and wants to carry your burdens. Tell him just how you feel just like the Psalmist did."

Though the words made sense and Ruth seemed to bask in the wisdom on his behalf, Clayton could not release his awful feeling of having been ripped off. His son had been taken from him! He could not hope to rejoice by releasing such an intimate wrong. So few things in this world are purely good. Bruce's life, he felt, was one such thing. He saw, and could still feel, the purity ... the wholeness ... the sacredness of his life. Now Bruce was gone. *How can that be right? How can I live in a world so unsafe and untrustworthy that allowed such an unjust abomination to occur?*

Beemer beseeched his editing mentor in a margin note: *I can feel Clayton's anger. This is not his imagination. This is a real feeling. I'm scared for the hero of my biographic book. After hearing, but not really accepting, such wise and loving counsel from his pastor back home, will he ever be able to trust THE BOSS again?*

The weathered editor responded: One human reaction does not the person make. It's important to differentiate a subject's reaction from his response. Right now, Clayton is reacting to the painful loss of his son with the feeling of anger. In the days, weeks, months, years to come, he'll need to come up with his response. Depending on your subject's willingness to go through the grieving process required for a healthy recovery, he may grow from these angry feelings, or they may haunt and harm him the rest of his life.

Beemer replied: *But that's not fair. Clayton didn't choose for this to happen. Why should he be required to accept it?*

The editor wrote: What THE BOSS allows to happen is up to THE BOSS. All I know is that no matter how dire a subject's circumstances, they eventually always have the choice to hold on to their resentment or let it evolve into a growing opportunity. That's not to diminish the pain they endure, but rather, to ensure that life always goes on. You needn't worry you'll lose your protagonist. Your subject has shown the proclivity to adapt. Be attentive to how THE BOSS woos him toward trust and hope again. Report and observe.

Clayton and Ruth tired of telling their story over and over but not of the love that came through those phone lines. In total, they received over eighty phone calls throughout their hospital stay. The sheer volume alone spoke of how much they were loved.

A Paul and Annette Griffith stopped by to visit. They said they weren't sure if they'd find Clayton and Ruth there but wanted to give it a try. Clayton and Ruth didn't recognize them. The young couple greeted Kevin and Kimberly affectionately. The kids responded in kind. "These are the people who prayed with us," Kevin reported.

Annette shared, "We've never stopped at an accident before. We've always thought we'd just be in the way. But this time was different. We both felt like God wanted us to stop." She looked to her husband.

Paul said, "For such a chaotic situation, it felt like there was a divine orderliness to it all. Everyone seemed to have their own task to help with. I was drawn to your one son right away." He looked around the room, "Duane, I think his name was. He was terribly upset. I could tell he had a head injury. Is he okay?"

They explained he was fine but in another room.

Annette picked up the thread. "Some were holding blankets to shade you from the hot sun. Some of us were praying. An older Spanish gentleman with a tattoo was holding Kimberly. It was like God broke down all barriers and prejudices to use whoever made themselves available. After you all went to the hospital, a whole bunch of us gathered your belongings, which were scattered along the road, and placed them in your van. I hope you'll get them."

They had. Dean and Bonnie had collected all they could find in the van, boxed it up with Kevin and Kimberly's help, and readied it for their eventual trip home. Ray and Kay would peruse the accident scene even more closely later, gathering all the tidbits they could find, from Un-Game cards to a camping pan.

Jack Willis visited them again that afternoon, assuring them that his church would do whatever they could to help them, including providing a place for Ray's family and Kevin and Kimberly to stay. Clayton marveled at how so many people were taking care of them while he could do so little for himself or his family. Though he was grateful, the agonizing grip of anger made it extremely difficult to express genuine appreciation to all who showed their love to them. Knowing this, but unable to change his feelings, added to his tumultuous guilt instead of easing it.

One thing that helped ease Clayton's angst was hearing about Kevin's tear-cleansing embrace with Kay. He had been worried about his oldest son. Kevin said he just laid his head on her shoulder and cried like a baby, evidently releasing the floodgates of grief.

Fourteen-year-old Duane moved to the room adjoining theirs. This lifted Clayton. Though Duane participated in their conversation, he fell asleep often and did not remember what was talked about, including any memory of his brother dying. The road rash on his legs and arms annoyed him almost as much as his troublesome hospital gown and catheter, which he tried ripping off on several occasions. He ate very little until Monday's noon meal. Then at 2:00 p.m., he said, "What's for dinner?" Ruth gladly called a nurse, and Duane ate ice cream, two custards, and a 7-Up soda. Their missing teenager was finally returning. Clayton felt some relief from his paralyzing anxiety.

Roland, Ruth's brother, called to tell them that their neighbors, a small group, and relatives were all taking care of the yard and the house. Ruth tried to insist that they not trouble themselves over such trifles. But Roland told her, "These people are grieving over your loss too. They need to feel like they're doing something for you. Don't rob them of their giving."

Clayton felt like a bumbling ingrate. He and Ruth prayed that night that they could be gracious to those giving them so much despite the pain that everyone involved was experiencing. Ruth prayed for God to "help us through the valley of the shadow of death." She also asked for God to maintain their love for one another and to give them the strength to help their children through all their mixed-up feelings. Clayton, so lacking in communication skills, realized that he needed his wife now more than at any time in their marriage.

Clayton was overwhelmed at all the responsibilities he so keenly felt but knew he could not yet fulfill. But each moment of each day, he gained a little more resolve to answer the calls of husband, father, friend, employee, Christian, and man.

Kay, a career nurse, explained to Clayton and Ruth the technical terms of their various conditions. She also ran an important errand for Ruth. Tuesday was Kimberly's tenth birthday. Kay went to the store and bought a birthday cake because, "no matter the circumstances," Ruth said, "you can't ignore a ten-year-old's birthday." They all had a little party for her in their room. Kimberly described to her parents her delightful adventures from earlier in the day when she and Kevin were treated to a horseback ride with new friends from Bible Way Fellowship.

On Wednesday, July 11, 1984, two happy things occurred. Not only was it their twentieth wedding anniversary, but they were also released from the hospital. Clayton felt disloyal over the inappropriate joy these momentous occasions produced in the midst of his great sorrow.

That evening, they joined Jack for a prayer meeting with about thirty members of his church. These caring people held their hands, prayed, sang, cried, and shared together. The loud, charismatic, and heartfelt experience was like no church meeting Clayton had ever been a part of. The precious encounter heightened Clayton's confused emotions when he learned of many of the church members' military support. Then, to top off their giving, they gave Clayton and Ruth an envelope with a letter and ten one hundred-dollar bills—$1000.00! The people he had always judged as out of God's will were meeting all his rawest needs.

The letter, in part, read, "We, as the body of believers at Bible Way Fellowship, want to express our love to you at this time. We consider it a great privilege that God has chosen us to minister to you and your family. Please accept this token of our love to help you return home and to get things settled there. As God has richly blessed us, so we in return want to richly bless you ... " The love and encouragement Clayton and his family received that night rocked their topsy-turvy world.

Afterward, Kimberly gave her parents the remainder of her birthday cake, calling it their "anniversary cake." They celebrated as a family at the home of a gracious host family from the church. Still wound up from all the whirring events of the day, after the kids went to bed, Clayton and Ruth debriefed with Ray and Kay (who turned out to be wonderful listeners), an exercise they'd need to pursue and participate in regularly in the weeks and years to come.

Beemer wrote to his editor: *Wow! I still feel this nagging pang of hostility that Clayton is carrying around inside him, but I also feel a surging love from all those THE BOSS has sent to lift him and his family up. How can a person hold such powerful contradictory feelings inside?*

The editor replied: The strong emotions you're having only feel contradictive. They're all from THE BOSS. They're made to work harmoniously, not combatively. And they're not meant to be held inside a human. They're meant to be experienced, understood, and expressed. It takes the typical human a while to get it. Some never do. Yours is actually doing quite well under the circumstances—despite the unsettledness he's presently feeling, of course.

Instead of driving their van home, they flew home on a big jet. To Clayton, it would be like starting all over again. Would he ever get his bearings back? Would he find the strength to carry on? He recalled all the excitement his family had enjoyed preparing for this trip. Then he realized, with a knot in his throat, the adventure was still on. It just wasn't the adventure he'd planned on.

23

SUPPORT RECEIVED AND GIVEN
GRACE IMPARTED

"**W**ell, that's hard to verbalize," Beemer said in response to his editing mentor's question: "How is your subject feeling?"

"He's got so many different intense feelings; it's hard to know where to begin. Anger is certainly at the forefront. Bewilderment, fear, overwhelmed, gratitude for others' kindness, familial affection, exhaustion, anxiety, unfairness—they're all vying for his attention."

"What about sadness?" the chief asked.

"Yes, I purposely didn't include that sly rascal. Of course, Clayton is sad. But after his body experienced that weird shock sensation thing in the hospital and he realized Bruce was truly gone (which took at least forty-eight hours to absorb), he's not really been feeling a lot of sorrow. Strange, isn't it? He feels violated, like a part of his body has been removed, yet he's not really feeling sad."

"Not as strange as you might think. These foreign feelings of forlornness can easily upset the equilibrium of the system. When there is no solid ground to steady one's stance, often the subject rejects the scariest emotions from their storehouse."

Beemer scowled with one eyebrow raised. "Can they do that? Just up and throw out an emotion they don't want?"

"Yes, but no. No matter how convenient and wise it appears at the time, I've never seen an instance where the hidden emotion doesn't eventually come back to haunt them in some form or fashion. Until they can identify the culprit, accept its significance, and deal with its magnitude, they will never elude its role."

"Hmm, so Clayton isn't really *not* feeling his sadness. He's just denying its proper place."

The editor in chief nodded.

"So, how long before he starts to really feel his sadness?"

"That all depends on the subject, his awareness of his handicap, and his desire to become healthy."

Beemer squinted and pursed his lips. "Are we talking a few days, weeks maybe?"

"Maybe. Maybe years. Maybe never."

"Never?" Beemer winced. "Surely, my subject won't wait forever to feel one of the most basic human emotions."

The mentoring journalist raised his eyebrows as if shrugging his shoulders. "Let's hope not, for his sake. But these things can be tricky. Grieving is not an easy beast to anticipate. Observe and report. Quit trying so hard to make him your hero. Let him be who THE BOSS has made him to be."

Beemer sighed. "I don't get why he has to go through all of this death thing anyway. Why should any human have to maneuver through such a brutal phenomenon?"

"Death is part of life, Beemer. We don't fully understand the circle of life. For whatever reason, death makes life more meaningful."

Clayton and his family flew into the Cleveland airport at 10:30 p.m., Thursday, July 12, where they were greeted by Ruth's siblings and Clayton's brother Lee and his wife, Vera. They finally arrived at their clean, upkept home at 11:30 at night.

Clayton felt his already anxiety-ridden life swing further out of control when the car wouldn't start first thing the next morning. Relying on yet another good Samaritan, Clayton accepted a ride from their neighbor, who drove the family to the cemetery to pick out a plot for Bruce's burial.

The stress continued throughout the day. They talked with the youth pastor who would be conducting the funeral service regarding all the necessary arrangements. Decisions galore!

Next, they went to the funeral home to view the body. The sight of Bruce's swollen face and sagging cheeks horrified them. *This was not the boy they knew!* For an hour, they fretted, prayed, cried, and discussed their concerns. In the end, they made the hard choice not to have an open casket at the viewing. They did not want friends and family to remember Bruce this way.

Totally worn-out, the family went home and tried to relax for the rest of the day. Various siblings stayed with the family at all times, preparing meals, answering the nonstop phone calls, running errands, and just making sure they were present. These were such helpful gestures to the overwhelmed family! But each breath Clayton took felt restricted, like he could not take in a full breath.

Early on the morning of the funeral, Clayton and Ruth heard muffled sobs from the room upstairs where Bruce had shared a room with Duane. Clayton followed his frantic wife toward the noise. They found Duane crying his eyes out. Ruth rushed to hold him and asked, "What's the matter?"

In-between sobs, Duane blurted out, "I wished for a room by myself. Is that why Bruce was killed?"

Clayton's heart sank. He watched Ruth's tears stream down her face as she assured her son that his request was normal and not the cause of Bruce's death. Clayton got in on the end of the hug but did not have the words to guide his son. He felt bereft of answers.

The sharing service with loved ones in the morning was touching, if not joyous. Ruth's written memories of her son, read by a friend, included his adept construction of birdhouses at camp and his mastery of origami birds out of paper. After scripture reading, prayer, and a summary of Bruce's active life, those attending shared their fond memories of Bruce.

Peter Dunn, Clayton's boss, made note that many of the memories spoken of were linked to Bruce's love for birds. He then mentioned the nuthatch that had been darting in and out of the sanctuary, flying up and down the brickwork next to the cross and over and under the casket. He concluded, "This free-flying marvel is no doubt God's message to us to ease the pain we are all sharing."

A friend read the following dedication to Bruce that Clayton had penned.

We as a family are grateful to God that our injuries were not worse, that we were having a great trip, and that God has so wonderfully sustained us through our physical and emotional pain. Our pain has been great. We have cried a lot and have asked lots of questions, but we have continually been blessed by God's people all along the way. These people have taught us how large a family we really belong to.

We have been blessed and cared for by complete strangers. Some were white, some black. Some were Mennonite; many others were not. Some persons were large; others were small. We were taken care of by the timid, the liberal, the conservative, the evangelical, the charismatic, and even some non-Christians. Our faith in God's people has been greatly enhanced. God has a large family.

Regarding our loss, Bruce was very special to each of us in his very own special way. Our twelve years with him will never be forgotten. He has meant much to each of us. His gifts of wit, warmth, mischievousness, and kindness will be missed. His many contributions to our family unit will be a great loss. We loved him deeply; therefore, now our hurt is deep. He worked, read, rode the moped, and lived with intensity, but my last view of him was one of calmness and peace. Because of our mutual love for each other, we have the privilege of carrying many, many fond memories that bless and sustain us.

God has chosen to call Bruce early, the reasons for which we will not know until later. We only know that God knows best.

We deeply want to thank each of you for your support, concern, and the many ways you have cared. Each of you is very special to us. We deeply want to share and show our appreciation. We want to give as we have been given to.

The days ahead may yet be our hardest, especially when our thoughts wish for Bruce's presence. God works through people. When we cry, hold our hands. When we want answers, listen to our needs. When our faith wavers, tell us you understand. When we express sadness, anger, or grief, tell us, it is okay.

Again, we as a family wish to express our deepest appreciation. In our hour of almost total emotional devastation, you have been especially near to us. You have helped, blessed, and ministered to our needs in most meaningful ways. For this, we want to praise the Lord and wish you God's continual blessing.

Afterward, everyone shared a lunch provided by church members in the fellowship building. Elno, Clayton's brother, led the burial service at the cemetery.

In the afternoon, the public memorial service welcomed a packed church. A highlight of the ceremony was singing performed by Clayton and Ruth's small group, which many referred to as "angel voices."

On Sunday night, Clayton and Ruth left the kids with their Uncle Roland and took advantage of Ruth's mom's anniversary gift money by staying overnight at a Ramada Inn. The timely evening rested their weary bodies. They did their best to reconnect though their grieving needs differed significantly.

On Monday, Ruth's mom and stepdad Clare encouraged them with their presence and wisdom. That evening, Clayton's step-in parents, Phares (Homer's brother) and Lucille (Bertha's sister), also lightened their hearts by joining in their mourning. Respected parents are a healing balm when life is harsh.

Later in the week, the family spent some R & R time at Laurelville Church Center, once again considered their haven. They wrote a lot of thank-you cards, did some reading, participated in selective camp activities, and generally recuperated from the previous weeks' trauma and decision-making.

Beemer noted in the side margin to his chief: *Wow! I remember thinking how horrible LCC was in its unfair treatment of Clayton and his family. I thought Clayton losing his*

*job was about the worst thing that could have happened to him.
In comparison to losing a child, I guess Clayton figures finding
peace in an old battleground is better than holding a grudge.*

The chief wrote back: I'm continually amazed by the fascinating ways THE BOSS's creatures find healing. The
master plan is magnificent.

And might I remind you that you have fallen these two
times right along with Clayton? And, right with him, you
are recovering nicely.

Beemer recalled his superior's prediction of his "impending fall." He
had no words to respond.

Twenty-four days after the accident, Clayton went back to work, though
only for eighteen hours that first week. Getting back to a semblance of a
routine was good, in that it helped distract him from his pain. However, it
did little to mask the loss. He returned full-time a week later.

For the first forty-five days after the accident, the family received at
least one card a day from a loved one, tallying over three hundred in total.
Clayton's employer, long-time friends, extended family, church family, and
many mere acquaintances extended the grace he needed. And though
deeply appreciated, the attention also tied them to unforgettable tragedy.
Clayton felt forever marked in the community.

Each member of the family grieved differently and dealt with their own set
of circumstances. Kimberly had lost her best friend and personal protector.
One evening, when asked to set the table, Kimberly set out place settings
for six as she always had. When the family sat down to dinner, the obvious
vacant setting brought the reality of her missing confidant crashing down
on her.

Duane dealt with random seizures for a year after his head injury, com-
plicating his physical and emotional recovery.

Kevin had to fight off the demons that he was the driver when the horrendous accident occurred. He may have felt more alone than any of them. The next summer, to find some solace and independence, he lived with the Christian roofer/youth minister (and his family) in Oregon who had helped him at the scene of the accident.

Ruth did her best to meet the needs of her children and to graciously acknowledge all who showed sympathy. Exhausted, she also keenly felt the sorrow of losing her son. She often released her torrent of tears in the seclusion of her showers.

Clayton did his best to keep the uncomfortable and alien feelings at bay. To be the father to his kids, the employee, and the Christian figure he wanted to be, he refused to succumb to the jumbled-up pain inside him. Occasionally, he realized how tenuous his noble presentation to the world was. One day about a year into the grieving process, an employee called out, "Bruce!" to another employee. Clayton's ears perked up, and he immediately looked for his forever missing son. Unable to cope with the instant remorse, sorrow, and anger, Clayton exited the plant, sobbing uncontrollably.

> Sometime later, Beemer wrote this note in the margin: *I know grieving is necessary for this species, but how long is this going to take? Will Clayton carry this awful thing around with him like a ball and chain the rest of his life? When will he be normal again?*

> The editor wrote back: Grieving takes as long as it takes. There is no set time. Observe your subject and report his unique experience. Whatever way he responds is normal. Keep in mind that a human does not suddenly get over grieving. Some aspects of the memory will always remain embedded in their biology. Most subjects eventually learn to function fully despite the unforgettable experience.
>
> Where is your subject in the process?

> Beemer: *Well, afraid to lose his faculties again, Clayton did not allow himself to process all his complex emotions right away.*

He simply got angry—angry that he had his sixteen-year-old son drive while he slept on the floor, angry that the wonderful vacation was cut short, angry that Bruce was taken, angry that he didn't get to say goodbye to Bruce, and angry at THE BOSS for letting it happen. He tried to smother all those angry feelings. But he couldn't help secretly asking THE BOSS questions: "Why did this happen? Why Bruce and not myself? Did I sin somehow to cause this? Are you even real, God?"

So, basically, he went into the funeral angry, afraid, and questioning—not aware of his sadness. Which was strange because he did cry some. But it was crying more from the compassion so many expressed for him and his family than for the grief he felt from losing his son.

After counseling and coming to grips with his denial, he finally (ever so gradually) has allowed himself glimpses of that nagging elephant in the room—sorrow. His gradual grieving process has been like a boy knowing, but not really seeing or understanding, that he is becoming a man. I think he's just now, over three years out, in touch with the sadness of it all.

About three years after losing Bruce, Clayton and Ruth's friends Les and Trish connected them with a Catholic couple who had lost a daughter in a car accident. With Les and Trish's presence and willingness (though they had not lost a child), the three couples met every other week to share their experiences and struggles. The effects encouraged and uplifted each of them.

Soon, they opened the group to others, eventually growing to between twelve and sixteen couples. Ruth was the driving force of the group, while the core group steadily remained active in structuring the meetings. Some attendees came just three or four times, while many attended for months. Clayton pursued this one endeavor more out of compassion than from his old hounding pursuit of *being better than his brothers, Elno and Marion.* He found that helping others through their pain brought him hope and healing, too.

Beemer wrote a side note: *This grieving thing sure took (is taking) a long time, but I've got to admit you were right— THE BOSS's system sure is incredible! To think that Clayton was just looking for anything to heal the wound of his loss, followed the breadcrumbs of grief groups, and found hope through expression in relationships. Then, by leading others through their grieving process, he found the strength he sought in the first place. What a wild journey! Not exactly like William Clark in his Lewis and Clark expedition, but it's been adventurous just the same.*

The editor returned his musings with: It looks like your subject has learned to be authentically and humbly vulnerable. Definitely a BOSS-like trait.

Tell me, how has he dealt with his anger?

I'm glad you asked. Like his grieving in general, his anger has slowly diminished. I wouldn't say he's conquered it exactly, but it appears to have little sting anymore. He used to feel anger at his dad constantly, for instance. But, after the accident, putting his son to rest, and dealing with the anger he felt over that very real experience, the anger at his dad no longer seems to carry much significance.

Similarly, I think that once he realized that all his anger regarding Bruce's death could, in the end, be directed only at THE BOSS, he finally (slowly) let that go. I think, compared to God's grace from above, as Clayton calls it, holding onto anger has little to offer him any more.

What grace from above does Clayton credit THE BOSS with?

From the very moment when the van stopped rolling, Clayton saw THE BOSS's mysterious hand through it all. To name a few things: Kevin landed beside Clayton to say he was sorry.

Clayton was kept from seeing the carnage around him outside the van. Christian folks surrounded the accident, helping each family member according to their individual needs. The Assemblies of God Church adopted their family when there was no Mennonite church that could. Clayton relearned the blessing that those different from himself (religiously, economically, racially, politically, and so on) are as helpful, valuable, and necessary as himself. Roy's, Dean's, and Ray's families were close enough to drop what they were doing and drive many miles to assist them. At home, neighbors and others took over their care. Their neighbors, the Sprungers, had gone through the same grief and steps with a grandchild only weeks before and were an invaluable help to them. Then, there was the bird at the funeral, Laurelville's restorative atmosphere, his employer's patience, and Kevin's summer of employment with his gracious hosts in Oregon. And that's not to mention all the love and support they received from people everywhere, nor the fact that they lost only one member of the family, and everyone else recovered.

That's quite the litany of gratitude. You've done your homework well.

Regarding his anger, how did he deal with all his unanswered questions?

Well, he never really got answers to most of them. Again, the overwhelming care he got from so many people and the grace from above basically outranked his unanswered questions. Being more on the cerebral side, a biggie that he came to grips with was that, when natural laws are broken (like falling asleep at the wheel), bad consequences occur. It's the nature THE BOSS set up. If it were not so, Clayton couldn't count on anything. But relationships now mean even more to him than they did before, more than trying to get everything all figured out. Life is temporary. Now is the time to live, not a time to wish reality was different.

And what about his anger at his dad? Do you honestly think he's overcome that completely?

As near as I can tell. Why do you ask?

These familial issues tend to have a long shelf life. Some have dubbed such phenomena generational curses. Be aware of its nastiness if your subject suddenly finds he's stuck in inescapable patterns.

Okay. I don't foresee that, however, as he has no need to cover that ground any longer.

PHOTO COLLECTION
PART II: 1964–1984

Clayton and Ruth's wedding in 1967. They were married by Clayton's oldest brother, Elno, and Clayton's brother-in-law, Irvin Nussbaum.

The Homer and Bertha Steiner family on the day of Clayton's wedding. Clayton is in the front row on the far right.

Clayton graduates from Goshen College in 1967. He
and Ruth lived in the college trailer court.

Clayton teaches fifth grade with fellow teacher Abe Willems in 1967.

*Clayton as director of the Walnut Hill
Daycare Center in Goshen, Indiana,
welcomes his pupils with their parents in 1970.*

*The Mennonite Voluntary Service (VS)
gang in Champaign, Illinois, in 1976.
Clayton is on the top far right. Ruth is
on the left and is holding Kimberly.*

*Clayton with his customized
Clayton's Chimney Care van
that he bought for his chimney
sweep business in the early 1980s.*

Clayton's children, Kimberly and Bruce, had their tonsils removed on the same day! They're all smiles on their way to the hospital in 1981.

Clayton's four children play in the sandbox in Champaign, Illinois. (Left to right: Kimberly, Kevin, Duane, & Bruce)

From the same cloth, the Steiner family in Voluntary Service in Champaign, Illinois, in 1976. (Back row: Clayton and Ruth. Front row, left to right: Kevin, Bruce, Kimberly, & Duane.)

The Steiner family on a Voluntary Service retreat in Arkansas.

Bruce explores a playground around age five.

Bruce in kindergarten.

Bruce loved playing on his Little League baseball team.

Bruce was a big help in the kitchen.

Taken at the Homer & Bertha Steiner reunion right before leaving for their trip out west.

The last photo of all four children together by themselves, taken while in Carlsbad, New Mexico. (Left to right: Kevin, Duane, Kimberly, & Bruce)

The first professional family photo, taken in 1984 after Bruce's death. (Left to right: Duane, Ruth, Kevin, Clayton, & Kimberly. Bruce's photo is pinned up in the back.)

PART 3
OVERCOMING

24

CAREER DILIGENCE
THE REWARD OF RELATIONSHIPS

The constant pull of the grieving process tempted Clayton toward depression and futility. Life just made little sense some days. If not for the counseling therapy, loved ones, and a purpose in his job, he likely would have given in to hopelessness. Gradually, working in the family atmosphere of Wood Décor every day, filling orders, making decisions, and following a plan gave him the structure to hold onto while his wild emotional roller coaster ran its course.

He took his managerial position seriously. One day, Clayton discovered that an employee had taken a small box of staples home with him. Clayton asked the owner what to do about it. Peter Dunn told him to fire the employee. Clayton understood, but he also knew that this young man counted on this job to provide for his family. Maintaining integrity within the company, Clayton knew, ranked higher than turning a blind eye and inviting corruption. He fired the man and felt awful about it. A manager's job never promised to be easy.

Peter once called Clayton into his office to ask him to stop his divisive complaining, claiming it was undermining Peter's authority and the company's efficiency. Peter said he made his decisions based on what was best for the company, and when Clayton bad-mouthed his decisions, he compromised the company's integrity.

Clayton vehemently disagreed with his BOSS's assessment, denying he "complained" but promised to watch his p's and q's. Walking out of Peter's office, Clayton did some soul-searching. It did not take long to realize that his boss was right; he had, in fact, done his share of complaining. He recognized, without realizing it at the time, that he had found some perverted sense of control or pride in showing others that he knew better than the head cheese.

Remorse and shame followed him home that night. Repenting from his negative attitude toward management, he decided he would henceforth represent management in only a positive light, dedicating his allegiance to its prosperity and not to his selfish pride. The lesson he learned was hard, but one he needed to learn. He was grateful for the lesson.

Peter noticed the change in Clayton's demeanor and soon promoted him to be the retail store and restaurant manager. Clayton enjoyed the new challenge. He learned how to deal with customers, account for the bookkeeping, and work as a tight-knit team with his dependable top employees, Ruth and Sandy.

After he had worked for Wood Décor for eight years, it became apparent to Clayton that the company was not going to make it financially. One day, Peter once again called Clayton into his office, but this time, it was to inform him that the company would be taken over by a new owner and that everyone's job was in jeopardy. The next day, Clayton picked up the shrewd new owner at the airport. The following day, Clayton was let go. Again, without a job, he was forced to start over.

> Beemer wrote in the side margin: *What? Again? How is Clayton supposed to get anywhere? It's like he's just spinning his wheels. He's forty-four years old. At least half his life is probably over. If this is typical for humans, it's a wonder more don't just give up. He was so faithful and productive. It's so unfair for him to lose his job.*

> The editor responded: Yes, it's unfair. All humans are presented with unique circumstances from which to grow. Status need not be the definitive evaluation of the

circumstance's value though. THE BOSS evidently thinks that each subject has more to gain through occasionally not getting what they deserve. Observe and report what your subject learns.

To fill his time while job hunting, Clayton worked at improving his Moser house by laying a fancy fireplace in the living-room corner. The huge project took nearly four weeks.

During the end of that time, through a connection with their neighbor, Clayton landed a job at ARE, a start-up company of about fifteen employees that manufactured fiberglass and aluminum caps and lids for pickups in nearby Mount Eaton, Ohio.

Clayton started out building the molds for the caps and lids. He soon moved up to designing the molds. Duane and Kevin got in on the action on Saturday mornings, waxing and rewaxing the molds. Eventually, Clayton took charge of establishing a lab to test the incoming material for the fiberglass products. His attention to detail and insistence on accountability impressed Aden, his boss, so much that he promoted Clayton to plant manager.

As the manager of twenty-five employees, Clayton needed new skills in this fast-paced environment where each employee needed to stay focused on the task at hand. The challenge to stay ahead of continuous new orders, communication breakdowns, human error, and morale issues fed Clayton plenty of stress. He continually fought with his slow processing nature in this whirlwind environment.

His uncompromising faithfulness and dedication to quality continued to open doors within the company as he changed hats numerous times. One promotion landed him in charge of quality control. While in that capacity, he constructed measures that were recognized and passed by ISO and Lean Manufacturing, authorities in the fiberglass industry.

As quality control manager, Clayton moved with ARE to their new plant in Massillon, Ohio, twenty-five minutes from his home. This huge 1994 venture instantly tripled their business. To manage the overwhelming growth, management asked Clayton to oversee the purchasing department. He ordered millions of dollars-worth of material each year. To do this efficiently, he systemized the operation through spreadsheets to track quality control, a huge progression for the expanding company.

As Clayton gained more and more trust and responsibility at the workplace, his bank account finally began to grow. In the eighties, while he was still working at Wood Décor, he had become interested in the stock market, reading all he could, and he taught himself to invest shrewdly. As he made more money with ARE and his children became responsible for their own finances, he risked more and made more.

Beginning in 1993, Clayton was ready for a new type of first-time investment. He wanted to build a subdivision. At the time, his brothers Lee and Roy owned his dad's farmland and were renting it out to farmers. Clayton told them of his subdivision idea and offered them fair market value for the property, which they accepted. After struggling to orchestrate the complex scheme on his own, he came across a well-known Mennonite contractor who was willing to not only help him with the project but also loan him some needed funds. In return, Clayton agreed to give him half of the land to develop his own houses on. Within six years, Clayton had contracted twenty-two houses on his half of the land and named the development *Steinwood*.

Beemer wrote in his side margin: *Clayton was so out of his depth on this, it's not funny. For a guy who takes a long time to process things and sometimes appears slow, he did really well on this risky project. I think THE BOSS is going to be super proud of him for this successful project!*

The editor responded: Beemer, THE BOSS still doesn't love him any more or less for his accomplishments. THE BOSS is proud of Clayton! Not those houses. THE BOSS is more interested in what Clayton was feeling and how he handled all the obstacles along the way. How did he handle the obstacles?

Beemer: *What makes you think he had any problems? He's an amazing guy!*

Editor: Beemer! These are people we're dealing with. They're always dealing with problems. If not their own, other people's.

Beemer sighed ... very uncomfortably.

Surprisingly (to Clayton), many local farmers opposed the Steinwood venture along the way. They cited added traffic, water runoff, turning prize farmland into housing, and pricing their farms out of future farming possibilities as potential problems. Their protests were loud, unapologetic, and (in some cases) hostile. To head off their vehemence, Clayton installed a pond and later spent $12,000.00 complying to the Township Trustee's requests, causing him to take out another loan. Moving forward, Clayton had to double down on his resolve. It felt like him against the world.

One time, two fellow church members came by his house to tell him in no uncertain terms, getting up in his face and pointing their fingers, that he was out of line for turning perfectly good farmland into a whoremongering get-rich-quick scheme. Clayton had never received such a tongue-lashing in all his life. Twice, he received anonymous letters telling him that he should be ashamed of taking farmland out of production, that he was a poor example of a Christian, and that he would pay for his selfishness.

Clayton wondered at the value of being a Christian at times throughout the whole ordeal. But in the end, after prayer, humility of heart, and advice from his pastor and other community leaders, he decided to be like Jesus and turn the other cheek. Except for a homeowner who later sued him for a runoff issue (which was dismissed), Clayton was delighted that he stuck with the project as he did.

Beemer replied in his side margin: *And that is how a hero handles adversity.*

Back at ARE, in 2000, Clayton helped lead successful efforts to curb climate change by controlling the carbon dioxide emissions. Several years later, he contributed to the innovative discussions of incorporating robots to make production more efficient. Toward the end of his career, ARE opened a fifth plant in Reno, Nevada. Clayton flew there on four different occasions for week-long stints to set up the quality control and purchasing flow.

A perk that Clayton appreciated at ARE was the biannual fishing/golfing trip around Lake Erie that his main supplier gave his employer and him (with Ruth). One year, Ruth caught the biggest fish the fishing company had ever caught. These events strengthened Clayton's marriage and his bond with his employer and supplier. Nothing broke up the monotony of the job like an expense-paid weekend with his wife!

Clayton thrived on taking salesmen to task. Getting the upper hand made him feel victorious over his *slowness* complex. He knew when salesmen were sloppy and not well-informed. Clayton enjoyed doing his homework and asking questions that made them squirm. If they did not know their product well or understand the needs of his company, Clayton used their unpreparedness to his advantage. In these cases, many yielded to his demands or, at the very least, left with their tails between their legs, forced to study their jobs more thoroughly. Either way, they were often at the mercy of Clayton and ARE's needs. Of course, ARE loved the results.

In the meantime, many years passed and Clayton's sons were now in their twenties. Kevin was selling Spectrum products and Duane sold health and life insurance. When some salesmen learned of Clayton's connection to the sales industry through his sons, they found the connection unbelievable. But eventually, in part because of these connections, the salesmen and Clayton learned to work together and developed a mutual respect and friendship. Some even contacted him after their retirement just to touch base.

Aden or Ralph, the owners, wrote out yearly report cards for their employees. Clayton always received high marks. A few of the accolades throughout the years were that Clayton "willingly takes on new assignments and works well with outsiders," "[is] very dependable and thorough," "puts in whatever hours necessary," "develops excellent spreadsheets," and "stays motivated and works independently." In response, one year, Clayton wrote "ARE continues to be an exciting place to work. I feel this past year has been one of my more fulfilling years at ARE. I have sensed that many persons see me as a positive and stabilizing force."

Beemer wrote in his margin notes: *Finally, after feeling like a schmuck from his dad, being fired at LCC, starting over in the job market several times, and losing his sense of purpose after his son died, he finally feels good about himself. And those who matter in his life (his authority figures) recognize his significance and have expressed their approval of him. I guess there's not much else to add.*

But why does my telling of it come off so flat? It's like he's (or I'm) missing something. Or accomplishment is not all that it's cracked up to be.

The editor in chief responded: Why do you think your depiction of Clayton's employment accomplishments comes off flat?

I don't know. Maybe I didn't add enough flair. Do you think if I added a few more of Clayton's employers' attaboys and spruced them up a bit more, like he walked on water or something, he'd come off as more stupendous?

No. Stop. Don't revert to immature writing habits. Colorful language is encouraged, exaggeration is not! Remember, your mission is to accurately report an earthly being's life for THE BOSS's Great Hall of Annals. Have you forgotten?

No, Sir. I mean, yes, Chief … That is to say … maybe I forgot for just a fraction of a human second. But I remember really good again now. I will continue writing honestly … no matter how unimpressive my subject looks.

Why do you describe your subject as unimpressive? He's shown integrity throughout his working career. Not all subjects achieve success and respect from their employers and fellow employees like your subject has.

Yes, but … I don't know … it's just that it's taken a lifetime to get here. I mean, I doubt they'll erect a statue of him for being a faithful employee. Is satisfaction for a job well done as good as it gets?

Though the annal you are presently writing is covering his employment, do not forget the hundreds of other aspects that make up your subject's life. Whether you think those other aspects matter or not, you need to consider what THE BOSS delights in and write from that perspective— not from your hero juxtaposition.

So, what does THE BOSS delight in?

All aspects is the short answer. But what does the BOSS care about more than anything else?

Love, I suppose.

LOVE is a good answer. Do you think THE BOSS places more value on Clayton's employment success than how he loves people?

No.

Maybe that's why your annal is falling flat.

Hmm, that's worth considering.

And remember, if Clayton's life were a movie, you'd be the videographer, not the director.

Part of what made Clayton so effective in his job was that he learned to respect everyone, whether they were his employers, fellow employees, subordinates, or outside parties. He had grown up thinking that only those who thought as godly as he did mattered. But through his experience with the Algerian Civil War, the different VSers at Champaign, the diversity at Laurelville Church Camp, and the parade of supporters throughout Bruce's farewell, Clayton learned to see and treat others with as much value as himself, whether they believed as he did or not.

This was significant because when he had first started his job in 1985, ARE was made up of ninety-five percent Mennonite or Amish-born. He naturally understood and accepted them. In the 2000s, when the company grew to be eight hundred strong with only one percent relating to Mennonites, Clayton could have easily shrunk back from the differences or, worse yet, judged the *worldly pagans* for their sinful lifestyles, which would have caused resentment and disharmony. Instead, he chose to proceed like Jesus would have, treating others as he wanted to be treated, erring on the side of acceptance rather than judgment. And, as to not hinder his employer's mission, he explained what he believed only when asked.

In his Sunday school class, Clayton often shared his *in the world* ARE experiences. His peculiar stories of non-Christians' behavior opened the eyes of many, though it closed the eyes of a few in disgust.

For most of Clayton's life, he strove to please his dad. Because his dad never expressed appreciation for Clayton's accomplishments or efforts, Clayton sought approval from other authority figures. Receiving that approval at the end of his career scratched that long-anticipated itch, an itch, ironically, that no longer needed to be scratched with the same intensity. What mattered to him more than his career success were the relationships his career produced.

The list was long. For starters, at ARE, Aden Miller topped the list. Not only Clayton's employer, Aden also became a trusted friend, always looking out for Clayton's best interests. Clayton looked to Aden as something between a brother and a father figure.

The two Dons were also among Clayton's prized relationships. These fellow employees, though contrasting radically in religious views and personality, conversed with each other and with Clayton for many years during breaks and lunchtimes. This strange threesome helped Clayton respect those with different views.

Ken Smith, a solid employee with a Native American heritage, freely shared his life experience, impressing Clayton with his candor. His daughter suffered from a chronic illness, which occupied his time away from ARE. His loyalty to ARE and Clayton benefited all.

Charlie, Clayton's sidekick, did not have the finer side of life handed to him. Bearing a criminal record, many of his former enemies later worked for him at ARE. Religion or God held little interest for this man who enjoyed tobacco, alcohol, and swearing. Curiously, Charlie became a buffer between Clayton and some of the wilder employees, and they developed an unexpected mutual respect for one another.

Then there were the supervisor Bills. Though Clayton bristled at Bill V's boisterous style, they learned to appreciate the other's contrasting demeanor. Later, Bill V even confided in Clayton regarding his wife's illness, which eventually forced him into retirement.

Bill A, a true encourager and problem solver, became Clayton's new supervisor. He taught Bill A the computer skills he needed for the quality control end of things, while Bill showed him how to problem-solve and motivate employees through honesty, care, and a hands-on approach, a style that Clayton did his best to emulate.

The conglomeration of these salt-and-pepper relationships motivated Clayton to be the best version of himself on all accounts. Through diversity and comradery, relationships meant the world to him. He knew people could have their bad side, but he also learned what a family could accomplish if they treated each other respectfully.

In 2005, at the age of sixty-five, Clayton injured his shoulder moving a product. December 5 was his last day at ARE. He had the damage surgically repaired later that month and officially retired on January 13, 2006. ARE threw a big party for him, replete with email messages that expressed the company's appreciation for him. Among the many notes were: "It has been a great pleasure working side by side with you for over fifteen years. I want to thank you for everything you have done for me personally." His last secretary wrote, "WOW... I can't imagine us without you. You're fun to be around and always so nice to me ... I will truly miss you." One person who worked under his supervision wrote, "It has been a great learning experience working for you. Thanks for the fiberglass knowledge you shared with me." Another fellow employee wrote, "Things just aren't going to be the same around here without you." And Clayton's favorite email came from a salesman who relied on Clayton's business for his livelihood: "You will never know how much you will be missed."

Through Clayton's steadfast tour of over twenty years at ARE, he gave of his time, energy, thought, will, and character, not only to his job but also to the people along the way in that journey. In return, he was loved. There is no greater reward.

25
RETIREMENT
REACHING FOR VITALITY

After the familiar dread and self-doubt from another awkward routine inspection visit from the editor in chief, Beemer threw some questions at his mentor.

"So, Chief, now that Clayton is sixty-five and retired, do you think he'll be one of those typical statistics who enjoys the leisure life and becomes a lazy, self-indulgent blob?"

The squat, sober editor palmed the back of his domed head. "Where did that come from? Has your subject given any indication that he's going to live a sedentary lifestyle now that he's retired?"

"Well, no," Beemer admitted. "But I've read enough to know that these humans tend toward self-indulgence. I mean, it's kind of the American dream to retire and suck martinis by the poolside, isn't it?"

The chief scowled. "Martinis? Does your subject even drink?"

"No, not really."

The old journalist shook his round head. "Beemer, what are you asking? Get to the point. I don't mind answering your questions, but I've got mounds of work in front of me. Entertaining mindless incongruities is not on my list."

"Sorry. The thing is, Clayton feels a little … I don't know … nervous about all of this. I think maybe he's afraid."

"Afraid of what?"

"I don't know exactly. I think maybe he thinks he'll be a couch-potato statistic. I'm a little worried my hero is in his downhill slide into the abyss."

The wise critic clasped his intertwined fingers around his substantial girth. "And what if he is? You're not the author of his story."

Rebuffed, Beemer quickly nodded. "Right."

The informed editor closed his eyes momentarily as he rubbed his wrinkled forehead. "I don't see your subject's character falling to sluggardly narcissism."

Beemer's mouth hung open. "Huh?"

"I don't think Clayton will fall to the temptation of laziness or selfishness. He has shown he wants to be the best person THE BOSS can help him to be. I don't expect his conscience will change now that he's retired. Your worries are more those of an anxious mother than of a chosen chronicler of THE BOSS."

Beemer blinked—several times. "Good … I think."

The editor in chief said farewell and left without so much as acknowledging his apprentice's awkward, ashamed countenance.

Beemer sighed. Why did he always forget that this biographic book was not his own but THE BOSS's? He hated disappointing his revered tutor.

A few years prior to retirement, Clayton met up with a second cousin from Kidron at a Mennonite conference. James Lehman had become the head librarian at the respected Eastern Mennonite University. Clayton had long admired James and his classic book, *Kidron-Sonnenberg, a Haven and Heritage*, which had been instrumental in Clayton's interest in writing and becoming a historian himself. James had gladly discussed with and directed Clayton on numerous occasions throughout the years.

At this particular conference, when Clayton asked James and his wife, Dorothy, what they recommended for retirement, they instantly endorsed the International Guest House (IGH), and they went on to share their delightful adventures as hosts for two terms at the Mennonite hostel in Washington, DC. Clayton wasn't even sure what a hostel was. They explained that though hostels are rare in the States, they flourish in much of Europe. The premise was that travelers could board inexpensively and share common amenities, such as bathrooms and meeting areas, in the same building.

James suggested Clayton and Ruth talk to the chairperson of the board of directors, who just happened to be at the conference. They met her, and she cordially invited them to visit and apply for a one-year term. In the summer of 2005, a year before their retirement, they complied and visited DC to see if the position might suit them. After a two-night stay at the International Guest House, they were impressed and intrigued with its mission of serving all walks of life. Make no mistake, the rigors of the job would be demanding and stretching. They met the other members of the board and filled out applications before they left.

Soon after they arrived home, they received word that they had been hired for the voluntary position at IGH. They gladly accepted. After Ruth's thirty-year career as an elementary school teacher ended on June 2, 2006, they obtained renters for their house and moved to Washington, DC the next month.

The long ago, but familiar, feelings Clayton had experienced when he left for Algeria, Goshen College, and Champaign came flooding back on the car trip to DC. He was nervous, excited, and in the clutches of a vulnerable future he knew not of. It was invigorating to wonder at the possibilities again!

The International Guest House welcomed all guests with open arms, limiting each stay to two weeks. Twenty-five percent of the guests were returnees, twenty-five percent were students attending classes or seminars, fifteen percent were in town on business, and the rest were tourists taking advantage of a great deal.

As host and hostess, Clayton and Ruth's responsibilities were to register the guests, assign duties to the three other temporary staff members, buy groceries, take care of finances, report monthly to the board of directors, and set the overall climate and direction of the house. They not only worked at the quaint, uptown house, but they lived in it as well. The staff dwelled on the second floor, while the guests stayed on the third.

Learning all the sundry tasks that needed to be fulfilled to accommodate their guests took time, diligence, and effort. But after a while, Clayton and Ruth felt they were not only living up to the mission of the Guest House—providing *a home away from home*—but they were making it their home too. The physical demands of the job did not allow them to get bored, just as filling food allergy requests, giving directions, cleaning spills, or listening to a guest's problems did not allow them to become complacent. Staying on their toes was mandatory!

Clayton particularly enjoyed the 8:00 a.m. breakfast that all guests were encouraged to attend every morning. Each day, if there were new guests, Clayton introduced himself and where he was from, then opened the floor to the staff and guests to do the same. One morning, they accommodated their capacity of fifteen guests around the table from twelve different countries. Often, the conversations lasted till after 9:30 a.m. Sometimes, total strangers walked out the door together, toured the city, and returned together. Clayton couldn't help but smile at this hub of co-mingled neighbors from around the world.

Another highlight was the 9:00 p.m. teatime. Those who wanted would join in the downstairs living room for tea where the discussions frequently picked up from where the breakfast conversations had left off, generally becoming more in-depth and personal. Clayton always learned something about another country or area that he hadn't known about before. The information he learned was riveting, but the people made the interaction fascinating. He twice connected with visiting Algerians. Once, a transgender male bravely shared his unique outlook and discriminatory experiences with them at teatime. He slept in the men's room upstairs, left for the day, then came back looking like an attractive female. His curious story spoke to Clayton of how harsh the world is on so many people and the need for Jesus-like compassion toward those who are easily disregarded.

In what little free time they mustered, Clayton and Ruth took in the sights of DC, visiting free museums, monuments, and attractions. Their familiarity came in handy when friends and family visited. For Christmas, Clayton's family (now including two grandkids from Kevin) all stayed at the guesthouse. They had a marvelous time. A couple of Ruth's relatives came on as staff for a couple of weeks, *sharing the load*, and making the house seem even homier to Clayton. In the fall of 2007, Clayton and Ruth finished their extended-term and returned home, drained, but filled.

After a year of relative calmness, they decided to indenture themselves to the rewarding work of serving their church through the ministry of the IGH for another year term. This second term topped even their first incredible year. They knew what to expect and how to do all the functions required of them. Still young enough to handle the busy atmosphere, they thrived on serving their guests and learning about God's love through them, his creation.

After completing their year-long commitment in 2008, Clayton and Ruth returned to IGH several times to train or relieve hosts and hostesses for a week or two at a time. Clayton found this correspondent role fulfilling. Being needed and valued felt nice.

Travel had become another interest that enchanted Clayton and Ruth and enhanced their relationship. Prior to retirement, they had enjoyed four different trips out of the country. The first was to Nova Scotia. They then had the opportunity to visit England; they also had gone to Ireland and Wales. A special trip was enjoyed when they went to Clayton's homeland in the Alps and Switzerland with his brothers Marion and Roy and their wives. After their commitment to IGH was completed, they drove to visit their daughter, Kimberly in California. Later, they went with her to Yellowstone, Glacier Park, and southwest Canada. They loved to travel!

As is common with many men Clayton's age, his prostate began giving him problems in the spring of 2009. Slow and painful urination led to frequent doctor visits, where his doctor informed him that such symptoms are usually not cancer related. Clayton began taking prescriptions and supplements; however, his prostate-specific antigen (PSA) levels kept increasing. In September, they finally took a biopsy. The results came back positive.

After Clayton received the bad news and discussed the alternatives with Ruth, Beemer called for his dependable supervisor.

"Hello, Beemer." The editor in chief wobbled and back-peddled into the bedroom wall, grasping for purchase to steady his failing equilibrium.

"Chief!" Beemer yelled and ran toward his old mentor. "Are you okay?"

"Nothing a little time won't settle," Chief said, leaning fully against the wall, his glasses dangling from one ear. "These transports will be the end of me yet. My swoops down here are more of an *oops* these days."

Other than holding his leader's outstretched arm, Beemer didn't know what to do. "I'm sorry. I shouldn't have called you down here. I'm just not very good when someone is in crisis." He looked at his chief's meek position. "You're not going to die on me, are you?"

The shallow-breathing journalist looked up at his rookie colleague. "We don't die, Beemer. We're not human, remember? We just switch jobs if we must."

"Oh, yeah." Beemer nodded sheepishly. "But wait—you might not be my editor someday?"

The aged chronicler drew in a deep breath and connected his glasses properly to the end of his nose. "Not if I make too many more of these horrendous transports."

Beemer shook his head guiltily. "Well, I wouldn't have except … my subject is dying. I'm afraid he won't complete his hero mission. How do I prepare for this?"

The tenacious manager frowned, then he shook his head and closed his weary eyes. When he opened them, Beemer hadn't disappeared. "As I've stated too many times to mention, you aren't in charge of his … mission … or story … or life. You report what you observe. No more, no less." He waited for his rebuff to sink in. "So, what makes you think he's dying soon?"

"He has cancer."

"What do the doctors say?" asked the elder reporter.

"I don't know yet."

"There is no way to predict the results without a complete diagnosis. And even with a bad diagnosis, you can't be sure how Clayton will respond," said the chief. "I've seen anything from utter resignation by the subject, leading to premature death, to instant and complete healing, undoubtedly by THE BOSS."

Beemer blinked several times. "So, what do I do about the not knowing?"

"The same thing Clayton must do. Deal with whatever information you receive as best you can."

"But what if ..."

The veteran chronicler held up his hand like a stop sign. "Save it, Beemer. We're not in the business of *what ifs*. We're reporters. If you can't handle the not knowing or possible tragic end your subject may have, you're in the wrong department. Perhaps you want to be a greeter at Heaven's Gate since you're so entranced with the future."

This time Beemer's hands flew up. "No, no! I'm made to be a chronicler."

"Then chronicle. Don't predict."

"Yes, sir ... I mean, Chief. Sorry. I'm a bit unnerved. I'll get it back. Don't worry." Beemer forced a smile.

Beemer looked away when he felt his superior herald look through him. Chief said, "What's bothering you, son?"

Beemer drew a long breath. "I guess ... I don't know ... I can't bear to see Clayton ... you know, enter Heaven's Gate. Not yet anyway. Now that I know how he feels and thinks, it doesn't seem like it's time yet. He can't die. He's got so much life in him still. Is he being punished? What did he do to deserve this? And what about his kids, his wife, his friends, his church, his fellow travelers ... everyone who relies on him? This isn't fair!"

The editor nodded. "This is exactly how Clayton is feeling. He's scared, bereft, confused. I know it feels disorienting, but you've got to remember that you're feeling Clayton's world."

"But I don't like it."

"You don't have to."

Then, almost as an afterthought, Beemer asked, "Can I ask you something?"

"Sure. While I'm down here, now's the time."

"This imminent death thing feels so awful. Why would THE BOSS ever want humans to go through such lonely terror?"

The master of written rhetoric looked over his glasses. "There's a number of things to unpack with that buckshot sentence. First, THE BOSS doesn't *want* people to suffer in the sense that cruelty brings The Almighty Creator delight. Second, THE BOSS is never about *loneliness*. THE BOSS is always about *enduring together*. Too often, humans choose to be alone in their fear instead of depending on others to share their scary burdens or guide them through daunting obstacles.

"As far as death goes, as near as I can tell, the finality of death in their earthly lives accentuates the wonder of life. In a word, life is precious."

Beemer scowled. "You mean, Clayton could end up enjoying this cancer thing?"

The master reporter smirked and shook his round face. "No, I doubt that will ever happen. But it may make him a stronger person."

"Hmm. Covering a human can sure be unsettling. I never know what's going to happen to him."

"Yes. Now, you know what Clayton feels like."

Clayton learned that the particular prostate cancer he had was the fast-growing kind. The doctor insisted that he immediately get X-rays and scans to determine if it had spread outside the prostate. Thankfully, it had not.

Of the three options presented to him (all of which held major potential downsides), Clayton chose to have the prostate surgically removed, thereby eliminating cancer completely. Through pre-surgery tests, results showed that his platelets were low. This concerning news sent him to another doctor who diagnosed him with chronic lymphocytic cancer (CLC), a life-threatening disease, making the surgery even more imperative. One of the dangers the doctor warned of was the twenty-two percent chance of losing all erectile function, a similar percentage to the other options. But Clayton was told, the latest state-of-the-art, DaVinci computer-guided machine that they would use during the surgery would hopefully decrease that bleak percentage.

During surgery, Clayton's heart stopped unexpectedly due to a major vasovagal response, which is a fancy term for fainting due to a sudden decrease in blood pressure. His breathing became slow and weak.

Heartsick, Beemer, resigned to losing his first subject, wrote to his editor in the side margins during surgery: *Is my new assignment ready?*

Beemer expected an immediate response. None came.

The doctors resuscitated Clayton through artificial respiration, which lengthened the surgery. After the surgery was over, the head surgeon matter-of-factly informed Ruth that Clayton, "is now fine, though he gave us a little scare when his heart stopped." He said they would need to keep him in the hospital longer than anticipated, though they released him the next day.

To Clayton, the traumatic event and the hazy couple of weeks that followed felt like an out-of-body experience, like the story was happening to someone else. Though determinedly grateful for the success of the surgery, he couldn't shrug off the annoying sense of more bad news to come. After being derailed by cancer so unexpectedly, much like the feeling he had when he had lost his job at Laurelville, he felt little control. An unaccounted-for dread ruled his inmost thoughts.

Beemer wrote his editor: *Clayton's dread feels real. His foreboding suddenly won't allow him to maintain the positive attitude he tries so hard to live by. Do you think humans can know when something bad is going to happen?*

The editor: I've known some to occasionally display an intuitive sense. But premonitions are not always reliable. Some people have thrown their lives away chasing hunches they are convinced are real. Still, it does appear that THE BOSS has, at times, given many a brief look into the future. The problem is that it is extremely difficult to know which notions are reliable and which ones are bred from unreliable sources. A human's mood, past experiences, education, biochemical imbalance, and others' opinions, all affect a person's perception.

Monitor Clayton's emotions. Whether this is an instance of him knowing future realities or not, it's his reactions and responses that matter. Don't get caught up in predicting. If Clayton trusts his dread, that is up to him, not you. Observe and report.

Concerned with his complete recovery, Clayton kept every doctor's appointment. When things were not progressing as expected, he made additional appointments. When the doctor's uninspiring pep talks failed to encourage him, he changed doctors. As time waddled on, Clayton slowly clothed himself with the dread he'd tried so hard to avoid. His fear that he'd lost his manly functions forever sunk in like a seeping acid rain.

Depression overtook him. More doctors and more doctor visits ensued. He tried numerous antidepressants and anxiety meds. None of the combinations appeared to help.

Beemer wrote: *I don't get it. Why is Clayton so depressed? He's been given a new lease on life, and he's pouting about the minor functioning of his male anatomy. Why can't he just let it go and move on?*

Beemer, there's a lot you don't understand about these humans! THE BOSS made men to feel virile. They feel most masculine and connected with their partner when they can share their most intimate parts with one another. From the time they become men, THE BOSS wired them to have hormonal needs. When that system Clayton has learned to count on to help him feel alive and strong breaks down, its destabilizing. This isn't just a physical issue here. This involves his emotions, psyche, and spiritual nature through and through.

Hmm. I guess I didn't realize how a physical thing can flow into a kind of a spiritual thing. No wonder he's so frustrated. He shared his seed through Ruth to give the world the wonderful hope of his children. Now, it feels like hope has vanished.

So well said, my boy! Hope is vital for these humans.

Okay, I get why this is such a big deal. But why is he so afraid of telling anyone? Seems like he would want to tell everyone so they could all support him during this trying time. I get the feeling he doesn't want anyone to know, like he's embarrassed or something.

This is not something humans talk about openly. THE BOSS made them to feel modest about their bodies in public. Now note, modesty is different than shame. They can be modest and enjoy physical intimacy privately. There's a fine line between the two poles of private and public awareness sometimes. But naturally erring on the side of modesty in public is generally the safest road to travel. Clayton is appropriate and wise to be as discreet as possible with such personal affairs.

On July 29, 2010, Clayton, with seven-year-old grandson Kyle (Kevin's son) in tow, dropped Ruth off at the door of a Walmart in Wooster. Clayton and Kyle ran some errands before parking near the entrance to pick Ruth up. They got out of the car to meet Ruth inside. Without warning, Clayton dropped like a sack of potatoes, hitting his head on the pavement.

Beemer quickly pulled out his biographic notebook and wrote: *Oh no! Oh no! Oh no! I think I'm losing him again. I'll stick with him no matter what, of course, but you should probably be looking for a new assignment for me. Sure wish I could do more than observe and report right now. This has got to be really scary for little Kyle.*

Clayton didn't remember anything after the fall when he awakened in the emergency room. Ruth was at his side to tell him what had happened. The doctors assessed that his heart had stopped momentarily, and the bump on his head kept him knocked out. They transferred him to the specialized Cleveland Clinic.

Kimberly immediately flew from California, and Kevin drove from Indy. Both were prepared for the worst. (Duane could not get away.) They found their dad, though comfortable, looking horrible with black and blue discoloration around his eyes.

A day later after doing tests, Cleveland Clinic found the heart stoppage was due to a conflict between depression medications. They told him if he dropped one of the prescriptions, he would be fine. No long-term damage would result.

Four days later, he went home. His purple face eventually returned to its natural color. The joy of life and feeling the love from those who loved him touched Clayton. But, eventually, the brief encounter of restored life acted as an accelerant to his depression, adding guilt for still feeling depressed about being stripped of his manhood.

Clayton was also not sleeping well. He had trouble concentrating. Routine chores dropped off his to-do list. He had little drive to accomplish anything or think of anyone else's needs. One day, Ruth bluntly and forcibly told Clayton, "Something has to be done!" Her needs were not being met. She could not continue living with him in his depressed state.

Her harsh words and resolve startled Clayton. He had felt bad for her only in the sense of his diminished intimate output, not her genuine need for companionship and understanding. This kickstarted his resolve to get back into the game. His depression had robbed him of his passion to love, learn, and grow. He finally aimed to change instead of wallowing in pity.

Clayton found two different professional counselors. One specialized in marriage counseling, the other in medical counseling. To Clayton's surprise and delight, Ruth joined him in many of his sessions. The marriage counselor helped him pick up and meld the severed pieces of his self-worth. The medical counselor helped him face and confront the cause of his depression—the severing of his manhood.

Clayton made an appointment to have a penile implant surgical procedure to regain functionality a week later, in early 2011. The recovery time took three months. Nearly two years had passed, but through effort, research, helpful consultation, and tenacity, Clayton finally felt like the man he wanted to see in the mirror. Six months later, he ditched the depression pills!

When Clayton's health felt satisfactorily restored, and he regained his sense of vitality, they resumed their joy of travel. Over the next couple of years, they visited Guatemala and Belize; a Sight and Sound theater production in Pennsylvania; New York and the New England states with Kimberly; and The Holy Land with Clayton's brother Marion and his wife, Ellen. Life again felt full and adventurous for the Steiners!

In 2014, Clayton and Ruth decided it was time to downsize and move from their retirement house to a more hassle-free retirement home. They did not want to be caught unaware like others they had known, whose health or children had dictated their move. When the lumber-drying business, which was an eyesore, encroached on their backyard, potentially devaluing the future of the property, they knew it was time to seek other living arrangements. They found their best option in Orrville, eight miles from Kidron, in a community called OrrVilla Retirement Community. Not only would the layout and adequate green space meet their needs, but they knew many of their potential neighbors in the close-knit community.

What sealed the deal for them was the combative attitude that they were experiencing with their recent pastor and many in the congregation at church. They felt their long-time, stable community was becoming too judgmental and inflexible. Moving helped them out of the jam. So, in May of 2014, they moved and quickly involved themselves in various community programs, fitting right into the neighborhood.

> In the margin, Beemer wrote: *Well, it looks like Clayton and Ruth are set for the next twenty or thirty years. Clayton may just go out in a cloud of glory yet, renowned for his empathetic outlook and wise decisions. It's a great feeling to know that he has overcome so much in his life and can handle whatever is thrown at him in the future.*

The editor: Don't count your chickens before they're hatched. (That's a colloquialism you should look up.) Fortune-tellers turn into false prophets, who end up losing their jobs! Observe and report.

Beemer gulped. The strange admonishment stared back at him. Clayton was gaining such palpable confidence in the twilight of his life, curbing his optimism for his subject seemed... well, unreasonable. He wondered, *Why shouldn't I be excited for his near future here?* He'd ask Chief the next time he saw him.

26

THE DIAGNOSIS

BATTLING THE UNEXPECTED

The move to the independent senior living center in OrrVilla took more out of Clayton and Ruth than they had anticipated, which was ironic because part of their rationale for moving was to make the aging process easier. Ruth found recovering from the exertion particularly difficult. Days after the move, unusually exhausted and sore on her left side, she saw her family doctor, who sent her to a cardiologist because of a concerning heart murmur. The cardiologist assumed the sore side was a pulled muscle from the move. He was more concerned with her blood pressure. He ran some inconclusive tests and referred her back to her family doctor, who then referred her to a general surgeon. The general surgeon diagnosed the pain in her side as a pulled muscle as well and saw her two weeks later when he again gave her the same diagnosis. He told her to give it more time.

Two months later, the pain on Ruth's side had not subsided. X-rays showed no gallstones or urinary tract infection, but they did show an unidentifiable mass on her pancreas. The doctor ordered a CT scan.

Ruth emailed her children to pray for "this uncertain time."

The CT scan came back negative, so she was again sent to the general surgeon who again told her it was a pulled muscle. He wanted to see her in another two months.

Clayton could only shake his head at the merry-go-round game of tag these doctors were playing. Ruth confided in him that she knew something was not being diagnosed properly. On her own, she researched Crohn's Disease, Ulcerative Colitis, cancer, and other diseases that might be causing her mysterious symptoms.

In October (six months after their move), when the ultrasounds that her gynecologist ordered came back negative, he sent her to a gastroenterologist for a CA-125 test to test her blood for cancer. A foreboding on the possibilities surrounded Clayton and Ruth. Unfortunately, they would not know the results till after the weekend, on Monday, they were told.

After deliberating over the wisest use of their time, they decided to go ahead and go to the planned Algerian Pax Reunion, which was being held a few hours away; they were determined not to be ruled by fear. On the way there, they got the call. Clayton pulled over, and Ruth put her cell phone on speakerphone.

The nurse said the CA-125 marker was too high, and they expected cancer. The news hit Clayton hard! His wife had cancer! *Was this a death sentence? Or just the incidental kind that could be cleared up with a few injections or something? Maybe there's some other explanation. After all, these doctors don't really seem to know what's going on half the time.*

Shell-shocked, he tried to concentrate on what the nurse was saying but grasped little of it. *What was his role?* He wanted to take charge, be above it all. But there were so many possible negative scenarios. So much he didn't know. So much doubt about his adequacy!

Whatever else she said, the nurse told them that the results had been sent to Ruth's gynecologist, Dr. Sherock. Ruth called him. He caringly told her, with no sense of urgency, that he had ordered a CT scan but that it wouldn't be until Friday. He suggested they enjoy their reunion plans and not worry about the rest.

Dazed, Clayton and Ruth sat in a silent car on the side of the road, as if to say, "Now what?" Refusing to tuck their tails and run home to fret, they proceeded to their destination. Clayton's mind was a whirl of raging activity the rest of the way there.

At the Pax reunion, Clayton met up with many old friends from long ago as well as many people he'd never met. The interactions were pleasant, however awkward, knowing the pain and stress his wife was under. They sat off to the side, so Ruth could sit in a rocking chair and raise her feet.

The fear and confusion Beemer felt through Clayton reminded him of the trauma Clayton had experienced losing his son, Bruce. Remembering his own panic back then and not wanting to lose his chronicler's edge now, he reflexively called his editor for some on-the-job training while the Pax meeting unfurled.

To his chagrin, a young, gangly woman with spongy hair approached him. A heavenly being other than his old, bald, squat editor had never contacted him on earth before. Beemer didn't know whether to greet her or ignore her.

She smiled warmly and welcomed herself by gently grasping Beemer's shoulder. "Hi! I'm Maammy," she said. "I'll be your new editor in chief."

Beemer's startled response drew a whimsical cackle. "Sorry for the sudden switcheroonie," she said. "It couldn't be helped. What do you need?"

Beemer gazed at this young, bubbly woman. All he could think to say was, "Where's Chief?"

"He's been reassigned. These transports just got to be too much for the old coot." Then she added, conspiratorially, "I mean that in a reverent way, of course."

Beemer's eyes widened. "He lost his job because of me?"

"Oh, no. He's been doing this for thousands of years. It was bound to catch up with him sooner or later. You're not the only one who's called him down here willy-nilly, you know."

"Willy-nilly? I thought I was using restraint."

"Well, sure you were. You're just a rookie, though, right?"

Beemer nodded mechanically.

"Well, there you go. You were just doing your job, and he was just doing his—visiting you every time he looked around." Maammy crooked her neck. "I hope I can last as long as he did."

A scowl covered Beemer's face. "So, you're saying he was demoted 'cause I can't figure things out on my own."

Maammy laughed wholeheartedly. When the joyous outbreak finally ceased, she laid her hand on Beemer's shoulder again. "Well, of course I am … about the *you can't figure things out* part, not the *demoted* part. He's been promoted as a trumpeteer for the heavenly orchestra. Of course, as much as he loved editing, he probably saw it as a demotion. But you were just the straw that broke the camel's back. Don't take it personally. Just laugh it off. That's what I do."

Failing to find any humor in the situation, Beemer said, "But I didn't even get to say goodbye. This is so … sudden … and unfair."

"Aww. You were fond of the old rationalist, weren't you? That's sweet. A lot of his chroniclers found him a bit harsh."

"Well, it was hard to get a good *atta boy* out of him. But I learned to appreciate his grainy wisdom, however rough it was. He called a spade a spade. I trusted him. He never let me settle. A real stickler for accuracy and truth."

"Sounds like you're chronicling THE BOSS's way," said Maammy. "No reason we can't keep that practice up. And have a little fun along the way." She giggled like a school angel.

"Will I at least be able to still write to him?"

"Sorry. Heavenly employees don't cross crafts. His full attention will be on trumpeting-in the new guests. A full-time business, that."

"So, I'll be all alone on my biographic book?" Beemer looked panicked.

"Heavens, no! I'll be right here anytime you need me."

Beemer grimaced. "You? Do you even know how to write a book?"

Maammy guffawed like there was no tomorrow.

"Why are you laughing?" Beemer asked.

Maammy wiped her eyes. "Because it's better than giving you the what-for for being so rude. It's obvious your being down here with only humans has affected your manners. You've forgotten how THE BOSS's structures work, haven't you? The *Heavenly Chronicle* would never place anyone incapable of editing its primary source of existence as its editor in chief. That would be ludicrous. Do you know what ludicrous means?"

Beemer ashamedly nodded.

Maammy chortled out her nose. "Okay, then. Enough with the reproaching and reprimanding. You work for THE BOSS; so do I. My job is to help you chronicle the best account possible so THE BOSS can enjoy the memory of your beloved subject forever. Now, before we go any further, to make this relationship come to that end, we need to clear the air on any confusion. So, have at it."

"Confusion?" is all Beemer could muster.

"Yes. One of us is confused here. And I know it's not me. So, tell me what you're confused about so we can get on with the chronicling of THE BOSS's work of art."

Beemer swallowed. Blinked. "Ah … okay, ah, how long have you been an editor?"

Maammy giggled. "I'm a rookie too. You're my first assignment. But don't think that means I lack experience. I was a chronicler for 3,652 years. Moses was one of my first subjects. Ever heard of him?"

"Holy Moses!" Beemer couldn't blink. Then, he couldn't stop blinking.

"Well, he wasn't actually holy. He was a bit of a stinker at times, to be frank. That whacking the rock was so immature. And he avoided his leadership role for so long there at first. But that was his story. What else?"

Beemer cleared his throat. "Ah … I may have trouble calling you Maammy." He eyed his new editor suspiciously. "I kept calling Chief, sir because he seemed to be so formal. He hated it when I did that. I finally broke the habit … mostly. Now, you seem more informal but want to go by ma'am."

"I don't go by ma'am. I go by Maammy—as in a respected and nurturing mix of madam and mommy. I'm not just your superior; I'm your friend."

Beemer did not know what to do with this conflicting information. Chief was a lot of things to him. But friend? He couldn't see it. To relieve his confusion, he noncommittally said, "Okay." Then he observed his subject, Clayton, looking blankly out the window at the darkness of night, lost in his torment and anxiety.

"No, it's not," Maammy came back.

"It's not?" Beemer wondered aloud. "It's not what?"

"It's not okay. Something's still eating you. Come on. Out with it."

Beemer gulped. "It's just that … well … I don't know as I can be party to such a discriminatory nickname."

"Discriminatory? Whatever are you talking about?"

Beemer worried that his worry about being offensive had offended his higher-up. "Well, it's just that, down here, that's a derogatory term that one race used to call another race's enslaved nanny. I believe it's thought to be unkind and tactless."

Maammy frowned for the first time since Beemer had encountered her. Then, she smirked. "Beemer, I'm touched that you want to be so sensitive, but we are not humans. Heaven has no prejudice. Just because you're down here observing this human race does not mean you get to act like one."

"Yes, ma'am ... mee." Beemer's fearful eyes met her annoyed ones.

Then Maammy chuckled, and the tension faded instantly. Beemer found the humor as well and joined her in the laughter.

"Beemer," Maammy finally said, fondly cupping his shoulder again, "I know Chief was a diligent character and this job requires some diligence, but that doesn't mean we can't enjoy the process. Sometimes, it helps to loosen up a bit. Always being tight and rigid will only weaken the great stories of THE BOSS's children, not improve them. I've found this fun approach helps one to feel the full character of the subject, which is what this project is all about. At least, that's the way I roll." She looked at her new pupil with a glint of motherly hope in her eyes.

Beemer stepped back and exhaled, his serious demeanor deflecting the impact of her words. This approach would take some getting used to. He nodded, doing his best to buy into his new supervisor's positivity.

Maammy said, "Okay, now that that's out of the way, what did you call me down here for?"

Beemer nearly blurted, "But I didn't call you down here. I called for Chief!" But fortunately, he refrained. Instead, he jiggled his head and forced himself to remember his predicament with his subject. He stood motionless for a long, uncomfortable moment. "Ah ... Clayton just found out his wife has cancer. It's obviously a huge deal. But he's kind of shell-shocked. It's like he's so afraid, confused, and wondering how he should handle things that he's numb. I'm afraid he's going to wig out like he did when his son died thirty-one years ago. That was some kind of awful! I wasn't ready to go through that mess with him then. I'm afraid, well, unsure, what's going to happen now or how Clayton's reactions will influence me ... my chronicling."

Maammy stared back in an odd manner.

Beemer said, "You aren't up on my case, are you?"

"No, it's not that," Maammy assured. "I've read everything you've written, and every note Chief wrote on your case. I am certainly up to snuff. I just find it curious that, like Clayton, your first reaction is to be more concerned about your duties than your subject."

Beemer narrowed his eyes, searching to find her meaning.

Maammy jiggled her head to reboot. "No worries. We'll cover that later. I'm reminded of all the cases I took on and all the times I went through the trauma of my subjects. Those were difficult times. I won't lie."

The concern in Beemer's stare dissipated.

Maammy smiled, apparently throwing off the trying memories. "But I made it through every case, even that one with Chrysippus."

"Chrysippus?"

"You've never heard of Chrysippus? He was a stoic philosopher in ancient Greece. Many of his teachings on logic, physics, and ethics are still taught today. Now, he was a real serious guy. Ironically, though, at the height of his career, he witnessed a drunken donkey trying to eat figs off a fig tree and laughed so hard he keeled over and died. Just like that. Laughed himself to death. Let me tell you, I was not prepared for that sudden job reassignment."

Beemer looked on, stunned.

Returning from her gaze into the past, Maammy said, "But don't worry. Those kinds of freakish things are rare. Just let happen what happens. Ours is not to hold to some perfect theory, but to discover and interpret."

Beemer blinked several times. "So, I may get socked in the gut again if Clayton loses it while his wife is battling for her life, but I should just accept that as part of the job?"

"Technically, yes. But it does help to know how these humans generally operate and who your subject is at his core." She looked at Beemer matter-of-factly. "You do know your subject inside and out by now, right?"

Uneasy with being put on the spot, Beemer stammered, "Uh ... sure," then quickly added, "unless he goes into shock again or does something bizarre."

"Well, all bets are off if the erratic happens, granted. But why is he so distressed right now? What's he feeling and thinking?"

Beemer narrowed his eyes and looked at Clayton, sitting next to his bloated wife. "He loves his wife more than anything in this world. Now she's hurting and afraid. He wants to comfort her but doesn't have a clue how to. I think he's angry that it's all out of his and their control. It's unfair! He wants to fight but doesn't have the right tools. That makes him feel defeated … and scared. What if he doesn't have what it takes to fight this? What if he loses his wife? Such a future is beyond his comprehension. He can't let things go there. Fighting the unknown is just too horrifying and lonely!"

Maammy smiled warmly, laying a gentle hand on Beemer's shoulder again. "See, you do know your subject. This terrible event is terrifying for Clayton, and, therefore, you. Discover and interpret. That's what you just did. Now chronicle this biographically."

Beemer slowly nodded his head.

"You got this."

With that, she stepped away and said, "It's time for me to go. Now, if you have any questions, any concerns, just call me or write a question in the margins of your biographic book. I'm not as busy as Chief used to be yet. I don't at all mind coming down and chatting with you a while. Enjoy the journey. Discover and interpret."

Beemer helplessly watched her go, unsure what to make of her. He tried to find comfort in the joy of the discoveries he'd uncover, as Maammy encouraged, but the unmistakable pang of disappointment clung to him like a wet blanket. He had just lost his reliable confidant! The betrayal and despair he felt consumed him.

Like Clayton, Beemer wondered if he had the moxie to perform his role surrounded by the uncertain darkness that he felt all around him.

As it turned out, the Algerian Pax reunion was the ideal place to process the initial findings of a cancer diagnosis. Upon sharing their personal news, the mixed group exuded concern and grace—the very responses Ruth and Clayton needed in their overwhelmed state. Clayton felt far from *fixed*, but the empathy he felt helped him feel loved and protected from the fiery darts of hopelessness and untethered fear.

Friday was a long time in coming. After the CT scan at 1:00 p.m., Dr. Sherock called them at 3:30, informing them that the excessive fluid shown on the scan likely indicated cancer, but they needed to see an expert. He made an appointment for Monday with an oncologist in Akron, forty miles away.

> Beemer wrote to his new editor in the margin (though he had little confidence she could reply half as helpfully as his old editor): *What's with these doctors? Why did it take them so long to come up with a diagnosis? Aren't they supposed to know what's going on? All they seem to do is run lame tests and refer people to another doctor, or they make a later appointment to retest the same misguided notion. It all seems like a big joke!*

> Maammy wrote back: Keep in mind that all doctors are human. Humans tend to think of them as having above-mortal status, which is totally unfair. Many diseases and conditions are mysterious and stem from physical, emotional, mental, or psychological origins. It's not easy diagnosing accurately. That being said, some doctors, if they don't know the answers, simply regurgitate their best possible assumptions as if they were facts. It's always up to the patient to continue seeking answers and the right doctors for their life.
>
> It sounds like Clayton and Ruth are doing all they can to get to the bottom of things.

Over the weekend, Ruth informed their Sunday school class of the diagnosis. Clayton read over the email before she sent it. She asked for prayer for wisdom in the many decisions ahead. Quoting from her *Reminders from God* devotional, she noted that "His Spirit supplies the wisdom and strength for the journey ahead."

Clayton communicated the news to their kids and their pastor, Carl. Their pastor would relay the message to the congregation that Sunday morning. The kids were shocked and very concerned.

As Ruth's abdominal pain increased, her sister-in-law Gladys came by one evening to listen to their fears and questions and pray with them, which was a big help. The next night, they asked their previous pastor's wife, Ruth Detweiler, to come over. She was a fifteen-year ovarian cancer survivor and mentored a healthy approach to overcoming the battle. This attitude was a Godsend in Ruth's time of need!

The excruciating pain Ruth felt as she waited for the oncology appointment came from a grainy fluid buildup, according to the oncologist. This pain was a classic sign of ovarian cancer as it turned out. As stunning as the pronouncement was, at least now they knew what they were up against.

Dr. Robin Lasky was assigned to be their primary oncologist. Clayton and Ruth immediately took to her and felt blessed to have caring, knowledgeable staff in charge of their recovery. Their attitude surfaced in what Clayton wrote in his journal that night, "We are blown away by the journey we have been forced to take that we did not request … We will depend on our family, God, church, and our friends to carry us through this journey."

Beemer wrote to Maammy, more to voice his own thoughts than to get a worthwhile reply: *I noticed Clayton is treating Ruth's disease as if he's battling it too. He mentioned "we" instead of "she." How could this be? He is separate from her. His body does not have cancer, hers does.*

Maammy replied: Marriage doesn't always produce this strong sense of togetherness. But when it works like THE BOSS intended, they genuinely feel the other's fear and anguish.

Beemer wrote back: *But you don't understand. Their personalities are way different from each other. Clayton is quiet, contemplative, introspective, reflective, and not terribly articulate. Ruth is the opposite on all accounts. How could Clayton feel her inner pain when he sees the world so differently?*

Maammy: That's how THE BOSS made things. Love has a way of connecting on the deepest of levels. The more a couple commits to one another and practices humbly sacrificing for the other, the more their hearts are joined and their hardships mutually felt. I don't know how. I just know it is.

Dr. Sherock called to check up on Ruth and to apologize profusely for not finding the cancer sooner.

Before the exploratory surgery on October 22, Pastor Carl, Clayton's son Kevin, and Kevin's wife, Mandy, joined Ruth and Clayton in the prep room. Carl prayed and hugs and kisses were given all around.

Left to wait for hours, Clayton, Kevin, and Mandy grabbed a bite to eat at Hardee's. Together, they explored the possible outcomes of the surgery. "Yes, Ruth has given the doctors a copy of her living will," Clayton told them. He asked them to ignore his tears, explaining that Ruth's pain and everyone's outpouring of care overwhelmed him. "I'd rather be a widower," he said through a cascade of tears, "than to see her in long-term pain and not able to enjoy life." Sharing his guts, he admitted to already grieving— not expecting her death but knowing their lives would never be the same.

Beemer felt a heaviness that he couldn't place. Taking his new editor up on her offer to "call if he ever needed anything," he reluctantly asked to speak with her.

Maammy waltzed into Hardee's to greet Beemer while Clayton was in the bathroom. "That was quick. Finding the cancer scare a little too unnerving, are we?"

"No. I mean … yes. I mean, it is unnerving for Clayton … and, therefore, unnerving for me … I guess. But … " Beemer lost his thread of coherence before it started. Why did this new authority figure elicit such confusion in him?

Maammy threw her head back and cackled. "Flustered like a true rookie. Don't worry, I needed my editor to hold my hand for my first dozen bio-graphic books or so. Don't feel belittled by it all."

Beemer did. But he wasn't about to let this replacement know that.

"What can I help you with, Beemer? Can't identify some emotion Clayton's having while he's contemplating the big changes that are likely coming his way?"

Beemer wished it were that simple. He sighed. "Maybe. But to be honest, I'm having trouble focusing."

"Oh? You aren't taking on too much of Clayton's emotions as your own, are you?"

"No. At least, I don't think so."

"So, what's causing the confusion?"

"Confusion? Who said anything about confusion?"

Maammy smiled as if placating a toddler. "Beemer, I may be green at editing, but I know when I lost focus as a chronicler, it was because I was confused about something—whether it was grammar, my insight, the subject's societal norms, or THE BOSS's plan; whatever the source, confusion always blocked my flow. So, what's confusing you, my fine novice?"

Beemer bristled at her condescending habit of always acknowledging his lack of experience. And being right. He lowered his head. "It's not fair," he muttered.

Maammy squinted through her smile. "Excuse me?"

Beemer looked at her and firmly said, "It's not fair."

Maammy nodded. "Okay. You're right; cancer's not fair. At least not from the human perspective. Or ours either, for that matter. Why exactly THE BOSS allows it to happen is above my pay, but …"

"No," Beemer cut her off, "that's not what I meant. It's not fair that Chief is suddenly not my editor anymore. I relied on him to see me through. Now he's gone. I didn't want him to leave, and I didn't expect him to leave. He was the only boss I ever knew. I'm so disappointed, hurt, and angry that I can't concentrate."

The ever-present smile on Maammy's face melted away. In fact, if her cheery disposition was capable of displaying displeasure, she was displaying that. "Beemer, THE BOSS is the only one we call BOSS. We'll start there. Do you remember that?"

"Ah … yes, ma'am … mee. I knew that … I know that. Sorry. I meant no disrespect. It just feels like I've got a screw loose or something."

Maammy squinted at her new student. "I hear you," she finally said, nodding her head. "You started to have a bond with the old general, didn't you?"

Beemer shyly nodded.

"Nothing wrong with that. Except, your job isn't to idolize your editor. It's to write for THE BOSS. Is this the kind of problem that requires a reassignment?"

Beemer's demeanor instantly flipped. "That won't be necessary. I'm sure this is just some form of writer's block. I'm probably getting too into my subject, like you said. I must have been so focused on his story that I thought it was my own."

When his vomitus reply finally ended, Maammy looked at her uncharacteristically apologetic apprentice suspiciously. "Uh-huh."

Beemer swallowed and his eyes roamed aimlessly.

Maammy said, "It sounds like your emotions are doing a little exploring on their own. Are you aware of where that could lead you?"

Beemer's eyes widened. "Ah … I'll get it under control. I'll just stop …"

"No, please don't," Maammy interrupted.

"Huh?"

"Your having such obvious strong feelings for Chief shows that you're thinking of someone other than yourself. That's a good thing. The kind of thing this job requires. That means genuine empathy is right around the corner. When you can write with empathy, you've mastered your craft. I've already put in a motion to the *Heaven's Chronicle* board to make empathy the fourth E in the *Threeseez*. I think it's just a matter of time before they'll adopt it."

Beemer's mouth dropped. "I told Chief they should add education to the *Threeseez*."

"Well, there you go. We might as well make it the fiveseez right here and now."

Beemer smiled wide. Then he caught himself and furrowed his brow. Why was he smiling with his irreverent superior? "But I thought us chroniclers weren't supposed to have emotions."

Maammy laughed. "Imagine someone trying to deal with things if they didn't have emotions?"

Beemer couldn't. He looked over at the men's room and rubbed his chin. "You know, I think that's exactly what Clayton has been doing. No wonder he's so anxious. He's trying not to feel—when he feels so much!"

"Especially when he feels so much for someone else," Maammy added.

The ache of missing Chief enveloped Beemer anew.

"So, we're okay then?" Maammy beamed her comforting smile.

"Yeah. Thanks for coming down. I'll focus my focus on Clayton's focus from here on out."

Maammy cackled generously. "There's my prodigy. Now, don't be afraid to feel. And if you need to work through any more confusion, don't hesitate to call."

"Yes, ma'am … mee."

Maammy chortled, waved, and disappeared.

Beemer breathed a strange sigh of anxiety and calm. He missed his old editor fiercely. He felt ripped off and defenseless—like Clayton felt when he lost Bruce. But there was something about the unorthodox, playful disposition of Maammy he longed for. Yet, he found himself resisting her warmhearted manner. But why?

Clayton walked out of the men's room just then, his expression dour, his countenance humble and nervous. He ached for his partner. Beemer knew just how he felt.

He suddenly thought of Clayton as a youth, feeling empathetic, gentle, and caring like his mother, but also absorbing his dad's wrath and shame for feeling those (what he deemed as) womanly traits. *What was one to do with feelings one thought one shouldn't have?*

At 3:30 p.m., Clayton, Kevin, and Mandy met in the consultation room with Dr. Laskey after surgery. Mandy took notes. The medical staff had drained one-and-a-half liters of fluid and found cancer cells throughout the abdomen, including on the surface of the liver, ovaries, and gallbladder. The fallopian tubes were so enlarged that the doctor couldn't even make out the ovaries. But X-rays showed no cancer outside the abdomen.

The best news came when Laskey said, "This journey will have a happy ending!" The sound of that bolstered Clayton's morale like seeing new life sprouting from the ground in the spring after a harsh winter. The doctor saw no reason why Clayton and Ruth couldn't proceed in planning their fiftieth anniversary celebration trip to Costa Rica with their family at the end of December.

At 4:30 p.m., Clayton found Ruth looking healthy, in good spirits, and without pain. Relief flooded his soul! He gushed with joy when he felt her life-giving touch and contemplated the many years they'd still have together.

Knowing his other kids were distraught from a distance, Clayton called Duane and Kimberly to inform them of their mother's status. Sharing the news created a bittersweet bond. Later that night, he emailed his extended family through his niece Cindy. After journaling, he hit the hay after 1:00 a.m., exhausted, but encouraged.

Not at all a big fan of seeing blood, observing physical pain, and seeing needles, Clayton was profoundly thankful when they installed a port in Ruth's arm for a one-site infusion, blood test, and administration of medicine the next day before her first chemotherapy. The first chemo went as expected. Doctors told them that the minimal side effects would increase as each of the chemo sessions unfurled every three weeks over the next few months.

When they got home the next day, they did their best to relax. Clayton couldn't help but sense the same out-of-control feeling he had had after Bruce's accident. He was not calling the shots. He had to rely on the medical community to make the life-or-death decisions and actions to save his wife. Would they save her, when they hadn't been able to save his son? He didn't know. There were many reasons to mistrust and resent this situation. But instead of fighting the system and all its flaws, he determined that it would be best for his family to trust and encourage it.

To settle their angst about Ruth's stage-three cancer status, Clayton and Ruth took different approaches. Ruth found a semblance of control through researching online all the ins and outs of her ailment. Clayton found peace by busying his hands in the flower beds around the condo. As a couple, they took walks and cuddled a lot, reassuring each other that they'd make it through this trying time together.

Though they could not risk Ruth's immune system through personal contact with their friends, their Sunday school class faithfully provided meals until Duane, Duane's wife, Janet, and Kimberly arrived. Ruth and Kimberly had many wonderful mother/daughter times playing the piano together at the house. Each family member stayed their allotted time before they had to get back to their personal commitments. Clayton joined Ruth in Skyping their children when they weren't present.

Perhaps the biggest boost in the form of support came through *CaringBridge*, an online resource that connected them to friends and family across the globe. Clayton kept up with informing their loved ones by posting developing information on CaringBridge. Ruth and Clayton derived much encouragement reading all the kind and supportive replies. They each responded through emails to the overwhelming support.

Ruth took the next chemo like a trooper, Clayton told the Geisers. Dr. Laskey again reiterated her firm belief that this would end well. As expected, however, Ruth began losing chunks of hair when she showered. She and Mandy had gone to the wig store proactively and picked out a wig. Clayton and Kevin affirmed her choice.

To Clayton's surprise, a few days later, Ruth's hairdresser shaved her hair off. She came home with a donated wig from the beauty shop. No one raved over the new look. Ruth ended up dumping that hairpiece, and whenever she had company or went out, she wore the one she had picked out. She was bald most of the time around home. That took some getting used to for Clayton. To show solidarity though, he shaved his head as well.

On November 17, a swollen leg that had been bothering Clayton finally disturbed him enough to see a doctor. It turned out he had a blood clot that had been induced by a blood disorder; he had to remain bedfast until the swelling went down. He would need to take a blood thinner for the rest of his life. But other than the temporary, life-threatening danger the blood clot had presented, the tangent did not sidetrack them long.

Duane and Kimberly came in support of the December 4 chemo treatment. Dr. Laskey was pleased to report that the blood tests had come back better than when they first started the treatments—a sign that they were beginning to beat this ugly monster! She again gave her full release for their Costa Rica plans at the end of the month.

A week later, Clayton and Ruth excitedly drove to Indianapolis to watch their granddaughter, Kristin, perform a leading role in her annual high-school concert. To their dismay, the redness around Ruth's port became inflamed and sore. On the morning of the concert, they decided to visit the ER. Not only was the area around her port infected, but her bloodstream was also infected. To make matters worse, her blood pressure and temperature were both too high. Because the flu had just arrived in their area, Ruth needed to stay isolated to prevent the risk of her depleting her immune system. This meant not even family could visit. Needless to say, they missed their granddaughter's concert.

Of more concern was the threat of canceling their fiftieth anniversary trip. Fortunately (though not a day too soon!) a temporary port was okayed by Medicare, the medical supplies arrived, and Clayton was taught how to administer the medicine before their trip. A major setback avoided!

To add to the chaos, during the port dilemma, Clayton had to go to a doctor in Indy about his sore leg again. It felt like everything was going wrong at once. But, to Clayton's embarrassment and relief, the doctor diagnosed the cause of the pain to Clayton's exercise regimen of incessantly climbing the hospital stairs, not another blood clot. The doctor issued elastic stockings for Clayton to wear throughout the upcoming trip to prevent future blood clots.

Oddly enough, all the annoying health scares only enhanced the Costa Rica trip. Ruth, of course, was limited in what she could do, but the kids all went out of their way to look after her needs. Clayton felt the family time was extra rich, bonding them like never before. He was pleased to be able to faithfully administer Ruth's antibiotics through the complicated daily procedure, and he chuckled inwardly at their two grandkids' fascination.

On January 8, Ruth had surgery for a full hysterectomy, which Dr. Lasky reported went better than expected. The chemo had done its job, allowing for a clean operation and not requiring any other organs to be taken. The only small cancer spot she found outside of the removed female parts, she removed with an argon gun. She expected that only four to six more full chemo treatments would be necessary.

Ruth recovered slowly, but nicely, from the surgery and in time for the next chemo treatment on January 29. They began attending church again, sitting in the back and making a quick getaway at the end of the service. Plugging back in felt marvelous.

Kevin and Mandy joined them for the fifth chemo infusion in Akron and, other than a little nausea, Ruth went through it all with flying colors.

After the final chemotherapy on March 13, Dr. Laskey said all signs continued to look optimistic for full remission. Clayton and Ruth felt ecstatic! No more full-day trips to the Cooper Cancer Center! No more threat of losing Ruth! Except for some minor maintenance infusions every twenty-one days, the main hurdles were nearly all behind them now. It was time to rejoice! To celebrate, Kevin and Mandy joined them at Papa Bear Pizza Oven. The air felt lighter. The days seemed free of worry. Life was back on track!

To give back for all the ways so many had helped them, Ruth and Clayton began training with Stephen Ministries to minister to those with life crises. They were overjoyed to share their wealth of good fortune!

27
BEING WITH
DETERMINATION

The birds were singing. Flowers were popping through. Clayton and Ruth felt like they had new life! However, just a month after Ruth's official defeat of cancer, she felt fatigued and sore in her stomach at her routine CT scan on April 10, 2015. Clayton and Ruth, skittish after cohabitating with the cancer scare for the past eleven months, looked to the professionals for an accurate analysis, in particular, to their trusted doctor. When she was informed of Ruth's concerns at the infusion appointment a few days later, the chipper Dr. Laskey, though surprised, suspected the symptoms were lingering effects from the hysterectomy. She made a June 1 appointment with the GI surgeon.

By the end of that month, the pain had not subsided, but increased. Reluctantly, Ruth informed Laskey, who ordered an X-ray. The results came back negative. The familiar roller-coaster ride began anew.

Ruth had more blood tests. At Ruth's next infusion appointment on May 5, Clayton and Ruth anxiously awaited the blood-test results. The C-125 cancer marker had been only thirteen at her last reading. This time, it read sixty-two. It should have at least been less than thirty. Clayton's heart sank. He wondered if he had heard right.

Dr. Laskey evidently felt similarly, saying it must be a *false reading*. She immediately ordered another C-125 as well as a CT scan. Sensitively expressing her concern, she told them that even if the number was correct, there were numerous other possible causes. Clayton felt shaken but cared for.

When the highly anticipated results came back a couple of days later, the cancer marker came back at seventy-eight, even higher. The CT showed no tumors but revealed ascites. Ascites, they learned, was the medical term for the fluid buildup that is usually caused by cancerous cells. Cancer appeared to be back!

The dooming news rattled Clayton to the core. They had just escaped the smothering tunnel into the light only to return to another tunnel, one without a light at the end of it yet. Fear ran through Clayton's mind before he knew what hit him. *What had gone wrong? Why had the cancer come back so quickly? What had they done or not done to deserve this? Had they been misled? Had they trusted unwisely? Had the medical profession made wrong decisions? What was going to happen next? Could they handle this?*

Beemer did not like the scene unfolding in front of him and nervously called down Maammy (hoping against his better judgment) to guide him through the tenuous situation. She swept down gracefully.

"Hi, Beemer. Bad news for Clayton ... or you?"

"Clayton," Beemer announced, a little more indignant than he intended. "His wife was just diagnosed with cancer again, and Clayton's about to lose it. All sorts of unhelpful, unanswerable questions are going through his mind. I'm afraid they're going to short-circuit his system and cause his emotions to run amuck."

"And if they do?"

Beemer frowned. "Then he may go into shock again or something. Mercy, he may go crazy for all I know."

Maammy smiled, pursed her lips, and nodded her head. "He could." She raised an eyebrow. "If he does, are you willing to write it all down?"

Beemer's frown twisted into perplexed confusion. "Well, yeah, if I have to, I guess. Does that happen to humans very often?"

Maammy shook her head. "Not often. From what I've read about Clayton, I don't see that happening. He's pretty grounded."

"Then, how's a human supposed to cope with such incredibly horrible news? This is way outside of Clayton's hopes, dreams, and comfort level."

"That it is," Maammy agreed. "Humans can go a number of different ways. If a human isn't tied into THE BOSS, family, friends, church, or at least one substantial relationship (and even then sometimes), well, that human will likely turn to substance abuse, accusations, despair, or even suicide. Clayton appears to have *all* those prescribed relationships. That's rare! I expect he'll see his need to rely on them soon enough."

"I hope so."

"Why is that?"

"Because he's still in line to be a hero somehow. I don't want him to blow it like William Clark's business partner, Meriwether Lewis of the famed Lewis and Clark Expedition. He had money woes and died of gunshot wounds of his own making. A crying shame, that. To think that the man who led that wonderful adventure eventually besmirched his incredible efforts by killing himself."

Maammy nodded. Then said, "Why isn't your first concern Clayton's wellbeing instead of this biographical book?" She smiled widely.

Beemer reddened.

Surely, Beemer thought, *THE BOSS, too, would want Clayton to be a hero.*

When the shock of the unthinkable lessened, Clayton wisely shooed the unanswerable questions from his mind and asked smaller, more practical ones. *Should Ruth stay home all the time again? How much exercise should she get? Is it alright to invite our kids to our next doctor visit?*

Clayton and Ruth again found their best source of encouragement through *CaringBridge*. Friends heard quickly and wrote back all sorts of supportive replies. That weekend, they joined an Ovarian Cancer Survivors Support group on Facebook, which helped them feel plugged in and anchored. When Kevin and Mandy said they'd join them at the next doctor consultation on May 11, Clayton and Ruth were teary-eyed thankful!

Mandy wrote a page and a half of notes at the appointment with Dr. Laskey to discuss the latest findings and to plan how to move forward. Clayton didn't enjoy much of their favorite doctor's message but did appreciate her candor. She admitted (and apologized!) to being caught off guard by the relapse but was ready to defeat the disease again.

This time she would use slightly more aggressive chemotherapy, though it would not cause hair loss. She wanted to start as soon as possible—May 19, which was in just over a week. Likely reactions were sores on the hands, feet, and mouth. "If this doesn't arrest the cancer," Laskey told them, "and I'm confident it will, I have other tricks up my sleeve." She went on to say that Ruth's excellent physical condition, her healthy living habits, and her relatively young age all tipped the ledger in her favor. Clayton appreciated the optimism. It was his lifeboat. Before they left, Dr. Laskey led her tearful audience in a group hug. Kevin and Mandy insisted they go out to Starbucks afterward to de-stress and debrief. It was an excellent idea!

Ruth called their pastor, asking him to assemble the church leaders to anoint her with oil and pray as the Bible stated in James 5:13-15. Before the anointing, Pastor Carl asked Clayton about his thoughts on the ceremony. Clayton told him he was there to support and love his wife and knew that her healing was in God's hands. The pastor then asked Ruth if she believed God wanted to heal her and if she would accept any form God chose to heal her. She said she did and would. Carl then poured the bottle of oil onto his fingers and pressed them to her forehead. The group prayed for her healing. During the strange meeting, Clayton noticed an unusual calm come over Ruth. He had never been to an anointing service and hoped her peaceful demeanor meant God was healing her. But he wondered if she was preparing to leave this earth—and him.

Clayton could not accept such a thought. He would not entertain such a devilish notion! As much as Clayton and Ruth shared, both in words and actions, he could not bring himself to discuss the possibility of her death with her. The subject seemed too presumptuous, too raw, too final. The closest he got was to ask her, off-the-cuff one night, "What would you think of me remarrying someday if you died first?"

Short of dismissing the feeler, she said, "Be careful."

Clayton didn't know what to make of the cryptic reply, other than to assume she was thinking of some of their friends and acquaintances who had gone through ugly marriages, separations, and divorces after remarrying. So as not to poke the bear, he let the comment lie.

> Beemer wrote in the side margin: *Why do you think Clayton can't talk to his wife about her possible death? I thought they shared everything at this stage in the partnership.*

> Maammy wrote back: It sounds like Clayton wants so badly to be the supporting husband that he's afraid that if he opens the door to the possibility of death, even a crack, it might swing wide-open and focus on the dangerous negative. He probably prefers safety. To his credit, it's usually best to stay positive.

> Beemer: *I think he thinks the dicey subject will be too much for Ruth right now.*

> Probably so. But the truth is likely that she needs to discuss it with him (or someone), and he is too afraid that he'll not hold up under such unnerving contemplation.

Beemer did not like Maammy's comment. It painted Clayton as a coward rather than a hero. Like Clayton, Beemer chose to keep his thoughts to himself, afraid any comments might somehow backfire on him.

Kimberly joined them for the May 19 chemo session, where nurses placed ice bags on Ruth's hands and feet to prevent blistering. Meanwhile, her C-125 score had risen to 107. Clayton saw Ruth handle it all like a trooper.

Pain and stress prevented Ruth from getting a sound night's rest. Clayton programmed the earbuds Ruth had received from Kimberly, so she could listen to music to help calm her to sleep. It helped!

Clayton ached to see Ruth give up so much. To him, his wife was a dynamo. Always on the go and on the giving end, she thrived in fulfilling tasks. Now, she had to give up gardening, caring for the house, and the church choir (to name a few)—all things that she drew strength and joy from. Dealing with her unfair, devouring fatigue was beyond difficult; it was crippling. She did find comfort in the Robert L. Lynn poem entitled, "What Cancer Cannot Do," which proclaimed that cancer cannot take away love, hope, faith, peace, confidence, friendships, and memories. Ruth wrote the author and got his blessed permission to post the poem on *CaringBridge*.

The C-125 marker shot up to 154, then 274 after the next two infusions—a trend that did nothing for their morale. The sores in Ruth's mouth and the rash below her breasts added to the woes. Pain and fatigue gained momentum. Dr. Laskey believed things would still turn around, but she told Ruth, "At any time, if you think the treatment is worse than the disease, just say the word and we'll stop." Ruth said, "Stay the course." Clayton was proud of his wife, the trooper!

Pain meds helped some with the sores. The rash under the breasts was eventually evaluated as ringworm, which added another item to the list of prescribed medications. The pain on both sides of her abdomen became so great that sleep evaded her. Laskey finally referred her to Supportive Services to deal with the multitudinous symptoms.

Kevin and his family visited during this dark time. Time with the grandkids cheered Ruth and Clayton's somber mood. Duane and Janet's visit right after Kevin left helped lift the mood as well. Ruth wrote on *CaringBridge* that "love is the best medicine, and I am getting a lot of it."

Because friends and family made such a huge impact, Clayton and Ruth longed for that input into their lives. This was the one area Ruth was willing to spend her limited energy on. With that desire and God's inspiration, they got the okay from Laskey to attend a Mennonite World Conference in Harrisburg, Pennsylvania, at the end of July. Their attendance encouraged them beyond their wildest hopes. The singing was divine. Meeting up with old friends from all the places they had lived (especially the International Guest House) uplifted their spirits like nothing else could. The venture was so successful, they began planning their next trip—a family outing to Disney World!

Beemer wrote to Maammy: *Isn't this a bit too optimistic? It looks like they're just setting themselves up for a big flop. Surely Ruth won't be able to hold up to such a trip by then.*

Maammy responded: Sometimes a carrot dangled in front of the mule is more valuable than the cargo the mule is packing, simply because the cargo is of no value if it never moves. In other words, humans often need something to shoot for to motivate them to live. Maybe this unrealistic plan is the best thing for them.

Beemer hoped so.

Ruth's Aunt Eunice from Pennsylvania encouraged them with a visit the following week, and Kimberly came the week after that. Clayton marveled at how Ruth continually got inspiration from loved ones at exactly the right times. He smiled in his heart at God's wisdom.

Then, he learned of Dr. Laskey's need to take maternity leave after her next visit with them. Clayton and Ruth grieved at the news though Laskey assured them that her replacement would take good care of them until she returned. Clayton wondered at God's wisdom at times such as these.

Kevin, Mandy, and Kimberly joined Clayton and Ruth for the next monumental meeting with Dr. Laskey regarding Ruth's current and future status. Mandy once again took meticulous notes. Laskey admitted that the cancer had not yet relented. However, she believed that it was still confined to the abdomen. During the consultation, she asked Ruth straight out, "Do you want to continue the fight?"

Ruth, without hesitating, said, "Yes."

In response, Laskey said that numerous routes were available, but she recommended the chemo drug Gemzar, noting its possible negative side effects, but stating that all the other options had equally negative challenges. While Clayton and Ruth agreed to her recommendation, they also asked if this was a good time for a second opinion. Laskey's response was that they could certainly do that if they wanted, but she knew of no magic bullet or smoking gun that would arrest the cancer.

Perhaps the most worrisome note came when Laskey suggested they look into palliative care—a medical branch devoted to the comfort of the patient with a serious illness, not necessarily to curing the illness. Clayton knew the inference of "palliative" included the care of dying patients, but he refused to dignify the thought.

After the soul-rankling meeting, Laskey hooked them up with a cancer psychologist who went by the untitled name of Clarice. To Clayton's surprise, Ruth was taken with the counselor right off, saying "we'd love to" when asked if she and Clayton would like to get together regularly. Clayton recalled her reluctance to receive counseling early in their marriage when Clayton had found it vital.

> Beemer wrote to Maammy: *Do humans always go to counseling when they're faced with hard times?*

> Maammy: Not that many, honestly, though it's a wise thing to do. Of course, the wisdom completely depends on the counsel. They need to make sure their counselor is qualified and fits their needs.

> *But why would Ruth submit to professional counseling now when she was always so leery of it before? She's never really wanted to figure out the "why" questions all that much. Nor has she tried particularly hard to help Clayton figure out his inner struggles. So why now?*

> Well, did it help them in their marriage before?

> *I think so. Clayton thought so. It certainly helped Clayton. But Clayton always got the feeling that she looked at the whole thing with wary eyes.*

Maybe she saw how much it helped Clayton in his time of despair and now welcomes a similar outcome. She may not be wanting to know the whys of what she's feeling but rather how best to handle this life-threatening situation—for her loved ones' sakes as well as her own.

Ruth and Clayton began meeting with Clarice weekly. Clayton felt like she was a Godsend, giving sound advice. And better yet, Ruth was eating it up, learning how to cope with the possibility of death that was lurking at her door.

They also met with Clarice individually on occasion. Clayton was excited but also nervous to meet with her privately because he worried about the dam inside him that seemed ready to burst at any time. On his first meeting alone with her, Clarice asked him why he wanted to meet with her.

Clayton sighed. "Well, I want to love and support Ruth to the best of my ability. But, some days, I think I'm about to lose it. I'm not sure I have the inner strength to lead her the way I'm supposed to."

Clarice's eyebrows raised briefly. Then, she smiled warmly. "And how are you *supposed* to lead her?"

"I don't know," admitted Clayton. "Be the rock she needs to hold onto, I guess. She means everything to me. She's always been there for me, and I'm going to give my all to be there for her—now, when she needs me the most. I never want to look back and think I didn't give her my all."

"What about you, Clayton?" Her gentle smile remained.

"Me?"

"What do you need?"

Clayton took a deep breath and let it out. "Ahh ... it's not really about me right now. I just want Ruth to get well. Whatever I need to do to make that happen, I'll do."

Her smile turned more empathetic. She nodded slowly. "That's a very loving attitude."

Clayton looked blankly back at her. Her smile returned.

Finally, she said, "We all have needs, Clayton. It's admirable that you want to wholly love your wife as she battles for her life with cancer. But that doesn't somehow cancel out your needs."

"I can get my needs met later … when she gets through this terrible cancer thing."

"And how long will that take?"

Clayton's expression became sterner. He fidgeted in his chair.

Clarice continued. "Another week or two? A couple of months? A few years? The rest of your life?"

"I don't know!" Clayton blurted. He closed his inflamed eyes and shook his head. "Whatever it takes."

Clarice let his despair hang in the air.

Clayton said, "It's just that … well, I'm tired. I shouldn't be, but I'm so sick and tired of her being sick. Sometimes, I feel sorry for myself. Like it's about me. But it's not about me. It's about her getting better. I need to figure out how to keep my focus on her and her needs and not on me." Clayton's tears then flowed like a river.

"This is hard, Clayton. It hurts to see a loved one suffering. It's natural to want to ease their pain. Noble even. But we're not made to gallantly hold up the world and totally lose ourselves. It doesn't work like that. At some point, you need to take care of Clayton, or Clayton won't be able to take care of anyone."

"I'll do it after."

"After what?"

Clayton looked at the counselor as if challenged. He looked away. "After she gets well."

His decree was met with silence. "Fair enough," Clarice finally conceded. "I'll hold you to that. After this is over, you will need to take wholehearted care of yourself.

"Until then," she went on, "you've got to take a realistic approach, so you don't burn out and become unable to be that pillar you want to be for Ruth."

Clayton relaxed. He thought maybe he liked this counselor.

"First of all," Clarice said, "stop trying so hard to be her hero."

Beemer wrote in the side margin: *But what if Clayton is the hero?*

Maammy replied: Relax. The kind doctor is not saying he
isn't or won't be. She's just encouraging him to stop trying
so hard to be the hero. Words you could stand to hear.

Clarice continued, "Ruth needs your presence more than anything. She
needs you to *be with*. You can do that only as yourself. If you try to be
someone you're not, she'll sense your phoniness, and you won't *be with*;
you'll be apart."

"But what if I'm afraid of something or don't know what to do?"

"Share that with her. You're both scared and unsure about a lot of things.
Why pretend otherwise? Be honest. She'll gain much more strength from
you joining her where she is than if you're proclaiming some pie-in-the-sky
ideal she can't relate to."

"Hmm."

"Be authentic! This is good news, Clayton. You can be yourself. And by
doing so, you get to share your worries, fears, and needs with her as well.
It's a win-win."

Clayton left relieved and encouraged, though he was still a little skeptical.

A week later, Ruth struggled more through the next Gemzar chemo than
any prior treatment. The golf-ball-sized lump on her left side, the doctor
assumed, contributed to her cramping and extreme fatigue. New rashes
popped up after treatment number three, and four was scrubbed due to her
low platelet count, though they resumed the treatment a week later.

While suffering through the awful and harmful treatments, Clayton
and Ruth, along with their children, still held out for their coveted family
vacation to Disney World in Florida. After so much thought and planning
for the expedition, they worried about what the doctor might say. At the
September 7 meeting, before the next chemo treatment, they nervously
broached the subject. To their delight, the doctor was all for the diversion,
telling them, "Don't let cancer stop you from living!" and "Make as many
memories as you can!"

The grind of the weekly Gemzar infusions continued through September
21 when the doctors wanted Ruth's body to have a three-week break, so
her immune system could build back up. As the treatments progressed, her

platelet numbers increased and her C-125 numbers decreased, just as they all had hoped.

Because the oncology staff was so slow to hand over second-opinion references, Clayton finally broke out of his complacency and talked to a friend in the field who knew a friend who knew a doctor, and so on. Desperately wanting encouragement, they finally visited a reputable oncologist in Cleveland. Kevin and Mandy joined them. Their posse wanted to know if they were taking the best approach and if there were any experimental drugs that they could possibly benefit from.

After reading Ruth's records and giving her a physical exam, the doctor told them they were receiving the best possible traditional treatment. After Gemzar, he did know of another drug they could try. But he said these treatments would not prolong her life; they would just make her quality of life better. He said the mass in her side was cancerous, but he was confident cancer would not kill her. Clayton found his answer cryptic and discouragingly unhelpful.

> Beemer wrote to Maammy: *I'm not sure Clayton knows what's going on here.*

> Maammy: Do you?

> *Well, it looks to me like Ruth is dying. The second doctor seemed to tell him that, but Clayton didn't want to hear it. He still thinks she'll pull through this.*

> And you don't think she will.

> *I think it's unlikely even though THE BOSS is certainly capable of proving me wrong. But Clayton refuses to consider any other outcome other than her living even though he suspects that Ruth believes she'll die from this, despite her huge effort to fight to the bitter end (for her family). Is Clayton's stubborn optimism wisdom or fear?*

Maybe both. I suspect Clayton is playing it safe, thinking he's wise to hope and afraid not to.

A few days before the family get-together, Clayton and Ruth flew to Florida to acclimate Ruth and spend time with Duane and Janet, who lived in St. Petersburg.

Ruth rented an electric cart at Disney World so she wouldn't get totally worn-out. The family stayed together in the mornings, visiting the milder attractions. Clayton and Ruth went back to the onsite condo to rest in the afternoons while the younger generations busied themselves with the more active festivities. They spent the evenings together, doing family things, mostly in the condo. Clayton felt that the bonding they experienced did more for the entire family than any amount of money or good fortune could have. Ruth seemed deeply moved.

Renewed, it was nonetheless hard to start up where they left off when they got home. Clayton almost convinced himself that Ruth was not in much pain or suffering from numerous side effects any longer. Of course, she was. Her good attitude and their family experience had merely masked those issues—at least, for Clayton, for a time.

In their first meeting with the doctor when they got back, they learned that the reason Ruth couldn't eat much or keep the food down was that fluid was again pressing against her stomach. They drained 3.3 liters! The Gemzar steadily decreased her C-125 numbers but appeared only to slow the progress of the cancer, not stop it.

One night, the incessant vomiting became so awful that Clayton took Ruth to the hospital down the street. Right after Clayton called them, Kevin and Mandy made the four-hour trip through the night and caught them still in the ER. Ruth was dehydrated and nauseous, the doctor said. The ER staff hydrated her and gave her anti-nausea medication through her port. Clayton and Kevin were not as passive this go-round. They pummeled the poor doctor with questions. "What if she gets dehydrated again?" "What if she gets nauseous again?" "Isn't there anything else that can be given?"

The badgered doctor hemmed and hawed awhile, then said, "Well, there is one other medication that is supposed to work well with pain and nausea that I learned about in medical school. But I've never prescribed it. Do you want to be my first patient?"

Of course, they did! "What was it?"

"Medical marijuana."

Clayton's jaw dropped. He had never used street drugs and never intended to. Kevin and Mandy right away said, "If it works, why not?" The doctor said it was completely legal in the state of Ohio. So, Clayton and Ruth okayed the drug. The result? Ruth didn't vomit for the next few days and finally got some rest. *God works in mysterious ways,* Clayton thought.

Clayton's daughter-in-law, Janet (Duane's wife), arrived on October 24, ready to stay for as long as needed.

The next Gemzar infusion on the 29th turned Ruth's tongue white and made her throat sore. The doctor strongly encouraged Ruth to pursue palliative care options as her symptoms were expanding. When they contacted the office they normally received their palliative care from, they were told that the office was so busy they wouldn't be able to make an appointment for four days. This was unacceptable, so Clayton contacted another county. This office, after learning of Ruth's history and that she was presently not keeping food down, threw the hospice option on the table. Clayton did not appreciate the suggestion.

On *CaringBridge,* Clayton told their followers that Ruth's second battle with cancer had just passed a year. He thanked all those who had encouraged them in word or deed and conveyed that, though the journey had been difficult, it had also been filled with joy along the way. Without intending to (for Clayton was still holding onto *a good outcome*), in describing Ruth's many ailments and the doctors' bleak reports, he was basically leading the readers to expect her death relatively soon … though he could not, or would not, see it himself.

On November 4, at Janet's direction, Clayton called the ambulance from the hospital located down the street. The staff at the hospital noted Ruth's dangerous dehydration again and immediately began an IV drip. From there, she was transported to the Akron City Hospital where she could be cared for by her oncology team. The head doctor said it might be time to pursue hospice care because all these complications were just going to make her life shorter and shorter.

This unfavorable notice hit Clayton hard. He didn't think a member of the team he trusted would be so heartless as to suggest Ruth's fight might be ending here. He still believed.

> Beemer wrote to Maammy: *He still doesn't get it. Does this guy deserve a medal or a bop on the head?*

> Either way, you can't deny his determination and his undying love for his wife.

> *You're right. There's heroism in this somewhere. I'm sure of it.*

Mercifully, they installed a Denver Drain through her abdomen to constantly drain the fluid. This cut down ninety-five percent of the vomiting.

Dr. Laskey returned from her maternity leave a few days before Ruth's release from Akron. Laskey gave her heartfelt, tear-filled apology that things were not ending well—as she had predicted. They exchanged hugs and shared a precious moment that only a doctor and patient could under such circumstances. Clayton heard the exchange from out in the hall and thanked Laskey for her kind and compassionate care when she exited the room.

Wayne County Hospice came to the hospital to explain hospice and to have Ruth sign the necessary papers to accept their services. Reluctantly, she signed the papers. And as Ruth signed, the dam in Clayton finally began to crumble. The reality of Ruth's fate finally got through to him. Ruth would not recover. She was dying.

Beemer immediately knew something was up. Clayton was in danger! He called Maammy for help.

Maammy flew down in an instance. "Has the truth come a knockin'?"

Breathless, Beemer nodded.

Maammy smiled. "Breathe, Beemer, breathe. You've got to be alert enough to record this for THE BOSS. Now remember, discover and interpret. Your discoveries will lead to great insights. You'll figure it all out later. For now, just be with."

Beemer watched Clayton excuse himself from Ruth's hospital room, telling her he needed to use the bathroom.

By himself in the public restroom, the crumbling dam within finally burst. Clayton punched the walls, screamed, cried, and stomped around. He wanted to destroy something. He had not let go of his pent-up emotions since Ruth's diagnosis so very long ago. Frustration, hostility, and rage poured out of him as he had never experienced before. The morbid purity of his emotions both scared and soothed him. Letting it out aroused danger but doing so also loosened the death grip of fear—at least it was a start.

Clayton carried on for twenty minutes. He oddly recalled his old neighbor, Lores Hostetter, who had lost two wives, telling him how he'd gone into the barn on occasion to, "holler so loud the neighbors could hear him." Clayton suddenly knew what he'd felt.

Beemer sighed after it was all over. He still had a job. Clayton would live through this. His hero was still alive!

Clayton washed his face after his *reckoning with reality* and joined Ruth in her room. She seemed at peace. Clayton thought maybe he was too. He figured she'd been making peace with all of this since her anointing with the church leaders all those months ago. The realization was sobering. She was being a good trooper, following God's path, never complaining, always willing to hope for the impossible, and encouraging her loved ones through her will. It was her unshakable constancy that gave him strength. And here *he* was trying to be strong for *her*.

At home, they tried to make things as comfortable as they could for her. On good days, they helped her walk outside to view and smell the roses she had replanted from their Benville house. One special evening, they heard the Central Christian Music Choir at the OrrVilla meeting hall. At that point, Janet or one of the family members was always present with them. Clayton and Ruth were so thankful for that!

Earlier, when Ruth had been feeling better, she had decided to make comforters for her grandkids, Kristin and Kyle, with the help of Sue Hofstetter and the sewing ladies at church. She and Sue had picked out the material she wanted, and together, they decided on the layout. Ruth decided she would complete at least sixteen knots for Kristin's age and thirteen knots for Kyle's age while she still could. She had sent out an invitation to their close friends, announcing that she would be at the church on Saturday afternoon, November 21, and would appreciate their help to complete the comforters. Reading between the lines, everybody knew that this was an invitation to say farewell to Ruth and vice-versa before she died.

When that Saturday afternoon arrived, Clayton, Kevin, and Mandy made the Herculean effort to get Ruth dressed, into a wheelchair, into the car, and to the church. Their love for Ruth made the chore irrelevant. Ruth was eager, ready, and determined to finish the comforters, show her love for her grandchildren, and say goodbye to her many friends who had carried her burdens for the past thirteen months. It was a joyous occasion mixed with sadness. Over thirty people, male and female, came to work on the comforters and to say their goodbyes. Everyone took the opportunity to talk to Ruth personally while she knotted the comforters. With the help of others, she did put in sixteen knots on Kristin's comforter and thirteen knots on Kyle's. It was a laborious undertaking on her part, but with the same characteristics that she demonstrated throughout her life, she finished the task with tenacity and perseverance. With her mission completed, she was ready for home.

Clayton marveled at Ruth's accomplishment. But as he approached home, he felt out of his depth. Though they had had the foresight to call hospice before they left the church to meet them at home, Ruth was so exhausted that she could barely move. He parked in the driveway knowing full well he could not budge his near-comatose wife. Thankfully, Chris, a nurse from hospice, pulled in behind them. He joined them in the car and asked several nitty-gritty questions to assess the situation. With earnest compassion, he told them death was coming sooner than later. They had two choices. They could either go to hospice now, or he could get them a hospital bed and oxygen for home. As tired as she was, Ruth made the call. She asked to be taken to hospice.

Clayton questioned this decision to himself as it seemed to invite an impersonal touch to her journey. But he left his thoughts unsaid.

> Beemer wrote in the margin: *Why is Clayton shrinking back now when his wife needs his strength the most?*

> Not all thoughts should be spoken. If he had insisted she stay home, he would have overridden his wife in her most vulnerable state and added all kinds of stress on himself and his family. How do you think his wife would feel if she made their lives miserable during her last days?

> *They could probably handle it as long as they needed to.*

> Maybe. But this way, they will leave the caretaking to the experts and be able to just be with. I think Clayton will realize this when the stress of the moment clears.

Ruth said her emotional goodbyes to OrrVilla. The home had served them well during the past year-and-a-half.

When they entered the doors of hospice, a deep pang hit Clayton. He was actively putting a dagger in his hope to save Ruth. The management of Ruth now lay in the hands of hospice, and of course, God. Strangely, with all the sorrow, there was an odd freedom accompanying the moment too.

A steady stream of friends and family visited for the next four days. The medical staff medicated Ruth, making her more comfortable than she had been in a long time. Ruth's sisters-in-laws, Gladys and Karen Geiser, visited most of the days. Their kids, of course, hung out as much as possible.

Ruth wanted personal time with each of them, making her farewell heartfelt and personal. It appeared to bless all parties, including Ruth.

Clayton sensed that neither he nor she needed their personal farewell talk. They had spent most of their lives together. To the best of their ability, with the help of Clarice, they had shared their deepest selves with one another these past few months. To try and top that with a goodbye speech seemed unnecessary and painful.

Clayton and his children were ready for her pain and discomfort to end. Ruth was ready to go. They all verbally gave her permission to give up and move on. Her children's words and faithful presence were her rewards for being a loving mother.

Ruth fell into a peaceful and painless coma during her last eight hours. Her favorite CD played in the background. At 5:15 p.m. on November 25, Janet noticed Ruth's breathing becoming laborious. She notified a nurse who came into the room and concurred. She gave Ruth an injection, and a minute later, her breathing stopped. Her battle was over.

Clayton was the first to speak. All his family except for the grandkids were present. He said, "Thank you, God. It is over. Let's move on."

Clayton's children left the room one by one. He kissed Ruth on the cheek one more time and said goodbye. Then he walked out the door and closed it behind him.

The nurse went in to clean the body and the funeral home arrived. Clayton wanted no part of seeing Ruth's body being carried out. He and his children left the hospice, the place that had served them so well. Out into the cold November air, he walked to his car alone. That night he slept better than he had in some time, and the next day, Thanksgiving Day, proved that a person could be immeasurably sad while also being deeply thankful.

Clayton witnessed his kids step up and take charge in preparation for the memorial celebration. Kimberly contacted everyone taking part. Kevin prepared the slide show on PowerPoint to show at the service. Duane printed just the right pictures and matted them to put on and around the casket. (They decided to have a closed casket, so people could remember Ruth as the robust, caring person she was, not the emaciated figure her body had become.) Mandy and Janet gathered things for a display table that people could view.

Thankful and in awe of his family, Clayton suddenly realized he was without a job. So, he set out to write the obituary (since he'd already written five for other family members) and to plan the order of the service. While he was at it, he wrote a tribute to his wife of fifty-plus years that would be read at the service. He considered it his therapeutic labor of love, spending many hours on the work of art.

Clayton was awestruck by all the guests that chose to attend the informal calling service. Many came from a great distance. And many encouraged Clayton with their kind words of how Ruth had graciously influenced their lives.

The service of remembrance took place after the burial on Sunday. A friend's rendering of Proverbs 31, another's singing of "I Shall Rise Again," and the content of Pastor Carl's sermon all fit Ruth's legacy perfectly. Clayton's tribute capped the ceremony off, just as he had hoped. He waxed about her many fine qualities and all the loving gestures she had shared with so many. Personally, he mentioned how grateful he was for her being "the spark that lit his way." He would miss her "hugs, smile, listening ear, friendship, companionship, and positive attitude." And he asked her to "please give our son Bruce a special hug!"

Though the service was all Clayton hoped it would be, he wasn't prepared for its length. Wanting to honor Ruth, Clayton didn't think leaving in the middle of the service to pee showed much reverence. So, he held it. By the end, he nearly wet his pants.

The promise he had made to his counselor of "taking care of himself when this is all over" popped into his mind. Heavy-hearted, but grateful, he guessed his new life was beginning right about then.

28

GRIEF

DEATH'S PERPETUAL GRIND

Clayton went through the same ritual every time he went to bed. He gazed at Ruth's picture on his dresser, remembering her beauty, inside and out. He recalled her stirring touch and life-giving hugs. Then, he looked around the room and admired her womanly touch, evident from the selection and positioning of the wall hangings to the quilt on his bed. The bed! Everything about Ruth and that bed made him feel like royalty. It was his shrine, really. Sleeping in that bed was the only way he knew to keep the love he had known and lost from fleeing his now-fractured life.

Clayton often lay sleepless in his bed. Memories of his former life as a married man ran through his mind like a waterfall cascading over the mountain's edge. He remembered his boyish crush on her when he was becoming a man. She had chosen him though he was so naïve and insecure. Their honeymoon was unremarkable, but fabulous. The kids she had birthed and they had reared were wonderful from day one. But the addition of the children had drawn their attention away from their marriage and accentuated their differences. Clayton breathed sighs of relief, knowing they had escaped calamity. They could have easily gone over the edge, bitter at each other's lack.

What righted the ship? he wondered. Certainly, his desperate decision to seek professional counseling helped. But he knew it was much more than that. He remembered their mutual full participation in a Mennonite

Marriage Encounter in 1986. *What was it about that weekend that made it a catalyst for the rest of our married life?*

Somewhere in the recesses of his memory, Clayton recalled that Ruth, to fulfill an exercise, had written a letter regarding her feelings about her eventual death to her spouse that weekend. As best as he could piece her response together, she wrote something to the effect of "I don't want to die because I feel there is still much unfinished business. We lost Bruce, but it could have been me or you, too. What a relief when I came to, to see you with my eyes. You were still alive. I would not be alone. If you had been killed, I would have found it very difficult to go on. I feel that, in many ways, we are having a rebirth in our marriage and want to experience the *true joy* that comes with *love, no matter what.* I love you and hope to spend many more years with you. Then, I hope when it's our time to go we can both go quickly and close together." Clayton thrilled at the memory of the *true joy* of their love, but he ached at the thought that they did not *go* together. He still remained in this lonely world. A tear trickled down his cheek.

They had also completed an exercise that weekend in which they wrote down *what they liked about each other.* Clayton smiled at the recollection of Ruth's varied responses. She liked his desire to grow and not get in a rut, his pursuit to make the marriage as strong as it could be, and his commitment to God and the church. He remembered the great boost to his ego that gave him then. But he wondered what good it did him now.

Then he remembered their commitment to thankfulness from 1990–92 when they each wrote a daily thank-you note to the other. *What a source of encouragement those were!* The notes covered the whole gamut—from his taking care of the cars and the lawn and her faithfully cooking meals and cleaning the house to his massaging her feet and commitment to the marriage and her snuggling the night before and being a super mom. Basically, the most themed notes revealed her need for his time, acceptance, and support and his need for her presence, encouragement, and companionship. They both thrived on being heard, desired, good parents, and physically intimate.

Oh, the connection we had! He'd have to go through all those notes and letters they had given each other. Some day. But at this point in Clayton's life, he did not have the energy to dredge up more sorrow—as beautiful as the memories were. He was sad enough just thinking about them in bed.

It was interesting to him that they had written so much to each other in the 1990s and the 2000s but so little after 2010. He thought, *We must have gotten so good at communicating our love on paper that we finally just spoke the words to each other. Our love matured so beautifully through the years! How am I ever going to make it without her?*

Beemer wrote to his new editor in the margin: *It's been two weeks since Ruth passed away. It looks like Clayton is getting worse instead of better. Can a human die of a broken heart?*

Maammy replied: Yes. THE BOSS has made them with a strong need for companionship. Though the scientific reason for it is beyond them, their emotional system impacts every fiber of their being.

Would Clayton have been better off if they hadn't been so close-knit, so dependent? His kids once told him he was too "joined at the hip." Maybe they were right.

Perhaps. But the pain Clayton is going through now may have been worth the joy and comfort they received throughout their marriage. Quality of life is subject to each human. We cannot judge such matters.

Beemer missed his old editor's direct replies. Maammy's sentimental approach scared him.

A few days later, Clayton awoke extra low on energy and hope, essentials to a life well lived. Fear and desperation wormed their way in, and he did not like it. Not knowing where else to turn, he called Clarice, the psychologist through whom he and Ruth had found help during Ruth's exhausting illness. She fit him in the next day.

After the perfunctory greetings and logistical affairs of how Clayton had been filling his days, Clarice asked Clayton why he wanted to see her.

He said he didn't really know, but that he didn't seem to have any purpose anymore. All he thought about was Ruth and all the ways he missed her. He didn't think he could go on like that much longer and wondered if she could help him stop obsessing about his loss.

Clarice sat up straight, notepad in hand, watching Clayton fidget. "We all cope with loss differently, Clayton. I can share some general coping skills with you, but they may bounce off you like a pebble off a windshield. To best help you, it would help me to understand how you have handled trauma in the past, and what worked and what didn't. Would you mind sharing with me some of the hard things in your life and how they affected you?"

"Sure. Like what kind of hard things? I grew up on a farm. I had to do chores every morning. Then I worked for a bricklayer. Those were hard things. Is that what you mean?"

The prim and proper Clarice chewed at the side of her lip. "Not exactly. What I mean is, what kind of hard things in your life happened to you that made you terribly sad or upset? What kind of things changed your life without your consent? What bad things happened in your life that confused, angered, or threatened you?"

Clayton's heart suddenly began to beat faster. His mouth hung open until he finally blinked and looked away. "Okay ... " The first thing that came to his mind was his abrupt dismissal from Laurelville. After recounting to Clarice the humility and despair of that life-altering debacle, he shared the horror of Bruce's death, which she had already heard from Ruth's perspective.

Clayton watched Clarice, who looked up from her note-taking and waited for Clayton to continue. He searched his mind for other tragedies but came up empty.

To cover the awkward silence, Clarice said, "Your son's death must have been excruciating. Death is so difficult to accommodate."

That rattled his brain enough for him to restart. "Oh, my mother died in 1990. That was hard."

"Oh. Were you close to your mother?"

"Yes! Well … actually, not so much as we had been when I was growing up. She was the best mother. I really connected with her. Then, when I moved away and when I learned how I was still depending on my mother's love and approval and placing that on Ruth, I kind of pulled away. When she died, I felt extra bad because I had let her down when she needed me most. She was always there for me, but I wasn't there for her." He shook his head. "That still bothers me."

"Why did your mother need you?"

"Well, I was the youngest of eleven. When I left, she pretty much had to deal with my dad on her own."

Clarice wrinkled her face in confusion.

"That's kind of a long story," Clayton said. "Let's just say my dad wasn't the best company. I'm sure she was lonely. She was very confused and helpless toward the end of her life. It was so terrible for her life of empathy and giving to end so pathetically! I wish I had included her more in my busy life."

Clarice nodded.

"Then there was my sister Arlene. She died in 1988. I kind of saw her as my second mother. Mom had so much to do when I was younger that Arlene often watched over me. Then, when I got married, she and her husband, Irvin, were pastors near where I lived. We spent a lot of valuable time with them. When she was diagnosed with cancer, they moved back to Kidron where we lived. The remaining time I spent with her was really special! But it sure did make her death, a year later, that much harder. She was only sixty-one. That sparked my midlife crisis."

Clarice stretched her face, top to bottom. "Your midlife crisis?"

Clayton cleared his throat. "Yeah. I'll get to that in a bit. But Arlene's death sure made me wonder about life and needless suffering."

"And what did you come up with?" Clarice asked.

"I don't know. It's like, what's the point? Seven of my eleven siblings have died so far, and each death hit me extremely hard. Since I'm the youngest, I'm really worried I'll have to watch them all pass before me. Is waiting for heaven worth all the pain this life hands us?"

Clarice looked up from her pad and raised an eyebrow. "The death of loved ones hits us all hard at some point."

"Yeah. Some are harder than others, like in my oldest brother, Elno's family. His second child was what they called at the time a *blue baby*. They cared for him as best they could, but he died when he was three years old, a day after my fourteenth birthday. That was one of the first funerals I went to. What was the purpose of his life?

"Elno also had to endure a stillborn baby, and his young-adult, adopted son died in a horrible train crash. Then, in 2005, Elno also suffered through skin cancer radiation treatments, which resulted in some gruesome skin grafts. But he fought through it—only to fall and break his hip in 2007. His balance was a problem after that. Once, he showed me the exercises he did to strengthen his equilibrium. That was the last time I talked to him. One day, he walked out his front door, fell back, and hit his head on the steps. He didn't survive."

Clarice gave him a caring expression.

After sharing how Elno had always been an encourager, supporting his efforts like a good dad would, Clayton said, "Is this what you're wanting?"

"Yes. I think this may help you get in touch with your feelings of loss and suffering. Sometimes, we discard the messy things of life, opting to value only the happy times. But the truth is, enjoyable and hard times are equally important. Both are necessary and good."

Clayton looked at her incredulously. *Good?* he thought. *What's good about any of this?* His resolve suddenly became to show her how tragically impactful others' deaths had been on him.

"I didn't find much good in Ruth's mom, Grace, dying in 1995. She and her sister were visiting a doctor friend and his family in Arizona near the Mexico border. Now, keep in mind, Ruth respected, emulated, and deeply loved her mother. And my kids all adored her. She spent so much time and effort getting to know them and blessing them. Kimberly, my youngest, lived with her in Florida at a critical time in Kimberly's life when she helped her transition into adulthood. Grace's thumbprint was all over my family."

"We all must die some time or other," said Clarice.

"Not like that!" Clayton snapped, more forcefully than he intended. He swallowed and cleared his throat. "I mean, her death was awful. She went with a group to Mexico for the day to visit a friend. After passing through the US immigration authorities, they headed for their car in the parking lot. In the crosswalk—not in an alley or jaywalking in a street, but in a crosswalk where they were supposed to walk!—she was struck by a vehicle that was rapidly backing up. The car knocked her to the ground, ran over her, and dragged her fifteen feet before crashing into a cement wall. The only good thing about the whole thing was that her sister, who was behind her, and her friend and her small kids, who were in front of her, were not touched.

"They rushed her to the hospital where the friend she had been visiting happened to be the attending physician on duty. Grace had multiple bone fractures, contusions, a collapsed lung and bladder, and who knows what all else. Her doctor friend sedated her and had her helicoptered to the nearest big hospital.

"We got the call about her accident while we were at the supper table. Ruth was horrified. Grace, of course, didn't last the surgery and died of internal bleeding, *just as any younger person would have*, said the doctor.

"I would not call that *good*," Clayton railed.

"Nor would I," Clarice replied.

After a long moment, Clarice asked, "Is that pretty much it for the bad stuff in your life, then?"

Clayton frowned and proceeded to build on his head of steam. "Death doesn't stop. It keeps on taking.

"The Geiser plane crash in 2000 was even more tragic."

"The Geiser plane crash?" asked Clarice. "Who were the Geisers?"

"That's Ruth's maiden name. Her younger brother Roland, and his twelve-year-old son, Andrew, along with Ruth's nephew-in-law and his twelve-year-old son crashed just after the small plane they were in took off from a private airstrip on the way to Cleveland.

"The pilot and three of the passengers died. Roland, somehow, survived. He frantically made his way out of the wreckage and began yelling for his son and trying to lift burning metal in desperation. As a result, Roland was put into an induced coma for a couple of days and hospitalized for about a month with life-threatening injuries and burns.

GRIEF

"His wife, Karen, meanwhile, and the other surviving mother/wife, had their entire world turned upside down. Ruth graciously came to their aide, helping these precious young women pick up the broken pieces of their shattered lives, and find that even amidst this senseless tragedy they could know grace from above."

"I bet Ruth was good at empathizing with them," Clarice offered.

Clayton's hostile demeanor shifted. "Yes. Yes, she was. She was made for that type of situation as a matter of fact. She always knew just what to say and how to say it when someone was hurting."

"And the fact that she had," here, Clarice paused and retracted, " … that you both had … lost a twelve-year-old son all those years before must have helped her resonate with them."

"Yes," Clayton said again. "Who would have ever thought two more twelve-year-old Geiser boys would die in a terrible accident? Each boy accepted the values of their parents in word and deed and were on their way to becoming productive and responsible adults. The magnitude of the thing was—unbelievable. A person couldn't have thought up such a tragic story."

Clarice nodded, cautiously. "This must have been a big deal for the small Kidron community."

"You got that right. There was a parade of cars out to view the site that next day. I couldn't believe how strewed out the wreckage was. I have no idea how Roland survived."

"That's pretty amazing alright," Clarice agreed.

"Then, to take care of his burns … it was awful! It was too painful to even think about, let alone watch. All those skin grafts and raw flesh!" Clayton winced and shook his head. "Months later, we invited them out to Florida and observed his wound-care ritual. I don't think I could have handled that. I'd have passed out every time they touched me."

Clarice asked, "Were they bitter?"

Clayton thought about that. "No, actually, they ended up not being. We had a lot of experience by then with our grieving classes. Both families joined us in the groups. I think we influenced them … for the good." Clayton looked up and met Clarice's understanding expression at his use of the word, good.

Clayton went on, "Roland and Karen ended up leading burn-survivor groups. They had a tremendous influence in the Amish community, who generally don't talk freely about tragedy or have the resources to deal with such things. It was quite beautiful actually."

Catching Clarice's smiling eyes, Clayton regained his own tragic recollections. "My sister, Dorothy, died in 2011. Now, she suffered. She had scarlet fever, pleurisy, and rheumatic fever as a kid, then tuberculosis in high school … a couple of times. For, like, four years she had to go to a sanatorium by herself. They ended up taking part of her lung out. One surgery required fifty-two stitches."

"Oh, my," said Clarice.

"Yeah, she had it pretty rough. I think she fell behind socially, and she had it rougher than any of us really knew. But she finally married this cute-as-a-button guy named Calvin when she was forty. He was maybe 105 pounds soaking wet. They weren't ever in charge of anyone's committee, to be sure, but they had each other. Though they had much to complain about, their love seemed to be enough.

"Then her heart gave out, and I was called to the hospital. My sister Norma and I watched as they shocked her with those defibrillator paddle-things to no avail. She died holding Calvin's hand. It was so sad. I felt so helpless."

Clarice looked sad. Clayton rolled on. "Then 2015 was the real killer. I lost my wife, two brothers, a sister, and a sister-in-law—three of them within three days of each other!"

Clarice's eyes widened.

"In January, my brother Roy's wife, Vesta, died unexpectedly from pneumonia after a short bout with the flu. Then, three days later, I lost George and Vi, whose health had both been deteriorating for some time.

"But this all still shook me big time! It all happened on the heels of us processing Ruth's emotional battle over her first bout with cancer. I did not have the luxury of mourning or letting down my tough veneer … for me … or for Ruth, I'm not sure which. All I knew is that I had to get in there and deal with all the duties as a brother, especially for George, since I was the executor of his estate."

"Why was he your responsibility?"

Clayton rubbed his chin and sighed. "Well, my brother Ken was actually in charge of his affairs after my parents died. He did an unbelievable job! I'm amazed at how well he handled George. But Ken's health began to fail, so I took over."

"Was that a troubling responsibility?"

Clayton didn't know how to answer that. "George was ten years older than me. I was told he was always a little slow, quite a bit slower than all the rest of us (who were never considered fast thinkers by any means). I think maybe he was strong-willed as a young child. But my dad was real good at breaking a kid's will. By the time I came along, George was quiet, reserved, and never spoke unless asked a question. School didn't work out well for him. Some people thought maybe he had some mental retardation. I don't know. He behaved well enough, but he showed little emotion—even less than the rest of us. My kids once said that he seemed like a zombie sometimes. He was real good at routine things like chores, but he never had any aspirations of his own. In fact, at his funeral, all his nieces and nephews commented on how disturbing it was that he had never been encouraged to be himself. I've always wondered how much of his God-given soul was beat out of him early on."

Clayton shook his head. "I didn't do all that much to help him really. I left him at home to deal with my dad on his own. I could have done something."

Clarice asked carefully, "Did your dad hit him or something?"

And there was the question. Clayton took a deep breath. "Well, *I* never saw it. But my siblings say he beat George—unmercifully, at times—before the age of six. But he did look after George's basic needs after he quit farming. Dad got him a job at Horst Machine where he worked. George was a janitor basically. They worked there for twenty years.

"After my dad died, George became a ward of the state. I remember a state psychologist coming out to interview him to assess his mental capacity. George could not answer the simplest questions. I'm sure the many put-downs my dad threw at him did nothing for his mental health. He stayed in several group homes and ended up in a nursing home at the end."

Clayton paused and took a long breath. "George's death was unbeliev-ably sad. But then Vi's death on that same day took the cake. I remember crying right there on the phone when my niece Bonita told me the news." Clayton shook his head slowly.

"Vi was the most vibrant person I knew. She made everyone around her smile just being herself. Like my mother, she had the kindest heart, but she also had this hilarious personality that just made you laugh. She had these funny expressions like, *Good Governor* and *Uncle John* for exclamations. And she could twist a phrase like no one else! I think what made her so endearing was her ability to laugh at herself. The joy her life spread was immeasurable!

"I remember the tender times we had staying up late into the night when we visited each other. She freely shared herself with me.

"Her kids' laughter, teasing, and joking gave our Steiner family reunions that much-needed spark. At her funeral, I was impressed with the deep grief her kids showed because it illustrated just how much my big sister meant to them.

"Vi was known to always have a cherry pit in her mouth. Always! Her family made fun of her all the time for this, but she just laughed along with them. To honor this quirkiness, they placed her stash of cherry pits in a jar on the top of her casket." Clayton smiled fondly at the gesture.

"But toward the end of her life, this energetic, optimistic lady got struck down by some awful dementia disease called Lewy body. It caused her to have no filters and act out in the strangest ways. It was hard to see my sister show such ugly traits when her whole life had been a model of caring and good nature. So, when she died, though I was glad her and her family's suffering had ended, it was a hard pill to swallow, saying goodbye to such a mighty life force."

Clarice said, "I can see how that would be difficult."

"And my siblings' deaths basically doubled because I've also had to bury their spouses who became as close to me as my own brothers and sisters."

"Yes, so many deaths."

"Ken died that same year as George and Vi—a few months before Ruth. Another strain I could not fully deal with while aiding Ruth. He was my closest brother in age. We shared the same bedroom; we played in the creek, damming it up; we ran naked in the rain on our roof; we shared most everything when we were younger. He covered my chores even more than

George, I think. I often bullied him into doing the chores I liked least, and Kenny didn't hold it against me. My personality was more dominant than his humble disposition, and I often took advantage of that, like when I'd pull the one-legged milking stool out from under him then run away from him faster than he could chase me. For some reason, I used to get him to chase the stray balls I'd hit with the bat when we played ball together. When we made hay, Ken was the one with the hard job of picking up the bales while I drove the tractor. More than once, I remember choosing the biggest piece of pie before he got the chance to take it. He could have so easily resented his smart-alecky little brother. But he chose kindness instead.

"About a year before his death, we spent the day in a car, roaming the countryside we grew up in. I was amazed at all the people and stories he remembered when provoked by the houses and local scenery. I thought I was the historian, but he knew things that I'd never known. His warmth when sharing his essence with me that day was a small picture of how he treated me my whole life. I miss him." Clayton's eye's watered again.

"Kenny's wife, Mae, took such wonderful care of Ken, who suffered from CBD, a degenerative disease that slowly made him an invalid. They were a couple just made for each other. The love they shared and showed warmed my heart like Mom's fried mush."

"I'm glad you can remember all the good from those you've lost," said Clarice. "We need to hold onto all the positives we can. Sometimes, they're the only things that keep us afloat. You've sure had your share of deaths in the family. I may need to come to you for advice when I get to your age."

Clayton puffed out an unexpected chuckle.

"I didn't mean to rush you," Clarice went on. "Was that it for the major difficult deaths in your life?"

Clayton nodded. "I think so." Then he looked up and said, "No, wait. There was one more." He sighed. "How could I forget?

"Ruth's younger brother, Al, was one of these larger-than-life type guys. He had a lifelong commitment to serving the church and was a worldwide traveler. As a young man, he served with Mennonite Central Committee's Pax program in South Korea and then in Pakistan instead of doing military service. In 1975, after serving with MCC in Bangladesh, he took a year and a half to travel around the world on just his motorcycle. That trip took him across Asia, the Middle East, and Africa. Along the way, he sometimes stayed with missionaries, volunteering to fix things for them in exchange for a bed and a homecooked meal.

"After his last child left home in 2000, Al and his wife, Gladys, joined the Mennonite Mission Network to serve in Afghanistan. While they were there, Al found an Afghan business partner named Shukur. Together, they started and ran Engineering Associates, a company that made water turbines to generate electricity for Afghan villages, many of which had never had electricity before.

"In 2008, just as he and Shukur were leaving an Afghan funeral to return to Kabul, he was ambushed by armed men. They tied up Al and Shukur and held them for ransom. Shukur was released a few days later, but Al was held hostage for fifty-six days. His captors would release him from his blindfold and ropes only long enough for him to go to the bathroom. Much of the time, he could only lay on the ground, bound. Back home, Gladys and members of the Kidron Church met nightly to pray for his release. The FBI met with Gladys many times. Finally, in the dark of night, daring US military commandos stormed the compound where Al was held. They killed the guards and hoisted Al into a waiting helicopter. He was debriefed in Kabul before being flown back to Kidron."

"Sounds like a movie," Clarice said.

"It could have been," said Clayton. "I remember well that emotional reunion with his siblings in his Kidron home. He was clearly shaken and physically weak, but he was happy to be home safe.

"Al being Al, with his commitment to serve the Afghan people, he chose to return to Afghanistan less than a year later. He said that while he was in captivity, he faced death head-on when his captors read him his last rites. When they didn't kill him, as he lay on the cold earth by himself, he could not help but visualize what Afghan projects he would like to be involved with if his life was spared.

"After six months at home, he returned to continue his hydroelectric service to outlying villages. Four months later, Al was again ambushed. This time, the assailants shot and killed Al and his Afghan partner on the spot. His body was picked up by locals and returned to Kabul.

"This guy's commitment, bravery, Christian witness, and heart for the less privileged boggles the mind. And he was shot in cold blood! Just like that! My kids were all torn up about it. That was a really hard one to swallow."

Clarice took a long breath, letting the silence linger. She finally said, "Death is unbelievably hard."

Clayton nodded, then added, "I remember at his funeral a friend played "I've Been Everywhere," the Johnny Cash song, but with different lyrics indicating the places Al had traveled to and lived." He half-chuckled. "What a fitting tribute."

Clarice smiled charitably. "I'm sorry you've had to endure so many deaths. They will all be embedded in your memory forever. They can't be taken from you, and we won't try to do that here. Our goal is to acknowledge the pain and sorrow and give them their appropriate due. No more and no less. It's a matter of perspective."

She set her notes on her lap and resettled her sitting position. "What other hard stuff, other than deaths, have you gone through?"

Still in a state of melancholy, Clayton was caught off guard. "Ah, what do you mean?"

"Well, have you gone through any other difficulties in your life?"

Clayton sat back and riffled through his memory. "You mean like the Laurelville firing?"

"Yes."

"Let's see. There was my prostate cancer scare. I thought I might not be around anymore for a little while there. That was definitely hard. And then, there was all that business with my midlife crisis ... "

"Yes. You mentioned that before." Clarice looked at the clock on the wall behind Clayton. "I want to give this its proper due. Maybe we can go into that more next time. Our time's about up."

She looked through her notes. "I don't want you feeling more discouraged than when you came. You've shared a lot of painful events in your life. Let me ask you this, how did you get through all of them?"

Clayton's brow furrowed. "Well, I guess God with his people helped me."

"And won't He with his people help you through this unfortunate business of losing your wife?"

"Yeah, maybe. But this seems worse."

Clarice nodded. "It does. It does. But what's the worst thing you can imagine happening to you?"

"Living without Ruth."

"Really? Is it possible that you might be having a little tunnel vision? Seeing only what your attention is understandably drawn to?"

Clayton frowned, not comprehending.

"What if you had an accident and lost all your limbs? What if you slowly lost your brain function over the next ten years? What if you had to go through the Holocaust?"

Clayton looked at his psychotherapist, dumbstruck.

"Look," Clarice said, "I'm not asking you to dwell on such morbid fears. I'm just encouraging you to look at life with a wider brushstroke. Don't get stuck convincing yourself that your tragedy is the end-all. It isn't. You're an overcomer, Clayton."

"But I don't feel like an overcomer. I feel like I've lost my best friend, and there's no reason to go on."

"And that's legitimate. Normal, even. Feelings always lag behind the mind and will; grief is a process. You must be patient and wait for all phases of your body to align through healthy comprehension. Rushing it won't help, trust me."

Clayton breathed heavily. "So, like how long? It seems like I should be over the sadness of this … yesterday."

Clarice smiled as if it hurt. "Clayton, I won't lie. Grieving is hard. It doesn't have rules that tell us exactly when it will end. It could be a while yet."

She let her words settle like steeping tea. "Your first answer was that God with His people helped you. Do you think that God's people are up to helping you through this challenge?"

Clayton closed his eyes. He knew the correct answer. He didn't know why he didn't want to answer it. Finally, he admitted, "Yes."

"The question is, then, are *you* up to the challenge?"

Shame tickled Clayton's pride.

"I think you are," Clarice answered for him. "You just don't know it yet because your emotions are lagging. In the same way our physical bodies naturally heal from, say a broken bone, our emotions eventually heal from the grief of losing a loved one—if we give them the time they need."

Clayton soaked in all the wisdom though it all seemed too much to take in at the time. He left Clarice's office drained. In his weakened state, he didn't know if he had the strength to overcome. But he did find comfort knowing his irrational feelings of despair were a necessary part of healing. This knowledge gave him the will to trust the uncomfortable process. So, that is the path he took. He trusted that, someday, the sad ache in his heart would lessen, and he'd once again have a vigor for life and joy.

Beemer asked his superior a question in the side margin of his biographic book: *Is it standard procedure for a counselor to ask her client to think about his worst fears?*

Maammy responded: Ha! Whatever works, right? I wouldn't say it's standard practice. In fact, I'd call it unorthodox. But, sometimes, drastic measures are used when the patient is stuck. I thought the therapist did a rather nice job of diverting his spellbound attention.

Yeah, after being with him all his life and feeling and thinking what he does, it's easy to get that tunnel vision. All the awful deaths of loved ones that he's experienced kind of just seeped into his overall vision. I hadn't really thought about how much they've impacted his life. I was lulled into thinking that he was just a regular guy. But to withstand such grief, he must be a hero—ya think?

Beemer, write Clayton's story—not yours!
But to answer your question from THE BOSS's perspective, yes, Clayton is a hero. Not because he's so exceptional but because THE BOSS sees all these humans as heroes and delights in all the good efforts they make.

I just hope Clayton doesn't take a nosedive in his mourning over Ruth. Things look pretty dark right now. What's to prevent him from giving up?

Nothing. He may. It's happened to others. It's a possibility that these humans must live with. Life is not simple or easy. There are a billiondy scenarios to which this could go. Overcoming the bad ones thrills their Maker. Of that, you can be sure!

A billiondy? Beemer wondered how she could just make up a word like that. Or even scarier, if she thought that was a word.

29
CRISIS MODE
DOING OR BEING?

A couple of weeks later, Clayton followed up on his previous appointment with Clarice. The encouragement he'd received from that last meeting had not snatched him from the jaws of the blahs as much as he had hoped. The unsettling sense of loss was a merciless taskmaster. The process toward peaceful acceptance, he helplessly realized, would take time. But he hoped another visit with a counselor would help him understand what all he was up against and clear some of the cobwebs that his fear had strewn throughout his mind.

After some small talk, Clarice said, "To help you navigate through the traps in your head, I want to continue marking those times in your life where you felt stuck—when you were afraid everything was falling apart. This will help me know what things you'll need to overcome moving forward."

She grabbed her notepad and pen. "Perhaps you could tell me a little about what you referred to as your midlife crisis."

Clayton took a long breath and nodded. "Well, there's several things. It's hard to pin it on just one thing."

"That's fine. Tell me all the factors that led to it."

Clayton said, "I think the first thing was soon after Bruce's death. My oldest son, Kevin, wanted to take the car to go see his girlfriend Mandy. I told him he couldn't. I remember thinking he needed to obey because I was his dad and that was really all that mattered. But he thought I was being unreasonable and decided to take the keys and go anyway. I told him, 'No, you're not.' He grabbed the keys. I grabbed his arm. He grabbed my hand. Long story short, we wrestled over the keys in our kitchen. He won. He took off in our car. I sat on the kitchen floor, suddenly realizing that my son was stronger and faster than me. He was seventeen and wanted his independence. I was, what, forty-three at the time? I had suddenly lost the upper hand and that scared me."

"Why do you think that scared you?"

"I don't know. I guess I liked being in charge of my family, feeling necessary. But he needed to be in charge of his own life—and soon."

"Did you keep fighting him after that?" Clarice asked.

"Not in the physical sense. I gradually got on board with his independence. Seeing my firstborn leave for kindergarten was hard but seeing him leave for college was brutal. I dreaded relinquishing the other two in the coming years."

Clarice said, "How much of losing Bruce had to do with your fears of seeing Kevin leave, do you think?"

Clayton thought about that. "Hmm ... Well, I know I hated losing Bruce. I guess having another taken from my charge probably did bring back some of the same fear. I never thought of that before."

"So, that was the beginning," Clarice said. "What else contributed to that hard time in your life?"

"Well, a couple years later, Duane graduated. That wasn't my favorite time of life. A Mennonite college would have been my preference for him, but he chose a Baptist-affiliated school for its youth ministry program. I couldn't even influence my own son to go where I wanted. I remember grilling the administrators at that school with theological questions when we went for a visit, hoping I could find major faults in their structure. They handled my rants well. I ended up conceding and tried to encourage Duane to go for it. But I felt pretty weak in the whole thing."

"What else was going on around then?"

"My dad died a couple years before that. That did nothing to help me. But the real hard blow came when my sister Arlene died in June, soon after Duane's graduation."

Clarice nodded and looked back in her notebook. "Yes, you mentioned that last time. You were quite fond of her. Your second mother, so to speak, right?"

"Yes. It seemed like the people I looked up to were leaving me. For some reason, it made me feel unimportant, unnecessary."

"Now, your mother passed a couple of years after Arlene, right?"

Clayton nodded.

"Had she been able to encourage you?"

"Not so much by then. The mental problems she had gone through made her more of a dependent her last few years."

"And what about your dad?"

"He was gone."

"I know," said Clarice, patiently. "What I meant was, was he a source of encouragement? Did you miss his wisdom and support?"

"No!" Clayton said, too emphatically. He felt his heart begin to race. "He wasn't really the supportive type."

"I can't help but think there was something more about your father that you're not telling me. Is there anything you'd like to share about him with me?"

Clayton did his best to settle his uneasy breathing. He swallowed hard. "No, not really. He wasn't a very strong influence in my life by then. His passing was more of an inconvenience than anything else. You know, a drain."

Clarice nodded her head slowly. "A drain. Like, you had to acknowledge his presence (and now, lack of presence) in your life, but nothing more."

"Something like that. Just another reason to be sad."

Clarice stared at Clayton's restless gaze. "Well, we may need to go a little deeper on that in the future." She looked back to her notebook.

Beemer wrote in his margin notes: *Clayton is lying here. Why would he do that? His dad had a huge impact on his life. And he still thinks about him a lot. And most of those thoughts have a significant influence on his mood and outlook. He should be honest with his counselor, not coy and hide it from her. Why would he willfully mislead her?*

Maammy replied: Whoa! Don't get so high and mighty here. Just because he's not disclosing all the facts does not necessarily make him a liar. Is it possible he's convinced himself that his dad had little pull in his life?

I don't see how. Unless he just wants to believe it so much that he's wishing it into truth.

There you go. Sometimes humans are so beat up by a problem that the only way to defeat it is to deny its magnitude and treat it like a house cat instead of a lion. I doubt that he's purposefully trying to deceive her. He's probably trying to protect himself from more pain.

But if he doesn't deal with it full-on it's just going to fester and continue to hinder his progress, right?

Right. Sometimes, they must learn the hard way and wait until they are hurting so bad their only alternative is to confront the truth. Be patient. You've got a lifelong learner. He'll come around.

"So," Clarice continued, "your defined roles as father, son, and brother were suddenly changing. That's disorienting—and scary. What else?"

Clayton rubbed his chin. "Well, I wasn't excited when Kimberly was about to graduate from high school and go to Eastern Mennonite University in 1993. But to encourage her, I started running with her. She was on the track team. However, she soon outpaced me, and I felt incapable, like she didn't need me as her father anymore. I felt that my job as a dad was more or less done.

"I was depressed for quite a while after that. Thought I'd never crawl out from the weight of that, honestly." Clayton smirked. "My old counselor, Floyd, used to like to put cute little names on things. He called this my 'empty nest syndrome.'"

Clarice said, "You obviously made it through that difficult time in your life. It may help you to reminisce about that a little. How did you manage to crawl out of it?"

"Well, time probably was the biggest factor. I finally had to adjust to the way things changed. Staying frustrated and sorry for myself wasn't good for anyone. I had to look at things differently. For example, around the time that my boys got married, I thought I could help them by giving them unsolicited advice. That didn't fly. All that did was make them resentful and want to get further away from me. Duane finally brought Kevin along to tell me that I needed to let them be adults. That was hard to hear. But I heard it and backed off. When they got married, I slowly realized I wasn't losing my sons but gaining two daughters-in-law."

Clarice smiled.

Clayton continued, "Of course, projects helped me get my mind off my gloom too. The biggest project came from turning the family farm I grew up on into the Steinwood Development." Clayton explained how delighted he was, after all the setbacks, to successfully develop the community. He went on to tell her about buying Grandpa and Grandma Geiser's Florida home after the Geiser estate was settled, which required that they go there at least twice a year to clean and remodel. And he couldn't leave out how being busy with church and the historical society in Kidron helped too.

Before he expounded, Clarice broke in. "I'd very much like to hear your journey with your church and the community another time. But just to summarize, you enjoyed your involvement with them. Am I catching that right?"

Clayton nodded and looked off into nowhere in particular. "Pretty much. That kept me motivated. I was often up late at night working on projects for them and wanted to wake up early just to get their books in order."

"This is very helpful," Clarice crowed.

Confused, but mysteriously heartened, Clayton asked, "And why is that?"

"Well, I see a pattern. One we can work with. I think you're a man who likes order. You like to keep books. You like things done the right way. That's important to you. You don't mind doing things over and over again, every day, because there's a rightness to it. A comfort. It's the glue that holds the greater picture together. Is that right?

Clayton gave a sheepish grin. "That's pretty accurate. Is that a bad thing?"

"Not at all. Of course, if you let it rule you, it could be. None of us are machines. Change and adjustment are mandatory in this life. But, if you can see that tendency in yourself—to gravitate toward the routine—and are willing to change to improve, well, there's hope. You've shown that you can *crawl out* of your ruts. Life can once again be joy-filled and boundless."

Clayton wasn't comprehending much of her exposé.

Clarice said, "I'm seeing a pattern here. Tell me some of your other midlife crises." She crinkled her fingers for air quotes.

Clayton blinked out of his confusion. "Um, I had the same experience right after I retired. Floyd called it my *kiss my career goodbye crisis*. I felt directionless, defeated, goal-less. It just sapped the energy right out of me."

"And how did you climb out of that one?"

"Well, that one was pretty easy. We got involved in the International Guest House, and all of the sudden, I was busy, meeting people, and felt needed."

Clarice smiled and nodded. "You had purpose again."

Clayton nodded too.

"What other things drained you of purpose and hope?"

"Uhh … when I got my prostate cancer, I felt like the rug had been pulled out from under me. Floyd called it my 'creepy cancer crisis.' Suddenly, all the things I was involved with didn't seem to matter. Life took on a whole new perspective—an ominous, terrible one."

"Okay." Clarice took a deep breath as if to put a period on his comments. "I'm not referring to any of this as a 'midlife crisis' because that's kind of a vague, and often misrepresented, term. I think what you were dealing with is much closer to an *identity crisis*. You see, it's important to feel like you belong. Or, if you aren't sure you belong, to find a role you can identify with. Identity is key. By finding identity in a role, you feel needed and valued; you feel successful. This is normal and healthy—to a point.

"The problem arises when your role is taken from you. Who are you then? When your identity is wholly based on what you *do* and not on who you *are*, you can feel like a fish out of water if your circumstances change. You're suddenly uncomfortable in your own body, learning just how inadequate you are in so many unfamiliar ways."

Clayton looked on, engrossed, but unsure.

Clarice went on. "You have learned to adjust. That's good. When times changed and your old routines no longer worked and your identity as a father, employee, or healthy man faded, for whatever reason, you learned to find new routines to identify with. That works.

"But a less painful way would be to be okay with who you are from the inside out. Tasks are necessary and can be rewarding. But if you could grasp that you are valuable just for who you *are*—beyond what you *do*—well, then the hurdles would be less harrowing and less time-consuming to adjust to."

Clayton looked like a deer in the headlights.

Clarice smiled warmly. "I know this is a lot to take in. You won't get this all at once. We'll keep working on it. You've got time."

Clayton nodded routinely. "So … what do I do in the meantime?"

The smile on Clarice's face widened. "There you go, worried about what you should be *doing* again. I'll guide you through some steps to take. But, for now, just rest. Don't overthink things. Let these nuggets of truth sink in. I don't know why our brains aren't generally capable of just flipping the switch and changing when we want to. Usually, it takes some hard knocks or extreme soul-searching and a lot of time. I'd say you're primed for such a change."

> Beemer wrote in his margin: *I don't really understand this role identity thing. Why would humans find their identity in what they do? Why not just be who THE BOSS made them to be and do things out of necessity or joy—not for credit or place.*

> Maammy: For whatever reason, humans tend to judge others by what they do more than who they are. They expect the same judgment from others. So, they often do all they can to look impressive. It can be a vicious cycle if they get caught up in it.

> *But why would they want to look impressive when THE BOSS sees them wholly on who they are? Whatever caused Clayton to go the performance route?*

You're asking questions you can answer yourself. Hint: go back to his early environment.

Oh, yeah. He was trained, above and beyond anything else, to obey. In his house, according to his dad, he was only as good as his performance. I guess it makes sense that he identifies with what he does. His feelings and thoughts all got squashed. His worth totally depended on his ability to do things well. No A for effort for him. But he was an immature kid then. He's a full-fledged adult now. Can't he see the harm such performance identity causes him and just change it?

No. He's human. Their condition mandates that they learn these things through experience and deep insight before their mind can change. What's your excuse?

Beemer didn't reply. He felt like a fly caught in a spider's web. Was he guilty of finding his identity in how well he wrote? But clearly, this was different because he was hired to write for THE BOSS. What kind of employee would he be if he didn't want to write well? This rookie editor was sure getting on his nerves. Where did she get off pointing the finger at him when he just wanted to write well for THE BOSS?

Clayton left the session numb. Not heading in a definite direction or pursuing something sounded uncomfortable. Resting, waiting, being patient all sounded like torture. But he also heard hope in Clarice's message and wondered what it would be like to outlast this grief he could not ignore and to someday be joy-filled and boundless. He decided the hope was worth the wait, however long and painful.

Though it was not "doing nothing," he did find a rather sedentary action that felt similar to waiting. As he had when Bruce died all those years ago, Clayton found rest, understanding, and direction from learning through books. He first read a classic grief book called *The Five Stages of Grief.* Then, he read a devotional with practical tidbits of daily advice like "be your own best friend; do not harm yourself being your worst enemy; and widen your circle of friends. Be vulnerable and love others." These soothed Clayton's gloomy woundedness, scratching an unseen itch.

Looking for more meat, he read *Grief and Sexuality—Life After Losing a Spouse*, which had been written by a Mennonite author, Rachel Nafziger Hartzler. She had interviewed many widows and widowers, both Mennonite and non, and found that the overwhelming majority of both males and females ranked sexual intimacy high on their list of grieving factors. Those that remarried considered touch to be the main component in wanting to remarry. So engrossed in the information, Clayton reread many of the sections two or three times. He missed the intimate touch of Ruth so much at times that he thought he'd burst. It was easy for him to scold himself for his animalistic desires of the flesh (as he'd heard in many a sermon). But here, in Hartzler's book, he read that he was normal. She encouraged her readers to embrace their sexual desires as God's gift—a need that God had given them to fulfill.

So, that longing in him was real and okay. Now what?

In stepped the renowned author, Brené Brown. Brown reminded him that he could accept himself just as he was. Her books encouraged him to step out and be vulnerable—a real counterintuitive eye-opener for Clayton. She taught that a healthy person believes they are good enough just the way they *are;* they don't have to *do* anything to prove their worth to the world.

This head knowledge was all good and healing—at least it triggered the healing process. But the void between his reality and the tranquil promised land still seemed a world away. The days remained gray; the nights dark.

He couldn't help feeling out of place, like the odd man out. Church, his supposed sanctuary of peace, suddenly made him feel more self-consciously single than anywhere else. All he could see were couples. His peers were coupled. Old couples were *so cute* together. Even the very young were finding partners right and left, it appeared. When he walked into the room, everyone noticed he didn't have a partner. At least, he noticed and got the vibe that everyone else thought the same. He soon figured out that those he felt the most comfortable being with (those that felt the least awkward to converse with) were other singles. So, at church services, he did his best to find other singles to sit next to. This generally helped his fish-in-the-bowl sensitivity though he soon learned that he should not sit next to a female single two Sundays in a row because people began talking about their potential pairing. He didn't know if he was extra sensitive or if his church family was that insensitive. Either way, singlehood brought many unwanted strings attached, many that chafed.

As much as he wanted to live the victorious, be-himself life, aside from identifying as a good worker, father, and husband, who was he? He wondered.

Journaling helped him express the pangs in his journey. Through writing his thoughts and experience, he better understood what he was battling. In March, four months after Ruth's passing, in one journal entry, he asked the question "Who am I as a single?" In response, he wrote:

1. *I cry easily.*

2. *I get lonely and depressed easily.*

3. *I have trouble sleeping.*

4. *It is hard to remember the good because I hurt so badly.*

5. *I want to live my own life, not somebody else's.*

6. *I want my grieving to help me be a better person.*

7. *I want to give myself grace rather than blaming myself.*

8. *I need courage to show up and be seen.*

Though not overly optimistic, he was nonetheless honest (at least on occasion) with himself if not yet to the world in general.

The war within to accept his grieving and move on in his singleness was sincerely expressed in a journal entry on (what would have been) his fifty-first wedding anniversary, July 11, 2016. Though never the poet, his lonely heart leaped onto the page as follows:

1. *On one hand, I very much feel loss and the need to hang on to the pain.*
   On the other hand, I feel the need to move on.

2. *On one hand, I feel like a teenager in an adult skin, learning all over the meaning of life and love. On the other hand, I am caught with my grief feelings.*

3. *On one hand, I want to take care of my own emotional and social needs. On the other hand, I need a female companion.*

4. *On one hand, I feel like I am in a new chapter in my life. On the other hand, I feel like I am still stuck in the present chapter.*

5. *On one hand, I enjoy my new freedom as a single. On the other hand, I do not like to be single.*

6. *On one hand, I can handle my loneliness, lack of a companion, and lack of a marriage partner. On the other hand, these things are as hard as ever to handle.*

7. *On one hand, I feel grateful for this opportunity to reinvent myself, to have a new beginning. On the other hand, my old ways feel very comfortable.*

8. *On one hand, I want these mixed feelings to just go away. On the other hand, I would not be true to who I am if they did.*

The nonstop dichotomy within continued to boil. Though not finding cemeteries particularly nostalgic, he nevertheless finally visited Ruth's grave with Kevin and his family. After he and Kevin reflected on Ruth's life, Clayton inexplicably began to cry. He didn't plan to or really even want to. But neither did he prevent the honest flow. The grief of his loss for Ruth seamlessly flowed into his grief for Bruce, whose tombstone stood next to Ruth's. He ached and longed for them both.

Walking through his endless tears, he found his mother's tombstone. The torrent began anew. The two women he cherished most were gone. They had influenced him more than any other people on this earth. And now, their bodies lay in the earth. The realization overwhelmed him. The more he bawled, the more he hurt, and the more the conspicuous outburst cleansed his soul. He didn't understand it. But he imagined his young grandkids would remember their grandfather crying like a baby at Grandma's burial site for the rest of their lives.

A similar mysterious victory came when Kimberly helped Clayton go through Ruth's closet. He hadn't dared go through it on his own. Her things seemed sacred or too personal ... or something, he didn't know. Kimberly wisely brought out all the clothes and personal items and laid them out in the living room. The goal was to get rid of as many things as he could, but this necessary chore seemed to go against every fiber of his being. In the end, he held onto four blouses and two dresses that he found especially lovely. The process was a strange rite of passage that he couldn't explain. A few months later, he gave those remaining clothes away to a charity, which he felt was a triumphant gesture.

So often, Clayton burrowed inward, attacking his poor choices or lack of ability as leading causes to whatever unfortunate circumstances he found himself in. Such cycles of debasement usually led to regret, which led to questioning his very existence. But something was catching on because that summer he began shedding the blame, writing in his journal once:

I am who I am.

Following up on the coaching from Clarice and the books he read, he proactively pushed himself to stay busy. Though it obviously did not clear his mind of all his grief, it often lessened the painful, helpless mind-wandering considerably. Most weeks, he volunteered, doing bookkeeping for a charity called Connections. Archiving and updating the books for his church and writing another grant for the Kidron Historical Society kept him occupied for months. In his spare time, he also digitized all his siblings' memorial services. When the weather got nice, he planted roses with the help of a friend. Then, for most of June, he worked on the archives at the International Guest House. The busyness certainly helped him cope.

Probably the most valuable thing, especially as time went on, was his connection to people. He had always coveted his alone time. But being alone all the time was way too much of a good thing. He craved companionship though he didn't always know it. The advice from his counselor and books to seek help and friendship from others nudged him to open up to others more and more. His main support person, Randy, the chaplain of OrrVilla, came to his house weekly for at least an hour during the critical months. He encouraged Clayton early on to trust that Jesus was walking with him through his grief and that Jesus enjoyed hearing his sorrows and joys. Later in the year, after a visit with Randy, Clayton wrote in his journal: *I'm still grieving, but I'm starting to feel normal. If I was not grieving, I would not be human.*

He also found time for occasional breakfast meetings with different acquaintances such as his neighbor, his former pastor, the former hospice chaplain, and several other friends. They all filled in as the friend he needed at the time.

Two support groups helped him feel connected. One was a six-week course on grief, which was sponsored through hospice. The other was a men's grieving group. He also was involved in an interesting Bible study in which he was usually the only male among four widowed women.

He continued to meet with Clarice till he felt equipped enough to grieve blamelessly. She often harped on the theme that it was okay to be happy. It sounded obvious, but Clayton found all sorts of reasons to complicate that simplicity ... to which she also constantly replied, "stop overthinking." Clayton was learning that it was okay to be needy, happy, and grieving, sometimes all at the same time.

> Beemer wrote to his new supervisor: *You know, as I'm writing all of this, it strikes me that Clayton is doing a lot of things with a lot of people. Is it normal for a grieving person to be so involved and connected with people?*
>
> Maammy: Ha! Good observation. No, not really. Though, sometimes, people become so involved (so busy) that they lose their own identity. This scenario is totally opposite of the majority who become hermits and are totally wrapped up in their own pain and have nothing to do with the outside world. It sounds like your man is feeling the true feels and doing the right dos.
>
> *It's interesting that he still seems to feel alone even though he's giving himself to so many. He not only wants human*

companionship (like THE BOSS made him for), but he also puts a lot of effort into learning and seeking help. Yet, he's still suffering. What happens to those humans who don't take the proactive approach and just wallow in their grief or ignore it?

Some make it out okay, eventually. Most do not. Your man is doing a lot of things well.

That's my seeker! He'll be a hero yet, don't you think?

Careful. THE BOSS knows when you oversell something. Just write his story honestly. And remember, THE BOSS heroizes the character, not the performance.

The past identity that Clayton had enjoyed the most, perhaps even above that of *doing* a job well, was being Ruth's husband. After months of grieving the fact that he was no longer Ruth's husband and never would be again, he was finally ready to accept the alternative. It was time to move on.

Then it was time to ponder some questions. First, could he be satisfied staying single for the rest of his life? He wanted to simplify his life by saying yes. But honestly, he knew otherwise. He needed companionship … often, deeply. He needed to bounce his ideas, broken thoughts, and nonstop feelings off a caring confidant. He needed touch. He missed the everyday touching, hugging, and caressing, as well as the intimate times between a man and a woman. He had sexual needs, and that was okay!

Then, the next questions were, when and who should he marry? This brought a whole new kind of stress to his life, albeit a rather thrilling kind. Beyond the logistics of the venture were the soul-searching ethics of it all. Ruth had warned him to *be careful* when Clayton asked if he should remarry after she passed. Would he be trashing their covenant of fifty years if her "be careful" meant he shouldn't remarry if he was unsure?

How was a man of integrity to go? He wished he could ask a father who knew.

30
CHURCH MATTERS
HOLDING ON AND LETTING GO

Clayton sat in the counselor's office, somber and a little anxious. He felt ready for the next step, which is why he had made this appointment. But never having been at this crossroads before, apprehension clouded his outlook.

Clarice greeted him. "It's good to see you again. It's been, what, over a year since I last saw you?"

Clayton nodded. "Yeah, I think that's about right."

"The last time I saw you, you were in the thick of grieving Ruth's unfortunate death. She centered your whole life, as I recall. You were basically rudderless. Then, we dealt with other hardships in your life and your identity crisis. How have you navigated all of that?"

Clayton took a deep breath and attempted to smile coolly. "I took your advice and settled into the grieving process. I was in no hurry to rush it. There was a sweetness to lingering over her memories every day. Every night, I gazed at her picture and recalled all the touches she made that turned our bedroom into such a special place." His eyes watered.

"That sounds beautiful," Clarice said, brushing a strand of her golden, impeccably groomed hair from her forehead. "That must have been very healing."

"It was. I felt like we shared that lonely time together. Only she and I knew all we went through in our fifty years together—more than that, really, if you count our growing up together in the same community. It was … I don't know, bittersweet."

"So, the pain wasn't too much for you to bear?" Clarice asked. "God helped you cope, would you say?"

Clayton nodded. "God, and His people," he amended. "There were a lot of lonely nights. I missed Ruth so bad sometimes I thought I'd lose my mind. We conquered a lot of hard things in this life. We had a great family. I was rich. I am rich, having gone through all of that with Ruth."

Clarice smiled. "That's very encouraging." They held each other's gazes for a moment. "So, what brings you here today?"

Clayton said, "The last time we met, you told me there would be a time when I'd be ready to face the world on my own again."

"And has that time come?"

"Yes." Clayton nodded once. "I slowly had the desire to get out there and start my life again."

"Good. Staying home and to yourself is necessary for a time, but getting involved in other responsibilities and with other people is so critical. How do you intend to start this movement forward?"

"Well, I've already started it." Clayton looked at the counselor's intrigued expression. A little panicky, he changed his tack. "Actually, I've read some widowerhood books that encouraged me to stay active. So, I've kept up with gardening the flowers around the house that Ruth nurtured as well as planting some of my own. I think my house is the most beautiful one in the neighborhood."

Clarice said, "That's marvelous."

"Soon after Ruth's death, I returned to the International Guest House (IGH) in DC for a month to organize and digitize their historical records. Later, in 2016, I took an Amish crew with me to remodel the basement. Then, earlier this year, I went back to celebrate fifty years of IGH's existence. It was a great weekend. I made a fifty-page picture booklet of all the staff, volunteers, and board members that served IGH during those fifty years. I also gave a speech at the main event on Sunday."

"My, I'd say you fought through your grieving to pull all of that off."

"And I've taken a lot of walks, been to a lot of widow groups and a couple grieving workshops and took a trip to see all my nieces and nephews."

"That's great. How many nieces and nephews do you have?"

"Well, I have thirty, but I didn't go see the ones in Alaska and China."

Clarice's jaw dropped. "My, you have been busy! That's certainly a good start to redefining yourself."

Clayton heard his counselor's confirming tone but knew he needed to shoot straight with her. He searched for the right words. "But something's missing. It sounds bad when I say it. It feels like I shouldn't even be thinking it. But I feel, I don't know … kind of empty. Like there's got to be more to life than honoring my wife in heaven with fond memories every day." Clayton's eyes widened, and he forced himself to look into Clarice's steel-blue eyes. "Is that bad?"

Clarice said, "No. It's a normal feeling. Why would you think it's bad?"

"Because Ruth meant so much to me. If I just discard her memory, aren't I discarding her presence? Aren't I saying her love was not enough for me? It feels sacrilegious or something."

Clarice pursed her lips and frowned briefly. "When Ruth was alive, you needed to be more *present* with her. Now, you're holding onto that presence though she's not here to be present with." She paused. "Clayton, grieving is necessary. Cherishing memories is important. But don't mix the memories of Ruth with her actual presence. Ruth is gone. That is reality. You can't maintain a viable relationship with a memory."

Clayton's head dropped as he let out a breath. "I know." He sat back on the spacious sofa. "Even though her memory and the love I felt for her feels sacred, I decided I needed more."

"And what does that mean," Clarice asked, "'needed more?'"

Clayton sheepishly looked at his folded hands before he said, "I used a dating app and met someone."

The counselor jutted her sharp jaw out as her eyes widened. "Good for you. How is that going?"

"Good." Clayton winced. "I mean, she's nice. I like her. But I'm not sure if it's a good idea."

"Why is that? Are there some red flags?" Clarice tilted her head and squinted.

"No, nothing like that. At least, not about her, specifically."

Clarice's eyebrows drew together. "You sound skeptical. What's holding you back?"

Clayton took a full breath and closed his tired eyes. "I'm not sure this is right."

"Why is that?"

"I feel guilty."

"About what?"

"About marrying another woman."

"Marrying?" Clarice leaned forward. "You're getting married?"

"No! I mean ... I don't know. But we're headed down that road, it sure looks like. And I'm not sure I'm supposed to be headed this way."

The intelligent counselor narrowed her eyes and stared at her client. "Would it make you happy?"

"Probably."

"Will it make you a better man?"

"I think so."

Clarice's forehead wrinkled. "I don't think I understand. I thought you were over the heavy lifting of the grieving."

"I am ... I think. But should I be? What if Ruth didn't want me to be done with grieving over her yet?"

Clarice asked, "Would Ruth care if you got married again?"

Clayton's eyes watered. He shrugged.

"Oh," Clarice intoned with understanding. "So, you didn't discuss this with Ruth before she passed?"

Clayton tried to smile but could only manage a wayward grimace. "Well, we tried to discuss it, but all she really said was, 'be careful.' I'm not really sure what that meant. She was sick and had other things on her mind. I didn't want to force her to think about her death, so I kind of just avoided the topic."

"And now, you don't know if she'd be okay with you marrying again."

Clayton nodded.

"Would she want you to be happy?"

"Yes, but ... "

"Would you want her to marry if you had left first?"

"Of course, if she wanted to."

"Let's think about this. You want to marry; you think it would improve your life, and you wonder if that might somehow offend her? Clayton, I have no doubt that the bond you and Ruth had was some kind of special. But you need not limit your future because of it. It was real, yes. It happened. Nothing will take that from you. But the marriage is over. If she loved you as much as you think she did, don't you think she'd delight in your happiness?"

Deep in thought, Clayton pondered her wisdom.

Clarice asked, "How long did you grieve?"

"Ever since she died. Over two years ago … so far."

"That's substantial," said Clarice, nodding. "And good to note that grieving, in some sense, never ends. But at some point, one is ready to find one's own identity separate from that grieving. Remember how important our identity is? It sounds like you're there. Not too many people that I know genuinely grieve as long as you have. I'd say you honored her—are honoring her—above and beyond. And that's not to say you can't continue to honor her through another marriage. Her influence on you is forever. You wouldn't be able to forget her if you tried. And I don't see you trying. You don't need to pretend like you've forgotten her. You haven't."

Still confused, Clayton said, "That all sounds really good—to honor Ruth even if I remarry—but what do I do with everyone else and my responsibilities?"

"I don't follow."

Clayton explained, "I'd like to agree with you that this might be best for me, but I'm not sure my kids and my friends at church will see me dating a gal from another state as wonderful."

"And how will they see it?"

Clayton drew his chin up, tightening his lower lip. "I don't know. But they might think I'm being foolish. Like I'm disgracing Ruth or something."

Clarice lifted an eyebrow. "Well, you won't know until you tell them. It may be a shock to some of them, you're right. But you're not in charge of their reactions. If they love you, they'll support you, or, at least, they'll try. If they're totally against it, you'll need to explain yourself, then listen to their concerns. It may help you to have some resistance. The key is to communicate—bounce this off them. Are you a hundred percent convinced about getting remarried to this … what's her name?"

"Jeanne."

"Are you sure getting married to this Jeanne is what you're supposed to do?"

"Not positive yet, no. But I will say she's a catch. Whenever I talk to her, I feel known. I've not found many people who I enjoy being with so much and who both accept and challenge me. She's pretty awesome!"

"Then seek input from those you care about. Talk to those who have your best interest and see if they might see some aspects of your decision clearer than you do. Talk to those who have gone through this before and learn from their experience. Network your concerns, so it's not you against the world."

Clayton furrowed his brow. "That makes sense. It seems so counterintuitive though. I keep thinking I'm all alone in this. That's why I found Jeanne in the first place. I forget that I have loved ones around that still care about me. Why not use those resources?"

Beemer interjected in the side margin: *Why would Clayton want to marry again when his first marriage was near perfect?*

Maammy responded: I hardly think their marriage was perfect. Where did you come up with that notion? Does Clayton believe that?

Beemer: *Well, I know it wasn't perfect. I guess, now that I think about it, Clayton did have a lot of frustrations to contend with, especially early on in the marriage. But he tackled most of those through counseling and working at them with Ruth. After observing Ruth's funeral and hearing all the well-wishers since then, I think it's easy for Clayton to view so many people's comments on their "wonderful marriage" as doctrine—like it really was near perfection.*

Is that why he's thinking of getting married? Deep down, he knows the marriage wasn't perfect, and he wants to improve on what he had?

On the contrary! I think he thinks it was wonderful and he misses the special bond he had with Ruth so much that he wants to recapture that hopeful sense of matrimony.

But could he ever find anyone as good for him as Ruth?

Wrong question. Regardless of the answer, a second marriage can potentially be a marvelous thing. Will it take work? Yes. Will it be worth it? Maybe—only if she is a good match, they mutually want it badly enough, and they're both willing to put in the work. It could be an over-the-moon experience, but it may end tragically. It is a risk. How adventurous is he?

Beemer didn't know. But he liked the prospect of Clayton being adventurous … like William Clark. Or, come to think of it, like his great grandpa C. B. Steiner. Beemer had never really considered the connection before, but through Clayton's research, he remembered Clayton learning of his great-grandfather's amazing trek out west at the age of sixty-nine. He sold all his goods, gave up the pastorate he had faithfully served for over thirty years, and said goodbye to his farming livelihood to move his family to Oregon (before cars!) in 1875. Now that was adventurous! Beemer recalled many adventurous Steiners in Clayton's ancestry. He only hoped that such a spirit would kick in with Clayton.

Clayton brought his finger to his lips, searching for what to say next. "Umm … what about routines and responsibility? Would it be good for a man my age to up and leave all of that and begin new routines and things all over again?"

His counselor raised her brow, displaying her probing eyes. "You're using drastic language here." She looked at her notes. "You're seventy-five now. You sound like you're cutting all human ties and moving to Mars. Why don't you break it down for me a little here? Tell me your concerns and what you mean about routines."

Taking a full breath, Clayton looked around the delicately adorned room without seeing any of it. "All the things I do every day to help me organize and stay settled. I'm a creature of habit. I need routine, or I go a little nuts. In the past, I'd get out of sorts when I'd get thrown off my routine of doing the same things at the same time every day, like putting the coffee on, having my prayer time, drinking my coffee, having devotions, eating breakfast, reading the news, and catching up on my emails. Those are things I basically do every day. When I don't do them, it kind of upsets my equilibrium. If I got married, all my routines would change. Would that be good for me? Or am I just asking for trouble?"

"Well, Clayton, that depends on your perspective. If you're committed to your (she hunted for the right term) *intricate* routines and convinced you can't alter them, you'd better stay single. But taking charge of one's life and where it's heading is more important than the security of habitual defaults. If you find the treasure of shared needs in a committed relationship, your pet routines probably won't mean as much as you think they do. Knowing you, you'll just find new ones. Sometimes, doing fresh, new things in our lives can free us from our stale patterns. It's like a kid riding a bike for the first time. Life is suddenly a new adventure worth going after with zeal."

Clayton nodded, liking the word picture. "What about the responsibilities and commitments I'm a part of?"

Clarice asked, "Like what?"

"Like my church and the Kidron Historical Society. In a way, they define who I am. Is it alright to just walk away from those? Wouldn't that be really bad for me ... and them?"

Clarice sat back, her tongue exploring her back molars. "Clayton, it's been a while. I don't think I can answer that without a little more background information. Perhaps it's time for you to tell me about your spiritual journey, particularly your personal history with the church. This will help me know what you're thinking. Sometimes, when we pursue God through the religious systems of church, we can get a little stuck in our thinking. From as early as you can remember, what's your experience with the church been like?"

Clayton looked back at her for a long moment. After closing his eyes to retrieve his memories, he said, "My dad taught me to obey and go to church. I knew that before I could walk, I think."

The trained psychologist immediately began writing something down on her notepad.

Clayton went on to explain how they went to church whenever the doors were open when he was a child, how his dad never let them speak ill of the church or the pastor, how his dad forced him and his siblings to listen to his awful, demeaning devotions twice a day, and how he wasn't to associate with people from other, wayward, Mennonite churches.

Not being from a Mennonite background, Clarice wanted to know what it was like being Mennonite but not associating with certain other Mennonites.

Clayton explained that it was difficult as a kid not "crossing the road from their grade school because they would be on the bad church's property," and how he "couldn't talk to certain kids from those congregations." The bishop of the Mother Church lived on the property adjacent to him and their families never spoke to each other. It had seemed normal until he met some respectable Christians from other churches, notably in Algeria and through Bruce's death. He slowly saw that God was never in such shunning. But, he hadn't known better then. He believed his dad and trusted and liked his bishop, Reuben Hofstetter, who fell in step with such rude shenanigans.

When Clayton was sixteen, in 1957, the next most influential mentor, Bill Detweiler, became a part of the Kidron Mennonite pastoral staff. His solid leadership and charismatic style grew the church from four hundred members to eight hundred at its peak. Bill built bridges with the other churches, the community, and non-Mennonites like no other.

Clarice set her pad on her lap. "Without going into too much detail, bring me up-to-date with how you were specifically involved in your local church."

Clayton hardly knew where to begin. He chose to share his involvement with the numerous small groups he participated in and led and how that was where the church connected like a family.

Clarice interjected, "So, this family concept was important to you even at church. How long did you participate in small groups?"

Clayton thought about that a moment. "Well, from 1979, when we arrived back here, through about 2013 when Ruth and I were mentoring a young couple's group before she got sick. Then, we had to back off.

"This past year, I helped the other leaders revive that group. Though I was still grieving, I began to learn how to function as a single in a couples' world. The group did a great job of accepting me though I felt like the odd man out."

Clarice scribbled on her pad. "What other ways were you involved at church?"

Clayton shared the numerous committees he had been on and led—the Witness and Service Committee, the Gift Discernment Committee, the Constitutional Revision Committee, and the Seventy-fifth Church Anniversary Committee, to name a few. When a job needed doing or a situation needed attending to, the Mennonite Church assigned a committee to it. That's how their cogs turned.

Clayton then described the mission trips he had volunteered on, the few sermons he had given, his satisfying term as secretary of the board minutes, and even a Sunday School he had led that touched on taboo and sensitive topics such as homosexuality, war, tithing, and so on.

Clarice looked up from her notes. "Is there anything else you want to add about your robust involvement in your church?"

"No."

Clarice grinned. "Okay. Well, you certainly are dedicated to your church. It's a wonder you had time for anything else."

"There is something else," Clayton broke in.

Clarice's mouth hinged open. She cleared her throat. "Okay."

"Not with church. But I did have time for something else. I've been involved in my community too."

Clarice slowly nodded. "Oh, yes. You mentioned community responsibilities." She settled back in her high-backed chair, took a deep breath, and said, "Go ahead," pen to her pad.

In 1994, he had promoted and acted in a play, *Unto These Hills*, written by some local writers, which encapsulated Kidron's past. His knowledgeable enthusiasm was noticed and appreciated, and later landed him a position on the board of the Kidron Historical Society. A few years later, he became the treasurer, which he excelled at, as bookkeeping had been an interest and skill of his since his high-school days.

The first thing he did as treasurer was update the archaic system by digitizing the books using Quicken software. In 2006, years after he had retired to volunteer at the Guest House in DC, he fielded several calls from the board president, eliciting advice for the books and direction for the society.

While on the Historical Society board, Clayton helped implement two major projects. First, they erected an awesome Heritage Center in the heart of Kidron, using Ruth's relocated childhood family farmhouse. Clayton spent many hours preparing the building and being a docent upon its opening. The main and most expensive attraction in the museum was Clayton's dad's curly maple secretary desk. Presently, Clayton was writing a twenty-some-page article on the history of the house in honor of Ruth and all the work she put into the project.

The Society also created the Sonnenberg Village near Clayton's family homestead. They moved six original buildings, including a blacksmith shop and the old Sonnenberg Church, onto the premises. Clayton raised over $100,000.00 in grants for the Village.

To commemorate the Sonnenberg one-room schoolhouse that Homer and all Clayton's siblings attended, which had closed in 1950, Clayton organized a reunion for all former students and their significant others in 2014. Of the forty-six living alumni, twenty-nine attended, coming from as far as Texas and Kansas. Four of Clayton's six remaining siblings attended and shared many a heartfelt story. Clayton's brother Roy surprisingly shared the most and the most comically. Clayton felt wonderful about the uplifting reminiscing that occurred at his behest.

Clarice stopped scribbling. She locked eyes with Clayton. "I can see why you'd want to stay put. You've put a lot into your church and community. I imagine it would be extremely difficult if you were to pit a future love of your life against all the encouraging involvements you're into."

Clayton winced. "Except they're not all encouraging."

Clarice's eyes widened. "Oh? What's not encouraging?"

"Well, I've been kind of seen as the rebel at church."

The counselor's forehead sunk, narrowing her examining eyes. "Is that a rebel with a cause … or just a rebel?"

Clayton gave a painful smirk. He sighed deeply. "Good question. I thought I always had a cause. I tried to be as diplomatic as I could in various church meetings, trying to share my views of scripture and what I saw as God's heart. But many looked upon me as *liberal*, as if that were a dirty word. I think the mainstream majority thought I didn't have a cause ... other than to stir up trouble and be some sort of extremist."

"You don't strike me as an extremist."

"I'm not. But some of these people view the Bible differently than I do. I feel their literal interpretation does not allow for a loving God to accept and encourage all people. They are re-enacting the Kidron split of 1936 all over again from my point of view."

Clarice frowned and ducked her chin back.

Clayton realized he needed to explain his understanding of how the Kidron church had split away from the mother church so long ago and the dismal consequences it wrought. After explaining that, he shared how he just now was learning to love people from other denominations and Mennonite affiliations. That distrusting, hateful, elitist attitude had wreaked miserable effects on his life and, near as he could tell, everyone else's lives. This was why he felt so compelled to speak out against the two main areas of contention.

"And what areas were they," asked Clarice.

"Homosexuality and conference affiliation."

An eyebrow raised on Clarice's typically stoic veneer. "You're for or against homosexuality?"

"I'm for allowing people to love who and how they want with no strings attached and not treating them like they're diseased because of their love tendencies."

Clarice nodded. "That's reasonable. Certainly not extremist for most of society these days."

"Exactly. And it's the stance our Mennonite conference is openly discussing."

"So, the *mainstream* in this case may part ways with the Mennonite church?"

Clayton nodded sadly.

"And what do you think?" Clarice asked.

"I love being a Mennonite and think we should stay the course. The Mennonite/Anabaptist emphasis has always been military nonresistance, a strong sense of community, and service, all things I see in the gospels and other writings of the New Testament. I think this unique approach should be embraced, not stifled. But the church can't serve those they don't accept."

"Curious. So, have your siblings gone down a similar path?"

"Well, not so much on these issues. Interestingly, of the eleven children of Homer and Bertha Steiner, I'm the only one that stayed in the home church of our parents. But you should note that all of us have been active in our churches wherever we were living. My oldest brother, Elno, was a Mennonite pastor for over forty years; Arlene was a Mennonite pastor's wife for over thirty years; Lee sang in several Mennonite choirs; and Vi attended a Mennonite-related church all her life. All the other siblings were active members of various denominations. Nearly all of the next generation are active churchgoers too, several as missionaries and pastors.

"I feel blessed and thankful for the religious heritage of my parents and the privilege of serving the Mennonite Church in Voluntary Service for more than seven years. I make no apology for being a Mennonite. Despite my hiccups with the church over the years, its unique emphasis squares with my beliefs. Kidron Mennonite has enriched my life. It met my social needs, helped rear my kids, and utilized my giftings as a Sunday school teacher, historian, and secretary. Many a Sunday, I came away well fed!" Clayton looked out the window, melancholy.

"And now?"

"And now … it seems like *I'm* the one going against the grain, the enemy of the majority. To be true to who I am and who I think God is, I stand for what I think is right. Then, we fight. I love them and I think they love me. But I don't like fighting."

"Clayton, are you trying to worship the church or God?"

Clayton grimaced at the absurd question.

Clarice said, "Church is a structure. It is a tool to serve and praise God. It's not God himself. Sometimes, separating the two brings clarity. Sometimes, distancing from one may draw you closer to the other."

The weight on Clayton's heart lightened. Yet, to even consider that his lifelong relationship with his home church might be ending wrenched his mind.

The conversation stalled. Clarice broke the silence. "Clayton, it sounds like you're also fighting something else. You want to keep the good things the way they are but move away from the bad things. But, sometimes, you've got to make a clean break from both to progress. Your fight is with staying or going."

"You mean with the church?"

"Well, yes, but also with staying true to your lifelong commitment to Ruth or going with the best life you can live today. Is your life static, unyielding to change? Or is change inevitable and necessary for health and well-being? The battle is on."

Clayton's eyes closed and his shoulders slumped. Reluctantly, he finally said, "But what if I'm just using the uncomfortable feelings at church as an excuse to leave and start a new life with Jeanne?"

"What if you stay and your life becomes more miserable? Maybe this is your answer. As painful as leaving your home church would be—the church you've given so much of your time, energy, and heart to—maybe joining Jeanne in a new direction is your solution."

Clayton's body froze, and his heart began racing.

Did these physical reactions mean such a move was wrong, and his fear was rightfully kicking in? Or was he just amazed and excited that God had worked things out so magnificently?

He left Clarice's office, hoping and praying it was the latter.

31
WHO'S AT FAULT?
ANGER FLESHED OUT

Back at the counselor's office a week later, Clayton told Clarice, "I think I've decided that Jeanne is God's answer to my prayers—both for my companion needs and for my need to exit my church."

Clarice smiled. "Good for you! Has that freed you up?"

"Yes." Clayton returned his therapist's smile. But then, he couldn't help but add, "My only concern is that I'm doing this too quick. I'm not used to making such a huge decision based on my emotions. Trying not to over-think it, I keep asking myself, should I, or shouldn't I?"

Clarice nodded. "Going with the heart is difficult when you've decided with only your mind most of your life. This is not the first time I've heard you use *should* and *shouldn't*. Sometimes, it's not so much a matter of should or shouldn't, as *want*. You can want things, you know. That's allowed in this life. Do you want to be with Jeanne?"

"More and more every day. My longing is almost embarrassing."

Clarice chuckled. "Clayton, you don't need to be so disciplined that you become a machine, devoid of desires. You aren't a naughty little boy in constant need of his father's direction and correction due to willful defiance … are you?"

Clayton froze. His unblinking eyes held fixed on the family photo of Clarice's wholesome family on her desk. He recalled the painful kick to his shins by his father under the table during those awful devotions when he was only three years old. Tears welled in his eyes.

The veteran psychologist saw the visceral reaction. "Clayton? Tell me what's going on."

"My dad ... " The tears fell freely. He couldn't finish his thought.

Clarice nodded imperceptibly. "At the beginning of explaining your church experience," she looked at her notepad, "you said, 'My dad taught me to obey and go to church.' I sense there's some underlying pain in this. Why don't you start there and help me try and understand where you're coming from?"

Clayton wiped his sodden face and looked away. Eventually, he said, "I thought I was over this. But it keeps coming back. My first counselor helped me realize that I had a deep anger problem concerning my dad. Then, when the anger kept rearing its ugly head, I had to spend time on it again with a different counselor—Floyd. I discovered that my dad laid out a horrible worldview for me—one that convinced me that I was only as loved as how well I performed.

"But as hard as I tried, all my life, I couldn't obey well enough to get my dad to express his love for me or show his pride in me. Sure, I made mistakes and rebelled like any kid does. But I was a pretty straight arrow when it came right down to it, especially as I got older. I did everything like my brothers Elno and Marion would have. Better, in some cases, just like my dad wanted. Served in the church and on behalf of the church, just like he preached. I even dedicated a family heritage book I wrote in his honor. Did I ever get praised for any of this? Did he ever even mention it? No! You'd have thought my whole life was a waste, judging by his lack of acknowledgment."

"That must have hurt," said Clarice.

"Yes, it did. It made me angry. But I didn't even know how angry it made me until my counselor brought it to my attention. He called it my "burying my dad's approval crisis." I was having marriage difficulties and had a bad job attitude and had no idea my anger was at the root of much of that. I just bottled the bitterness of my dad's unfair treatment inside me like a personal torture chamber, too intimate to make known to anyone, even myself."

"Did the revelation of the power your dad's unjust treatment held over you change you? Did you see the world differently?"

Clayton thought about that a moment. "Well, yes and no. I grew up thinking I was never enough. It helped to know that that was faulty thinking. But I don't think it really helped me get over the hump of getting rid of the anger. I thought I could only feel good about myself if I did things right and well, which I couldn't always do because I'm not perfect. If anything, understanding all of this made me even angrier at my dad. I spent a lot of time fuming over all the ways he made me feel insignificant and how I never felt safe or noticed."

"So, have you held all that anger in up to now?"

Clayton said, "Well, kind of, I guess. I basically let go of it for a while there. When Bruce died, I realized how precious life was. My priorities changed; I think. Instead of focusing on all the love my dad didn't give me, I think I focused more on the love I did have with my wife and my kids and all my friends. The church body came through a hundredfold in that. My dad's rejection conveniently seemed insignificant."

Clarice said, "So, you thought you had put that part of your life behind you."

Nodding, Clayton took a tentative breath. "Pretty much. Then, more often than I care to admit, that anger at feeling stupid from his insensitive belittling comes back and sets me off. Even my natural disposition of processing things slowly makes me feel less than I'm supposed to. It doesn't take much for me to instantly become moody, depressed, then defeated from feeling inept. I hate it!"

Clarice gently nodded her head. "You know, it's fairly common for people to perceive their heavenly father's view of them in the same way their earthly father views them."

Clayton winced. Horrified, he closed his eyes, hoping to close off the oncoming rush of emotions. He could not. His tears turned into sobs. The onslaught was uncontrollable. Embarrassed and shaken, Clayton could not control the ensuing storm.

His supportive counselor gave him all the time he needed. When his waterworks were but a drip, she said, "When you're ready, tell me what scared you so much about comparing God to your dad."

418

The tears fell afresh. Finally, Clayton said, "If I see God like I see my dad, that would mean I'll never get close to Him. I can't think of a worse thing."

"That's scary alright," Clarice agreed. "Was there anything you appreciated about your dad?"

Clayton said by rote, "He taught me how to work hard."

The counselor and the patient looked at one another, both waiting for further discussion. When none came, Clayton said, "I respected my dad, but to be honest, I think I felt more hate for him than love." Tears trickled down again. "Do you think I hate God?"

Clarice smiled soothingly. "No, I don't. I think you love Him so much that you fall apart at the thought of not loving Him."

Clayton wiped his reddened eyes again. "I never felt like a full man in my dad's eyes. I think I felt more like my mother when he looked at me."

"And what was your mother like?"

"My mother was accepting, tender, and caring. I was always more empathetic, like her. That made me confused, wondering if I was more like a woman or a man."

The wise counselor said, "Or more like God?"

Clayton lifted his downtrodden head. He wanted to bathe himself with those words. But he was afraid.

Clarice asked, "How did your dad's passing affect you?"

Clayton closed his mouth. "Like I said last time, his death was kind of at the start of my midlife crisis … er, uh, I mean, my identity crisis. I didn't take it real good."

"I vaguely remember you not wanting to share much about it. Please fill me in."

Clayton said, "I cried like a baby at his funeral."

"That's understandable."

"No, it's not." Clayton sounded more authoritative than he planned. He cleared his throat. "What I mean is, I didn't cry because I missed him. I cried because I would never know his approval or feel his fatherly love. My longing would *never* be met. So, along with him that day, I buried my hopes of ever being his appreciated son, the man I longed to be."

"That must have been lonely."

Clayton nodded. "Yeah, I think I tried extra hard after he died to prove my worth to those I admired—my bosses, my coworkers, my pastors, my influential friends … It got to be exhausting. I think I eventually realized that I didn't have to earn their love. There were plenty of people in my life who loved me just for being me. Unconditional love is much better than conditional love."

"I can't argue with that," Clarice agreed.

"Sometimes I wonder, though," Clayton continued, "all those years when I was seeking praise from my dad and from anyone in authority really, was I a big phony? As a Christian, I'm supposed to major in humility. Was I just serving the church for status and place—to be noticed and appreciated? Sometimes, I wonder if all my church service was a waste of time, me being selfish and the church being a critical institution."

Wearing her imagined judge's hat, the therapist said, "I'm sure not all your motives were pure. And I know the church is flawed. But your service was not for the church. It was for real people with real needs. I don't care how messed up you may or may not have been, your service made a difference in people's lives. It doesn't get much more Christ-like than that."

Clayton gave a half-chuckle, trying his best to accept the praise.

Clarice scratched her scalp. "So, were you ever able to put your dad's failure to be the dad he could have and should have been to rest after you buried him?"

Clayton's breathing became uneasy. "Not really. I thought I did. I planned to. I tried to. But my anger and hatred just seemed to grow." He looked down at the floor, then up to his counselor briefly before staring back at the nondescript carpet. His pulse was racing, and he could hardly breathe. He didn't want to share what was bottled up inside him, but he couldn't contain the pressure any longer. He finally just let it all out. "That anger was at its all-time high when I learned about his … inappropriate behavior with my sister." He looked up to his counselor's rapt attention. Clayton wanted to run.

As delicately as possible for such an explosive topic, the two fulfilled their uncomfortable roles as inquisitor and informer. The counselor asked her perceptive questions with grace and respect. Clayton answered as forthrightly and fairly as he could.

The long and short of it was that a couple of years after Homer died, one of Clayton's sisters received some inner healing. Through her freeing experience, she remembered some unsightly memories from her childhood—memories that included her dad's unwanted advances and a somehow knowable image of another sister possibly overpowered by his forced aggressions. That first sister called another sister; together, they approached the third sister about possible sexual abuse perpetrated by their father—a horrendous accusation they both, regrettably, sensed had happened.

The sister initially denied all allegations. But upon further probing, she finally broke down and disclosed the repeated incest, how she couldn't stop it, and couldn't tell anyone about it. With little to no animosity toward her dad, she said she was glad that, if it had to be anybody, it was her, so no one else would need to go through such shame.

Her dad (Clayton's dad!) had preyed on the innocence of his daughter! He lived his life like he was above it all, preaching to his family how they should live righteous lives, "not lazy and ungodly like the Zuerchers." Everything about that was despicable in Clayton's eyes!

"Yours is a hurting, hateful anger," Clarice confided, "that will take an army of God's angels to fight."

Clarice then proceeded to help Clayton navigate the murky waters, picking up where the counselors before her had led him in his forgiveness for, and freedom from, his dad's missteps. Each step Clayton took in his recovery drew him closer to the man he longed to be.

The tricky part had always been to find the right people to confide his confusion, anger, and disappointment to and who not to. Certainly, not everyone needed to know this horrific story, heaping onto the victims' remorse. The victim, in this case, was not only the specifically exploited sister but the entire family that had to bear the shame of their father's incomprehensible actions.

> Beemer wrote to his new editor: *Clayton has sure tried his best to not share this terrible story with just anyone. Is that necessary? I mean, it happened. Why not let everyone know the truth? Wouldn't it help people to understand him better? I'm afraid, like so often in his life, he's way too good at stuffing the uncomfortable things, only for them to come out sideways in the end.*

Maammy responded: While stuffing his emotions is no way to deal with his painful past, to share this situation willy-nilly with just anyone could affect his siblings. That's really not fair because the atrocious actions of their father were not their fault, and they shouldn't be required to justify, condemn, or even explain his inappropriate behavior.

It sounds obvious that it's not their fault. But I don't think Clayton believes that. I think somehow he feels the blame for his dad's behavior. This is so unfair.

I'm sure you're right. And the burden of such unwarranted shame no doubt weighs him down more than he knows. Let's hope he can see the false accusation pit he's fallen into and THE BOSS's escape route to climb out of it.

I'd also like to note I see your compassion for your subject. Instead of trying so hard to make him look impressive, you're identifying with his struggle. That's growth!

Thanks. I'm trying.

Clarice looked at Clayton after his confession. "Clayton, do you feel responsible for how your dad acted?"

"What do you mean?"

"I mean, your dad was not perfect, obviously. Yet, I get this impression that it was your life goal to honor him as if he were perfect. So, when you hear about or remember his faults, do you conjure up excuses for him, so he can still be worthy of honor? Is it up to you to make his life reputable?"

Clayton gave his deer-in-the-headlights stare.

"Let me ask you this," Clarice went on, "was the relationship between your mom and dad one that you admired and wanted to emulate?"

"Not in a million years." Clayton shook his head. "I wish!"

"I sense some anger. Do I sense some regret?"

Clayton jumped on the question. "Of course, I wish it was different! I've wished all my life it was better. But it was utterly dis … " He tried again, "dis … "

Clarice helped him out, "Dysfunctional?"

"Yes, dysfunctional. And nothing could change that, no matter what."

Her elbow on her forearm, Clarice rested her chin on her thumb. "'No matter what … you did?"

"Right!" Clayton nodded.

"You do realize, don't you, that your parents' dysfunction was not your fault?"

Clayton returned a blank, questioning glare.

Clarice said, "You were the child. They were the adults, in charge of their choices and their actions. There wasn't a thing you could do to change their insufficiencies because their dysfunction wasn't your fault."

The hidden ache in Clayton's heart suddenly became exposed. Painful to the touch, the sore felt oddly, miraculously soothed. The unspoken shame of his parents' incompatibility was finally addressed and … appropriately categorized. Their actions, their inadequacies, their misdeeds belonged to them—not him! The startling truth hugged him like his mother's love.

> Beemer wrote to his editor: *Wow! Were Clayton and his counselor reading our correspondence? Finally, the right notes are played to lighten Clayton's soul from that torturous sense of responsibility for his dad's mistakes.*

> Maammy: Yep! I guess we know a little how THE BOSS must feel when humans recognize Truth and use it to make their lives better.

> *Do you think this will wipe out all the guilt and shame he feels for not intervening in his parents' relationship and saving his mother from his dad's relentless accusations?*

It's a good start. Taking the guilt of his mere existence as the cause of his dad's abusive actions out of the equation is huge.

Will Clayton be able to completely forgive his dad now and move on?

Yes, if he's patient and willing to work at it.

Did you notice this eye-opening freedom occurred only after he fully divulged his dad's shameful behavior? There's something to be said for facing one's demons, fears, and untruths.

I hadn't thought of it like that before. These humans are a complicated bunch. Doesn't this kind of make a mockery of the whole "trusting authority" thing, though? I mean, here Clayton was, trying to obey, honor, and impress his dad all his life—just like he was taught—just like he did to all authority. Then, come to find out, the whole gig of obeying his dad above all else was a fool's errand. Who's to say which authority deserves obedience? Maybe none of them do.

This should certainly show Clayton the importance of questioning his loyalty to authority and lessen his exhausting impulse to impress them. But at the end of the day, if an authority is proven trustworthy (through personal experience, other's trusted references, and dogged accountability), Clayton will be much better off trusting good authority than mistrusting all, though the process can be confusing.

Clayton left the counseling session, drained. The gamut of emotions he felt had penetrated him as no prior session had. He felt ravaged but empowered.

As the weeks moved on, the epiphany of his innocence regarding his parents' shortcomings (particularly his dad's hypocritical missteps) gave him peace, hope, and confidence. He wondered why he had been carrying the burden of their strife as his own for so long. Why hadn't he untethered from this damaging assumption thirty years ago? The unanswered query wearied his soul. He only hoped that, somehow, others would learn from his slow grasp of such an imprisoning impairment.

> Beemer asked Maammy in the margin: *Do other humans get trapped thinking they're to blame for how their parents behave?*

> Maammy: I'm afraid humans get stuck thinking they're at fault for many things they have no control over. Most have no idea they're entwined in flawed logic. Worse yet, many who sense something is off in their judgment don't have the tools to diagnose and correct the problem. If one's initial environment never taught them to look for problems or how to find solutions for misguided thinking, the chance of that person overcoming their issues by themself is slim.

> *But Clayton's upbringing didn't teach him to look for such incongruencies or encourage him to look for help through counseling. In fact, most of his family and church peers looked down on such instruction. Clayton figured most people from his environment thought only crazy people went to counseling, and those that did go were, at best, being tempted by worldly psychologists and straying from God's Word. Though he gained a great deal of perspective, and therefore strength, from most of his therapy, he dared not share his time "on the couch" with too many people lest they label him as disturbed or secular.*

> *So, was he just lucky that he benefited from professional counseling, or was this a heroic act that sets him apart from his community? Do you think THE BOSS will be proud of him?*

There you go labeling again. I think the fruit of his actions answers itself. Clayton's uphill swim to seek wise counsel definitely paid off. But THE BOSS doesn't need you to label Clayton's actions as heroic to know he is valued. Discover and interpret does not mean you tell THE BOSS how to think. Discover Clayton's changes and interpret how he's grown. No more, no less.

32

OPENING UP

RISK AND ADVENTURE

Beemer wrote to his editor in the side margin: *It looks like Clayton has opened himself up to see what's on the other side of widowerhood. I'm all for him being adventurous, as you know, but is it possible he's being a bit too risky? He could get himself into a lot of trouble if he's not careful. Wouldn't it be safer just to stay single and be involved in his church and community like a good little faithful servant?*

Maammy wrote back: Of course, it would. But love is an amazing thing. If he follows its beckoning wisely, the payoff could be tenfold. Then again, it could lead to heartache if he's unwise. Time will tell. But life is meant to be lived. Might as well take the risk and live it!

As much as Beemer wanted to find fault in his superior's logic, he found himself agreeing with her wholeheartedly and pictured Clayton rescuing a damsel in distress.

Before Clayton met Jeanne, he strategically navigated the widower-toward-companionship scene as best he could. Which, to Clayton, felt both noble and novel—and a lot of awkward. The phrase, "fish out of water," came to his mind on more than one occasion. He didn't necessarily know what kind of companion he wanted, for example: what she should look like, what type of personality she should have, and other details. He just knew he needed a companion.

Life in its grieving state, as difficult as it was to maneuver the uncomfortable feelings of loss and aloneness, eventually offered a sense of calm through the comfort of routines and a steady schedule. But it also got boring! And the loneliness never lessened but grew in intensity. So, he finally decided to take the bull by the horns and change his circumstances ... or at least try to.

The first alternative was to look in his own backyard. Not literally, of course, but it made sense to discover who was available in Kidron before looking all over the country. The few options he observed were either not his cup of tea, or he was not the sugar they needed in theirs.

The next logical step was to attend several local Wayne County Singles Club meetings. Options were limited and the possibilities too questionable. So, he broadened his scope and attended the Cleveland Singles Club. Though he finally got some bites in the form of emails and pictures, the women's reasons for being in the club and their general outlook on life differed too vastly from his to consider seriously following up on their leads.

Frustrated at his inefficiency in finding a compelling prospect, his daughter Kimberly came to the rescue. She saw how clunky the Cleveland Singles website was and suggested he up his game by subscribing to eHarmony, a much more versatile and efficient dating app via the Internet (a relatively new technology for Clayton's generation, but one he became unusually adept at). To use it effectively, he needed to express his personality, outlook on life, needs, and desires in what the website called a profile. He enjoyed the introspective challenge and opportunity to organize his intentions in answering eHarmony's profile questions. His non-negotiables, he decided, were that the person had to be a female Christian, of similar age, and open to new ideas. Now, instead of randomly looking for a suitable partner via looks and a greeting encounter, the app cut out all those who didn't suit his profile and found all those in the system who matched his major requirements.

eHarmony soon gathered around one hundred names of women in Ohio and Indiana for his perusal. He quickly narrowed those down to a dozen and began communicating with them over the Web. After some key obser-vations, he decreased the field to five. The pick of the litter soon became Jeanne Belote from Elkhart, Indiana. They chose each other's profiles on November 26, 2017. Jeanne had hopped on the website just for the weekend, exercising their *free* promotion. Sometimes being at the right place at the right time pays off!

They chose to email each other outside of the eHarmony app. Before they knew it, they were writing pages—frequently. For Clayton, she checked all the boxes, and she seemed genuinely interested in him. He just had to meet this gem!

Clayton suggested they meet for coffee in Elkhart on December 4 when he would be on his way to see Kevin in Indy. She readily agreed. The ren-dezvous turned out splendidly. They each told their stories.

Jeanne's husband of ten years had died a year before. She had one child, Stephanie, aged thirty-nine. Before retirement, Jeanne had led a solid nursing career, specializing in wound care, and had given many seminars and consultations. Losing seventy percent of the hearing in her right ear had resulted in a cochlear implant a year prior to meeting Clayton, and she used a hearing aid in the left ear. She was scheduled to undergo surgery for other issues the following day. None of these physical issues particularly scared Clayton because he was so drawn by her interested demeanor. It was obvious that she genuinely cared for people.

Clayton was taken that they both came from large families. While Clayton was the baby of eleven children, Jeanne was the second oldest in a family of nine, much like Clayton's esteemed sister Arlene. He saw a similar nurturing personality in Jeanne.

At one point, Clayton touched Jeanne's arm as a kindly gesture. Later, Jeanne recalled how that touch awakened her heart.

> Beemer wrote in the margin: *What an odd thing. Why would she be so influenced by a touch? And why was he so enamored with her caring disposition? He met with three other women on this trip, and they all had intriguing personalities too, or they could have been interesting if he'd delved into their stories a bit more. It was like there was zero mojo going on with them.*

But with Jeanne, he picked up this unrelenting harmony. Is the melody of love always this irrational?

Maammy wrote: Ha! You're not going to figure out why these humans fall in love. I've seen people fall in love for the craziest reasons. In this instance, Clayton's initial environment held a lot of dos and don'ts and harsh criticism from his dad. Anything smacking of that, he wants to stay clear of. Perhaps, the other ladies displayed some authoritarian or rule-structure influences that turned Clayton off. What felt the safest and most life-giving to Clayton when he lived at home was his mother's caring love. Jeanne's wafting that in spades, it appears.

Beemer was, again, awestruck with his editor's insight. He didn't care much for her unprofessional manner, but she sure understood these humans more than he did. Maybe, just maybe, he could be more caring like her.

That visit fueled Jeanne and Clayton's mutual interest even more. The emails deepened, and the phone calls began. Sometimes, the calls lasted over two hours. They enjoyed sharing their life stories and learning about each other.

Clayton shared his dating adventures with his kids. Ironically, their response was initially the same as their mother's—*be careful*. This time, Clayton understood their intentions and appreciated their concern. They were not suggesting his motives were wrong, but rather that he not make avoidable mistakes in judgment. "Be careful, cautious, and pick wisely," was their consensus. Each did not want Clayton to try and replace their mother. Their main concern was that he did not get hurt. Clayton appreciated their hearts for him. It encouraged him to feel safe, loved, and free to enjoy the dating process.

As Clayton thought about his family's concerns, he was reminded of the tumultuous years his boys had gone through when they each went through divorce. As their parent, he had hoped they would work through the issues and make their marriages work. But, after it became obvious that wasn't going to happen, he had ached for their losses. He had struggled not to be judgmental, and while not always successful, he had, in the end, chosen to love his boys through the agony they experienced. He knew, now, that his family was trying to help him avoid that kind of pain.

> Beemer wrote in the margin: *I can't imagine THE BOSS was too impressed with Clayton's wimpy hands-off approach here.*

> Maammy: On the contrary. Your man just took the high road! He loved his boys the best way possible under the unfortunate circumstances.

Beemer smarted from the rebuff at first, then he delighted to think that THE BOSS delighted in Clayton. Was he, Beemer, overthinking this hero thing?

Clayton accepted Jeanne's invitation to spend New Year's with her in Elkhart. He was thrilled to learn of their mutual interest in church involvement and serving others. Wanting to rejoice with her through her triumphs and help her through her struggles became a natural inclination, he found. And to think the reverse would be true encouraged him beyond his dreams. Just maybe, this marriage thing could work again.

He often thought of Ruth and the special bond they had forged. Wanting to duplicate it, yet longing for a fresh new adventure, he struggled with how to proceed accordingly many a night.

Slowly, through his many encounters with Jeanne, his fears began to fall away. In his journal, Clayton wrote:

1. *Jeanne is enlarging my heart. I can love her like I did Ruth. My heart can hold Jeanne in my arms and heart without shame, guilt, or reservation.*

2. *I am entering a new chapter in my life. I am ready to close the last chapter.*

3. *Ruth's death has released me from the marriage bond. In the eyes of the state and the church, I am no longer married and can enter another marriage without remorse or regret.*

Jeanne visited Clayton in Kidron on January 8, 2018. She seemed to genuinely enjoy the visit and told Clayton she regarded his Mennonite heritage as a plus.

Clayton loved that Jeanne warmed the hearts of those around her and how she made friends everywhere she went. He found himself entering into more conversations than he had in years, and he found that his social stigma of feeling slow and awkward lessened when Jeanne was around. Often, she deferred to Clayton when asked a question she could answer, bolstering Clayton's confidence.

In true Clayton fashion, they separately wrote out what they wanted in a new partner and marriage, and then they compared notes. Clayton wrote:

1. *Honesty in our feelings and dealings with each other.*

2. *To continue to be able to pursue our own creativity and paths.*

3. *That both can take full responsibility for their own lives; that is, to be comfortable in our own skins.*

4. *I want to add value to a new partner's life.*

5. *I want a new partner to be open to new adventures, be curious, and be a lifelong learner.*

6. *To be financially independent.*

Jeanne wrote what she wanted from a new mate:

1. *A listening ear: on daily happenings, my sorrows and successes, and my broader family concerns.*

2. *A social mate: going out to events, visiting friends and family, and hosting friends together.*

3. *Support in making decisions: making major decisions as equal partners and support in making small decisions.*

4. *Discussion partner: being open to new ideas and being a lifelong learner.*

5. *Stay healthy and fit: taking care of self in eating habits, weight, and related health issues, and doing exercises.*

6. *Making major purchases together.*

7. *Keeping assets separate but pooling income and daily expenses to pay the bills.*

The similarities and nuanced descriptions amazed and blessed them. Clayton thought it was as if they added subtitles to each other's lists. The weekend solidified their desire to move full steam ahead.

The fast pace at which things moved nearly took their breath away and shocked their kids. Because they knew most of their lives were behind them, they didn't want to lose any time. They liked what they learned about one another, and they were ready to take the leap. Singleness had played its role in each of their lives, motivating them to cooperate, cohabitate, and be life companions.

On Valentine's Day, 2018, Clayton wrote out his proposal and presented it to Jeanne outside an Amish store. It read:

"Jeanne, I am writing this letter to formally ask you to marry me. You are bringing much to my life, and I believe I am bringing much to your life. I believe we have even more to offer each other in the future. I am requesting you to be my lifelong partner, till death do us part."

Clayton then explained in numbered lists why he loved Jeanne and why he was choosing her as his soulmate.

Fortunately, Jeanne reacted exactly as hoped. She enthusiastically, without hesitation, said, "Yes!"

Real-life decisions rapidly unfurled from there. First—where would they live? Surprisingly, between Jeanne's home in Elkhart and Clayton's in

OrrVilla, they were both willing to graciously go where the other wanted. In the end, Clayton decided that his moving to Elkhart offered the best scenario. He already had dear friends in that area from his days at Walnut Hill Church, and he had planned to look for a different church, anyway, because of the strife at his own church.

Once they agreed upon that decision, Clayton put his beloved OrrVilla property on the market and prepared for the big move into Jeanne's home in Elkhart—no small task!

The wedding was the next hurdle. When, where, and who would perform it? They both felt strongly about the *who*. Clayton wanted his friend, Randy Murray, the OrrVilla chaplain, and Jeanne wanted her friend from her Lutheran Church, Father Ted. Instead of leaving one out, they chose both to marry them.

The wedding took place on June 30, 2018, outside a small retreat center in Goshen, Indiana, consummating their seven-month courtship. Only their children and grandchildren attended the intimate gathering, marking it memorable and special to the bride and groom. The in-laws on both sides warmly accepted the new spouse.

The reception at Jeanne's house the following Sunday entertained thirty-five guests, consisting mostly of friends from Walnut Hill, Trinity Lutheran, and Steiners from the area. Of special note for Clayton, two of his three remaining siblings and their partners, Marion and Ellen from Temperance, Michigan, and Norma and Jim from Jeromesville, Ohio attended.

Their three-week honeymoon included an unforgettable Alaskan cruise, kick-starting their adventurous union.

After the honeymoon, real life started. Clayton learned that he needed to back up his vow of working things out. Jeanne didn't always respond to him like he expected or desired. Sometimes, she responded to his hang-ups and shortcomings just as Ruth had, which put him on the defensive. Sometimes, she didn't respond favorably to some of his (what he deemed as) positive traits, though Ruth had. He found that he was having to navigate a complex and confusing assignment, one he promised to uphold.

Beemer wrote to Maammy: *I don't understand. These two were as giddy as schoolkids leading up to their marriage and on the honeymoon. They made music together. Why are they having so many petty arguments and hurting each other with blatant spoken observations?*

Maammy: Welcome to Marriage 101. Even though they have both been married a whole lot of years previously and are both mature beings in their own right, their notes together can be out of tune. That's evidently how THE BOSS set it up. I think they grow and harmonize only if they pass through this process of establishing their own needs while simultaneously learning to meet the needs of the other. It's a weird tag team match that makes them better people, their song a duet.

So, Clayton will just automatically become healthier if he bickers with his new wife for a certain period of time?

Ha! Doesn't he wish? No, there are no guarantees in this game. This marriage may fail. They're going to continue to have to work the kinks out every day. It's not going to be easy. A good marriage takes time and the willingness to be vulnerable and change.

But they may not have enough time at their age.

But they have experience and determination on their side. Are they the type to let a hurting comment lie?

Not so much. When one is hurt by what the other said, they usually let the other one know how they were hurt and why. And if the one that feels hurt doesn't know why, the other usually talks it out with them to figure out what the trigger was.

Wow! That's unusual. It's like they're their own counseling service. Is Clayton resenting her comments?

I don't think he's resentful. Sometimes, he gets mad at her directness. Then, he has to deep-dive into his feelings to figure out what's going on inside. Her patience with him usually helps him come out of the exchange having learned more about himself. Then, when she needs help on her short-sightedness, he's all the more willing to grill her on her stuff. I don't think she's offended by that, though she often responds with annoyance. I say that because she'll often end up crying and expressing how she's been wounded by something in the past but then is grateful for his insistence that she deal with it. It all seems so heavy.

Yes, it does. But if they can struggle through this communication process, they're looking at making some beautiful music together. I imagine THE BOSS is smiling. Discover and interpret.

Beemer thought about that. Clayton's not really done anything superheroic (at least from Beemer's perspective), yet THE BOSS delights in him and apparently loves to see him grow and find fulfillment. He wondered how much more amazed THE BOSS would be if Clayton did do something worthy of hero status.

Slowly, Clayton began to see the benefits of discussing their differences, as difficult as such confrontations tended to be. Jeanne's perspective, he found, often helped him see how malformed his reasoning was. For instance, Clayton often felt some form of shame in social settings; so, he shied from conversations and didn't smile much to keep from drawing attention to himself. He was self-conscious about his (obvious, he thought) overbite and constantly feared that his clothing was inappropriate for whatever setting he found himself in.

But Jeannie constantly told him he looked handsome, he had a great smile, and he had a wonderful heart that cared deeply for others. Of course, Clayton liked to hear this. But the foreign compliments did not sink in right away. A withering plant needs to soak up a lot of water before it becomes the beautiful flower it was meant to be. And to help Clayton cultivate a better self-image, she assisted Clayton in getting rid of some of his old clothes and encouraged him to update his wardrobe—an extravagance he felt unworthy of and an expense he found hard to rationalize. But, wanting to improve himself, he trusted Jeanne's wisdom. The more he soaked up her compliments and followed her advice, the more his self-esteem grew. And the more confidence he gained, the better life was.

Clayton wished the blending of the families felt smoother and more complete, but he also realized that the acceptance their kids had for the incoming step-parent was better than most remarried people experienced.

He still enjoyed his personal time of journaling, organizing budgets, and researching historical records. Jeanne sometimes wanted him to make himself available more in family matters. He tried to be himself *and* be a supportive husband. The line blurred at times. He didn't always make the best choices. Fortunately, Jeanne graciously helped him in his efforts.

Afraid of the worst, after observing some serious health problems, Beemer wrote in the margin: *Just so you know, it looks like it may be the big one for Clayton. He's in the hospital, and something's going on with his heart. His breathing is labored, and his legs and lungs are filling up with fluid. Not good!*

It sure seems a shame for him to go out like this. He was just starting to hum a beautiful song of this second marriage. After such a full life, I would've thought that he'd have gone out in a blaze of glory.

Then again, maybe I'm just fooling myself. He never was really famous or did anything that spectacular. He was just kind of an average Joe in many respects.

Maammy immediately came down for a visit when Clayton was in the hospital. "Beemer, I will not let you lose your position so early in your career!"

"Maammy?" Beemer looked up from Clayton's hospital bed in the middle of the night to see his editing supervisor in front of him. "What are you doing here? Are you here to heal Clayton?"

"No. That's not in my job description. I'm attempting to put an end to your suicide mission."

"What?" Beemer scowled, confused.

"If you continue to recklessly throw your subject under the bus, I will have no recourse but to take you off this assignment and strip you of your chronicling position. I'm sorry, but that's the way this works."

Beemer's jaw dropped to complement his bewildered stare. "What are you talking about?" He looked over at Clayton, sleeping. "I'm not trying to kill him. He's sick on his own accord … and almost dead. I can't do anything to save him, can I?"

"I'm not referring to his life. I'm referring to his biographic book and your graduating from your novice position by completing your first assignment." Maammy glowered at her underling—as much as she could with a dimple on her cheek and a twinkle in her eye. "It's the unsupportive, unbelieving, unhealthy vibe you're throwing off. THE BOSS can read that a galaxy away. If you think THE BOSS's precious child is failing or is subpar in any way, you are smearing this treasured book with accusation, gloom, and hopelessness. You're far enough along in your apprenticeship that we can't have this negative attitude. Sometimes you act like such a human."

Beemer gulped at the insult. "But I'm … I'm just wanting what's best for my subject. He's so close to being great."

"No. He is already great in THE BOSS's eyes. You don't have to *make* him great. Chief warned me about your fame preoccupation. Are you sure you're not the one who wants to be great?"

Beemer stood, speechless, crimson spreading all over his face.

Maammy smirked. "I thought so. This is serious, Beemer. If you want to keep this job, you need to report your subject's life, not your imagination. I know the aggravating hodgepodge of extreme emotions you're feeling is confusing. But there's more to it than you know. Only when you feel that exquisite pain of his inadequacy can you write THE BOSS's child's story. It's what you signed up for."

Beemer felt his heart pierced. His goals for Clayton were obviously not THE BOSS'S goals. "Yes, ma'am … my."

Maammy smiled helplessly. "You're a good nut, Beemer. Don't crack up now." She suppressed a giggle at her metaphor. "Write the truth, whether it disappoints you or not. Discover and interpret. Remember, you're interpreting THE BOSS's creativity in this dear creature, not your interpretation of how the subject misses the mark."

"Okay, okay." Beemer bobbed his head several times. "I'll nail it from here on out. I'll be sure to note his familial traits of THE BOSS while deeply feeling his flaws."

A snicker squirted from Maammy. She laid her hand on Beemer's shoulder. "I know you will. Tootles. Call me if you have any questions." With that, she was gone.

Beemer had not expected that dress down! He felt like his leash had just gotten shortened—big time. He couldn't afford to mess up like that again.

Still, he worried. *What if Clayton died right here, right now? Will I really get another assignment if he hasn't done something amazing yet?* He knew his editors told him otherwise, but he couldn't help but doubt something he hadn't experienced for himself.

Still, time was running out. Perhaps it was time to face the music and find some kind of rhapsody from Clayton's song instead of clanging the noisy gong of heroism out of step with a march he's not in.

Losing his pride, Beemer began identifying with the humanity of Clayton.

Clayton stayed in the hospital for four days in July of '19. Though the heart tests concerned him, he didn't feel like his life was in the balance. The doctors diagnosed that the lower region of his heart was not functioning normally, likely from age and the hot, humid conditions. They gave him some pills to keep the water buildup at bay and warned him to take it extremely easy in such conditions. While the pills helped with the water retention, the frequent urination after taking them each day wreaked havoc sometimes.

Eventually, Clayton found profound insight from Jeanne's comments and questions regarding his prepackaged responses to situations. He felt he was changing for the better. And he saw the same slow metamorphosis in Jeanne as well. They were becoming a team.

They enjoyed the opportunity to travel to see numerous friends and relatives all over the country when traveling conditions were safe. Ice and snow curtailed many plans, however.

Their month in DC at the International Guest House in 2019 created a memory that Clayton would always cherish. Just as he had with Ruth, he delighted in serving others alongside his wife.

On a visit to see Kimberly in the spring of '21, a peculiar idea began to form in Clayton and Jeanne's heads. What if they lived in California for the rest of their years together? Jeanne loved the sunny, mild climate with its many nut groves, vineyards, mountains, and fruit stands. Kimberly urged them to strongly consider the wild concept, which piqued Clayton's interest because it would allow them to live near his caring daughter.

When they went home, they discussed at length the possibility of moving. They thoroughly researched the area and made their lists of pros and cons. The pros of staying in their comfortable riverside home in Elkhart, Indiana, included:

1. *Only 30 minutes from Jeanne's daughter, Stephanie, and two and a half hours from Clayton's son, Kevin, with the grandchildren.*

2. *We love the backyard and deck with an awesome view and access to the Elkhart River. Lots of windows in the back provide a great view.*

3. *We have established friends. Jeanne has lady friends she meets with regularly at her Calico Point sewing club. Clayton has heartfelt friends at Walnut Hill Church and numerous relatives living in the area.*

4. *We love alternating between attending Jeanne's Trinity Lutheran Church and Clayton's Walnut Hill Mennonite Church.*

5. We have awesome neighbors.

> Beemer asked Maammy in the margin: *Why would Clayton want to leave all of that at his age?*

> Maammy responded: Maybe his adventurous spirit needs to be let loose.

Beemer suddenly looked at this venture in a new light. Maybe he wasn't seeing their reasons to leave well enough.

The reasons to leave the Indiana home were:

1. It was built in 1953 and needs periodic major upkeep, like the septic system we just replaced.

2. The washer and dryer are downstairs in the basement with no good place to move them upstairs (the stairs have become more challenging to climb).

3. It has only two bedrooms, with one being Clayton's office. A third bedroom downstairs does not meet code.

4. With its many windows, heating and air-conditioning are expensive.

5. We hate the winters (especially Jeanne!) She already fell on the ice, suffering a bad ankle fracture, requiring surgery with a plate and screws in her ankle.

6. Clayton has a rough time in the hot, humid summer months due to his heart condition.

> Beemer wrote in the margin: *Now there's a list that incites adventure!*

A few months later, they made another visit to California just to check out the housing situation and other practicalities. With a realtor, they checked out four different areas. Claremont, where Kimberly lived, was out of the question from the get-go because there was no way they could afford housing there.

The story unfolded a little like the *Goldie Locks and the Three Bears* children's tale. The first three areas all had obvious downfalls. One area was too crowded. One had too much traffic. One was too abstract or progressive or different from their concept of feeling homey.

But they finally felt comfortable when they entered Bakersfield. Away from the hustle and bustle of Los Angeles and with a population of 377,917, they were reminded of the small-town vibe of Elkhart. It had plenty of room to expand and had its own vineyards, citrus fruit farms, and gorgeous mountain views. Their water system far outperformed many of California's poor-quality water systems. And all the people they met in Bakersfield were unusually friendly. To top it off, Kimberly's boyfriend lived there, and it was only two hours from her, which, in California, was an average commute.

Of the ten houses they viewed in Bakersfield, they agreed that three of them could meet their needs. One sold before they could bid on it. The second was okay. But the third one was *just right*. Contrary to their conservative Midwestern tendency, after talking to Kimberly and weighing all the factors, they put a bid on the house (knowing their large offer might still be too little).

To their shock, the owners accepted their bid that same evening. The realtor informed Clayton later that another offer, which was higher than theirs, came in after the owners had accepted their bid. To Clayton, that proved that God's hand was in this crazy plan! They had a new house!

The major downside to this amazing California adventure was the very real possibility that Clayton would likely miss the passing from this life to the next of many loved ones in Indiana and Ohio. Realizing that he would probably have to say goodbye to many from afar in the years to come made him sorrowful. But, to him, the adventure of living and the thrill of laying it all on the line with his new bride was worth the pain that life would inevitably throw his way. Life was for living, after all.

Beemer in the side margin: *I'm stoked about this move! But just so I don't write my own truth, should I make note of all the negative things this move will likely inflame?*

Maammy: Like what?

Like his age and health for one.

That's two. And why are you suddenly knocking his adventurous spirit? Someone his age should be commended for tackling such a move. Didn't they visit California during the hottest time of the year? How did Clayton's health fare with that?

Yes, it got up to 115°F. He handled it every bit as well as a humid 85°F day in Indiana. But the move and stress of starting all over could really get him. He'll have to find new friends, new ways to serve others, and a new church or churches. He may not like a lot of things in this new environment.

But look at the opportunity he has to grow together with his wife. Are they buying this house together, or is he buying it?

They're buying it together. Clayton's financial adviser told him the move could improve both of their equity over time even though the cost of living in California is higher. He is pretty pumped about starting from scratch with her. At eighty years old, he feels younger for some reason. They even think they may enjoy swimming in their backyard pool even though he's never before been a swimmer.

Ha! Isn't that cute! The romance of older couples always gets me. The love THE BOSS has made available for these

humans just never ceases—if they look for it and are ready
to work at it.

As feared, Beemer noted how the actual move was even more traumatic than his life-altering move to Elkhart. Clayton stressed over the many decisions he had to make, like leaving his forty years' worth of tax documents behind. For an orderly historian, such sacrifices were monumental! Fortunately, Jeanne talked and walked him through the challenging ordeal.

On the other end, the *settling-in* process stretched Clayton's patience far beyond his expected limit. The trying decision to buy new furniture, for instance (a nagging resistance that Jeanne continually helped him fight), was only bested by the incrementally lengthened wait period for their orders (one of many COVID-19 consequences).

For all he was worth, Beemer wanted Clayton's last move to fit his hero's mold. But he finally knew better than to force that dying song. THE BOSS evidently had Clayton's own mold specifically picked out for him—one which Clayton's abilities, resources, temperament, and choices all suited. Slowly, after 80 years, Beemer was seeing glimpses of Clayton fitting perfectly into that mold. And as much as he fought the idea all throughout his life, Beemer finally saw the truth. Clayton didn't have to *DO* some grand thing to find THE BOSS. THE BOSS lived in Clayton where he was at, in his *BEING*.

Unbelievably, as never before, Beemer felt in tune.

33
LIFE LEARNINGS
RECORDING THE MASTERPIECE

Beemer waits till Clayton falls asleep to call Maammy down.

Maammy flies down instantly.

"Wow, you're fast," says Beemer.

"What can I help you with, Beemer?" She frowns. "Why are you smiling like a cat that ate the canary?"

"I have the best news ever!"

"Okay. I could use some good news. Sing?"

"First, I need to know something. Can I record another person's writing in my subject's biographic book?"

Her eyes narrow. "Yes, if it's pertinent. You know you can. You've already included some of Ruth's letters when he was in Algeria."

"Oh, yeah." Beemer snickers out his nose. "But what about a college paper?"

"A paper? You mean a newspaper?"

"No, a class assignment."

"I suppose. Beemer, what's this about?"

Beemer's smile turns lumpy.

"Beemer, are you crying?"

Beemer wipes the tears from his face. "Sorry, I can't help it. I'm just so happy."

Maammy's eyes widen to about the same circumference as her mouth. "We may need to take you to the heaven emergency room ... if there was such a thing."

"No, I'm okay. I just got a little carried away. Wait till you read this thing I got."

"What did you get? A cure for cancer?"

"No!" says Beemer, annoyed at a more outrageous answer than his. "I learned something from experience."

"*You* did? Or Clayton did?"

"I did."

"Hmm. That's usually a human thing. But go on."

Beemer swallows and stands up straight. "You know how Clayton had to die to his desire to be seen by his dad? And how painful that was for him?"

Maammy nods.

"Then, when he learned that not being loved by his dad wasn't his fault, he became well. Remember?"

Maammy's nods continue. "Sure do. He buried the sins of his father and received new life."

Beemer beams! "Well, that's what I feel like."

An eyebrow raises on Maammy's quizzical face. "Pray tell."

"Well, I finally admitted to myself (if not to you, sorry) that you and Chief were right. I've been making this story about my wishes and not about Clayton and how THE BOSS is sending grace from above to make his life full of hope and meaning. It's embarrassing to admit, but I had to die to my own ideas of the way I thought things should be. It wasn't very fun. I figured I was such a mess-up I probably had no business even being a chronicler."

"But? Please tell me you're giddy for a certifiable reason."

Beemer chuckles. "But then this happened." He hands his editor a stack of papers stapled together."

She takes the papers cautiously. "And what is this?"

"This is my dream come true after I died to it."

Maammy scrunches up her face. "I'm all for surprises, Beemer. But you're going to have to make some sense or I'm going to have to find an alternative line of work for you. Like maybe laying the streets of gold up yonder." She motions upward with her spongey hair.

Beemer's laugh chokes into a cough. "You'll understand after you read that."

Maammy looks at the papers in her hand and sighs. "Okay. But before I take these, I need to know that you're alright. You're scaring me. I don't feel good about leaving you here alone with your subject."

"No, don't leave. I mean, I don't need you to stay ..." Beemer's pulse quickens and his eyes dart around the room for the right words. "... because I'm crazy. I mean, I'm not crazy is why you should stay. I mean ..."

Maammy stares back like she is a first-time chronicler. With one eye raised, she says, "This crazy talk is not helping, Beemer."

"Please, just sit. I know I'm acting a little weird here, but this ... this ..." He finally points at the paper. "... paper has rocked my world. It's so ... I don't know, mind-blowing that I need to share it with someone." His watery eyes implore her.

"Okay, okay. Calm down. You'll be alright." She lays a gentle hand on his shoulder. "So, you want me to read this?" She waves the papers in front of her.

"Could you read them out loud, please? I need to hear the words from you to make them real. I was so sure of my judgment and plan that I couldn't see the plain truth right in front of me. This shows how wrong I was but how right THE BOSS is."

Maammy cocks her head back and frowns. Her eyebrows raise.

"Sorry. It's not as confusing as I sound. See, I fit this into the biographic book, and I think it fits better than anything I could have dreamed up. But I need you to confirm it so I don't go tooting my own horn again. Could you read it please?" Beemer motions to the chair.

Maammy sits. "Just read this out loud?" she holds the papers up.

"Well, actually, here." He yanks the papers out of her hand, throws them aside, then leaps to the biographic book on the desk. "You might as well just read this. I just put it in there." He opens the book on her lap and points to where he wants her to start. "I explain it right ... here."

Maammy reads out loud:

Clayton's granddaughter, Kristin, approached him, asking if she could interview him for her family sociology class. He, of course, welcomed the Zoom meeting with open arms. He had always enjoyed spending time with Kristin and wanted to help her in any way he could. Little did he know, their Zoom interview would last two hours. And that didn't include several follow-up emails that asked more challenging questions.

Kristin, a senior at Ball State University, was majoring in occupational therapy. Her typical escape of reading fantasy novels was put on hold as she imagined herself in her grandpa's world instead of a fantasy world. She told him that she had stayed up past midnight for the past two weeks just writing the paper and longed for the day she could go outside and go hiking with her friends again.

The assignment, according to Kristin, was to interview a personal acquaintance over seventy-five years of age and write an essay about what that person had learned in their life and how they have changed. She asked numerous preformulated questions suggested by her instructor as well as some of her own making.

After piecing all the details into the proper order and with the proper flow, she finally presented her rough draft to the professor. She let Clayton know that her professor really liked the presentation, but she needed to clean up a lot of grammar mistakes, tense errors, and theme definitions. Not being a writing major, she said she felt like giving up on the whole thing. But, she decided, having already put so much time into it, she might as well give it her best shot and see if she could make it something special.

A week later, in an email to her grandpa, she wrote:

Grandpa,

I finally finished my paper! Thank you so much for spending all that time answering all my silly questions. Your patience and perseverance to answer the questions fully made all the difference. I got an A! Now I should be able to breeze through that class the rest of the semester.

Besides getting a good grade, I learned a lot through interviewing you and then writing out my findings. I can't say that about many of my classes. Your life is amazing, and you are truly worthy of the time and effort I spent on this.

I hope I have as much wisdom and life experiences to share when I'm your age. I never tire of all your stories. You're an example for the ages!

I'm proud to be your granddaughter!

Love,

Kristin

Attached to the encouraging note, Clayton reads her following essay:

Learning to Grow and Change from My Grandpa

Most people make fun of their grandpa or are embarrassed by his behind-the-times, stuck-in-his-ways outlook. Some people I know don't even have a grandfather. However, I'm lucky. I have a real-life grandpa who I can make fun of (only on occasion) and who's still learning the best ways to live and grow.

I remember riding bikes with him and Grandma, vacationing in Costa Rica just before Grandma passed away, and seeing Grandpa flourish at family reunions. He has an enthusiastic heart for family and history that compels me to know my heritage as well. He also taught me one of my favorite pastimes—Sudoku.

I recently sat down with him (on Zoom) and asked him life's big questions. His answers floored me. It took him a while to come up with his reply to most of the inquiries, and he often needed to ask a few questions about the questions, but eventually, he came through with fascinating, well-thought-through answers. The following wisdom is what I received from him through the assignment—Learn from the Past: Interviewing an Elder.

Q: How have your goals changed?

My grandpa, Clayton Steiner, told me that as a young man, he wanted to make a huge impact on the world but had no idea how to do that. He felt small, not too smart, and limited. Traveling outside his home state of Ohio only a couple of times by the age of eighteen, he had no idea what opportunities lay ahead. His first semblance of a goal was to serve God through overseas mission work. That was the biggest dream he could imagine at the time, and through a Pax program through his church, he served in Algeria for two years, starting at age nineteen. Even at that early age, my grandpa was not afraid to challenge the boundaries in his mind.

He enjoyed serving the needy but realized that his immature heart and mind were extremely limited to meet those needs. He thought he'd pick up life skills like a carpenter does a hammer. But he learned he couldn't just bash things in with the hammer. Learning to skillfully use the hammer to build hope and safety around people was ultimately what mattered. To serve others, he needed to work on himself first.

Q: Which is more important—the mind, the emotions, or the will?

My grandpa thought about this question for a long time before answering, "To be honest, I don't know." Then, he went on to give story after story about how he got into trouble when he used one of those systems over the others.

He believes he was born extra sensitive, emotionally. But as early as he can remember, he thought such a disposition was wrong for a male to have. Without being told specifically, my grandpa got a clear message from his dad and his church that good Christian men do not get emotional. Strong men avoid, jump over, or plow through emotions, he assumed. He, therefore, bottled up his emotions.

It wasn't until he was well into his thirties that he realized he was dying from pent-up emotions. That is why, he said, when major trauma occurred in his life, like when his twelve-year-old son died in a tragic accident, his mother suffered mental illness, his marriage was struggling, he was diagnosed with cancer, his wife died of cancer, and his two adult sons were diagnosed with cancer a couple of months apart, he felt them deeply, but he tended to stuff such vital feelings down until recently. Now, life has much richer meaning with the use of his full emotions.

For him, thinking has always appeared to be more reliable than feeling. He was especially turned onto this concept when he went to college. Though previously considering himself unintelligent, college taught him that he could learn far more than he realized. It was in college when he first began one of his life's mantras—*I am a lifelong learner.*

However, leading with the mind alone led to trouble too, he found. Often, in his early years with my grandmother, Ruth, he made plans or decisions and assumed she would follow suit because he thought his logic was beyond criticism, only to find that he hadn't considered her feelings on the matter. As scientific as his mind worked, he found that it often lacked the human element of the heart.

His will to follow God, pursue goals, and complete tasks have also ruled him at times—with mixed results. He served a community, leading young volunteers on an extremely limited budget, for example, while raising four small children. Existing near the poverty line took guts, determination, and a deep trust in God to provide. But sometimes, like the time his confidence got out of hand and he suggested the camp he was working at needed to be overhauled, his will got the best of him, and he lost his job.

So, my grandpa concluded that the mind, the emotions, and the will are all important and necessary resources God has given us.

Q: How important is confidence?

My grandpa enjoys confidence. He says it has helped him accomplish some amazing things, like beginning a daycare project in a needy neighborhood and growing it into a model facility in the state. But it has also led to unavoidable humiliation, like the time he quit his steady job and set out to lead a struggling business back to prosperity. The venture failed, and he was forced to work for his previous company in a lesser position on the graveyard shift.

Humility, he says, is every bit as necessary and valuable as confidence. One makes one's production better. The other makes oneself better.

Q: What has been the hardest thing for you to navigate?

Tears immediately flowed down my grandpa's cheeks when I asked him this question. I told him right away that he didn't have to answer it if he didn't want to. He smiled through the tears and said he wanted to answer it.

In no hurry, he said he could think of a lot of things that have been hard in his life. "At times," he said, "all of life seems hard. Sometimes life gets you down, and you feel like it kicks you while you're down." Then, he wiped the tears and said, "But it's been worth every kick."

He told me the story of losing his son, my uncle Bruce, in the accident. I've heard this story all my life. It never gets happier. It's always sad. My grandpa doesn't pretend otherwise. He tells the truth. Tragedy is hard. He felt totally ill-equipped to handle it. Loss is no respecter of persons.

But he also is honest about how the sad, senseless misfortune contributed to his life. He can't appreciate enough all the people that helped him put his life back together again. The love he experienced during that lowest time in his life showed him that life is precious and worth pursuing no matter the circumstances.

Deaths, he said, in general, have been terribly hard on him—that of his wife of over fifty years being the most prominent. The finality of death in this life leaves an undefinable void he cannot explain. It just hurts like nothing else.

Of course, he knows, in his mind, that his deceased loved ones are in heaven and someday he'll see them there, but that realization does not always ease the ache of their present absence.

Q: What is most precious to you?

Without hesitation, my grandpa said, "Love and grace!" He went on to say how blessed he is to know the love of God in his daily life. The grace God displayed by sending his Son, Jesus, to live among us and show us the way to abundant living "boggles the mind," he said.

Then he mentioned how awesome it is to know that same love and grace of God in his interactions with people. He feels he is the luckiest man alive to have experienced such love with not only his first wife but also his current wife, Jeanne.

"But I think my greatest joy has been my kids," he said, looking directly into my eyes, "and my grandkids."

I didn't get the feeling he was saying this just to make me feel good. I think he was trying to genuinely share his heart with me. I was blown away. My grandpa really loves me! How does a person process that? Our eyes were both quite watery.

Q: Of what value has religion been to you?

This was one of those topics that my grandpa needed a clearer grasp of what the question was specifically asking. Religion, he thought, has a broad definition. It could mean many different things in many different contexts. I asked him what he thought religion meant.

He said he equates religion with structure. He thinks structure is valuable but not as valuable as what the structure is meant to hold. I made him explain what he meant. We had a wonderful, long discussion about church-and-state, Protestantism versus Catholicism, orthodoxy versus liberalism, religion versus personal relationship to God, and much about faith.

He's delighted that he has always followed the practice of attending church. But he does not believe he has the market on how to understand God. He thinks his understanding works for him just as other people's religion works for them, but we should always respect others' rights to believe however they want.

Q: How have other people's differences affected you?

My grandpa gave a big sigh and nodded his head. Before he could fully answer, he told me he needed to give a little background to his upbringing.

He was taught that those who thought differently than him and his church about the Bible were wrong and, therefore, inherently bad.

But when he saw people of other religions and other Mennonite denominations serving God with joy and resolve, he began to see the errors in his thinking. Also, when so many non-Mennonites helped them in their time of need after his son's death, he found that those outside of his specific belief system can be good, and maybe right ... at least for themselves.

My grandpa now knows that "the grace from above" doesn't require perfection to be accepted by his creator and others. He is a big advocate for seeing value in other walks of life. Though he knows he still subconsciously projects his perceptions onto people, he tries his best to include everyone into his circle of human dignity. That includes those who are not thought well of by the public, the physically or mentally challenged, the poor, and everyone that does not fit in a box. I think this is the coolest outlook!

He admits that he has a hard time with those who do not accept those outside their box, which puts him right back in the place of putting others not accepting different views in his box. I appreciated his candor. My grandpa doesn't pretend to have everything figured out.

Q: What role should authority play in people's lives?

My grandpa told me up front that "This is a hard one for me." I didn't quite understand his dilemma, but it evidently had something to do with his dad. He said things like "My relationship with my dad was not what it should have been," and "My dad never complimented me. I never thought I could please him."

He told me he had been convinced that obedience was his most important function in life. This meant that authority reigned supreme. His needs and desires were nothing compared to the authority he served. This made total sense to him until he learned that not all authority is good or right. Some authority is bad.

He found no authority (save God himself) was perfect. And unfortunately, he got much of his information about who God was (and what God required) from his church, its leaders, and his personal interpretation of the Bible—all flawed interpreters!

He still desires to follow good authority because he thinks authority is valuable and necessary to help make the world a better place. But because authority is not always good or right, he is very selective in who and what he follows.

He also noted that he is leery of authority claiming to know absolute Truth. Many religious and political leaders use such rhetoric. He innately doesn't trust them. He thinks we should always be searching for and fine-tuning our Truth beliefs, not settling for desired certainty.

Q: How important is money?

My grandpa smiled at this one, like he was not going to fall for the trap. He told me, "Money is not important. But how we handle it is."

From the time he was a young man, he liked to account for money. He likes to record spending, depositing, and withdrawing functions, and to report his findings in some sort of summary. Saving and investing are two of his favorite hobbies.

Money has always mattered to my grandpa, both when he had little, like when he was growing up as the youngest child of eleven on a modest farm right after the Great Depression, and now, when his nest egg allows him to live comfortably. He won't deny his fascination with it, but he also emphasizes that the Bible verse does not say "money is the root of all evil," but rather "the *love* of money is the root of all evil." He firmly contends that money is only harmful when one uses it unwisely.

Q: What contributions have you made to the world?

Because we were just talking about money, I was surprised that he didn't first mention all the money he's given to those in need and the church, as I know he has. Instead, he said, "I tried to be the best husband and father I could be. I think that's been my biggest contribution to the world."

He explained that by loving his family they have been better equipped to branch out into the world, making it a better place. I found this really cool because I'm part of that tree.

He's also tithed over a tenth of his income to God (before bills and taxes). But even more mind-boggling, he's given a tenth of his life's work to God by serving voluntarily through his church. I know it's common for many Christians to give a tithe of their income, but I've never heard of anyone tithing their time and livelihood.

Q: What will be your legacy?

This question confused my grandpa. He asked me, "What do I want my legacy to be?"

When I told him "No, what *will* your legacy be?" he initially told me that wasn't up to him. He assumed others would need to answer that. I asked, "What do you think others will think your legacy is?"

Sometimes my grandpa appears to be slow, like he has trouble under-standing. His brothers and sisters, I've noticed, have the same air about them. But my grandpa is not dumb. On the contrary, I think he's exception-ally bright, especially for someone his age. It's just that sometimes he gets a little stuck and needs a little time to sort out his misalignment.

After thinking about it, he said he often struggles with wanting others to see him in a specific light. He's spent an exorbitant amount of energy trying to fit into others' wishes instead of his own standards. Now that he's mostly conquered the temptation to always impress other people, it's hard for him to guess how he's impacted others.

Finally shrugging off his humbleness, he logically followed his life's breadcrumbs and eventually came up with a solid list. He thought most would see him as a hard, dependable worker, soft-spoken but always willing to engage, faithful to God and the Church, pacifistic, a good steward of money, a historian, open to new ideas, a lifelong learner, and able to change when necessary.

I can't think of a better legacy to follow, especially since he's not shouting these lasting gifts from the rooftops. He has just humbly lived out his life as best he could, one day at a time, and this impressive litany of contributions has resulted.

Q: What have you learned from life?

My grandpa loved this question. I think he'd have gone on longer if I had let him. He sent me a list in an email later. Learning and systematizing are two of his favorite go-to strategies.

He's learned that you take your family heritage with you wherever you go. Despite this fact, you can change your outlook though it takes much effort, time, and pain.

He's learned that learning helps propel you forward, instead of staying stuck. If you continue addressing the same problem the same way with the same results, you will continue having the same problem. Learning pulls you out of your rut and onto higher ground.

Mistakes and failures can either be devastating or opportunities to learn and grow. If you don't wallow too long in the suffering that failures produce, you can allow them to help you become a better person.

Serving others is much more valuable than merely serving yourself. Doing good deeds makes the world a better place—provided you don't get too wrapped up in your pride in doing so.

Family is wonderful. But controlling every aspect of the family unit is impossible, just as demanding each individual member to act and respond the same way is impossible. Your family is a living organism (even after the kids leave home) that teaches you more than you can teach it. Enjoy the unpredictable challenges.

Life is a push-and-pull lesson. Knowing when to do which is wisdom. If you can learn to let go when it's time to change and continue to grapple when it's time to stay put, you will remain sane and healthy longer.

If you define yourself purely on your position (the role you hold), you will struggle with your identity when your role changes. It's better to know and accept who you are, warts and all, than to identify yourself as your occupation or position in life.

Pain and suffering are inevitable. It is wiser to learn to grow through them than to ignore them or wish they never existed. You can suffer much more than you can imagine and can come out on the other side improved.

Justifying your own right at the expense of another's right is wrong. You harm the world when you insist that another must view the world as you do. It is far better to learn from the other's view and change your prohibitive views where possible.

Integrity takes a lifetime to cultivate. Honesty has no shortcuts. If you treat others fairly, your life will be worth living, and others will want to live it with you.

Messages of self-doubt and shame strangle, while messages of self-worth, thankfulness, and hope breathe life. You must do all you can to stop the lies of worthlessness and accept the lifeline of your inherent value.

Death is a part of life. Instead of denying its pain and sorrow, acknowledge it and allow it to add depth and gratefulness to your life. Life is a gift. Be thankful every day that you are alive and remember its many gifts.

God is good. The more you acknowledge God's power and participation in your life, the better your life will be. Through God's unconditional love and grace, you can enjoy yourself and grow unfathomably.

Jesus is our supreme example. His life was love and peace lived out. You should always search for ways to build others up, working toward peace and not demanding your own way.

Grace from above is for everyone. We need to spread that truth by showing grace to others.

Love is meant to be shared. You must give and receive love to be healthy. You can't merely imagine and remember love for it to be an impactful force in your life. You must work at relationships for love to make a difference. Selfishness and loneliness kill.

I've seen my grandpa laugh and cry. I've seen him angry and befuddled. Sometimes, he's blunt with his ideas. He's far from perfect. Life sucks for him just as it does for all of us at times. But he is not afraid to face it. He lives out his full humanity for me and everyone else to see. Though this has not always been the case, he's comfortable in his own skin. He's learned to appreciate himself and those around him.

My grandpa is an old man by the world's standards. Yet, he's still growing. He's still trying to improve. He continually wants to learn.

I saw him lose his wife of fifty years. It broke him. But only for a time. He fought his way through it, and now, he is loving his new wife and fully embracing life again.

He was angry at his dad for most of his life, he tells me. But he learned to forgive and be a better father, husband, and man than his father ever was. That took grit.

He is generally slow to speak, but when he speaks, he speaks his heart. I like to think I'm like that ... or am becoming like that. His words are true, and he's true to his word, combining honesty with trustworthiness.

I always appreciated my grandparents. They supported me in everything I did. I basically grew up thinking my grandpa was a kind man, doing the best he could. But this project has opened my eyes. He's had plenty of reasons to be bitter and angry. Yet, he remains kind.

My grandpa is more than my patriarchal forefather. He's my hero.

Clayton immediately felt the "grace from above" that had shined over and throughout his amazing journey. He could think of no greater reward than to be praised by his grandchild. After reading the email and Kristin's written assignment, Clayton cried.

And so does Beemer.

Beemer stands, waiting for Maammy's response. He is anxious, excited, nervous. What he should do with himself, he doesn't know. He folds his fingers on his breast and stares at his young editor.

When Maammy finally finishes, she looks at Beemer and warmly says, "You melded his granddaughter's paper in there nicely. Well done!"

Beemer beams! "Thank you! I thought you'd like it. I can't believe I didn't realize that he was a hero all along. Guess it was just rookie-itis." He laughs awkwardly.

Maammy nods and hands the book back to Beemer.

Beemer says, "Do you think THE BOSS will like it?"

"Of course. THE BOSS will be delighted to read about a precious human making such a huge impact on the world."

Beemer keeps on shining like the midday sun. "I'm glad."

Maammy stares at her student. "Is that it?"

Beemer wrinkles his forehead. "What do you mean? I can't be much gladder."

"No, 'Isn't he a great hero?' or 'I told you so' or 'guess I'll graduate for sure now, huh?'"

Beemer's mouth drops open. "Ah, no. I was wrong about all of that. That's the gladdest thing I'm glad about. This wouldn't be near as fulfilling if I hadn't died to that old dirge. That's what I learned—when you die to your vain, selfish desires, wonderful life grows around you."

A huge smile plasters Maammy's face. "Where has that rookie apprentice gone? I do believe I am seeing a grown, graduated chronicler."

The young reporter's mouth flings open again. "You mean? ..."

Maammy nods continuously. "No doubt in my mind. You're just the kind of chronicler THE BOSS wants. The kind that delights in seeing the subject grow and shine THE BOSS'S character wherever they go. The kind that writes from THE BOSS'S perspective, not your own. If I could pick favorites, I'd say you were my favorite pupil."

"Thanks , Maammy." Beemer squints. "Aren't I your only one right now?"

Maammy brightens. "Oh, see. You're sharp, too." She giggles like a school angel.

Beemer laughs along with her. "Thanks for hanging in there with me, Maammy. I know I was kind of stuck on myself. I thought I knew more than you did." He frowns sheepishly.

"Aah! I knew you just needed a little time to figure things out. I saw your real heart right away, as THE BOSS does. That's how we roll in this biz."

"I hope I keep learning and don't get stuck thinking I know it all."

"Good quest. Just remember you're writing *for* THE BOSS *about* THE BOSS'S children. All the books in the Great Hall of Annals Library are love stories that THE BOSS reads over and over again. And you've had the privilege of writing one. I can think of no greater motivation!"

With a tear in his eye, Beemer tilts his head at the irony. He has no words to retort.

"Now, I'll leave you to it," says Maammy. "Keep discovering and interpreting THE BOSS'S joy."

"I will."

With a smile and a wink, Maammy leaves Beemer to his thoughts.

Watching his sleeping subject, Beemer recalls how he doubted Clayton's resume. Though he'd watched his whole life unfold, Beemer had worried Clayton would be insignificant, ordinary. How silly he'd been!

This human may not have been the hero Beemer hoped he'd be, making his indelible mark on the world for all to see like the adventurer William Clark of the famous Lewis and Clark Expedition, but there is no doubt that he's far from ordinary. Try *extraordinary*!

To think he had thought that Clayton was too old to be a hero. Beemer smiles and shakes his disbelieving head. Clayton didn't need to do some amazing feat before he died. His long life had become a trough of wisdom. He sees that now … just as THE BOSS does. Now, if he could just share Clayton's life and wisdom with all the other humans on the planet.

But that is not his job. His job is to record this masterpiece for his Creator. Maybe THE BOSS has other plans to get it into the hands of people. *Stranger things have happened,* he muses. Who could fathom THE BOSS's ways?

If only Beemer could thank Clayton for his unique, fascinating life. For Beemer had learned and grown right along with him the whole time. They were soul-buddies after all!

For all our adventures, Clayton, here's to you! Beemer holds the biographic book high above his bed—toward heaven.

*If you have enjoyed this book, please leave a positive review wherever you purchased the book and/or on **Amazon, Goodreads, or Google**. This will help get this book into the hands of more people. Thank you!*

PHOTO COLLECTION
PART III: 1985–2022

The Homer Steiner children at the 1988 Steiner reunion. (Left to right (in age-order): Clayton, Norma, Roy, Marion, George, Dorothy, Viola, Lee, & Elno)

Clayton and Ruth Steiner get closer as they grow older (1990).

Clayton and Ruth with their family in 2013. (Back row: Janet [Duane's wife], Duane, Mandy [Kevin's wife], Kevin, Clayton, Kimberly, and Ruth. Front row: Ashe Kyle and Kristin [Kevin's kids])

Ruth spread so much love to her family and friends. This photo is from an arboretum near where Ruth and Clayton lived in Orrville, Ohio.

The International Guest House in Washington DC, where Clayton and Ruth hosted for two years after Clayton retired. It was their home away from home.

*One night at the Guest House, they had fifteen
guests from twelve different countries!*

*The Clayton and Ruth Steiner family at the Homer & Bertha Steiner
reunion in 2008. (Back row: Kimberly, Kevin, & Duane). Front row:
Ashe Kyle [Kevin's son], Ruth, Clayton, and Kristin [Kevin's daughter].*

Clayton and Jeanne (Russell) Steiner's wedding in 2018.

Clayton and Jeanne take a side trip during their honeymoon cruise to Alaska.

*Clayton and Jeanne Steiner enjoy sweet time
together during their honeymoon cruise.*

Clayton's two grandchildren, Kristin and Ashe Kyle Steiner, in 2016.

*Clayton visiting Washington DC with
his granddaughter, Kristin, in 2018.*

HOW THIS BOOK CAME TO BE

Clayton Steiner.

The unique making of this book bears explaining. As a young farm boy helping his mother grade eggs in the chicken coop, the twelve-year-old Clayton realized his propensity to understand family history "even better than his mother." Then, in the twilight of his life, with every bit of that same historian's heart, he wanted to build upon the impact of his previous genealogy book *From Switzerland to Sonnenberg*. Having kept every scrap of family history he could throughout his life, his next logical step became recording an account of his personal history to give to his children and grandchildren. But he wanted more of a professional rendering than his efforts alone could muster. Admiring his nephew Jere Steiner's creativity and knack for putting words to page, Clayton asked Jere if he would write his biography.

Jere, not yet accomplished enough to call himself an author, took on the challenge and let his vision fly. Though the heavenly characters were the genius behind the plot, they were far from parsed out. Because Clayton had not yet written out the last third of his life for Jere to outline, Jere basically plotted as he went along. Many backtracking changes ensued. The overall arc of the book became more complicated the more Clayton threw at him. When he finally completed the rough draft, Jere's head was spinning. He had written and rewritten so many themes, subplots, and nuanced vignettes that he was overwhelmed with how to tie it all in a bow.

Meanwhile, Clayton, the businessman, was researching who might help edit this monstrosity. By coincidence (or answered prayer), while visiting his brother Marion and explaining the dilemma they had with the book, Marion's granddaughter, Becca (Robb) Stutzman, heard the call. Her journalism degree, editing experience, and strong family drive compelled her to say, "I think I could help." Becca read through Jere's first edited manuscript and saw tremendous potential for a larger audience. Clayton was delighted. Jere was stunned.

All three relatives from three different family branches and three different generations made their unique contributions, but without Becca's editing, organizational, and attention-to-details skills, this leaky boat might have sunk.

The teamwork was beautiful, and our sincere desire is that you benefit from it.

Author, Jere Steiner.

AUTHOR'S NOTE

Throughout the book, Clayton and I (Jere) have sought to preserve history as much as possible. However, we have changed some names for their protection, made minor adjustments to the timeline where necessary, and fictionalized much of the conversation's content with the counselor. Please be assured that the overall narrative you have just read about Clayton Steiner is indeed a true story.

And yes, this story does tread on sensitive turf. Some readers may wonder why we chose to divulge such intimate details of Clayton's life and especially the tragic sins of Homer. In short, we want to do everything we can to help people heal from challenges similar to those Clayton has faced. We especially believe that harmful family secrets need to be recognized, faced, and defused.

Please note that the content of Clayton's biography is how *he* remembers it. Memory is a strange creature. We do not see memory as fact, rather as Clayton's best representation of the truth. Other family members would have written many of the stories differently. We know this because they don't remember some details herein the same.

This book shows Clayton and his family at their most vulnerable, sometimes painfully so, in order to offer hope to those carrying shame and debilitating burdens. As Clayton has demonstrated through participating in various grief support groups, to heal, people need to share their deepest pain with trusted allies. To bring those burdens into the light. To take away the destructive power of secrecy. To prove, once and for all—*you are not alone.*

ABOUT THE AUTHORS

Jere Steiner moved to Arkansas half his life ago to help start a church. Since then and for the past twenty-eight years, he's been a walking letter carrier with the Post Office. An exercise nut, he constantly pushes his physical body to the limit. He was a three-sport letterman in high school and now clocks about nine miles a day on his mail route. On his sixtieth birthday—for fun—he walked sixty miles, in one day!

Challenging himself has always been in his DNA. After attending a two-year Mennonite college, he spent a summer living in a tent in Alaska while working at a nearby sawmill. At age twenty-one, he rode his bicycle, averaging eighty-six miles a day, across the country to serve at a children's camp. The best part of the trip was meeting his wife-to-be, Jennifer Mishler, whom he married three years later. In their thirty-seven years of thriving together, his greatest thrill has been raising their three beautiful children into marvelous adults, an endeavor he's felt privileged to partner in.

At work, the daily grind of the Post Office (the rain, snow, heat, dead of night, and all of that), believe it or not, suits him. Though an adventurer, Jere also thrives in routine. As he's fond of telling people, he "figures things out" during the daily grind of his mail route. By that, he means he falls deep into his thoughts and basically waddles around in them until they make sense.

And sometimes, these thoughts actually lead somewhere creative and/ or remarkable. At special occasions, church functions, and reunions, he's known as the *skit guy*. He can't help himself; he often invents and performs one-of-a-kind skits to entertain people. He even used to drag his kids in on them until they were in one too many performances that flopped … or realized they weren't being paid enough.

Jere has always felt most alive exercising his creative gene. Since early adulthood, he's always wanted to write. But because he never received adequate training and even less encouragement, he put writing on the back burner until his kids grew up. He has had such a good time writing *Clayton's Chronicles* that he can't wait till retirement, so he can start knocking out more quality books!

Clayton has taken great satisfaction in organizing numerous historical records for various organizations, as well as publishing a family ancestry book. For his own records, he dutifully journaled his experiences throughout his lifetime, paving the way for this book.

Jere lives in Farmington, Arkansas, with Jennifer, his wife of thirty-seven years. Clayton and wife, Jeanne, live in Bakersfield, California.

If you wish to contact us or join the author's email list for future written works, please go to our website at: **claytonschronicles.com**

CPSIA information can be obtained
at www.ICGtesting.com
Printed in the USA
JSHW081812110623
42905JS00004B/16/J

9 781039 160743